Rachel Pollack's

Tarot Wisdom

SPIRITUAL TEACHINGS and DEEPER MEANINGS

A must-have book for an
—AECLECTIC TAROT

It doesn't get any better than this! Rachel Pollack has sorted, evaluated, and made connections among the many myths, traditions, legends, and conventions surrounding Tarot, crystallizing their essence into core concepts and a modern understanding guaranteed to deepen your readings and study.
—MARY K. GREER, author of *21 Ways to Read a Tarot Card*

A master work born of 40 years of learning, teaching, reading, and writing about the Tarot. Rachel's love of the cards and their history, mythology, art, stories and, yes, wisdom shines through every page.
—RUTH ANN AND WALD AMBERSTONE, directors of the Tarot School and authors of *Tarot Tips* and *The Secret Language of Tarot*

[Rachel Pollack's] *Tarot Wisdom* is, by turns, scholarly, personal, humorous, and wise. . . . It's the most lucid and comprehensive series of card-by-card essays since *Seventy-Eight Degrees [of Wisdom]*.
—MARK McELROY, author of *What's in the Cards for You?* and *Putting the Tarot to Work*

About the Author

Rachel Pollack is a poet, an award-winning novelist, a world authority on the modern interpretation of Tarot cards, and a Tarot card artist. Her novel *Godmother Night* won the 1997 World Fantasy Award. *Unquenchable Fire,* her earlier novel, won the Arthur C. Clarke Award.

Her thirty books include twelve books on the Tarot, including *Seventy-Eight Degrees of Wisdom*, often called "the bible of Tarot readers," and she is the creator of the Shining Tribe Tarot. Her books have been published in fourteen languages. Rachel lives in New York's Hudson Valley.

FROM THE AUTHOR OF
Seventy-Eight Degrees of Wisdom

O

THE FOOL.

Rachel Pollack's

Tarot
Wisdom

SPIRITUAL TEACHINGS
and DEEPER MEANINGS

RACHEL POLLACK

TAROT

Llewellyn Publications
WOODBURY, MINNESOTA

FIRST EDITION
First Printing, 2008

Author photo by Joyce Tudrin
Book design and editing by Rebecca Zins
Cover design by Ellen R. Dahl
Line drawings by Llewellyn Art Department
Tarot decks reproduced with kind permission of Lo Scarabeo:
Tarot of Marseille, Visconti Tarot, The Egyptian Tarot, Sola-Busca Tarot.
Rider Tarot card illustrations are based on those contained in *The Pictorial Key to the Tarot*
by Arthur Edward Waite, published by William Rider & Son Ltd., London, 1911.
The Shining Tribe Tarot and The New Golden Dawn Ritual Tarot
are reproduced by permission of Llewellyn Publications.

LIBRARY OF CONGRESS CATALOGING-IN-PUBLICATION DATA
Pollack, Rachel, 1945-
    Rachel Pollack's tarot wisdom : spiritual teachings and deeper meanings / Rachel Pollack.
        p. cm.
    ISBN 978-0-7387-1309-0
    1. Tarot. I. Title. II. Title: Tarot wisdom.
BF1879.T2P645 2008
133.3′2424—dc22
                                                            2008035624

Llewellyn Worldwide does not participate in, endorse, or have any authority or responsibility concerning private business transactions between our authors and the public.
    All mail addressed to the author is forwarded but the publisher cannot, unless specifically instructed by the author, give out an address or phone number.
    Any Internet references contained in this work are current at publication time, but the publisher cannot guarantee that a specific location will continue to be maintained. Please refer to the publisher's website for links to authors' websites and other sources.

Llewellyn Publications
A Division of Llewellyn Worldwide, Ltd.
2143 Wooddale Drive, Dept. 978-0-7387-1309-0
Woodbury, MN 55125-2989
www.llewellyn.com

Printed in the United States of America
on recycled paper, 15% post-consumer waste

Dedication

To Zoe Matoff, who set up the Intensive classes and then suffered through all the months of the book that came out of them—and to all the wonderful people who gave their time and knowledge and enthusiasm to the Intensive workshops, especially Carey Croft, Barbara Eres, and Scott Martin.

Nothing is learned except through joy.
Ioanna Salajan

Contents

Introduction

I FIRST ENCOUNTERED Tarot in early 1970 when a friend read my cards. By the time you read this, I will have worked, studied, and played with Tarot for more than forty years, the total of the numbered cards—ace through ten in each of the four suits—in the part of the deck known as the Minor Arcana. Because of Tarot, I have learned about spiritual and esoteric traditions I did not even know existed. I have seen many subtle surprises and truths in human behavior and have come, I think, to a better understanding of subjects like free will and even what we mean by "sacred."

Having written stories all my life, I became a nonfiction writer to tell people what I understood of the cards (my first Tarot book and my first novel were published at the same time). Through Tarot, I have traveled to many countries at the kind invitation of people who wanted me to teach. And I have met dear friends who have remained close to me for decades, no matter where we live.

That first book on Tarot, published in two parts in 1980 and 1983, was *Seventy-Eight Degrees of Wisdom*. It came out of a weekly class I was teaching in Amsterdam, in the Netherlands, where I lived for nineteen years. It seemed to me that I had developed an approach to the cards that I had not seen anywhere else at that time. Part of that approach involved using readings as the primary mode by which we entered the deepest levels of the cards' meanings, including spiritual and metaphysical truths and secrets. At that time, people tended either to do readings with formulaic meanings for each card or else study the cards according to a strict system of occult ideas. My own approach stressed psychology, myth, esoteric philosophy, and the interpretation of the cards that came up in readings as moments in someone's life, or a story, or a dream.

Over the years, many people have told me they found *Seventy-Eight Degrees of Wisdom* of great benefit. And yet, much has happened in Tarot since then. A vast number of new decks have been published, including my own Shining Tribe Tarot. Brilliant interpretations have emerged, along with decks and books that link the cards to specific mythologies or esoteric traditions. Material that had been kept secret for generations was finally published. We also know a great deal more about Tarot's history, so that statements I made in *Seventy-Eight Degrees of Wisdom*—for example, that regular playing cards derived from Tarot—I now know as simply not true.

Because so much has happened and my own ideas have developed so much, I thought it might be time to do a new book that would once again give a detailed interpretation of the entire deck, card by card. Actually, just as *Seventy-Eight Degrees* came out of my Amsterdam class, so *Tarot Wisdom* comes from a series of day-long workshops I taught called Tarot Intensives. In these classes, we spent an entire morning or afternoon looking at just one or two cards, bringing in a whole range of approaches—from comparison with many decks, to a look at how the historical meanings of the cards have evolved over the past two centuries, to readings inspired by the core ideas of a single card.

One of the special things we did in the Intensives was to go back and see what the early cartomancers (people who do readings with cards) gave as the meaning for each card. In this we were greatly aided by a recent book by Paul Huson, whose early work on Tarot, *The Devil's Picture-Book*, was one of my favorites when I was first learning the cards.

Huson's new book, *Mystical Origins of the Tarot*, is one of a group of exciting new works by various authors that attempt to bridge the gap between historical scholarship on Tarot and the tradition of occult or spiritual interpretation. Knowledge of Tarot history has taken huge leaps in the last decade. We now know far more about not only the origin of the deck but also the likely source of most of the pictures. At one point, the people doing this research seemed to have a kind of anti-occult agenda. That is, if they could disprove the claims of Tarot having a secret origin as a mystical doctrine, then all of the concepts and symbolism built up around it would be seen as meaningless. All of us who believe we see spiritual truth in Tarot cards would have to realize that it's just nonsense, that Tarot was invented as a game, nothing more, and all the rest is foolish fantasy. In reaction against this extreme view, some Tarotists have steadfastly ignored historical evidence. To them, Tarot comes from ancient Egypt, or Atlantis, or wherever else they have heard (see below for some of the examples), no matter what all those researchers say.

Huson and others, notably Mary K. Greer and Robert Place, have taken a different approach. They use what researchers have found out to create a fuller picture of the cards, recognizing that that picture should include the concepts that have built up around the Tarot since the eighteenth century (see below for a brief history) and the intriguing possibility that those first inventors of the *game* of Tarot may very well have conceived of the pictures as allegorical lessons.

One of the things that Huson has done in his book is list for each card in the deck the meanings given by the early cartomancers, beginning with "Pratesi." The name actually belongs to a contemporary historian who found a manuscript on Tarot that gave simple meanings for a fair number of the cards. The manuscript dates from around 1750, and since the earliest published meanings date from 1781, the anonymous text is the first known list of what today we call "divinatory meanings," and the earliest sign that Tarot cards were used for fortunetelling.

When I began to read through the various historical interpretations for each card—Huson takes us from Pratesi to the beginning of the twentieth century—I realized something amazing: for many of the cards, the older meanings were nothing at all like what we believe the card means today. Consider the Fool. Today we view this figure as a wise innocent making his intuitive way through the world. In earlier times, however, people saw him as a sort of schizophrenic homeless person. And I'm not referring here to card readers who knew nothing of Tarot's spiritual or occult meanings. These interpreters were in fact the very people who wrote the books and designed the cards. As I made these discoveries, it seemed worth our attention to look at how the interpretation of each card has evolved over time.

THE HIEROPHANT

LE PAPE · IL PAPA

THE HIEROPHANT V DER HIEROPHANT
EL PAPA DE HIÉROFANT

< RIDER & MARSEILLES *Hierophant*

ᵥ MARSEILLES & RIDER *Hermit*

L'ERMITE · L'EREMITA

THE HERMIT IX DER EREMIT
EL ERMITAÑO DE KLUIZENAAR

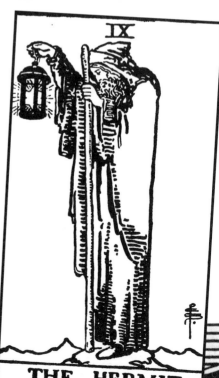

IX

THE HERMIT.

Terms

It might make sense to pause for a moment and explain my usage of two important words, occult and esoteric. For some people, occult means human sacrifice, devil worship, and other scary practices that mostly occur only in bad movies and the fantasies of Fundamentalist preachers. *Occult* simply means "hidden," and the term refers to a tradition and a set of ideas considered by its followers as a scientific description of different dimensions of existence. I use it primarily in reference to the symbols and concepts that have influenced Tarot for the past two and a half centuries.

Esoteric means "inner teachings or concepts"; its opposite is exoteric. In religion, the exoteric level usually means the moral codes and commandments, such as "Love your neighbor as yourself" (from Leviticus, quoted by Jesus as the basic teaching of the Law). Esoteric means the more subtle levels, that which cannot be explained in simple, conventional terms. So, to quote Jesus again, when he says, "Unless you become as a little child, you shall not enter the kingdom of Heaven," he probably does not mean that your body becomes smaller and healthier and you forget everything you've learned since second grade. This statement could be described as esoteric in that it cannot be understood literally but only on a symbolic, inner level.

I should add here that in various places in this book I will quote or refer to various religious traditions, in particular Christianity and Judaism. This is not in any way an endorsement of those beliefs; they appear simply because they illustrate the concepts we are looking at. The fact is, Tarot comes out of a Christian background—late medieval and early Renaissance Europe—and those were the ideas and images, such as angels, that gave rise to the pictures. And as we shall see in a moment, Tarot has become linked to Kabbalah, a mystical tradition that began in Judaism (which is why we sometimes see Hebrew letters on the cards), so that Jewish stories and symbols apply. But these are all on the esoteric level—they do not endorse or require belief in the outer teachings or rules. We also will look at stories and ideas from Paganism, ancient Egypt, Greece, Taoism, the Hindu gods, and other sources. *You do not have to believe in or practice any religion to read Tarot cards.*

One final note on esoteric: some people use this term to refer to a separate set of concepts and information from the normal one. For example, if you look up, say, the King of Wands, in some Tarot books it will tell you that it refers to a person, a man of a certain age and hair coloring, with a particular temperament. This might be called the exoteric level. Other books will tell you it refers to what is called "Fire of Fire" (explained later in the court card section), the astrological sign of Aries, and similar information. This kind of information some call esoteric, because it is not found in the usual descriptions. To my mind, however, simple information is never really esoteric, even if it comes from obscure or mysterious sources.

I think of esoteric as that which requires a level of understanding beyond what we can write down in a list. We need the outer levels to spark our responses to the cards, but those responses have to come partly from within. Tarot cards work so powerfully on our awareness because the pictures carry centuries of symbolic information and because they are *pictures*, so we can respond to them on a non-rational level.

There are two cards in the deck that show us the levels of exoteric and esoteric teachings. These are the Hierophant and the Hermit.

Originally called the Pope, the Hierophant shows us a church tradition, with disciples bowing down to receive the official word from the priest. By contrast, the Hermit stands in a high place, holding up a lantern of truth to those who climb high enough to see it and respond to it.

A (Very) Brief History of the Tarot

First of all, the deck itself: the Tarot consists of seventy-eight cards, in two parts, what are called the Major Arcana and the Minor Arcana (*arcana* means secrets—what is arcane, or hidden). The Minor cards are the four suits, usually called Wands (Clubs in regular playing cards), Cups (Hearts), Swords (Spades), and Pentacles (Diamonds). The suits have had different names through the centuries, and we will look at these below, but for now those four titles will be fine. The Major Arcana consists of twenty-two named and numbered cards. The numbers actually run 1–21, with an extra card, 0, the Fool. Some see the Fool as really separate, but most consider it part of the Major cards, which also bear the title "trumps," because in the card game of Tarot these will trump—triumph over—the cards from the four suits.

It may surprise some readers to learn that you can play a game with Tarot cards. Called by the French *les Tarots* or by the Italians *Tarocchi*, the game has been played for hundreds of years and is still very popular, with international leagues and tournaments.

Then where does the Tarot come from? Before giving my summary of what we know from history, I think it's worthwhile to look at the various claims that people have made—usually with absolute confidence—for the Tarot's origins. What follows is a list I compiled for an earlier book, *The Forest of Souls*.

> The Tarot depicts the sacred myths of the Romany (or Gypsies), disguised in cards for the centuries of exile from the Rom homeland in India—or Egypt—or outer space. The Tarot is a Renaissance card game inspired by annual carnival processions, called triumphs. The Tarot is a card game derived from annual processions, called thriambs, in honor of the god Dionysus, the creator of wine. The Tarot conceals/reveals the secret number teachings of Pythagoras, a Greek mystic who lived at the time of Moses and who influenced Plato. The Tarot depicts the secret oral teaching of Moses, who received them directly from God. The Tarot contains the lost knowledge of Atlantis, a drowned continent first described by Plato. The Tarot is a card game imported from Palestine and Egypt during the Crusades. The Tarot is a vast memory system for the Tree of Life, a diagram of the laws of creation. The Tarot hides in plain sight the wisdom of the Egyptian god Thoth, master of all knowledge. The Tarot shows Egyptian temple initiations. The Tarot shows Tantric temple initiations. The Tarot preserves the wisdom of Goddess-initiated witches during the long, dark centuries of patriarchal religion. The Tarot maps the patterns of the moon in Chaldean astrology. The Tarot was created by papermaker guilds who were the last remnants of the Cathars, Christian heretics brutally suppressed by the Church of Rome. All of the above, and more, Tarot writers have proclaimed as the one true, authentic origin of Tarot.

Curiously, of all these, the one given most credence these days is that of the symbolic card game, though people still argue (often vehemently) over the sources and original concepts of that game and its clearly allegorical images. Despite all the claims made for Eastern or mysterious sources, the original pictures come from well-known scenes, primarily religious, found in Northern Italy from the late Middle Ages.

The earliest-known deck, complete except for a very few cards, dates from 1450 in the city-state of Milan. Called the Visconti-Sforza, it most likely was painted by an artist named Bonifacio Bembo as a wedding gift for a marriage between two noble families (the Viscontis ruled Milan). We will use a contemporary repainting of this deck, the Visconti Tarot, as one of our sample decks for the various cards.

> VISCONTI
*Hierophant,
Eight of Cups,
&
Queen of
Wands*

So if the Tarot began its life as a card game, where did all these other ideas come from? And are they all worthless now that we know the "truth"? Clearly I do not think so, or I would not be writing this book. For one thing, remember the original paintings were symbolic images. They showed such subjects as Justice and the resurrection of the dead. They may not have come from Atlantis, but they originated in a very old tradition of pictures with many levels of meaning. And yet, this is not really the reason for all those wild claims. The reason is the power of myth.

In the latter half of the eighteenth century, a French scholar named Antoine Court de Gébelin published a massive study of esoteric traditions, titled *Le Monde Primitif*, or "The Primitive World." *Primitive* here does not mean crude or savage, but rather a more exalted state, a Golden Age. In volume eight of this great work, he made a surprising announcement. He told how he had gone to visit a friend of his, a certain Madame de la H., and she had told him of a wonderful new craze that was sweeping Paris, a marvelous card game called *les Tarots*.

When he saw the cards, Antoine was stunned, for he instantly recognized them as the pictorial equivalent of the ancient teachings of the Egyptian god Thoth, also known as Hermes. (See the Magician section for more about this figure and the term derived from his name, *Hermetic*.)

In his chapter on Tarot, Court de Gébelin developed some ideas of what the cards meant, and then he gave space to an associate, Comte (Count) de Mellet, who added his own concepts. Some Tarot historians, such as Mary Greer, believe that the whole story of the great "discovery" was in fact a cover. Both authors were Freemasons, and the Masons may have had an esoteric view of the Tarot for some time. For whatever reason, the society, or just the two men, decided to go public, and because the Masons are a secret order, they needed some plausible way to announce what they knew.

> Visconti
*Papesse/High
Priestess
&
Hanged Man*

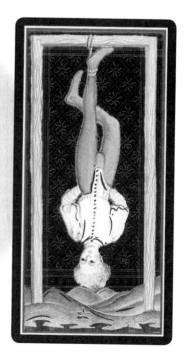

LE BATELEUR   IL MAGO

THE MAGICIAN   DER MAGIER
EL MAGO   I   DE MAGIËR

LA FORCE   LA FORZA

STRENGTH
LA FUERZA   XI   DIE STÄRKE
DE KRACHT

∧ Marseilles *Magician & Strength*

> Rider *Magician & Strength*

THE MAGICIAN.

STRENGTH.

The remarkable thing about this tale is not really the information, it's the very idea of it. That concept of a great secret hidden away in a humble card game has captivated people ever since the eighteenth century. It has become the Tarot's central myth, so that for over two centuries now, people have argued just what hidden wisdom the cards concealed. Everyone assumes it must be concealing something.

And the idea is hard to resist. Many of the early cards do, in fact, seem to suggest hidden meanings. For example, what do we make of a woman wearing the oufit of an abbess but the triple crown of the pope? Is this "Papesse" (female pope) just a satire on the church's all-male priesthood, or might it suggest something more complex? (For more on this card, see the High Priestess section.)

And what of the Hanged Man? Historians say the image derives from the habit of hanging traitors upside down by their feet, but notice his calm manner and almost serene expression in that earliest version.

By the time of Antoine Court de Gébelin and Comte de Mellet, the standard Tarot images were a style known as the Tarot de Marseille, named for the French port, though the style appears all over Europe. Here too we find subtle possibilities of symbolism. In the card we today call the Magician, the man wears a wide-brimmed hat that loops around like an infinity sign. So does the woman in Strength. In modern decks, we see an actual symbol above the heads of these two characters, but the suggestion comes from the Tarot de Marseille.

Its Own Tradition

The fact is, the Tarot does not really need an ancient source. Sparked by the concept that Tarot contained secret truths, people have developed a wide and complex tradition of symbolism and meaning from it. We will look here at just the barest outlines of this history. The two articles in *Le Monde Primitif* included suggestions that we might link the twenty-two trump cards—what we now call the Major Arcana—with the twenty-two letters of the Hebrew alphabet. Why would anyone want to do that?

The simple answer is that Kabbalah, the ancient tradition of Jewish mysticism that was picked up and adapted by Christian esotericists around the same time as the first known Tarot cards, treats the letters as sacred, involved in the very creation of the universe. According to Kabbalah's most ancient text, the Sefer Yetsirah (Book of Formation), the world was created with ten numbers and twenty-two letters. Since the Tarot's Major Arcana contains twenty-two cards, and each suit has ten numbered cards (ace—ten), the comparison is striking.

In the mid-nineteenth century, a French occultist named Éliphas Lévi (his loyalty to Kabbalah led him to take a Hebrew name) developed a more complete system of correspondences between Tarot and Kabbalah. Following Lévi, a man named Paul Christian (originally Jean-Baptiste Pitois) developed Egyptian imagery for the Tarot, along with ideas for what the cards mean that have influenced readers ever since. An artist named Maurice Otto Wegener created a set of Tarot trump images based on Christian's work, and this too influenced later Tarot art. A modern version of Wegener's pictures has recently been published as the Egyptian Tarot, and we will see this deck with the Major Arcana here.

Then, in 1888, a small group of esotericists led by Samuel L. MacGregor Mathers, Wynn Westcott, and William K. Woodman started a remarkable organization known as the Hermetic Order of the Golden Dawn. Using Tarot and a Kabbalistic symbol called the Tree of Life, the Golden Dawn synthesized a vast amount of information from many sources—Kabbalah, astrology, Neo-Platonism, esoteric Christianity, Freemasonry, medieval magic, Pagan gods, and much more. All of this served a great cause: to raise a person's level of being so that he or she could become a true magician. This was Paul Christian's idea of the Major Arcana, that it outlined the development of the "magus," but the Golden Dawn carried this project much further, creating powerful, complicated rituals along with their complex structure for Tarot. As we go through the cards and how to interpret them, we will encounter the Hermetic Order of the Golden Dawn again and again.

Ultimately, the greatest influence on modern Tarot comes from a single deck produced by two former members of the organization, the scholar and magician Arthur Edward Waite (who actually headed the Order for a time) and the artist Pamela "Pixie" Colman Smith. In 1909, the Rider company of London published their deck, which Waite called "true and rectified." The Rider deck, as most call it (its American publisher has titled it "Rider-Waite" which many of its fans have extended to Rider-Waite-Smith, or simply RWS), revolutionized Tarot through a change in the Minor Arcana. Previously, almost all decks showed only arrangements of symbols for the suit cards. That is, the Eight of Cups would display an arrangement of eight cups. Smith, however, painted a scene on every card.

< MARSEILLE
& RIDER
Eight of Cups

Suddenly it became possible to *enter* these pictures, to treat them as moments in a story. There is another reason for the Rider deck's power. While Waite and Smith's pictures contain a precise and detailed architecture of symbolism—every gesture means something, every tiny image, even the minute folds of an angel's robe—we do not need to learn all those details in order to appreciate the cards and use them in readings. The pictures alone can inspire us.

It was the Rider I saw in my friend's house all those years ago, and the Rider I learned and studied. Quite simply, that was just about the only deck available then. The other most influential Tarot deck of our time, the Thoth Tarot designed by Aleister Crowley (another former head of the Golden Dawn, and an enemy of Waite's) and painted by Frieda Harris, had just been published but was hard to find. Based more closely on the Golden Dawn than the Rider deck, and graced by often stunning art, the Thoth deck was actually created during World

War II but not published until 1969, and even then only in a small edition. Now it is known all over the world, with many who see it as the only true and genuine Tarot.

Since 1970, I have worked with and studied many decks, and of course designed my own, the Shining Tribe Tarot, inspired by tribal and prehistoric art. And yet, like so many others, I return again and again to the Rider.

Does it matter where the Tarot *really* came from? If we now believe it did not come into existence until some two thousand years after the ancient Egyptians, does that make all those Egyptian images and spiritual ideas meaningless? If the Kabbalist masters never heard of the Tarot, can we no longer use all those seemingly perfect correspondences? To me, it seems almost the opposite. By creating a myth of the Tarot's origins, Antoine Court de Gébelin and all those who came after him have *liberated the Tarot from time*. We can adapt whatever story or teaching or image fits to deepen our experience of the cards. In this book's section on the Major Arcana, we will discover tales and rituals from ancient Greece and Egypt, but also a Talmudic myth about two fallen angels. All of these come from long before the Tarot's historical beginnings. And yet, they match perfectly the cards' essential story of the soul, its exile, and its liberation.

Wisdom Readings

One more expression needs some explanation before we can properly begin. In various places in this book, you will encounter the expression "Wisdom Readings," usually in regard to spreads (formats for reading the cards) with questions about large issues rather than personal concerns. In other words, rather than ask the cards "How can I find my soul mate?" we might ask "What is the soul?"

The concept of Wisdom Readings is my own invention, and that question was, in fact, the very first one I did. Mary K. Greer and I were teaching together at the Omega Institute in upstate New York, where we have taught an annual class for twenty years. Some years ago, we had taken as our theme "Tarot and Soul-Making," a term invented by John Keats and developed in recent decades by psychologist James Hillman. I decided to ask the cards "What is the soul?" The answer was very striking: the Ace of Birds from the Shining Tribe Tarot.

Like an owl (the picture comes from an ancient Egyptian plaque), the soul is powerful and mysterious, and it "hunts" truth in the darkness of our lives. A few days later, I asked "What

< SHINING TRIBE
Ace of Birds
&
Six of Trees

is the Tarot?" and got the Six of Trees, a picture that shows a woman walking through a forest of strange trees painted with owl eyes.

From this came the idea that the Tarot guides us through the tangled woods of people's lives, what I call the "Forest of Souls." We will look further at Wisdom Readings in the final part of this book.

A Note on the Illustrations

The Rider deck illustrations used here are from the original black-and-white drawings. The Visconti, Marseille, and Sola-Busca decks are contemporary redrawings based closely on the original design.

The book that follows these words can really be summed up in a simple phrase—it is what I have learned about Tarot over the past forty years. To those who read it, I hope you will find it of value.

The Major Arcana

FOR A LONG time now, I have thought of the Tarot's Major Arcana as the great, neglected masterpiece of Western culture. Occultists speak of it as containing the highest truths and link it to the complex teachings of the Kabbalah and the Hermetica, the two linked pillars of esoteric tradition. For the general public, however, including the great majority of artists and thinkers, these twenty-two cards are simply part of a fantastic device for fortunetelling.

Kabbalah comes out of Jewish mystical practices and concepts, the Hermetica out of Greek and Egyptian ideas, with both strains noted for their dense intellectual ideas and detailed descriptions that seem to have gotten more and more complex over the centuries. We will look at some of this detail in this book, but not necessarily in systematic order. For example, each card in the Major Arcana is associated with various correspondences. These include a letter from the Hebrew alphabet, an astrological sign or planet (say, Gemini for the Lovers, Mars for the Tower), and a pathway on the Kabbalistic Tree of Life. I have included these at the head of each card description, and I could have added many more, such as musical tones, names of gods and demons, direction on something called "the cube of space," and so on. But I have kept it simple and not gone into detailed explanations of these correspondences for every card, choosing instead to highlight them where they seemed particularly important for that card's meaning. So, with the Fool, it seemed to me significant to consider its Hebrew letter, Aleph, but less so to look at the astrological planet, Uranus. On the other hand, with the Lovers, the sign of Gemini highlights the theme of Choice associated with this card, while its Hebrew letter, Zayin, did not strike me as vital. Those who want a systematic listing of all the correspondences for each card can find them in many books. Because of that, I have chosen to emphasize a thread of meaning, what I call *story*, that runs through the pictures.

By "story," I do not mean simply a once-upon-a-time tale, though in fact we can find the essence of many fairy tales and myths in these pictures. Instead, I mean a basic idea that lies at the heart of all that Hermetic complexity. This is the concept that we do not know our true selves, that we live in a kind of exile from the homeland of our genuine spiritual being. The Tarot, however, shows us the way of our return. To use another metaphor, we are asleep, in a kind of dream even when we follow our daily activities, but it is possible to wake up. By exploring the pictures of the Major Arcana and the ancient wisdom traditions that they open up for us, we can come to a point of liberation. In my own Shining Tribe Tarot, I changed the name of the next-to-last card in the Major Arcana from Judgement to Awakening. Going through the process of the previous cards, we truly wake up and then enter our true being in the final card, the World.

Does this mean that simply by looking at the cards and reading the descriptions in this book (or any other book), we will attain a genuine spiritual liberation? Of course not; if it was that easy, we would all become great spiritual masters. But I do believe that the cards can give us a glimpse of a truth that otherwise we might never know. And also, that they do indeed lay out a program for us that if we could really follow it, we would, in fact, awaken to our genuine place in the cosmos.

There is a term for the experience the Major Arcana describes—*anamnesia*, the removal of forgetfulness. Suppose you woke up one day and discovered you had no memory of who you are, or where your home is, believing you were someone else. Suppose, in fact, you'd existed in this state for years, and this realization that you do not know who you are was the first stage of your recovery. And then suppose that you found a blueprint of some kind for a process to rediscover all you had lost, that explained just how you had forgotten who you are, and more important, how to get back. That blueprint is the Tarot.

Do we know for sure that this story, as I call it—or for that matter, the doctrines of Kabbalah and/or the Hermetica—is the original intended meaning of the Major Arcana? No. Playing-card historians have made a strong case that the pictures come from standard allegorical images of the time, as discussed in the Introduction. But of course, those allegories were about *something*, and the something was generally religion. So there was always a certain spiritual content, but it's unlikely that they carried the highly specific and precise teachings of Kabbalah.

The Tarot's esoteric tradition actually begins with a story, Antoine Court de Gébelin's announcement, in 1781, that he had discovered that the ancient Egyptian teachings of the god Thoth, also called Hermes Trismegistus, were present in the world, concealed in the lowly card game of *les Tarots*. Such is the power of story that until the last twenty-five years or so, people just accepted the idea that the Tarot contained a secret doctrine of great power, they only argued over the details. What, they debated, should we consider the "true" Tarot, with the one and only correct set of correspondences?

The Hermetic Order of the Golden Dawn did not come along until the last years of the nineteenth century, yet even today many people consider its detailed correspondences not only the one real Tarot but a genuine picture of the universe. Others vote for some later version, especially that of Aleister Crowley and his Thoth Tarot, painted by Frieda Harris. Many European occultists, especially the French, choose the classic Tarot of Marseille and the correspondences and order of the cards described by Éliphas Lévi. But all these arguments assume, first of all, that the Tarot indeed contains secret teachings, and second, that only one version can be correct.

If, in fact, Tarot conveyed Hermetic doctrines, and those in turn represented a scientific view of reality, then yes, there would have to be a "true" order and list of meanings. After all, there is only one periodic table of the elements, beginning with hydrogen and ending with uranium (at least for substances found in nature), with the order determined by the number of protons and electrons found in each molecule. I do not consider Tarot scientific in this way. I see it as story, as myth.

Major Arcana 3

For the most part, where I look into particular correspondences, I follow the Golden Dawn. I also use their numbering of the cards. This is not because I believe they contain absolute truth or a correct astrological order, but because I think they contain valuable *meaning*.

As mentioned, the descriptions in this book come from a series of classes I did called Tarot Intensives, in which we moved, card by card, through first the Major and then the Minor Arcana, seeking to understand their messages and symbolism—or rather, their possible messages, for we did not restrict ourselves to a single concept but tried to look at the many layers in each card. As part of this work, we looked at what early writers on Tarot have said about the cards, aided by lists assembled by Paul Huson for his 2004 book *Mystical Origins of the Tarot*.

The remarkable thing about these early interpretations is that not only had the order changed for the Major Arcana, and sometimes the details of the pictures, but the assumed meanings had undergone huge shifts, sometimes almost reversing their original explanations. In some cases, the understanding that today we take for granted about a particular card did not even exist until the modern era.

This discovery only reinforced my belief that we understand Tarot best by looking at all its meanings. For me, these include associations, particularly with certain myths, that were probably never originally intended. As you read through these pages, you will discover stories that seem to me to run through the cards. They include the Kabbalistic myth of the Shekinah, the female aspect of God, separated from God the King, the male aspect; the Egyptian goddess Isis and her struggle to resurrect her murdered husband, Osiris; certain Greek deities, in particular Aphrodite, Apollo, and Hermes, who loom over the entire Major Arcana; the fairy tale of Rapunzel; a pre-Kabbalist Jewish myth of two fallen angels named Shemhazai and Azazel; and the stories and mysteries of the Greek goddess Persephone, who is kidnapped by Death to be his bride in the Underworld, and who returns for part of every year.

I do not claim that the original designers of the Tarot, whoever they might have been, planned the deck with these stories in mind. I'm not sure that the cards were designed with any specific tradition in mind. Instead, I think they set up a structure and used images that follow the basic pattern of our existence, so that almost any really meaningful spiritual tradition seems an exact mirror of the Tarot.

The argument for the Tarot's Kabbalist connections lies outside of any historical discoveries. It's structural: 22 Hebrew letters, 22 pathways on the Tree of Life, 22 cards in the Major

Arcana. Four worlds in Kabbalah, four suits in Tarot, each world with ten sephiroth, each suit with ten cards. Four letters in God's most holy name, four court cards in the Tarot. Add twelve astrological signs and ten "planets," and how could anyone think Tarot did *not* come from Kabbalah? And yet, you could take many other traditions and make almost as convincing an argument. The Tarot is a template of the soul's progress.

One thing we *can* say for the Tarot's historical origins: it came from a largely Christian culture. In that time of the early Renaissance, Greek myth and philosophy had begun to influence people, and there was an interest in the Graeco-Egyptian Mystery schools of Alexandria 1,500 years earlier. Nevertheless, Christian imagery and thought dominated people's imaginations so that we see in the cards angels, a devil, a pope, and the resurrection of the dead. Kabbalah, with its Jewish myth and its Hebrew names, became a powerful influence from at least 1781. As a result, you will find in these pages many references to "God," and Hebrew words, and such figures as the archangel Michael, who threw Satan into Hell, and Adam and Eve. None of this, not a single image or idea, requires belief in a particular religion. In fact, you may need to give up some of what you learned in your religious education to really hear what these pictures are saying, for like the Hanged Man, they often turn assumptions on their head. As well as Christian or Jewish terms, you will find Greek, Egyptian, and occasionally Hindu gods and goddesses, ideas and practices from modern Wicca and Neo-Paganism, and a few nods to science and geometry. If in fact the Major Arcana shows us reality, then like reality, it will not confine itself to any particular human culture or system of beliefs.

My own approach to the Major Arcana is structural. Because the Fool is zero, it stands apart from the twenty-one other cards, so that we can imagine it as the "hero" of the Tarot, who journeys through all the experiences. Twenty-one is a special number, three times seven. And here is where it becomes valuable to look into what I call the wisdom traditions of ancient cultures, to understand what makes those numbers important. I will be detailing some of the meanings as we go through the individual cards, so I will keep it simple here.

Images of three are found over and over in the world's mythologies and religious teachings. There is the Christian trinity of Father-Son-Holy Spirit; the Hindu *trimurti* of Creator-Preserver-Destroyer; the European Triple Goddess of Maiden-Mother-Crone, connected to the phases of the moon but also to the three Fates who determine our lives. And in modern philosophy, Hegel (and then Marx) developed the concept that ideas, and history, move through a process of thesis-antithesis-synthesis. To my way of thinking, all these come from one of the most basic facts of our existence, that we each share the genes of a mother and father. Father-Mother-Child is the most basic trinity.

This allows us to divide the Major Arcana into three levels. I see these as Conscious, Unconscious, and Superconscious. In each, the Fool will progress through seven challenges and lessons.

The first, one through seven, concerns the outer problems and concerns of life—growing up, dealing with parents and society, love, making our way in the world.

The second line involves self-knowledge and transformation. There is both a modern and an ancient model for this transformation. The new one is therapy, in which we realize that the self we have built up in life is not working and is not who we truly are, so that we seek to find our essential nature. The older is initiation, in which a person goes through a spiritual death and rebirth. Line two runs eight through fourteen, and if you look at the later cards—Justice, Hanged Man, Death, Temperance—you will see the very image of that initiation process.

And Superconscious? The very term sounds odd. We know about conscious and unconscious—or at least we believe we do—but super? It often strikes me that we have no model for this because it's not about ourselves. Not Me, but You. The third level of the Major Arcana, cards fifteen through twenty-one, concerns the cosmos beyond our narrow goals of self-improvement. This is why the final card bears the title World.

Three times seven. Seven is a remarkable number, for it connects us quite literally with the world beyond us. Ancient cosmology was built upon the fact that there are seven visible "planets," by which they meant heavenly bodies that move rapidly across the sky, at least compared to the background of the stars. These are the moon, Mercury, Venus, the sun, Mars, Jupiter, and Saturn. Since Earth was known to be a sphere (it is a modern myth that people used to think the Earth was flat) and these planets could be seen everywhere, they were assumed to exist in concentric spheres around the Earth. When a person was born, the soul traveled from the Empyrean, the place of God beyond the physical universe, through each of the planetary spheres in turn on its way to the new body. The configuration of each sphere against the constellations—the sign the planet was in at that moment—shaped the child's unique qualities.

Even though this cosmology is long vanished from our descriptions of Earth's place in the universe, the fact that there still are those seven moving bodies in our sky gives the old structure meaning. So does the fact that there are seven colors in the rainbow, seven chakras, or energy centers, in the human body—the exact same colors as the rainbow, but only when the body is upside down (see the Hanged Man)—and seven tones in the diatonic musical scale. When you find such concepts as "seven pillars of wisdom" or seven "heavenly palaces" (a Kabbalistic image—see the Chariot), they all derive from the powerful presence of seven in our lives. In America, people used to be considered full adults at the age of twenty-one, the same number of cards as the Major Arcana.

Three lines of seven. This allows us to compare the cards in interesting ways.

1	2	3	4	5	6	7
8	9	10	11	12	13	14
15	16	17	18	19	20	21

Each of the vertical columns can be called a triad, a term I learned from Tarot creator and writer Caitlin Matthews. Thus, 1, 8, and 15 are related to each other; and 2, 9, and 16, and so on. We will look at these triads as we go through the individual cards.

We can think of each of these lines as following the same development. The first two cards set out the basic issues. For example, in the first line, one and two, the Magician and High Priestess, symbolize the basic dualities of life—male and female, light and dark, action and stillness, conscious and unconscious. The middle three cards then show us the various challenges we face at that level. The sixth card depicts a powerful experience we can have, while the seventh shows something we can become. All this will become clearer as we move through the cards.

And finally, what does all this have to do with readings? Isn't that why most people turn to the cards, why we first became interested? All this talk of our true selves may be interesting in a lofty kind of way, but will it help us figure out how to find our soul mate? Well, yes. One thing it will do is help us understand just what a "soul mate" might mean, and to see how that idea, which may seem a modern talk-show fantasy, goes back at least as far as Plato. More generally, the best meanings for the cards derive from their symbolic truths. Too often in the past, people who've gone deeply into the Tarot's wisdom consider the practice of readings irrelevant or even insulting. As a result, when they do list "divinatory meanings," they may simply repeat old fortune-telling formulas, sometimes even contradicting their own understanding of the real truth found in the pictures. This can make the meanings trivial and hard to use in actual readings. For my own descriptions, I have tried to let the meanings grow naturally out of the cards' images, stories, and spiritual wonders.

The Major Arcana

Fool: 0

Astrological correspondence:
   Uranus

Kabbalistic letter: א Aleph

Path on Tree of Life: Kether
   (Crown) to Hokhmah
   (Wisdom), first path

Fool cards from
VISCONTI,
MARSEILLE,
RIDER, GOLDEN
DAWN RITUAL,
EGYPTIAN &
SHINING TRIBE

The Fool

WHAT DO WE SEE when we look at the Fool? What thoughts and emotions come to mind when it shows up in a reading? Is the Fool the wise innocent making his way through the world? Is he the hero of all those fairy tales where the foolish younger brother succeeds after the smart older brothers fail? Is he the symbol of instinct, the ability to do the right thing with perfect spontaneity, the free child unencumbered by fear and social conditioning? Is he the soul about to incarnate into a body to begin the long journey of life? Is he a symbol of mystical perfection? Or is he just a fool, a crazy person stumbling through the world?

Ask most modern Tarot readers about the Fool and they will speak of his spontaneity and freedom, his innocence and joy. They will say how he takes chances and can do seemingly impossible things because he acts on instinct (like the fairy-tale character), without the analysis and second-guessing that so often paralyze us when we need to do something important. Going a little further, they might describe the Fool as the hero of the entire Major Arcana, the character who moves through all the other cards. Many people describe the Tarot itself as "the Fool's journey," a title I have seen used (independently, with each person coming up with it on their own) for books, dance recitals, art shows, and workshops. This idea of the journeyer seems, quite simply, the natural response to the image—or at least in modern Tarot decks, for there we do indeed see a joyous free spirit.

This quality of the Fool as a free spirit is not just a concept. If we can identify with the Fool and allow the card to spark some of that spontaneity in ourselves, we too can do what is necessary right in the moment. The Tarot is not simply an intellectual or spiritual doctrine (though it certainly contains that, along with the original game that gave it life). Because it is composed of images and symbols, it can work on us in powerful ways that bypass the normal channels of our thoughts and behavior. Here is my own story of becoming the Fool, at least for a moment.

The first Tarot Intensive class I taught was on the Fool, presented as one of the monthly classes I have been teaching in New York City for over fifteen years. For an entire evening we talked about the Fool, shared experiences of what it's meant to us, in readings and in life. We looked at samples from different decks, experimented with Fool-inspired readings (see the end of this discussion for a Fool spread), and dug up some of its history.

At the end, a little later than I'd planned, I grabbed my things and dashed downstairs with only a short time to get to the train station and catch my train upstate, where I live. Of course I was late; under the influence of the Fool, it's hard to remember to look at your watch. Train stations, however, are not Fool-based (we might call them outposts of the Emperor, card four), and if I missed that train it would be a very long night.

The class in those days took place in an apartment on the corner of Second Avenue and Thirty-fourth Street, one of New York's busiest streets. When I came downstairs I saw a taxi stopped for a light on the other side of the road. In New York, taxis all have medallions on the roof (how magical sounding!) displaying their number. This particular cab was 722.

Now, seven is the number of the card called the Chariot, and a speedy chariot was certainly what I needed. At the same time, twenty-two, as well as being the number of the entire Major Arcana, is also the number of the Fool, the twenty-second card. Clearly, this taxi was the one for me.

The only problem was, if I waited for the light to change, it would take off in the wrong direction and I would miss it. And there were no others in sight. So I ran into the street. Thirty-fourth Street—3+4=7, the number of the cab—has five lanes of traffic, all of them crowded with fast-moving cars and trucks. I was halfway across before I heard the shouts, the people yelling at me from back on the sidewalk. With no awareness of what I was doing, I had run into traffic. People were not shouting from anger, but fear and astonishment. I kept going, dodging in between speeding cars, until I'd gotten to the other side and into my Chariot Fool taxi to take me to the train.

I am certain I could never have done that if I had not immersed myself in the Fool the entire evening. I would never have done it without the Fool's influence.

The iconic modern image of the Fool as a joyous innocent setting off on a journey comes originally from the Rider deck of Arthur Edward Waite and Pamela Colman Smith. Arms out, happy and carefree, the Fool appears about to step off a cliff. He is fearless, simply because he has never learned to be afraid.

In the Shining Tribe Tarot, I took this a step further (literally). Instead of a youth on the edge of a precipice, we see a young child flying through the sky. He has not set out to fly but simply to follow a bird. Not just instinct inspires the Fool, for instinct only works to satisfy basic needs, like hunger or safety. No, the Fool follows a path of *delight*, of fascination that is as natural as eating.

After I drew this picture, I met a woman who told me of a Native American teaching (I do not remember which nation) that each of us has a spirit child inside of us, and this child is the part of us that can fly if only we know and accept it. Some time later, I remembered something I had not thought of for many years. Around the age of eight or nine, I decided that I could fly if only I truly believed it, without doubt or fear or worry. And the reason I could not achieve such belief was very simple. The grown-up world had told me flying was not possible. Thus did my eight-year-old self understand repression, for flying was just a symbol of all the things my parents and my culture had told me were not possible. I still have not flown, but I

> Visconti &
Marseille
Fool

have done some things many people might consider impossible, including running across five lanes of Manhattan traffic.

There are deep and complex ideas around the image of the Fool, and we will look at them in a moment. First we should consider something as strange, in its own way, as a flying child. This is the question of how the Fool came to symbolize such purity and innocence. Consider two very early images, the Visconti Tarot and the classic Tarot de Marseille, long considered the standard of Tarot imagery.

They do not appear happy, joyous, or adventurous, but rather bedraggled and dazed. On the Marseille, instead of a frisky dog we see a cat biting him. Such a person does exist in our world, but not as a free innocent. Instead, we see this version of the Fool in the homeless crazy person, driven from place to place by society and his own delusions.

Now consider the earliest meanings given for the Fool, beginning in 1750 and carrying all the way to Arthur Edward Waite, writing first under the pseudonym "Grand Orient" and then under his own name in the book to go along with the Rider deck that brought us that iconic image of the radiant Fool with his sweet dog.

Some Fool Meanings

Excerpted from *Mystical Origins of the Tarot* by Paul Huson.

Pratesi's Cartomancer (1750): Madness.

De Mellet (1781): Madness.

Lévi (1855): The sensitive principle, the flesh, eternal life.

Christian (1870): Arcanum 0. Expiation. The punishment following every error... fate and the inevitable expiation.

Mathers (1888): The Foolish Man. Folly, expiation, wavering. Reversed: Hesitation, instability, trouble arising herefrom.

Golden Dawn (1888-96): The Spirit of the Ether. Foolish Man. Idea, spirituality, that which endeavors to rise above the material. But if the divination be regarding ordinary life, the card is not good, and shows folly, stupidity, eccentricity, and even mania unless with very good cards indeed.

Grand Orient (Waite, 1889, 1909): The Fool signifies the consummation of everything, when that which began his initiation at zero attains the term of all numeration and existence. This card passes through all the numbered cards and is changed in each, as the natural man passes through worlds of lesser experience, worlds of successive attainment.

Waite (1910): The Fool. Folly, mania, extravagance, intoxication, delirium, frenzy. Reversed: Negligence, absence, apathy, nullity.

There are hints here of our wonderful innocent, but mostly the image is of folly and even insanity. How did this change occur? Partly the answer lies in the very name. The French *le Fou* (and the Italian *il Matto*) actually mean "the crazy person." Some older commentaries speak of him as under the influence of the moon, which is to say, a lunatic. However, when we change Fou to Fool, we step into two powerful traditions, the holy fool and the court jester.

The idea of a holy fool is that of a simpleton touched by God, someone who can say or do profound things because he is not like the rest of us, not "normal." The jester is not a sacred figure, but he can say and do things that more established figures of society cannot, such as challenge the king. Just as with the Tarot Fool, the jester had no fixed place in the hierarchy. He was below all the nobles and yet he had a certain freedom, for in the guise of jokes he might say things no knight or lady would dare to express. In Shakespeare's great masterpiece

King Lear, only the Fool dares to tell the truth. At the same time, Lear himself, in his anguish at the overthrow of everything he believes, embodies that other Fool, or Fou, a homeless madman howling his pain in a storm.

Tarotists used to think that the joker in a poker deck was a remnant of the Fool (and thus evidence that ordinary cards were a stripped-down version of the Tarot). The joker usually appears as a court jester, and when we look at the classic Marseille card of le Fou, we see that despite his ragged state, he too wears the motley and bells of a jester. Nevertheless, research has indicated that the joker was an independent creation, coming out of a "gentlemen's club" in New York in the nineteenth century. At the same time, there are enough similarities that we might say that both the Fool and the joker come from the same archetype, that of the figure who gains a certain power by having no fixed place in the regular structure of society. In the Middle Ages, a time of rigid social classes, the annual Carnival allowed people to don masks and costumes and break at least some of the rules. Often the townspeople would pick some beggar or crazy person and crown him King of Fools.

In the game of Tarot (Tarocchi), the Fool—le Fou—is not actually part of the trumps (the Major Arcana). He stands alone, unable to capture any other cards, but he himself cannot be taken. When you know you cannot win the "trick" (a fascinating term—it means the cards put down on the table in a round of play), and you do not want to sacrifice any of your valuable cards, you play le Fou. When the winner of the trick scoops up the cards, le Fou returns to you, as if he has danced away from the net that caught the other cards.

The joker has no identity of its own. Instead, it becomes whatever it stands alongside. Put it with an ace and you have two aces. Put it alongside a pair of sevens and you have three sevens. There are people like that, who take on the identity of whomever they are with, and we tend to think of them as crazy—fou—and maybe that is the case. To be free of a fixed identity, of the illusion that our social personality is somehow the truth of who we are, is to achieve a spiritual freedom, the goal of much meditation, devotional prayer, and other practices. The trick is to stay free. The sane person believes in his or her ego identity. The crazy person may have no identity but takes on the qualities of whomever they are with. The true Fool stays free of all such limited beliefs.

This freedom is the goal of the entire Major Arcana—to shed the narrow beliefs in a limited "reality" and come to a sense of dancing freely in the world of flowing, ever-changing life, which is why we call the last card the World.

The Fool gives us a vision of such freedom at the very beginning, or rather before the beginning, for the Fool, 0, precedes all the other numbers. There is an interesting mathematical trick you may have learned in school. Take any number, any number at all, divide it by zero, and the result is always the same. Infinity. This is because an infinite number of nothings can fit into any something. One reason the modern version of the Magician, card 1, displays an infinity sign (a sideways 8) above his head is that this first something carries the memory of that glorious nothing.

There is a famous description of an electron as "nothing spinning." That is, it's useful to think of an electron (and other "elementary" particles) as objects, but in fact, it is more like a state of being. That state includes the quality of spinning. We might very well describe the Fool—our modern conception of it—as "nothing dancing."

Here is an exercise that may help you grasp a little of that elusive state. Find a quiet place where you can sit undisturbed and relaxed. Place the Fool from your favorite Tarot deck in front of you (if you only have one deck, then that's your favorite!). Perhaps do a short meditation to center yourself and detach from the usual chatter that fills our minds at any moment. If you are not used to meditation, it is enough to sit quietly and breathe deeply without forcing.

Think of the various roles you play in your life—your job, your responsibilities as a parent or a child or a partner. With each one, tell yourself—really, remind yourself, for you know this already—"I am not that. I am free. I am nothing." Think of all the things people believe about you, the things your husband or wife says so confidently, the pronouncements your teenage children make, the opinions of your boss or your neighbors. Tell yourself, "I am not that. I am free. I am nothing."

Think of the ways you describe yourself *to* yourself—kind, selfish, fat, smart, stupid, sexy, not sexy, loving, cruel, a success, a failure, a fake—all the ways we measure and judge ourselves. With each one, tell yourself, "I am not that. I am free. I am nothing." Even the most basic—a woman, a man, a body, a soul, a child of the universe—let go of them in the same way. If you do this for a while, you may come to moments of revelation, anything from "I am God!" to "I am infinite radiance" to "I'm really stupid." Do it long enough and you may want to cry or embrace the cosmos. Let go of all such moments in the same simple way. "I am not that. I am free. I am nothing." The Fool does not think of himself as innocent or free. He just is.

In Waite's list of divinatory meanings for the Rider Fool card (given above), he falls back on the old ideas of folly and madness. In his fuller description, however, he was one of the first to give us a sense of the modern view. "He is a prince of the other world on his travels through this one—all amidst the morning glory, in the keen air... He is the spirit in search of experience." He goes on to say, "Grand Orient has a curious suggestion of the office of Mystic Fool, as a part of his process in higher divination." Grand Orient is, course, Waite himself. It is worth quoting again, for it may very well be the origin of the idea of the Fool's journey: "The Fool signifies the consummation of everything, when that which began his initiation at zero attains the term of all numeration and existence. *This card passes through all the numbered cards and is changed in each*, as the natural man passes through worlds of experience, worlds of successive attainment." (italics added)

There are at least two ways to consider the Fool as journeyer. One is that the Fool—like all of us—begins life ignorant of his true nature. Some describe him as a soul incarnating into a body, and we should notice that he is not pushed or pulled or compelled, this prince of the other world, but is simply "in search of experience."

The contemporary view of the soul taking on a body is simply that being in the physical world and encountering the challenges of life is the only way to grow. Thus, the Fool begins at 0, empty of knowledge and experience, and develops step by step until he reaches its full attainment (at least, perhaps, for this lifetime) in card 21, the World. In fact, we do not need to embrace the concept of a soul taking on a body to see the Fool as someone who travels through all the experiences and challenges of the other cards. We simply can see such cards as the Lovers, or the Hermit, or the Devil, as kinds of experiences, what we all encounter on our own journey through life. "The Fool's progress" might be another title for this view of the Fool as the person who moves through all the different stages.

Looked at a slightly different way, we might describe the Fool as that within us which does not stop or get caught in any of the other cards. This is that concept of being free, being nothing. As implied above, we so easily make the mistake of believing we are this thing or that thing. If I am creative, then I *am* the Magician. If I am a boss, then I *am* the Emperor. If I feel trapped in some obsessive or abusive relationship, then the Devil controls me. The Fool is the vital and necessary answer to all this identification. You are not that, you are free.

The Fool reminds us to keep going. When we reach the kind of success and control symbolized in the Chariot (card seven), the Fool helps us find the inner Strength (the title of the card that follows the Chariot) to look inside and discover who we really are. When we have done that and discovered our "angelic" self in Temperance (card fourteen), the Fool sets us free to go down and face the Devil (fifteen).

The ancient Chinese text of the Tao Te Ching ("Classic of the Way") often seems to speak to us with the voice of the Fool. Here is what Lao-tzu, the legendary author, says of people's attitudes to the Tao, the Way (this and other quotations from the Tao Te Ching are my own renditions, based on various translations):

> The wise person hears of the Tao and practices it every day.
> The average person hears of the Tao and thinks of it now and then.
> The fool hears of the Tao and laughs.
> Without laughter, the Tao would not be what it is.

Lao-tzu also tells us, "Do nothing and everything will get done." And perhaps most famously, "Those who know do not speak. Those who speak do not know." This is not about secrets, but only an awareness that cannot be broken down into formulas and explanations.

To be in accord with the Tao is to be a Fool. More than simply an approach to life, the Tao is the very source of life, the perfect Nothing that precedes all the Somethings. In a passage that remarkably sums up the opening cards of the Major Arcana, Lao-tzu says, "Out of the Tao comes the One. Out of the One comes the Two. Out of the Two comes the Three. Out of the Three comes the ten thousand things." In Tarot terms: out of the 0, the Fool's emptiness, comes the first card, 1, the Magician, an image of energy flowing into existence. Since there is action it calls forth its counterpart, stillness, and thus card 2, the High Priestess, can be said to emerge from the Magician. Add 1 plus 2 and you get 3. That is, take the dual principles of the Magician and the High Priestess—light and dark, motion and rest, consciousness and mystery—and combine them, and you get nature, reality. This is card 3, the Empress. Out of nature comes all the rest of existence, what Lao-tzu calls the ten thousand things.

If the Fool is so perfect, why can't we just be that way? Why not move through life without attachments or plans, in harmony with nature and whatever is going on around us? Why is it so difficult to follow a path of delight? Some might answer that life itself is difficult, and without working at a job, we would not eat; without sacrificing spontaneity to the needs of our children, they might hurt themselves. This is all true; the Fool does not represent a practical approach to life's problems—unless you are so in harmony with the flow of life that you do what needs doing, including work and child care, without worrying about it, so that by "doing nothing" everything gets done. I have had moments of this, and it amazes me what can happen.

The problem of the Fool, of truly living that way, goes beyond the need to do unpleasant things. Ultimately, the Fool is not about taking off work and going to the beach. We cannot really be the Fool, we do not want to be the Fool, because the Fool has no personality, no self. There is no sense of I, or for that matter, of you or them. There is only movement, and which of us could live that way? We could not even call the Fool "enlightened," or free of ego, because the Fool has never known an ego from which to free himself. He does not even know he is a Fool.

Consider a newborn baby (the Golden Dawn envisioned the Fool as an infant). It comes out of its mother's body alert and conscious, able to make eye contact and bond with its mother. After a few hours, however, the eyes lose focus, the awareness disappears. For a time, it seems to function solely on physical needs, until fascination and curiosity begin to involve it in the world outside itself, while (hopefully) the parents' love and attention allow that curiosity to begin to develop a consciousness, a self. What happens that first day? Where does that original awareness go?

When a baby is born, it enters a new universe. Sensations, experiences, information overwhelm it until in a short time it simply shuts down. Something similar would happen to us if we suddenly became the Fool, for we would experience the world in its totality, without filters of logic, "common sense," and cultural descriptions of reality.

If the Fool represents something so unattainable and impractical, why even show it to us? Partly, the Fool allows us to recognize (re-cognize—become aware again of what we already know) that all our somethings are really nothing, that no label or measurement can ever describe the truth of who we are. This is something vitally important, and most of us forget it all the time. The Fool reminds us.

Almost all societies have a story of a lost paradise sometime in the distant past. The Fool hints at what living such a state might be like. In fact, some commentaries describe the Fool as Adam and Eve before the "fall." We are not talking about sin and disobedience here (that is the realm of card five, the Hierophant), but rather the soul in its pure condition.

The Fool does not exist alone. The Major Arcana follows it. One way to describe the Major Arcana is as a step-by-step process to allow us to regain the Fool's perfection, until at last, we rise up from limited consciousness and dance gracefully in the World.

To truly understand any card, we need to see it in readings. If we look through the deck we may think, "I don't care much for the Emperor, but the Fool looks great. I'll be like the Fool." As we have seen, no one can really do that, not fully, and certainly not all the time. But we all can have flashes of the Fool, and readings will show us moments and situations when a Fool response is exactly right. At other times, the reading might call on us to do something very different.

Here is another example from my own experience. In 1990, I bought a house in the Hudson Valley and moved from Europe, where I had lived for nineteen years. I bought the house very much under the influence of the Fool, following an impulse to live in a town I did not really know and buying a house because I fell in love with it. My schedule called for me to teach two extended workshops back to back right after I took possession of the house and then return immediately to Europe to ship my belongings.

During the two workshops, the Emperor came up in every reading I did for myself. It happened so consistently it became a joke with my students. I kept trying to figure it out, without success. Almost as frequently as the Emperor, the Tower appeared. This card can signify extreme circumstances, symbolized by a tower whose roof is struck by lightning.

After the second workshop, I came home at four o'clock on the day before I was due to fly to Europe. As I approached the house, something looked wrong, and as I came closer, my mind finally registered what it was. A tree had fallen on the roof.

Here was the "lightning-struck tower," as literal as it could be. And here was the need for the Emperor, for now that my Fool self had bought a house, I had to become an Emperor, a responsible adult compared to the Fool's eternal child. Remember how the Fool is 22 as well as 0? 22 is 2+2, which equals 4, the Emperor. Luckily (the luck of the Fool?), the damage was mostly external, and my insurance company said they could process the claim while I was away, and we could do the repairs when I returned. I had learned a lesson that there is a time for the Fool and a time for the Emperor. We have the Tarot to help us know.

> RIDER
*Emperor
&
Tower*

THE EMPEROR.

THE TOWER.

In all this we have looked at the Fool as the first card. Tarot tradition has not always placed it there. In Éliphas Lévi's Kabbalistic system, still followed by many today, the Fool comes next to last, between card twenty, Judgement, and card twenty-one, the World. We will look at this idea more closely when we come to that point, but here we might say that just as the Fool "leaps" into having a body—or to put it another way, into ordinary consciousness—so, at the end of the journey through that step-by-step process of the Major Arcana, we must take another leap, this time into the total consciousness of the World.

The position of the Fool becomes most important when we work with the cards Kabbalistically as pathways on the Tree of Life. Do we make the Fool the last card, the next to last, as Éliphas Lévi did, or the very first, as the Golden Dawn chose? The first card is the first Hebrew letter, Aleph.

For me, the idea of the Fool as Aleph has always made valuable sense. Consider its shape: א. Avigayil Landsman, a teacher and writer on the Hebrew letters, comments that Aleph resembles the blades of a windmill, a sort of spinning vortex (like the electron—nothing spinning). If we picture it turning round and round, so fast that the arms disappear (like the blades of an electric fan), we can imagine it forming a circle. A circle is one way to write the number zero, whose usual shape is an egg, as if all experience is born from it.

Most important in terms of the Fool, Aleph is a *silent* letter. It actually has no sound of its own, serving only as a carrier of vowel sounds. In Hebrew, only consonants are letters. If we wrote English this way, the word fool would be spelled FL, with a vowel marker to indicate that it's *fool*, and not *feel* or *fail*.

Aleph is like the intake of breath before we speak, the mouth open in preparation for whatever words will follow. The silence of the Aleph matches the nothingness of the Fool.

Above, we saw that that sideways 8 above the Magician signifies infinity. Modern mathematics uses a different symbol to notate infinity—the Aleph. Aleph is the first letter in an important Kabbalistic expression, Ain Sof (sometimes spelled En Sof), Without Limit. It represents the divine truth that is beyond all knowing, beyond even the Tree of Life itself.

Let us look a moment at some of the symbols that appear in different versions of the Fool. In many he carries a stick over his shoulder, with a bag. As a wanderer through life, without a home or a fixed place in the world, he carries all his belongings with him. Some Tarotists see the bag as holding his past lives, or the "self" that the rest of us wear as tightly as our skin. In the Rider the bag displays an eagle, symbol of the soaring spirit. The red plume he wears hints that his true home is the heavens. The Visconti Fool wears a whole array of feathers in his hair, as if this "madman" lives half in the kingdom of the birds.

The Shining Tribe Fool literally flies after a bird. Below, in the landscape, we see lines of energy snaking through the earth, with concentric circles to mark places of sacred openings to other worlds. In the Rider the Fool carries a rose, symbol of passion. He holds it lightly, freely, this prince of the other world.

With all this, what does it mean when the Fool appears in a reading? Its primary meanings are of spontaneity, freedom, the ability to act on instinct rather than careful planning. When the Fool appears, it may call on us to take a risk. If the reading is about love, it would say to take a chance and follow your heart. In work, it may mean to quit a job you dislike or launch a new project.

Here's the trick, however. The Fool indeed urges us to act without plans, to take chances. Does that mean we should do it? Here is where we have to judge such matters as the card's place in the reading and the other cards. If several other cards urge caution, maybe this is not the time to be Foolish. And if the Fool appears in answer to "What would be a bad approach right now?" then the card shows us what we need to avoid, not what we should do.

If the Fool does not seem to concern a specific action, then it might simply show us a way to be. The Fool is curious, joyous, eager, uninhibited. Childlike, the Fool also can be immature.

The card might come up as a description of someone else in the reading. If we ask about a new relationship, and the Fool comes up for the other person, it describes someone who can be delightful, free-spirited, often very loving, but not always reliable. There is nothing malicious about the Fool, he or she just does not like to make plans. If you seek commitment in a relationship, a Fool partner might be a bad choice.

When we reverse the Fool (for the concept of reversed meanings, see the chapter on readings), the first meaning becomes caution. This is not the time to step off the cliff. This meaning becomes reinforced when other cards of caution or maturity, such as Temperance, or the Emperor, appear in the reading right-side up.

Sometimes the reversed Fool can indicate that we have lost touch with our instincts. We may second-guess ourselves too much and avoid taking risks. How do we choose which interpretation best fits the situation? Partly we look at the other cards and see where the reversed Fool shows up in the reading. Such analysis, however, is not the only way. We also need to let our intuition guide us to the most useful meanings.

In this way, every reading involves the Fool, whether it actually shows up in the spread or not. For what could possibly be more Foolish than shuffling a deck of cards and asking it questions about our lives?

A Fool Reading

Do you want to know more about your own experience of Foolishness? Here is a reading based on the Fool. As always, we shuffle the whole deck and see which cards emerge. The questions, however, revolve around the idea of the Fool.

1. How have I been a Fool in my life?

2. How has it helped me?

3. How has it hurt me?

4. Where in my life do I need to be more Foolish?

5. Where will the Fool not serve me?

6. Where do I find the Fool outside myself?

7. What gifts does it bring me?

THE FOOL.

Magician cards from VISCONTI, MARSEILLE, RIDER, GOLDEN DAWN RITUAL, EGYPTIAN & SHINING TRIBE

THE MAGICIAN

The Magician

JUST AS WITH the Fool, the Magician has undergone a transformation over the centuries since the earliest Tarot decks. The most popular images today of this card show him as serene, powerful, with an infinity sign over his head and pointing his magic wand up towards the heavens as if to draw down divine energy. On his table lie the four emblems of the Tarot Minor Arcana, as if he is master of the physical world. He is indeed a "Magus," as Éliphas Lévi called him, and as Aleister Crowley titled the card.

Now look at the older Marseille image. We see someone dressed somewhat like a court jester. There is no magical infinity sign above his head, yet the curved wide brim of the hat subtly suggests that image.

Instead of the symbols of the four suits, the table contains an odd assortment of objects: a knife, a couple of plain cups or containers, and several balls or pellets, along with a bag of some sort on the side, reminiscent of the bag the modern version of the Fool carries over his shoulder. What are these for? The French name, *Bateleur* (in Italian *Bagatto*), often translated as "juggler," gives us the answer, for the word refers to a sleight-of-hand game played on the street with unsuspecting marks. The "juggler" places a small ball under one of two (or more often, three) cups, slides them around, then reveals where it is. When he invites someone to try it, the person usually gets it right the first two tries or so, but when serious money is placed on the table, the juggler's hands move much more quickly—sometimes dropping the ball into the bag—and the person loses the bet. People today who have seen this "game" played on the sidewalks of New York or London may be surprised to know how old it is or that it was the original inspiration for the Tarot Magician. Thus, the grand Magus of the modern tradition is revealed to have his roots in someone who is at best a street entertainer, and at worst a con artist.

Here are some of the odd ways in which this card has developed over time.

Some Magician Meanings

Excerpted from *Mystical Origins of the Tarot* by Paul Huson.

Pratesi's Cartomancer (1750): Baggatino, married man.

De Mellet (1781): The Mountebank.

Court de Gébelin (1773-82): The Thimble-Rigger.

Lévi (1855): The Hebrew letter Aleph, the Juggler. The Magus. Being, mind, man, or God; unity; mother of numbers, the first substance.

Christian (1870): The Magus: Will. In the divine world, the Absolute Being who contains and from whom flow all possible things; in the intellectual world, Unity, the principle and synthesis of numbers; in the physical world, Man, the highest of all living creatures.

Mathers (1888): The Juggler or Magician. Willpower, dexterity. Reversed: Will applied to evil ends, weakness of will, knavishness.

Golden Dawn (1888-96): The Magus of Power. The Magician or Juggler. Skill, wisdom, adaptation, cunning, always depending on the cards around it and whether or not it's reversed. Sometimes occult wisdom.

Grand Orient (Waite, 1889, 1909): The Juggler. Skill, subtlety, on the evil side, trickery. Also occult practice.

Waite (1910): The Magician. Skill, diplomacy, subtlety, snares of enemies, the inquirer—if male. Reversed: Physician, magus, disgrace.

Notice that the split between mountebank and magus goes through much of the history of the card, including Waite in his two versions. The first cartomancers all assumed it symbolized the street performer, and it is not until Éliphas Lévi that we see something grander. But look how grand! Not just Magus, though he introduces the term, but also "being, mind, man, or God." Paul Christian continues this theme, but notice how Mathers reverts to the Juggler and includes "will applied to evil ends, knavishness." By using the concept of the reversed meaning, Mathers is able to suggest the Magician/Juggler's good and bad sides. The Golden Dawn (founded by Mathers) includes "the Magus of Power" and "occult wisdom" but also "adaptation" and "cunning," both qualities of the "Juggler," that Baggatino with his table of tricks. Grand Orient (Waite) says primarily "the Juggler" but also adds "occult practice." And notice how Waite, writing under his own name, gives "snares of enemies" in the primary meanings, but also "physician, magus, disgrace" in the reversed.

Is there no way to reconcile these two images for the card, the mountebank and the magus? Surprisingly, the full meaning of the Magician, and perhaps the Tarot itself, may depend on knowing both the grand magician and the trickster. Both attributes are embodied in the name of a Greek god who can be said to be the patron of the Tarot, Hermes.

When Antoine Court de Gébelin and Comte de Mellet pronounced the Tarot a book of ancient Egyptian teachings (in 1781—see Introduction), they were referring to the Hellenistic city of Alexandria, named for Alexander the Great, where Greek ideas and images joined with Egyptian. The esoteric traditions that sprang up in that time (the period before the Roman Empire) were attributed to the Egyptian god Thoth, associated with writing, magic, raising the dead, and wisdom of all kinds. Early occultists called the Tarot the Book of

Thoth (a title used in the twentieth century by Aleister Crowley), with the idea that the god himself created the pictures and handed them to his human acolytes. The Alexandrians were Greek as much as Egyptian, and so they linked Thoth to a Greek god with similar attributes: Hermes, calling him either Thoth-Hermes, or Hermes Trismegistus, Hermes Three Times Great. Hermes Trismegistus was a god but also a great wise man, the legendary author of a complex series of sacred texts known collectively as the "Hermetica." And yet, the name Hermes is vastly older than the mysterious figure of Hermes Trismegistus from Alexandria some two thousand years ago. Even though Homer describes Hermes, whom the Romans called Mercury, as a son of Zeus, and therefore fairly late, Hermes may originally have been one of the earliest figures in prehistoric Greece, for we know he was represented not by grand statues but by rough standing stones. Mythographer Walter F. Otto said of Hermes, "He must once have struck the Greeks as a brilliant flash out of the depths."

This brilliant flash can be described as creation itself, the moment when the Divine says, "Let there be light." To quote the Tao Te Ching once again, "Out of the Tao comes the One," the oneness of the Magician, card 1, emerging—magically—from the formless Nothing of the Fool. The greatest magic act, writer Alan Moore tells us, is for Something to come out of Nothing.

For all that, the Greeks did not visualize Hermes as remote, or grand, or sitting on some high throne. Hermes was a god of both wisdom and knowledge (not the same thing), and it makes sense that the later Alexandrians would see him and Thoth as the same. But he also was a messenger, a guide to dead souls, an outsider, a prankster, a wild child, a symbol of the generative power of male sexuality—the Magician with his wand is the Tarot's primary symbol of masculine energy—and a thief.

The *Homeric Hymn to Hermes* tells how baby Hermes, the very next day after his birth, slips out of his cradle and goes seeking adventure. Hidden within the dynamic energy of the Tarot Magician rises a spirit of play, for creativity can never be dry and purely intellectual but must always contain an element of simple delight. Baby Hermes comes across a herd of cattle, and being a god of magic, he instantly recognizes them as belonging to his big brother, Apollo, god of the sun, poetry, prophecy, and civilization. Hermes makes off with some of the herd, cleverly walking backwards to confuse any trackers. After a wild barbecue he returns to his cradle, where he pulls his blanket up and puts on an innocent face.

Wise Apollo is not fooled but marches in and furiously accuses his baby brother of theft. "Me?" Hermes says innocently. "I'm just a baby. I was born yesterday. I don't even know what 'cattle' is." When Apollo, unappeased, takes Hermes before their father, all-powerful Zeus, Hermes says, "I'm a frank person, and I don't know how to lie." (trans. Charles Boer) He then swears a solemn oath: "NOT GUILTY, by these beautiful porticoes of the gods!" (Boer) Even as he says this, holding onto his blankie like an innocent babe, he winks.

Instead of being angry, Zeus bursts out laughing and orders the two of them—rational, grand Apollo and prankster Hermes—to reconcile. And then something special happens. For before he went after the cattle, Hermes created something. He saw a tortoise wobbling along and had a vision of what could be done with its shell. He killed it (there is a merciless quality to the Magician, tempered, at his best, by service), gutted the shell, attached reeds for a neck and strung seven strands of sheep gut down the length of it. Seven, remember, is the number of the planetary spheres and the diatonic musical scale, as well as the chakra centers in the body and the colors of the rainbow. Thus he created the lyre, the first musical instrument. When Zeus orders Hermes to make up with Apollo, Hermes gives him the lyre. In the ancient world, Apollo was known as the god of music, for harmonious sounds were thought of as the very essence of reason. But there is no beauty in harmony without inspiration, that flash of light out of the depths. And so, again, we get the Magician as dynamic creative energy.

Zeus then asks Hermes what he would like to rule over. Knowing very well that Apollo rules the great Oracle at Delphi, cheeky Hermes asks to be in charge of prophecy. Zeus refuses, but then Apollo says something remarkable. Prophetic vision may be out, but there are forms of divination that are older than prophecy, that of three sisters, the Fates, who were long skilled at prediction when Apollo was still learning. Thus, Hermes becomes the god of the very practice that dominates our modern use of Tarot cards, divination.

In recent years, Tarot divination has become *psychologized*, that is, the cards are seen as representative of psychological or emotional states. We might say, for example, that the Magician symbolizes creative energy, or the Empress strong emotions. Both these statements are true as far as they go, but divination also contains a quality of magic. The word *divination* itself derives from "divine," for in ancient times people saw divination as communication with the gods. Karl Kerenyi, one of the past century's great writers on Greek myth, described Hermes' ability to look at the tortoise and "see through" its present state to its future possibility as the lyre. This divine, or magical, quality of *seeing through* is just what happens in a Tarot reading.

We lay out the cards and, inspired by the images, see beyond the present situation to what is likely to develop.

There is a difference between oracular visions, under the rule of Apollo, and divination, under the rule of Hermes. The first, as practiced most famously at Delphi, depends on direct inspiration, often in a trance state. Divination uses a system, often some kind of casting of lots. In Greece, this might have meant using the letters as symbols of meaning, the way people have always used the Scandinavian runes (actually an alphabet) or the Hebrew letters. Tarot cards are a system of divination, an intermediary that we use to answer our questions and gain insight.

Though the Fates were very ancient goddesses, it is significant that they were women, and divination belongs to them. Many cultures have considered divination a woman's occupation, sometimes done by traveling diviners. In Scandinavia, the runecasters traveled from village to village, wearing cat's fur gloves and capes to partake of the magical psychic power of cats (compare the idea of black cats as "familiars" of witches). Today, while there is no shortage of men who read Tarot cards, the image of a Tarot reader often conjures up a "Gypsy" woman in colorful scarves. And those of us who teach Tarot workshops often comment how women participants will greatly outnumber men. The act of divination calls forth the feminine—in men as well as women. Divination involves sensitivity, psychic awareness, nurturing, and care (people who come for Tarot readings usually are suffering, or at least worried), qualities our culture considers the realm of women. And yet, while the High Priestess can symbolize, and even bring out, our psychic abilities, and the Empress our nurturing, the practice of divination belongs to the Magician.

In traditional Tarot symbolism, the Magician stands for the masculine principle—active, light, dry, rising upwards, tending toward oneness, conscious, and rational, while the High Priestess represents the feminine principle—receptive, dark, moist, sinking downwards, complex, unconscious, and intuitive. We sometimes see the masculine and feminine described as "positive" and "negative," but this does not mean good and bad. Instead, it refers to the positive and negative poles of electromagnetism, which exist together and allow energy to flow.

The very image of the number one, whether as the Arabic numeral 1 or the Roman I, suggests the male organ, upright and potent, just as the Roman representation of two, II, suggests the entrance to the female womb, where new life grows. When ancient peoples set up stones to represent the phallus—those upright pillars for Hermes, and similar columns for the Hindu god Shiva—or created pools and temples in the shape of the womb, they were not obsessed with sex. Rather, they understood that the life-giving energies of sexuality are a mirror of divine masculine and feminine principles. As above, so below.

This is a good point at which to stress that the Magician is not just for men, and the High Priestess just for women. The Tarot uses a very old symbolic system in which images of men and women symbolize particular qualities. At the same time, esoteric teachings have always understood, even when society believed in rigid gender roles, that true fulfillment lies in integrating both male and female energy.

Throughout life, we all fluctuate between different qualities all the time. One of the benefits of Tarot readings is their ability to show us what aspects of ourselves are active at any particular time. One day the Magician might appear to remind you of your creative energy or determination or clear mind, another time the High Priestess will help you acknowledge your intuition and inner wisdom.

The Magician's number, that I in Roman numerals, implies the conscious self, the ego (which is simply the Latin word for "I"). At the same time, magic, including the magic of divination, happens when we can allow energy to enter us and then direct it to manifestation. The ability to make ourselves a kind of opening for the magical energy of divination (or any other "magic") is symbolized in the Magician's posture, his wand raised to the heavens, his finger pointed to the ground. This posture often makes this card attractive to artists, healers, and other people who work with manifesting energy. Almost all creative people will say that when the work is going well, it's as if they're not doing it—some force, or energy, is moving through them, and they are simply the channel to bring the work into the physical world. With our modern emphasis on "intellectual property" (making creativity a branch of capitalism), we consider those statements quaint, or curious, just as we think the ancient opening of poems—"Sing in me, Muse"—is just empty words. Nor do we understand why so many spiritual texts were written anonymously or attributed to mythical authors (like Hermes Trismegistus, said to be a god). Just possibly these older peoples understood the magic of creativity more completely than us, a flow of energy symbolized in the Magician's posture.

Try standing this way. Take a stick, or a pen, or an actual magic wand, and raise it up with one hand while the other points earthward. Notice how it opens up the chest, how you can breathe more deeply. Now close the eyes and let yourself feel energy move through you, from the formless world of spirit to the solid world of matter. The Magician in a reading symbol-izes great creative and transformational possibilities.

The Magician's body also symbolizes the great Hermetic truth "As above, so below." The actual opening of the Emerald Tablet, literal cornerstone of the Hermetic teachings, runs like this: "That which is below is like that which is above, and that which is above is like that which is below, to accomplish the miracles of the one thing." (trans. Christopher Bamford)

Our small lives, which so often can seem random, or meaningless, are actually an organic part of the cosmos. This is one of the great teachings of the Tarot, and ultimately one of the reasons we do readings—not just to find out information, or seek guidance or self-knowledge (all of which are important) but also to demonstrate to ourselves that the universe is not just broken pieces. Things connect.

Along with the image of Hermes, there is another way to reconcile the two strands of the juggler/magus, and that is the figure of the tribal shaman. In the Shining Tribe Magician, we see a masked figure who causes a flower to grow in the desert as he channels down life from the sacred river that flows through the heavens.

Shamans heal the sick by journeying to the spirit world, and yet they were not above sleight-of-hand trickery to impress their "clients." The European explorers who first encoun-tered shamans in Siberia and other places sometimes described how they would observe the shaman palm a small stone before going into the tent of healing. After chanting and other magical actions, the shaman would pretend to reach into the sick person's body and pull out the illness—the stone hidden in his hand. To the European, this branded the shaman as a con artist. Only much later did they come to a more subtle understanding. The true healing occurs in trance, in the spirit world, but the sick person needs to see some tangible result. And so the shaman holds up the black stone to show the person that a healing has taken place.

When we refuse to see the connection between Hermes the sly trickster and Hermes the wise magus, we may end up with a dangerous split between the con artist and the philoso-pher. We see this sometimes in modern Tarot reading. The committed reader, sometimes with a code of ethics prominently placed on the wall, carefully avoids any trace of what is called "cold reading," the ability to elicit information from someone without actually asking, so that it seems like amazing psychic ability. To avoid any such trickery, they may block part of the essential communication that goes on in a reading. And by refusing to dazzle the client with something that might smack of trickery, they may hinder themselves from conveying the really important part of the information.

Many years ago, when I lived in Amsterdam and was first reading professionally, a very troubled man came to see me. He told how his happy life had fallen apart a few years back when he discovered he was psychic. Now, many people imagine such an awakening as thrilling, but they also imagine themselves in control of it. Unable to stop the sensations, emotions, and even thoughts coming in from other people, this man had suffered a breakdown and had lost his job and even his family, and now kept himself under control by taking drugs meant as antipsychotics (delusions and psychic experiences may come from similar areas of the brain).

At the start of our session, he asked me, "Are you psychic?" Thinking of my ethical standards, I told him no, I just interpreted the pictures. I didn't realize that he actually was asking, "Can I trust what you say?"

As so often happens with someone in serious need, the reading came out clear and precise. It showed the shock that had upended his once happy life, showed his frightened state, and most important, showed that he could be happy, and useful, and safe, if instead of suppressing his ability with drugs he found a teacher to train him.

As it happened, I knew such a teacher, a brilliant woman named Ioanna Salajan. She was in fact my teacher, for I went to her weekly combination class of meditation, Zen, personal growth, and psychology. It was Ioanna who said the words at the front of this book, "Nothing is learned except through joy." I only attended the weekly class, but friends of mine went to her intensive groups, where she focused on the esoteric traditions of psychic healing.

I told my troubled client about Ioanna, gave him her contact information, and told him as well that if she could not help him, he could go to her teacher, a near-legendary figure who lived in Denmark but taught in many countries. The reading offered great promise, but it meant he would have to give up his terror, go off the medication, and cultivate the very energy that had caused such anguish. And because I had said I was not psychic, he did not dare to trust me.

Does this mean I now say yes whenever someone asks if I'm psychic? No. I will say that psychic moments occur in readings, but I work primarily from the pictures. This is true, and it avoids the expectations that I will say something like, "On May 17, you will go to a party and meet a tall, black-haired man named Greg—" in other words, the kind of Tarot reader they've seen in bad movies. And yet, I try to remember that some people need a little razzle-dazzle to accept the genuine magic of the reading.

The infinity sign above the Magician's head (called a lemniscate) symbolizes the truth that life is eternal, without beginning or end, that nothing is destroyed but only changes form. "Energy is neither created nor destroyed" runs the law of conservation of energy. As a sideways number 8 it suggests "As above, so below," but also a variation, "As without, so within." The events in our lives reflect the inner truth of who we are. Paul Foster Case says in his book *The Tarot* that occult tradition assigns the number eight to Hermes (Trismegistus), the transmitter of divine teachings. Along with all these meanings, we might add that the lemniscate evokes the constant play of energy between Hermes the grand teacher and Hermes the trickster/diviner/juggler.

Karl Kerenyi says it is Hermes who puts things in our hands just when we need them. Such magical coincidence is a kind of divine trickery, and virtually everyone who commits her- or himself to a sacred or creative path will experience moments when something just happens to help them along the way. Merlin Stone (what a perfect name for a magician!), author of *When God Was a Woman*, told of how in the middle of her research she needed a certain book that was nowhere to be found. She tried used bookstores (this was long before the Internet), libraries, universities, all without success. One day she went to the supermarket, and as she walked through the aisles, she found an old book lying on the floor. It was, of course, the very one she needed. The Magician in a reading may signify such moments, especially if it appears with other cards that represent help or guidance.

Generally, the Magician in a reading signifies consciousness, will, and transformative or creative power. It suggests that in some way magic is present in our lives, or that we have the ability to bring about a magical change. If it comes up in a temporary position, such as "near future" in the Celtic Cross, we need to take advantage of this burst of energy, this flow of excitement. In a more long-lasting position, such as "outcome" in the Cross, it indicates a shift in life to greater power and creativity. It is a very auspicious card for an artist or writer or performer, for it symbolizes creativity itself.

As card one, it can indicate the beginning of something, and a very positive beginning, in particular the first actual steps to make it real, and the will to carry it through. The will of the Magician is unified and directed. The card also can indicate the ego and a desire to dominate, in particular with other strong-minded cards.

The reversed Magician may suggest an abuse of that strong will, even in some rare cases, so-called "black magic," used for destructive, selfish purposes. Remember that the Magician heads the triad that includes Strength but also the Devil. Conversely, the upside-down card can mean a weakening of the will, or lack of focus, or self-doubt.

The will or creative energy may be blocked or disrupted. This can result in weakness or confusion of purpose. It can lead further to apathy, lethargy, an inability to act. For artists it can mean a creative block. Sometimes the blocked energy can cause anxiety, or fear, or panic attacks.

Because the source of these situations is the reversed Magician, the problem may come from something the person needs to do, some decision or action the person is avoiding. It may involve taking a risk (especially when the Fool also appears) or going against family or social opinion (especially when the Hanged Man appears). Think of the Magician's posture as a lightning rod. If he allows the energy to pass through him and be grounded in action, or a decision, he experiences that magical joy. If he resists doing that, the energy stays inside, disrupting the system. If the Magician reversed comes up in a reading, ask yourself, "Do I doubt myself too much? Is there something I know I need to do? How can I serve the muse and the world?"

Here are two readings to understand magical power. The first is a Wisdom Reading to understand what magic means.

A Magician Wisdom Reading

1.   What is magic?

2.   How does it act in the world?

3.   How do we find it?

4.   How do we use it?

5.   How do we become magicians?

Lay out the cards in whatever pattern feels right to you.

The second reading is a personal reading to look at the same issues for yourself.

A Magician Personal Reading

1. What is magic for me?

2. How does magic act in my life?

3. Where do I look for magic?

4. How do I find it?

5. How do I use it?

6. How can I become a magician?

7. What will it mean to me?

LA PAPESSE   LA PAPESSA

THE HIGH PRIESTESS   II   DIE HOHEPRIESTERIN
LA SACERDOTISA   DE HOGEPRIESTERES

High Priestess: 2

Astrological correspondence:
    Moon

Kabbalistic letter: ℷ Gimel

Path on Tree of Life: Kether
    (Crown) to Tipheret
    (Beauty)

*High Priestess cards
from* VISCONTI,
MARSEILLE,
RIDER, GOLDEN
DAWN RITUAL,
EGYPTIAN &
SHINING TRIBE

THE HIGH PRIESTESS

THE HIGH PRIESTESS

The High Priestess

THE TERM *High Priestess* is modern, another inno-
vation of the Golden Dawn. Originally, and still
today in many European versions, especially the
Tarot de Marseille, the card is called Papesse, that
is, "female pope." The image of a woman wearing the pope's triple crown and holding a book
(open in some versions, closed or even locked in
others) goes back to the very first extant deck,
the Visconti-Sforza, whose pictures were without
name or number (the version of the V-S shown
here is a modern reconstruction).

We might assume that just as the unhappy Fou
became the wise, innocent Fool in modern times,
and the Juggler became the powerful Magician,

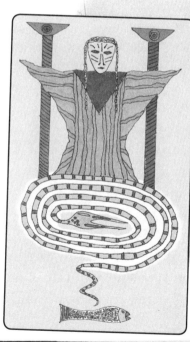

so the image of a High Priestess only emerged in the last century. A look at the history of the card reveals a surprise. The expression "High Priestess" goes back to the very origins of the Tarot's esoteric tradition, Antoine Court de Gébelin's comments in *Le Monde Primitif*.

Some High Priestess Meanings

Excerpted from *Mystical Origins of the Tarot* by Paul Huson.

De Mellet (1781): Pride, symbolized by her peacock. Idolatry.

Court de Gébelin (1773-82): The High Priestess.

Lévi (1855): The Hebrew letter Beth, the Female Pope. The house of God and Man, the sanctuary, the law, gnosis, Kabbala, the occult church, the duad, wife or mother.

Christian (1870): Arcanum II. The door of the occult sanctuary. Knowledge.

Mathers (1888): The High Priestess. Science, wisdom, education. REVERSED: Conceit, ignorance, unskillfullness, superficial knowledge.

Golden Dawn (1888-96): The Priestess of the Silver Star. High Prestess. Change, increase and decrease. Fluctuation (whether for good or evil is shown by cards connected with it).

Grand Orient (Waite, 1889, 1909): High Priestess. Nature, including generation and reproduction, fertility, change.

Waite (1910): The High Priestess. Secrets, mystery, the unrevealed future. The woman who interests the inquirer, if male; the inquirer herself, if female. Wisdom and science. REVERSED: Moral or physical ardor, conceit, surface knowledge.

Before we try to see what these concepts mean—before we try to look behind the "veil," or curtain, of the Priestess—we should consider that alternative title and image, the female pope. Was this a satirical, or subversive, response to an all-male priesthood? Many readers will know the story of Pope Joan, a woman who disguised herself as a man to become a priest, then rose to be elected pope. Whether this actually happened or was simply a popular legend, it may have given rise to the Tarot card of La Papesse.

And there is another possibility. In the 1200s, a radical movement sprang up in Europe, led by a woman named Guglielma of Bohemia. Guglielma preached that Christ would return in 1300 to begin a new age when women would be popes. Guglielma herself died before the great day, and so the Guglielmites elected a woman named Manfreda Visconti to be the first female pope. The year 1300 came and went without Christ making an appearance (at least as far as history records), and the church made its position on female popes very clear: they burned Manfreda at the stake. One hundred and fifty years later, the first known Tarot deck was created, commissioned by the rulers of the city-state of Milan—the Visconti family.

Did the Tarot secretly carry on the heretical teachings of Guglielma and Manfreda? Probably not.

But one thing we can say with some certainty: people seek balance, and even in the most patriarchal cultures, images of the feminine will find their way into art and stories and even religion. When the Catholic Church established an all-male godhead (notice that the very word suggests a head without a body), the people turned to visions of the Virgin Mary, a gentle figure who supposedly would intercede for them against the possible harsh punishments of the masculine God. The church resisted such efforts to raise up Mary, even as they used her popularity. Most people do not realize this, but it was not until 1950 that the Vatican officially set Mary in Heaven alongside her Son.

Many Renaissance images of Mary show her reading a book. Was Mother Mary herself one of the sources of La Papesse?

The Tarot, especially with the early cards, establishes a system of dualities—the Magician and the High Priestess, followed by the Empress and the Emperor. The Magician and High Priestess are the very model of duality in the Tarot. "Out of the One comes the Two," says the Tao Te Ching. We cannot have a north pole without a south, electricity cannot have a positive without a negative, light creates shadow. Thus, we can describe the Magician as light, reason, active, masculine, going outwards, and conscious, and the High Priestess as darkness, intuition, receptivity, feminine, going inwards, the unconscious. And yet, they cross over in subtle ways. The Magician's posture—one arm up, the other down—allows power to pass through him, so that the sense of active and creative comes from the Spirit (or the muse), not personal power or control.

And even though the High Priestess symbolizes the dark feminine (the Chinese idea of yin as compared to yang—"Carry shadow on your back, embrace light in your arms," the Tao Te Ching tells us)—the modern version shows her sitting between two pillars, one light, the other dark, so that she herself becomes the principle of balance. This is the genius of genuine symbols, that they can signify several things at once and the possibilities of their applications never really end.

Both the Papesse version and the Priestess include the sense of three in the headdress. The female pope's triple crown symbolizes Christ's reign on all levels. The Rider High Priestess wears the crown of Isis, symbolic of the three phases of the moon. More about this image in a moment. But first—

Here is another of my "mistakes" from my early days of Tarot (similar to telling the psychic client I was not psychic—see the section on the Magician). Some thirty years ago, I was giving private lessons to a young woman going through a difficult time. Frightening delusions would seize her, such as knives coming through the walls and fear of people wanting to kill her. The psychiatric profession might describe such a condition in terms of brain chemistry. In esoteric terms, we might say that the borders were breaking down between three levels—the archetypal world of principles, the lower realm of dreams, and the world of daily life.

One day, the woman came early to our appointment, and so as not to bother me she went for coffee in my neighborhood, a very old part of Amsterdam. The coffeehouse occupied a building scheduled to be torn down, so that huge pillars made from tree trunks shored up the walls on either side of the window. The very setting of a condemned building must have unconsciously symbolized for her the state of her endangered psyche. While she sat at the wooden counter facing the window, a black woman and a white woman sat down, one on each side of her. Panic seized her, and she rushed to my apartment. She told me that they seemed like demons to her, or more precisely, an angel and a demon fighting for her soul.

At that time a large number of black people had come to the Netherlands from the former South American colonies of Surinam and Curacao. In response, the Dutch, ever critical of racism in other countries, had shown a racist streak of their own. So when my student told me that a black woman was a demon trying to drag her soul into darkness, I made the great mistake of reacting politically, with the idea that skin color does not represent good or evil.

She listened respectfully and seemed to understand my point, but as I look back I'm sure what I said did not really reach her in a truly meaningful way. Only the next day did I realize what I should have done, which was to take out the card of the High Priestess, set it before her, and say, "This is the pillar of darkness. This is the pillar of light. And this is you sitting in the middle. They cannot harm you."

I'm not suggesting that just showing her that picture would have magically cured her of all her distress. But if images have trapped us, then images can free us. We can try to keep down

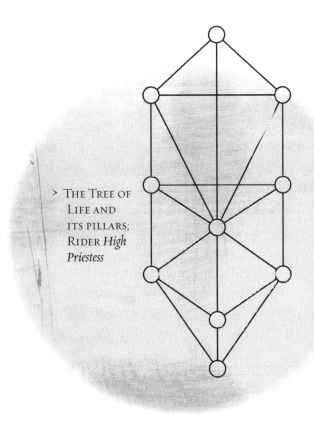

> The Tree of
Life and
its pillars;
Rider *High
Priestess*

the archetypal world by arguing with it, saying, "This isn't rational, this doesn't make sense." Or we can deal with it on its own terms and hope to travel through the experience. The Tarot gives us the archetypal in a form that we can use, for healing as well as self-discovery.

In the Kabbalistic Tree of Life, we find the masculine pillar of expansion on the right, the feminine pillar of contraction on the left, but in the middle is balance.

In the Tarot de Marseille, she sits before a curtain. In the later High Priestess card, in the Rider tradition, the curtain runs between two pillars marked B and J. The letters stand for Boaz and Jachin, which, according to tradition, were names of black and white pillars at the entrance to Solomon's temple in ancient Israel. The card subtly evokes Freemasonry, for the Masons set themselves the task of rebuilding the temple, but on the astral plane rather than as an earthly building. The two pillars also evoke the number of the card and the feminine principle, the entrance to the womb.

Pomegranates decorate the curtain. The fruit symbolizes the female, the Goddess, in many ways. Fecund, with many seeds, with red juice that resembles menstrual blood and a womb-like shape when cut open, it in fact contains estrogen, the female hormone. The plant has become popular in recent years due to the discovery of a high concentration of antioxidants, chemicals that can prevent cancer.

The pomegranate brings together Greek and Kabbalist symbolism. While the fruit appears in the myth of Persephone (more about her in a moment), the medieval Kabbalists envisioned paradise as *Pardes Rimmonim*, an "orchard of pomegranates." Our English word *paradise*, and the Hebrew *Pardes*, derive from the Persian word *paradeiza*, meaning an enclosed garden—like the Garden of Eden, originally considered a physical place in the world but with a counterpart in the heavenly, or astral, realm. As above, so below.

On the Rider card, the placement of the fruits suggests the Tree of Life, with the top triangle of the tree touching the top and points of the Priestess's crown. We can see the side sephiroth on either side of her, while the center ones are concealed by her body itself. Thus, she becomes the actual tree. And so may we, to the extent that we can embody the Priestess within ourselves. We will see this image—the body in the tree—even more developed in the Hanged Man and the World.

As mentioned, the pomegranate evokes the Greek goddess Persephone, and through her the most important rite of the Classical world, the Greater Mysteries of Eleusis (a small town outside of Athens). In the myth that underlies the Mysteries—and over time this myth has struck me as more and more significant to Tarot, whether or not the original designers thought about it—Hades, god of death, kidnaps Persephone to become his bride in the Underworld. When Persephone's mother, Demeter, compels the gods to allow Persephone to return to the world of the living, Death gives Persephone a pomegranate seed to eat, and because she has consumed food in the Underworld, she must return for part of every year (also see the Empress, the Wheel of Fortune, the Devil, and the Star). Thus the High Priestess becomes the mistress of the Mysteries, of death and the passage through death to a greater existence.

The Mysteries of Persephone are suggested even more strongly in the modern name for card five, the Hierophant, for that was the name of the priest who presided over the nine-day ritual. Thus we have a High Priestess and a High Priest, just as earlier decks contained a

Papess and a Pope. What exactly is the difference between a priest and a high priestess? Traditionally they represent the outer and inner aspects of mystical experience. The priest holds power over the tradition, the rules, the teachings. The priestess signifies levels of understanding that cannot be put into words or doctrines, that fall apart or just seem absurd if we try to describe them.

We've all had such moments. "I just can't describe it," we might say about a special experience. "I don't know how I know, I just do." High Priestess wisdom resembles such feelings, but of a different order because it involves divine truths. Such moments can give us a glimpse of her.

The curtain, or "veil," behind her in many versions reflects an occult image of the nineteenth century, "Veiled Isis," which becomes "Isis Unveiled" (title of a book by Madame Blavatsky, founder of Theosophy) when the great secrets reveal themselves. In the Rider tradition, the Priestess wears the crown of Isis, formed from two crescent moons, with a full moon between them.

Though the crown comes from Isis, it also represents the Triple Goddess of the waxing, full, and waning moon, physically present in the lives of women—Maiden, Mother, and Crone. This is not really a matter of symbolism, at least not an intellectual or artistic symbol. The phases of the moon are very real, and so are the phases of women's lives. *And they are the same thing*. They do not just resemble each other by some odd coincidence. Women's menstrual cycles follow the lunar cycle. Women's life cycles follow the same pattern as the moon. "As above, so below" is not just a slogan, or an ideology, or a metaphor saying that two completely separate things are like each other. It means they both belong to a larger existence. The Tarot does not just teach us concepts. It teaches us reality.

The Golden Dawn assigned the moon astrologically not to the actual Moon card but to the High Priestess, and in the Rider tradition we see the crescent moon at her feet. We might see in her the various moon goddesses of different cultures, in particular Artemis/Diana, who rejects marriage and social structures and lives freely in the mountains with her band of nymphs. Homer represents Artemis as a kind of rough tomboy, but in fact her worship and her image go back so far into prehistory that no one even knows the origin of the name. She signifies whatever is wild and free and ancient, yet she also comes to women in labor, to ease the pain of childbirth. As with Isis (and many other goddesses, including the Shekinah, the Kabbalist female aspect of God), paintings often depict Artemis with outstretched wings.

The curtain represents the "veil" over the occult secrets of existence. But look carefully at the Rider image. We actually can see between the pillars and the curtain, and when we do we discover no great temple, no ancient documents, no opening to the other world. Instead we just find water—formless, serene, fathomless. The ultimate mystery.

In modern terms, we name these hidden waters the "unconscious," but only if we distinguish it from the "subconscious," the mass of repressed thoughts, desires, and emotions that the conscious ego does not want to acknowledge. When we react with extreme emotion to some innocuous comment, the subconscious is acting out. When we get a sense of the wonder of life and can't explain it, we are touching the unconscious. *Unconscious* here means the vast sea of life beyond our personal experience, needs, and desires. Myths, inspirations of divine wonder, dreams that seem to come from a deeper place than the usual anxieties (the exam-time-and-I-forgot-to-study sort of dream)—these all give us glimpses of the unconscious behind the veil of everyday existence. We can link the High Priestess to Egyptian Isis or Greek Persephone. In Kabbalist Tarot, she also embodies a very important figure known as the Shekinah. The term originally meant (and still means, for older meanings live on) God's "indwelling presence," that is, the divine power alive on Earth and dwelling in the Ark of the Covenant (remember the end of the film *Raiders of the Lost Ark?*) in the center of Solomon's temple. Over time, the Kabbalists gave a more developed meaning to Shekinah—God's *female* aspect, who indeed lived in the temple and was partner to "the King," the male aspect of God, who dwells in Heaven. Above and Below, linked in the union—*Yihud* in Hebrew—between the King and the Shekinah. Raphael Patai, in his book *The Hebrew Goddess*, shows how many of the attributes associated with the Shekinah resemble those of such figures as the Babylonian goddess Ishtar.

Kabbalist myth further tells us that when the Romans destroyed the temple in the year 70, the Shekinah turned her back on the King (who, after all, had let the Romans destroy her home) and went into exile with humanity. Thus she becomes virginal, detached, yet dedicated, like the High Priestess. Part of our purpose as humans is to help restore Yihud between the two aspects of God. We do this through the union of men and women (or, really, any two lovers), as shown in the Lovers card, or through harmonizing the masculine and feminine parts of ourselves, our own Magician and High Priestess, as suggested in the World card.

Clearly, this is all very complex. What do we say when the High Priestess appears in readings? She may at times signify secret doctrines and teachings, or even the office of a priestess, someone who guides or inspires others. Modern Pagans have led the way in reviving the concept of priestess. The title does not simply mean a woman priest, for priest and priestess are very different roles. The priest officiates and directs, and in his best aspect directs divine energy to bless the people or the land. The priestess initiates; she brings people to the inner levels where they can discover their own mysteries. We can fulfill this role in ordinary life when we gently help others, especially those in a crisis, to find their own way rather than tell them what to do (or nurture and take care of them, as the Empress might).

The High Priestess card can signal something very deep awakened in us, especially psychic or spiritual awareness. In a class on dream readings once, a woman told how she'd dreamed that a shiny green jaguar came to her and led her into a room with an altar and a crown. The jaguar turned into a woman, who picked up the crown and set it on her head. I told her that this sounded very much like a dream initiation into a spiritual mystery. When we did the reading (for the method of using Tarot with dreams, see the chapter on readings) and came to the moment when the jaguar woman crowned her, the card was the High Priestess.

The priestess role of service shows us one aspect of the card. In another, it reminds us to be silent, to look inward and contemplate stillness. This can mean actual meditation or some other spiritual practice, but not necessarily. It just tells us not to rush about, not to try to solve things, not to get caught up. Most modern people run our lives between two states, action and relationship. We try to succeed, to be responsible, or we try to connect to family, lovers, friends in meaningful ways. The High Priestess card can remind us to stay with ourselves, to trust our instincts and intuitions. We don't need to act on them, and we may not be able to explain them, even to ourselves, but we can trust that sense of knowing.

Reversed, the High Priestess may call on us to get involved again in the world, especially if we've spent a time cut off from people, exploring our inner lives. There is a certain seductiveness in her silence, her separation, but if we stay too long in that state we can find it hard to get back our lives, our responsibilities, our relationships. The reversed card can remind us to be passionate, to commit ourselves to something or someone. We may need to make a decision or take firm action about something. In some contexts (depending on the place in the reading and the other cards), it may indicate pressure from people or a lack of respect from those around us.

A High Priestess Reading

1. What is deep within me?

2. How can I know it?

3. How can I be true to it?

4. What do I need to give out?

5. What do I need to keep within?

Empress: 3

Astrological correspondence:
   Venus

Kabbalistic letter: ‫ד‬ Daleth

Path on Tree of Life: Hokhmah
   (Wisdom) to Binah
   (Understanding)

III

Empress cards from
VISCONTI,
MARSEILLE,
RIDER, GOLDEN
DAWN RITUAL,
EGYPTIAN &
SHINING TRIBE

THE EMPRESS.

THE EMPRESS

The Empress

THERE ARE MANY trinities in religion. Though the ultimate triangle—the reason why the number three is so compelling—is mother-father-child, mythologies seem oddly to prefer all-male or all-female versions. Besides the Christian trinity of Father-Son-Holy Spirit, we find the Hindu Creator-Preserver-Destroyer, also all male. Women get their chance in the three Fates of Greece (matched by the Norns of Northern Europe) and the Triple Goddess of Maiden-Mother-Crone, whose aspects mirror the moon's phases of waxing, full, and waning, as well as the stages of a woman's life, from childhood, to child-bearing years, to menopause. In the Major Arcana, there are three primary cards of the feminine to match the

Triple Goddess—the High Priestess for the Maiden, the Empress for the Mother, and the Moon for the Crone. And yet, each of these actually carries all three qualities within her, whichever is emphasized. (For more on the Triple Goddess, see the High Priestess.)

Throughout these early cards, we have looked at a passage from the Chinese Tao Te Ching that matches the development of the Tarot images and ideas. Out of the Tao (Nothing, the Fool) comes the One. Out of the One (the Magician) comes the Two (the High Priestess). Out of the Two comes the Three, the Empress, passionate and life-giving, Earth as the Great Goddess. To complete the passage from the Tao Te Ching (see the Fool for more on this verse), "Out of the Three come the ten thousand things," that is, all of life, the outpouring of nature with all its wonder and energy.

We can see that formula—1 to 2 to 3—in another way. Quite simply, $1+2=3$; the physical world consists of the joining of the opposites symbolized in the Magician and High Priestess: light and dark, active and receptive, male and female, conscious and unconscious, positive and negative. None of these things can exist without its partner. Just as the Earth spins on an axis with both north and south poles, so the very molecules of our bodies hold together from the connection of positive and negative subatomic particles. While the Magician and High Priestess represent principles, the Empress signifies the reality that combines those principles.

In many mythologies we find the Earth, even the cosmos, described as a primordial being. The Greeks called the Earth Gaia and said she was the first to emerge out of the chaos before creation. The name, and something of the concept, has returned in the "Gaia Theory," which suggests that planet Earth is a single giant organism rather than a lifeless rock upon which living beings exist. Consider—you are alive, a single being, yet your body contains millions of bacteria and other independent organisms. Why not the planet?

In some cultures we read of a goddess whose body breaks up or is torn apart to make the world. Sumerian myth tells how Tiamat, a great dragon, or sea serpent, became oppressive to the gods, and so her descendant Marduk killed her and cut her in pieces to make the Earth. Many feminists and goddess historians believe that Tiamat was originally a benevolent Great Mother who made the world from her body, while Marduk represents the emergence of male power and its need to destroy feminine authority.

We find a similar story in Japan. Japanese myth describes the death of the first female, Izanami, and how her husband/brother Izanagi came to the Underworld to bring her back to life. But Izanagi became horrified by her worm-eaten body and ran away. Izanami chased him, and wherever she went, pieces of her decayed body dropped off to form the mountains, the forests, the seas. Is our world, then, the rotted corpse of a goddess? The very existence of life contains death, the destiny of every creature.

On one level such stories demonstrate our horror of death, which can turn us away from life. Culturally, they also establish patterns of male dominance, as when Marduk kills a supposedly oppressive Tiamat. In an earlier section of the Japanese story, chaos and monsters resulted when Izanami spoke first to initiate sex, and the "good" creation happened when her husband took the lead. In other words, the myth tells women to know their place.

On another level, however, if we strip away the patriarchal propaganda, the stories capture the powerful intuition that all the scattered pieces of the world, all the creatures and plants and rocks, all the individual *stories*, are really one life, one story, one being. We can describe the Major Arcana as a kind of blueprint of restoration, how we can bring all the broken pieces back together, *tikkun olam*, restore the world (as the Kabbalists say, and they're not talking about social progress), which is why we call the last card the World. The World is 21, and if we add those numbers, 2 + 1, we get 3, the Empress.

While a few modern Tarot decks depict the Empress as Gaia, most follow the imagery of the Rider version, which symbolically hints at two later Greek goddesses, Demeter, whom the Romans called Ceres (from which we get the word *cereal*), and Aphrodite/Venus. In the Rider, we see Demeter in the wheat growing all around her luxurious seat, for Demeter ruled over plant life. When Hades, the god of death, abducts Demeter's daughter, Persephone, to be his bride in the dark Underworld, Demeter stops all the plants from growing. Without plants the humans and animals will die, and without humans and animals, the gods will not receive any sacrifices. Zeus therefore sends Hermes (see the Magician) to order Hades to surrender Persephone. As we saw in the High Priestess, however, Persephone eats pomegranate seeds in the Land of the Dead and so must return for part of every year. In the Rider image, the Empress's robe displays pomegranates, but more as a symbol of fecundity than the Underworld. We will see aspects of this story again and again in the Major Arcana, especially in the Star, the bottom card in the Empress triad of Empress-Wheel of Fortune-Star.

Because she was willing to stop the world rather than give in to losing her daughter to Death, Demeter becomes the symbol of motherhood and its absolute devotion. The Homeric

Hymn that tells the story bears the title "Hymn to Demeter," not to Persephone, and in the nine-day ritual of the Mysteries, the celebrants all took on the role of Mother, experiencing the grief of loss and the refusal to accept the finality of death, and finally the joy of Persephone's return, with its promise that death will not become our final destiny.

The story of Demeter shows us the interconnectedness of all life, so that she, as much as Gaia, becomes the goddess of ecology. When this card comes up, we might very well think of our own connections to other living beings and our responsibility to nature. The Greeks saw Demeter as the goddess of law, possibly because she gave the gift of agriculture, and thus the laws of civilization. In the Tarot, we see law in the next card, the Emperor, but this is primarily human law, society and its structures. We can describe the Empress as the giver and ruler of the laws of life, from ecology to DNA.

The Empress is pervasive—the energy of nature, the devotion of the mother, but also sexuality, the power of passion. If we look at the Visconti and Marseille pictures, we see an eagle shield, symbol of the Hapsburgs and the Holy Roman Empire (for more on this image, see the Emperor). When we move to the modern versions, the shield becomes a heart emblazoned with the astrological glyph for Venus, known now primarily as the biological sign for female. The brightest object in the sky after the sun and moon, Venus appears soft and beautiful (especially compared to the angry red color of Mars), and so the ancients associated Venus with the goddess of love, whom the Greeks called Aphrodite and the Germanic peoples Freya. Friday is Freya's day, belonging to both planet and goddess, and thus a good day to express passion or perform any magic or rituals done under the influence of Venus—and Tarot readings about love.

Unlike some of the Greek deities, Aphrodite does not hold herself remote from the power over which she rules (Zeus seems to embody the "do as I say, not as I do" idea). Aphrodite can fall as wildly in love as any poor obsessed human. The Empress does not discriminate, does not hold herself back, does not wonder "Is this a good idea?" When you step into a room and all eyes follow you, and you know that anyone you want will go with you, you are expressing the power of the Empress. But she grips you just as well when you sit by the phone and wait for an answer to the five or ten messages you left on a lover's answering machine.

And you are equally in her realm when you look at your sleeping child and know you would kill to keep her safe.

Because the Empress signifies such powerful emotions, we can use her to energize or transform our own emotional lives. You can create rituals around the image (performed on Friday or when Venus appears strong in the sky, or well-aspected astrologically), or more simply, you can take your favorite Empress card from any deck and set her up on your dresser, look at her over a period of days, and see what she awakens in you. Write about your passions or emotional history and wounds, or let the picture inspire an affirmation. As well as emotional understanding, you can call on the Empress's life-giving energy to heal from illness. In ancient Greece, healing temples usually contained shrines to Aphrodite, for there is no healing without love—love of life, love of beauty, love and the desire to be whole.

To honor or even embody Aphrodite, wear gold or copper, for both were sacred to her in the ancient world (copper, a high conductor of electricity, was sacred as well to both Hermes and Isis, thus uniting the Magician, the High Priestess, and the Empress; people on Cyprus, where Aphrodite first emerged from the sea, used copper mirrors for divination). For Demeter, wear green and set out flowers. To honor both together, go on a picnic and make love in the fields!

Sometimes the Empress very specifically symbolizes "mother," either the influence of the querent's own mother (especially for people with "Mommy" issues) or the role of mother and mothering in a person's life. Appearing with cards that show children (such as the Sun), family, or fertility, the Empress may signify pregnancy.

Because the Empress embodies desire, she overlaps, in a sense, the Lovers card. The Lovers is 6 and the Empress 3, so that we might see the Lovers as the Empress doubled—passion in relationship. Though we sometimes assume that passion and desire exist only in relationships, they actually come from inside us. We need to love life and experience desire before we truly can fall in love.

Did the Empress always mean nature, passion, and motherhood? If we look at the historical meanings, we discover another interesting evolution.

Some Empress Meanings

Excerpted from *Mystical Origins of the Tarot* by Paul Huson.

De Mellet (1781): The Queen.

Court de Gébelin (1773-82): The Queen.

Lévi (1855): The Hebrew letter Gimel, the Empress. The word, the triad, plenitude, fecundity, nature, generation in the three worlds.

Christian (1870): Arcanum III. Isis-Urania: Action. In the divine world, the supreme power balanced by the eternally active mind and absolute wisdom; in the intellectual world, the universal fecundity of the Supreme Being; in the physical world, nature in labor, the germination of the acts that are to spring from the will.

Mathers (1888): The Empress. Action, plan, movement in a matter, initiative. REVERSED: Inaction, frittering away of power, lack of concentration, vacillation.

Golden Dawn (1888-96): The Daughter of the Mighty Ones. Empress. Beauty, pleasure, success, luxury; sometimes dissipation, but only with very evil cards.

Grand Orient (Waite, 1889, 1909): Empress. The sphere of action; the feminine side of power, rule, and authority; woman's influence; physical beauty; woman's reign; also the joy of life, and excesses on the evil side.

Waite (1910): The Empress. Fruitfulness, action, initiative. REVERSED: Light, truth, the unraveling of involved matters, public rejoicings; according to another reading [Mathers], vacillation.

De Mellet and Court de Gébelin both describe her simply as Queen, a term that can mean temporal rule or the Queen of Heaven, a very old expression, used, for example, to describe the ancient Hebrew goddess Asherah and the Christian Mary. The picture in the Rider suggests this idea, for she wears a diadem of twelve stars, as if to represent the zodiac. Yet Waite, in his chapter on the Empress (as opposed to just the divinatory meanings listed above) says "She is not *regina coeli*," the Latin for Queen of Heaven. He adds, however, "she is still *refugium peccatorum*, the fruitful mother of thousands."

As soon as we get to Lévi, we find the idea of nature and fecundity that Waite emphasizes in his longer text—"She is above all things universal fecundity." Paul Christian separates Lévi's "generation" into three levels, but all involve power and the ability to make things happen or come to life. Mathers emphasizes the idea of action in more conventional ways, including the

> GOLDEN
DAWN
RITUAL
Empress
&
Lovers

idea of plans, a quality that may seem against the spirit of the Empress as we know her today, for we think of her now as spontaneous and emotional. The Golden Dawn introduces beauty, pleasure, and luxury along with action and fecundity. Thus the Empress becomes the model of sensuality, one of the ways we still think of her. Notice that the Golden Dawn's Victorian spirit adds "dissipation" but recognizes this as a distortion, and "only with very evil cards."

As Grand Orient, Waite introduces the "influence" and power of femininity, but he also goes back to the original idea of Queen with his phrase "the feminine side of power, rule, and authority." And he takes the Golden Dawn's idea of luxury further, or maybe simplifies it, with "the joy of life." He also includes "excess on the evil side," without that hedge of "only with very evil cards."

Writing under his own name, Waite seems to revert to the earlier ideas of "action," though also "fruitfulness."

For myself, I would say that in readings the Empress represents, above all, passion. Whether as Demeter or Aphrodite, she shows us an embrace of life in all its messiness and horror as well as its beauty. She does not deny life's pain, but she reminds us we can love the world fully, without reservation. The Empress in a reading may indicate motherhood, especially, as mentioned above, with cards that show children or family. She may symbolize the total dedication and protectiveness of mothers, Demeter's willingness to stop the whole world to rescue her child.

The Empress can indicate love and desire, not necessarily for a specific person but simply the power of love itself. She often acts on impulse, according to feeling rather than careful judgment. She expresses herself powerfully, sometimes intimidating others, but only because they cannot match her passion. Apart from signifying a person, the Empress can indicate the lushness and beauty of nature, or rich surroundings, or the pleasures of the sensual life. Imagine a three-dimensional Empress card sculpted in chocolate, accented in gold leaf, and surrounded by flowers.

Reversed, the Empress becomes more cautious, or maybe just more thoughtful. In a sense, she veers more to the High Priestess, depending more on the intellect than the senses. She becomes less outgoing, less sensual. Sometimes this can mean repression, but more often it just says that life asks different qualities of us now. If the reading involves questions of pregnancy, the reversed Empress suggests problems with fertility or simply that now is not the time. It also may indicate difficulties with the querent's mother or someone in a mothering role.

An Empress Reading

1. What is my passion?

2. How have I expressed it?

3. How can I express it more fully?

4. What blocks me?

5. What frees me?

6. What do I nurture?

7. What does it ask of me?

8. What does it give me?

9. How can I bring together my passion and my nurturance?

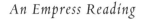

Emperor: 4

Astrological correspondence:
Aries

Kabbalistic letter: ה Heh

Path on Tree of Life: Hokhmah
(Wisdom) to Tipheret
(Beauty)

Emperor cards from
Visconti,
Marseille,
Rider, Golden
Dawn Ritual,
Egyptian &
Shining Tribe

The Emperor

TAROT INTERPRETERS HAVE seen the Emperor in two basic ways, and we cannot easily combine them because, in fact, they tend to be opposite. As a result, some choose one approach and ignore the other or consider it a mistake. This in itself is an Emperor attitude, for one thing both sides share is the belief in structure, rules, and the assumption of a correct way.

Here are the two interpretations, numbered. Emperor people like numbered lists: lists impose order on chaotic jumbles of reality.

1: The Laws of Society

The social structure. Rules, authority. Hierarchy and power, order and control. We see this vision to some extent in the Rider tradition's harsh, scowling figure sitting on his throne in a desert. A tiny stream flows behind him. In the Empress, we find a gushing river of emotion and feminine sexuality that disappears underground to flow beneath her throne, which looks more like a couch or a bed. In the Emperor, the water of life has become a trickle through a jagged land, with no flowers, trees, or grain.

In the older, less harsh versions found on the Marseille and Visconti cards, the Emperor displays a black eagle on his shield or crown; so does the Empress in many decks. According to Tarot historians, the eagle (and of course the titles of the cards) identifies them as the rulers of the Hapsburg Empire, which grew from the Holy Roman Empire that began in the year 800. That year, Charlemagne arranged for the Pope to crown him in Rome as successor to the Caesars. The very next card in the deck, these days titled the Hierophant in esoteric Tarots, originally (and still in most European decks) bore the title Pope. The Emperor and the Hierophant form an alliance, maybe a stronger one than the Empress and Emperor, who represent opposite though complementary qualities.

Technically, the Holy Roman Empire lasted until 1806, though its influence and power had long dwindled. Still, this gave it a thousand-year run, like Rome before it (what I cannot help but think of as the "real" Roman Empire). When Hitler called his regime the "third Reich" and said it would last a thousand years, he was claiming succession to Rome and the Holy Roman Empire.

Hitler and other tyrants corrupt the Emperor ideal—his power without his virtue and sense of service. Significantly, we need to turn to myth and literature for truly pure models of the Emperor. King Arthur, with his code of chivalry—"might in the service of right," as some call it—shows us such an ideal Emperor, and a number of modern decks have used him for that card. For many older Americans, Franklin Roosevelt represented a modern Emperor, a direct counter to Hitler and Stalin, with Eleanor a model of the Empress. A later generation saw Ronald Reagan that way, though many (myself included) would disagree.

2: Divine Law

The masculine aspect. This Emperor represents the abstract principles of creation and universal laws, such as the four basic forces of physics. When science or metaphysics looks at the world, they try to see beyond all the millions of actual things and events to discover the principles that underlie them. People used to consider such discovery a matter of logic or reason. That is, you pondered what happens in nature, removed yourself from all that messiness, and used the "higher" powers of intellect to reason out the principles. Modern science attempts to base itself on observation. You go out and collect data, or you do experiments, and from all this information you attempt to find, once again, underlying principles. The word "attempt" applies because scientists, like all human beings, tend to fall back on preconceptions and even prejudices. We are, after all, not Emperors but only humans, caught up in our lives and histories.

This more abstract version of the Emperor builds on traditions that show him sitting in profile. Kabbalists sometimes portray God the King, the male aspect of the divine, as just that, an old man on a throne, seen in profile. He does not look directly at us and so maintains a distance. Kabbalah texts often play on the idea of seeing the divine "face to face," in full revelation, and how overwhelming this experience would be. In the Bible, Moses asks to see God directly. YHVH, the unknowable Name, related to the four suits and the four court cards (usually translated as "Lord," though "Infinite" might be better), tells Moses he will die if he sees God face to face. But if he hides in a cleft in the rock, he may witness God passing by him. For the Jews, Moses was the greatest prophet (Christians and Muslims, of course, would vote for Jesus or Mohammed), yet he could not see God fully, because if he did, he would die to the physical world and move to a higher state, and the people needed him to lead them from slavery. Similarly, Christians believe God had to incarnate as Jesus to liberate humans from death (I would argue that liberation from *sin* was a later idea). The Emperor in profile represents a vision of the divine that is both meaningful and beyond human comprehension.

There is something else about the Moses story that we should notice, for it speaks subtly of the Emperor and Empress. From the earliest times of human understanding of symbolism, going back to the Old Stone Age, a cleft in a rock signifies the entrance to the body of the Goddess, the vaginal opening of Gaia, the Earth, source of life and rebirth. Thus, Moses

> VISCONTI
Hanged Man
&
MARSEILLE
Emperor
&
World

secures himself, anchors himself, in the Empress so that he might witness the passage of the Emperor.

In the Marseille deck and others, the Emperor crosses his legs to form the number four. This indicates that he rules over the physical world, for we can define our existence in terms of fours. There are four forces in physics—gravity, electromagnetism, and two nuclear. Four states of matter—solid, liquid, gas, and plasma. Four solar points in the year—two equinoxes and two solstices. Four planetary directions, caused by the planet spinning on an axis with a north and a south pole so that the sun appears to rise in the east and set in the west. Four human directions—right, left, before, and behind. Four limbs on the human body. Four points to make the simplest geometric solid (a three-sided pyramid). And for Tarotists, there are four suits in the Minor Arcana, the part of the deck that represents the physical world. All these fours, and the Emperor's crossed legs, symbolize the divine laws that govern the material world. We will see crossed legs again in the Hanged Man and the World.

The first three cards after the Fool form the basis of existence—the Magician and High Priestess as principles and the Empress as the outpouring of life when they combine. In Chinese terms, we might say that yang and yin, aspects of Tao, the Fool, join together to produce the "Mother of ten thousand things," the Goddess of Life. The Emperor, card four, signifies both the structures of nature that hold together those ten thousand things and the laws that govern them. This is the Marseille tradition.

In that tradition, the Emperor sits on a throne, but in some modern occult decks he still sits in profile, but on a cube. When we think of the number four, we think of the square, and a cube is a square in three dimensions. For modern Kabbalists, the cube also embodies the Tree of Life. This is because if we add up the surfaces, edges, internal axes, and center of a cube, we get twenty-two, the same number of lines on the tree and the number of cards in the Major Arcana. Modern Kabbalists call this the "cube of space," a term from Paul Foster Case, founder of a post-Golden Dawn group called the Builders of the Adytum (BOTA).

We do not find the cube in the Rider tradition. There the throne contains four ram's heads, symbol of the Emperor's astrological sign of Aries. However, we see a subtle reference to the cube in the Devil, for the Devil sits on a *half* cube, as if to signify half-truths, in particular the idea that only the material world exists, without spirit. And we see a hint of the cube in the Chariot, where the chariot itself appears cubic. However, Waite rejected the cube image for the Emperor, saying it "confuses ... the issues."

In most versions of the card, the Emperor holds a stick—a scepter of power—and an orb with a cross on top of it. In the Rider, the orb becomes an ankh, linking him to the Egyptian god Osiris and ultimately to Isis, for the ankh, the knot of life, belonged to the goddess. Isis as mystery appears in the High Priestess, while Isis as devoted wife and mother becomes the Empress, so that we see that for all his power, the Emperor cannot exist without the Empress. In the Shining Tribe version, he stands with empty hands, for his power comes from within himself and not from external symbols of authority.

The anonymous author of *Meditations on the Tarot*, a study of "Christian hermeticism," points out that the Emperor carries no sword or other weapon, so he has renounced compulsion and violence, ruling instead through the power of vision. "Where there is authority, i.e., where there is present the breath of sacred magic filled by the rays of light of gnosis emanated from the profound fires of mysticism, then compulsion is superfluous."

Now we will look at another list, Paul Huson's very useful assembly of early meanings for trump four.

Some Emperor Meanings

Excerpted from *Mystical Origins of the Tarot* by Paul Huson.

De Mellet (1781): The king.

Court de Gébelin (1773-82): The king.

Lévi (1855): The Hebrew letter Daleth, the emperor. The Porte (the Turkish Sultan's court), or government of the East, initiation, power, the Tetragram, the quaternary, the cubic stone.

Christian (1870): Arcanum IV. The Cubic Stone. Realization.

Mathers (1888): The Emperor. Realization, effect, development. REVERSED: Stoppage, check, immaturity.

Golden Dawn (1888-96): Son of the Morning, chief among the mighty. Emperor. War, victory, strife, ambition.

Grand Orient (Waite, 1889, 1909): Emperor. Logic, experience, wisdom, male power.

Waite (1910): The Emperor. Stability, power, protection, realization, a great person, aid, reason, conviction, authority, and will. REVERSED: Confusion to enemies, obstruction, immaturity.

Two things stand out—the assumption of earthly power by Court de Gébelin and de Mellet and the very early emergence (in Lévi) of the cubic stone idea. Thus, the two strains go back to the beginning. Lévi gives us a number of valuable ideas. Along with the stone, he links trump four to the "Tetragram" (Tetragrammaton), the sacred name YHVH, and the idea of four, or quaternary. He also brings in earthly power, the sultan, ruler of the Ottoman Empire, Christian Europe's main rival. This is ironic, for Charlemagne, the first Holy Roman Emperor, earned his title by stopping the Muslim army.

Paul Christian and Mathers introduce the idea of "realization," which we can see in the fact that it takes four points to create a three-dimensional object. Mathers also suggests the idea of immaturity for the Emperor reversed, something Waite picks up. As we saw with the Fool, we can consider that card—0—as the twenty-second card, and 2+2=4, so that the eternal child, the Fool, becomes linked to the archetypal grownup, who may act a bit foolishly when reversed (something we see in Shakespeare's *King Lear*).

Among the varied interpretations, the Golden Dawn may surprise us the most, for it seems to emphasize temporal authority with its "war, victory, strife, ambition," the very qualities *Meditations on the Tarot* tells us the Emperor renounces.

The Shining Tribe attempts to combine some of the variant ideas by showing us a shamanic Emperor, an emperor of the spirit world. The picture was inspired by a photo of a shaman encountered by Czar Nicholas II on a trip across Siberia. An image of masculine power, his head is that of a great stag, whose horns can symbolize branching ideas. He stands on a bull, inspired by the 17,000-year-old paintings of the Lascaux cave in France. We also see behind him a city for the creative power of civilization, and two black squares for abstract thought.

So far, we have looked at two versions of the Emperor. Let us look at two more, satisfying the Emperor's desire for order and lists of four things.

3: Daddy

Just as the Empress can represent the mother, so her partner can evoke the father. In some readings, the Emperor may indicate a person's issues with his or her father, or sometimes a mother who acts Emperorlike, which is to say authoritarian, stern, with an emphasis on rules. In traditional Western families, the father is the harsh one—"Just you wait till your father gets home!" women used to threaten their unruly children, back in the days before the majority of women worked outside the home.

We are born anarchic, pure "id," as Freudians say. For many, our mothers represent food and comfort and intimacy, while our fathers may embody the outside world. To overcome our fear/admiration of the Emperor's power, we need to somehow assimilate him. We need to become our own Emperor. When this card appears, we might ask a simple question: "Do you see this figure as something outside you or yourself?" If the latter, it means you establish your own rules, defend yourself and your territory, make an impact on the world. Some people find it valuable to visualize themselves as the Emperor on his throne or even to act it out. Find a thronelike chair, create a scepter, wear clothes that express power, sit in the posture, and let yourself imagine an empire spread before you. What sort of empire is it? How difficult do you find it to do this? What would you do first if you ruled an empire? If your immediate answer is "Abdicate and go on vacation," that will tell you a lot. So will "Execute my enemies!"

In the Fool's progress, the Emperor, the middle card of the first row of seven, challenges us in a special way. We need to come to terms with rules, which is to say society's laws and codes of behavior, but also our parents' judgments and demands on us. People can get stuck at the Emperor level in two ways. They can obey all the rules, live out a planned life, and never really develop their own personality, or they can constantly rebel and seek to break every rule, where they are still not making their own decisions.

The Emperor heads up a triad of special tests for each of the three levels. Below the Emperor comes Justice, in which we must face not society and its rules but our own truth and actions. And below that comes the Moon, the difficult journey back from mystery to the Sun light of day.

4: Zeus and Other Kings of the Gods

After the French Revolution, French Tarots did away with the Emperor and Empress, and instead called these cards Jupiter and Juno, the Roman names for Zeus and Hera.

Zeus is an obvious choice for the Emperor. Though he takes the sky as his primary domain, with thunder and lightning as his main attributes, he also exerts his all-powerful will on the people and events of earth. With his stream of lovers and divine or semi-divine children, such as the strongman Heracles or the beautiful Helen of Troy, he signifies aggressive male sexuality. The Greeks also celebrated the complexity of his mind, suggesting that humans, with our short life spans, and even the other gods, with their narrow concerns, could not penetrate the depths of Zeus's plans. Or, to give it a modern version, God moves in mysterious ways. Just as we can invoke Demeter or Aphrodite with the Empress, so the Emperor can bring the power of Zeus into our lives.

Here is a story of the power of Zeus the Emperor, from a trip I led to celebrate the Mysteries. To go from Athens to Crete, we took an overnight ferry, a journey back in time, for Cretan civilization was much older than Greece and was the source of the Mysteries described in the High Priestess and other cards. The myths described Crete as the birthplace of Zeus, describing how his mother hid him in a cave to keep his father, Kronos, from devouring him.

As readers who have traveled on a large boat will know, you do not feel it begin to move but only see the movement against the dock. Just at the moment we saw the boat slip away from land, a huge lightning bolt filled the sky and thunder sounded overhead. Seconds later, a downpour drenched the boat. Safe in our cabins, we traveled through the night, and when we arrived it was lightly raining. We found our bus and set out along the coast road for our hotel. Suddenly, my co-leader, Nicky Scully, cried out "What's that?" We looked through the window at the water, where a black funnel rose into the sky. Then we saw another and another. The driver pulled over, and we all got off to look. There were four of them, giant water-spout tornadoes several miles from land. Four is the Emperor's number, I realized, and I told Nicky, "Zeus is showing off. He wants us to know we've entered his world." The next day, the newspapers reported that nothing like that had ever been seen in the long history of Crete.

A number of decks equate the Emperor with the young, virile god of some Pagan cultures. In some traditions, the king embodied the god and in a ceremony would marry the goddess, the land itself. The Emperor joins the Empress, but just as in the sequence, the goddess is older, for the land exists forever, while handsome, young kings rise and fall, like the phallus, the ultimate scepter of the Emperor's authority.

We might argue that the Emperor in the Rider, who appears so harsh and controlling, has distorted the natural order by holding on to power after his youth and virility have faded. He has attempted to substitute a rule of authority for the basic law of nature that individual beings, rulers, and even societies rise and fall while the earth remains. However, this image of the card possibly distorts its true message, the greater laws and structure of existence.

In readings, the various meanings of the Emperor can apply. He may signify a powerful person, possibly benevolent but who expects obedience. The rules are the rules, he might say. More widely, the card can signify the power of society, its laws and customs, its expectations of conformity, and the idea that the system matters more than individuals.

And yet, there are those times when the Emperor simply means natural law. He may signify reason, abstraction, even science. In recent times, we have tended to distrust such qualities, their separation from emotion or intuition. We might remember that the occult tradition prizes those very same qualities, the ability to use reason rather than emotion, to see principles rather than details.

The Emperor may signify fatherhood and its importance in the querent's life. With cards of family difficulty, the Emperor may indicate a domineering father. With cards of generosity, however, he becomes a benevolent, loving father.

Sometimes the Emperor may indicate not a father but a husband, especially one who dominates a marriage or family. If both the Emperor and Empress appear, they may indicate a well-matched couple, two powerful people. And remember: the Emperor may be a woman, the Empress a man. Forgetting that, we may confuse a reading.

In work readings, the Emperor may indicate a boss, the company, the rules. But the card can mean the querent also, with his or her ability to take control or to defend territory. Sometimes only the Emperor's toughness and structures will work in a situation.

Reversed, the Emperor softens. He may become gentler, less insistent on rules and absolute principles. Often we find the reversed card preferable. With Justice right-side up, the Emperor upside down can signify a need to look at deeper issues, to find the truth of a situation rather than apply a set of rules. But the reversed Emperor also can signify someone who has trouble taking a strong stand, or who is too caught up in details, unable to discern principles. Sometimes the reversed card can mean immaturity or a reluctance to take responsibility.

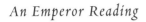

An Emperor Reading

1. How am I an Emperor?

2. How am I *not* an Emperor?

3. Where do I need to take charge?

4. What will help me do that?

5. How am I weak?

6. How am I strong?

7. What are the rules?

LE PAPE   IL PAPA

THE HIEROPHANT   **V**   DER HIEROPHANT
EL PAPA   DE HIËROFANT

Hierophant: 5

Astrological correspondence:
  Taurus

Kabbalistic letter: ו Vav

Path on Tree of Life: Hokhmah
  (Wisdom) to Chesed
  (Mercy)

*Hierophant cards
  from* Visconti,
Marseille,
Rider, Golden
Dawn Ritual,
Egyptian &
Shining Tribe

THE HIEROPHANT

5

THE HIEROPHANT

The Hierophant

FIRST, THE NAME. Originally, this card was called the Pope, and many decks, especially in Europe, still call it that. In some, the name has changed but the image remains, a pope blessing two disciples, usually monks. Some modern decks show the figure in conflicting ways. Many Italian decks show the Pope with suggestions of corruption.

Why the name change? Coming from the Golden Dawn, like so much else in modern Tarot, the new name replaces the implication of churches and religious authority with the idea of esoteric tradition, which takes its models from the Mystery schools of Greece and Egypt. "Hierophant" refers to the *Hierophantos*, the priest who directed the nine-day Eleusinian Mysteries. The Mysteries

IL PAPA
LE PAPE

V

THE HIEROPHANT
EL PAPA

DER HIEROPHANT

DE HIÉROFANT

began when the Hierophant displayed the sacred objects taken from the Athens treasury. The word means "He who shows [the sacred]."

Or at least that's the usual interpretation. Charles Stein, poet and classical scholar, argues in his book *Persephone Unbound* that Hierophant means "he who causes to be seen"—in other words, one who induces visions or leads people to experience visions. It takes a special mystical power to cause people to see sacred visions, especially when several thousand people all see the same thing at the same time. This power is not personal. It can only come from a tradition, one with great meaning and deep roots. If we look at this card and see only the social power of churches, we miss its true wonder. This is why I called trump five in the Shining Tribe "Tradition" and showed a circle of spirits in the form of stones. A genuine tradition can transform our individual experiences. In the card, green lines for life experiences enter the circle and change into gold for divine truth. We can also say that the gold of spirit changes to the green of people's lives. The five stones, the embodiment of the living spiritual Tradition, act as transformers of energy, connecting life and deep meaning.

The Mysteries probably came from prehistoric Crete, and from Eleusis they passed to the schools and initiatory groups of Alexandria, the Greek/Egyptian city where the Hermetic tradition originated. These schools became the source and model for the European secret societies, such as the Rosicrucians, the Freemasons, and of course the Hermetic Order of the Golden Dawn. And so we get the name Hierophant on card five.

And yet, the Marseille and most modern decks show a pope or a priest (a pope is, of course, the head priest). But what in fact is a priest? Our generally secular culture tends to think of the office as that of a spiritual leader, someone who helps his parishioners lead a moral life. In fact, while priests may serve this important function, the concept means something far more magical. In ancient Israel it referred to a hereditary caste, the Levites, who carried the divine power of YHVH into the rituals held in the temple in Jerusalem. When the temple fell, leadership passed to the rabbis, who were democratic—anyone can become a rabbi—but also not magical, despite occasional tales of rabbis who work miracles, including exorcism of demons and dead spirits.

Technically, the Jewish priesthood survives. Jews consider anyone named Cohen (or something similar, such as Kahn) a hereditary priest. Practice, however, limits the office to one moment a year, a ritual conducted during the Jewish New Year, when the various Cohens of the congregation, dressed in white robes, stand at the head of the people, raise their arms with the fingers in a special gesture, and chant/channel divine blessings. The people all stand but with downcast eyes, for the ancient tradition says that the power becomes so intense it can strike them blind. This is the oldest ritual in any Jewish service and is, in fact, a true Hierophant activity. *Meditations on the Tarot* calls "benediction," the passing on of divine blessing, the chief function of trump five.

In the Orthodox churches (including the Roman, known as Catholicism), the office of priest carries a magical meaning (I use the term "magical" here in the best sense, as sacred power). A priest is someone who can perform the sacraments, in particular the communion, the transformation of bread and wine into the literal body and blood of Christ. The Catholic Church argues that Christ himself gave the power to Peter, who passed it on to successors. Priests today still receive this power from a bishop, and once given, it becomes a part of his being, so that a defrocked priest may be forbidden from giving communion, but he is still capable of doing so. The Protestant Reformation moved in a similar direction as the early rabbis, that is, away from priests and toward ministers, people who do not claim any special powers, though some ministers, especially Fundamentalists, will claim to heal by "laying on hands," becoming a direct channel for divine power.

Modern Paganism has revived the ancient view of a priest as someone who embodies the masculine energy of the divine, while bringing back the concept of a priestess, a word that does not simply mean a female priest. A priestess embodies the feminine divine. Some modern decks, especially those expressing Pagan experience, have changed trumps 2 and 5 to High Priestess and High Priest. Remember that the original name for the High Priestess was Papesse, a female Pope.

The Hierophant becomes a partner to two very different cards. As an upholder of official traditions and teachings, he works with the Emperor, the enforcer of society's rules. As a true priest, a figure who channels divine power, he belongs with the High Priestess.

Today, the Hierophant tends to mean primarily the keeper of a tradition, especially the exoteric, or "outer," teachings, compared to the High Priestess's esoteric, or secret, revelations. Some people dislike this card, much the same as they dislike the Emperor. They see both as established power and therefore oppression. But if we consider the great teachers of mysticism and enlightenment—the Kabbalists, Sufis, Tibetan masters, Christian mystics such as Hildegard of Bingen or Meister Eckhart, they all arose from a tradition. If some strayed into territory that authorities considered heresy, they began with that firm foundation. Our ancestors give us a place to stand, texts which inspire us, a history of spiritual practice.

We find two distinct directions for this card—the priestly power of blessings and the concept of an outer tradition to match the High Priestess's secret wisdom. How did the early interpreters see it?

Some Hierophant (Pope) Meanings

Excerpted from *Mystical Origins of the Tarot* by Paul Huson.

De Mellet (1781): Jupiter. The Everlasting mounted on an eagle.

Court de Gébelin (1773-82): The high priest or chief hierophant.

Lévi (1855): The Hebrew letter Heh, the pope. Indication, demonstration, instruction, law, symbolism, philosophy, religion.

Christian (1870): Arcanum V. The Master of the Arcana or Sacred Mysteries, the hierophant or occult inspiration. In the divine world, the universal law; in the intellectual world, religion, the relationship of the absolute to the relative being; in the physical world, inspiration.

Mathers (1888): The Hierophant, or Pope. Mercy, beneficence, kindness, goodness.
    Reversed: Overkindness, weakness, foolish generosity.

Golden Dawn (1888-96): Magus of the eternal gods. Hierophant. Divine wisdom. Manifestation, explanation, teaching. Differing from, though resembling in many aspects, the meaning of the Magician, the Prophet (Hermit), and the Lovers. Occult wisdom.

Grand Orient (Waite, 1889, 1909): Pope, or Hierophant. Aspiration, power of the keys, the outward show of spiritual authority, the temporal power of official religion; on the evil side, sacerdotal tyranny and interference.

Waite (1910): The Hierophant. Marriage, alliance, servitude; by another account [Mathers], mercy and goodness; inspiration; the man to whom the inquirer has recourse.
    Reversed: Overkindness, weakness.

As usual, we find some surprises. Court de Gébelin introduces the name "Hierophant" at the very beginning and calls him a high priest, as if to say "This is not a pope but a more secret figure." For Court de Gébelin the Tarot was Egyptian, but Hermeticists of his time considered Greek and Egyptian mysteries the same given by Thoth/Hermes Trismegistus, and so he used a Greek name for what he considered Egyptian rites.

If Court de Gébelin introduces the Hierophant idea, Lévi brings in the emphasis on "instruction, law...religion." Paul Christian firmly puts him back in the occult but opens the door to combining the themes by saying that "religion" belongs to the "intellectual world." The Golden Dawn sees the Hierophant as not just a master of rituals but a "magus," saying he "resembles" the Magician, the Hermit, and the Lovers. They also label the card "occult wisdom."

As Grand Orient, Waite goes in the direction of "the outward show" and "temporal power" of religion, including even tyranny and interference. Under his own name, Waite introduces an important concept, "marriage." We will come back to this idea in a moment.

The picture has changed remarkably little over the centuries, even when people give it a different meaning. So let us consider the structure and the essential symbols. First, the gesture, the very symbol of priestly benediction, with its two fingers up and two fingers down. As with the Magician's one arm up, one arm down, it channels energy from the spiritual into the physical. But this is one hand and therefore a constant current of energy. "As above, so below" does not just mean that our life patterns mirror the astrological movements in the heavens, but rather that our lives are entwined with the divine.

We sometimes hear occultists talk of "evolution and devolution." By evolution they do not mean the movement from bacteria to fish to dinosaurs to mammals (though in my opinion, occult teachings take science into account more than organized religion does). Instead, devolution means the "descent" of spirit into matter, physical bodies, as symbolized in the Fool, and evolution the "ascent" of matter into spirit, as in Judgement.

Descent and ascent are metaphors, the movement not really up or down but a shift of energy. How do we experience this? In every moment, in our vital existence, our blood and our breath. "The blood is the life," Leviticus tells us, and in many languages the word for *spirit* literally means "breath." In Deuteronomy, Moses tells us that "It is not in Heaven or across the seas, but in your heart and in your mouth...that you might do it." Exoterically, this says that we cannot claim the Law is too difficult or exotic, we just need to commit ourselves emotionally and recite it out loud. But esoterically...in a remarkable book called *The Hebrew Book of the Dead*, the author, Zhenya Senyak, explains the statement this way: the divine, the sacred, does not exist separate and far away. All we need is the beating of our hearts and the breath going in and out of our mouths.

In the Rider image, the Hierophant sits on his throne between two pillars, recalling the High Priestess. But here, instead of light and dark, we see gray stone on either side. This suits the interpretation of the Hierophant as the keeper of outer traditions, who gives laws and rules but not inner truth, who in fact keeps people on their knees, ignorant and obedient. We might see the hand gesture as two fingers down for that half of reality kept hidden from the mass of people. Still, we might remember that in the Tarot de Marseille, the Popess does not sit between pillars, and so card five actually introduces the image of a teacher between two columns.

What do we make of the triple crown and three-armed cross? In church tradition (the Hierophant as outer teacher), they represent the Father, Son, and Holy Spirit. To some extent, these are just words (the satirical newspaper *The Onion* once ran a story titled "God to Phase Out Holy Ghost from Trinity"). We can describe them as realms of existence, what Paul Christian calls the physical, the intellectual, and the divine worlds. We also might think of mythological descriptions of the cosmos as Heaven, Earth, and Underworld.

Meditations on the Tarot gives us a more immediate interpretation, based on the idea of breath—"respiration"—as a connection to Spirit.

The three levels of horizontal respiration are love of nature, love of one's neighbor, and love of the beings of the spiritual hierarchies (e.g., angels).

The three stages of vertical respiration are purification (by divine breath), illumination (by divine light), and mystical union (in divine fire).

The Hierophant represents the first of three levels of teaching, one for each line of the Major Arcana (see opposite page's cards). This is the level of doctrine and tradition, an intermediary who connects Above and Below. The Hermit shows us a master of the inner pathways holding up the light that we might follow. The third level, at the bottom of the Hierophant's fifth triad, is the Sun, in which we experience direct revelation of the wonders of existence. In between the Hierophant and the Sun, the Hanged Man reverses the way we understand—from outer teachings to inner truth.

THE HIEROPHANT   V   DER HIEROPHANT
EL PAPA   DE HIÉROFANT

THE HANGED MAN   XII   DER GEHÄNGTE
EL COLGADO   DE GEHANGENE

THE SUN   XIX   DIE SONNE
EL SOL   DE ZON

< MARSEILLE
Hierophant,
Hanged Man
&
Sun

The Hierophant introduces a structural image that resonates throughout the Major Arcana, especially in the Rider tradition, where we see it in various Minor cards as well, but originally in the Marseille. This image consists of a figure between and above two others. The Hierophant/Pope sits above the two disciples, in the (Rider) Lovers the angel blesses the man and woman, the Chariot driver stands above the two sphinxes or horses. Later we will see the Devil above the enslaved demons, the Tower between the falling bodies, the Moon above the dog and wolf, and the Sun (in the Marseille) above the two children.

The High Priestess shows us something similar, but there she sits between the dark and light pillars, a figure of balance. Above suggests a control, the ability to mediate between dualities or rise above them and keep separate from them. Each of the triangular cards suggests its own kind of mediation or unification of opposites. At its best, the Hierophant uses tradition and teachings to help others. He shows them a path, and he unites Above and Below through that power of benediction. And the path serves him as well, for the rules and rituals of tradition help him avoid the ego trap of believing himself responsible for the spiritual condition of others.

What does all this mean for readings? In modern Tarot, we usually focus on the idea of a path that the querent is expected to follow. It may be what is socially approved or come from family or a partner or friends. This is the traditional way that does not require thought or independent action but simply following. Since modern society values freedom and initiative ("think outside the box," we hear over and over), we may automatically reject the path the Hierophant shows us or assume we would never just follow. And yet the path of tradition often goes back through many generations and contains great wisdom.

Sometimes what seems like nonconformity may conceal yet another automatic path, but one without the age-old wisdom. In 1970, when I first encountered the Tarot, I was teaching freshman composition at a college in New York State. At one point it seemed that every essay from every student included the phrase "Everyone is an individual." I wondered, if they were all so individual, why did they all say the same thing? Now I might say that they thought they had rejected the Hierophant but had simply found a new doctrine.

The Hierophant can mean a particular teacher or the educational system in some way. Sometimes it hints at marriage, probably because people go to priests to get married. The meaning becomes stronger with the Four of Wands, especially in the Rider tradition, for the picture suggests a wedding party. The Hierophant indicates what I call the "institution" of marriage, which does not always include passion or romance. Compare it to the following card, the Lovers.

The Hierophant can indicate the experience of benediction, that is, of giving or receiving some sort of blessing.

Reversed, the Hierophant suggests unorthodoxy. A person rejects the path laid out by society or family and goes his or her own way. This sounds attractive and often is very valuable. It also can lead to a lack of grounding or to gullibility. I've known people who rejected the concepts of society but then believed anything someone told them as long as it sounded alternative. Once, I visited a friend who told me excitedly of her discovery that a secret group of "masters" controlled the world. I asked her how she knew this, and she showed me a cheap-looking paperback book. I asked, "How do you know that writer is telling the truth?" She looked surprised. "I never thought of that," she said. This same person had rejected the claims of both religion and science as oppressive lies. The Hierophant reversed means freedom, but with freedom comes the difficulty of choice.

A Hierophant Reading

1. How has tradition affected my life?

2. What have I learned?

3. How have I broken with tradition?

4. What effect has it had on my life?

5. What do I have to teach others?

6. How can I fulfill this role?

Lovers: 6

Astrological correspondence:
  Gemini

Kabbalistic letter: ז Zayin

Path on Tree of Life: Binah
  (Understanding) to
  Tipheret (Beauty)

Lovers cards from
VISCONTI,
MARSEILLE,
RIDER, GOLDEN
DAWN RITUAL,
EGYPTIAN &
SHINING TRIBE

6

THE LOVERS   ♊

The Lovers

HERE IS A card almost everyone wants to get, especially in readings that ask that perennial favorite question, "When will I meet my soul mate?" In its modern versions, it speaks of love, deep relationships, fulfillment. But that was not always the case.

The older name, or at least theme, for this card is choice, and many people still see it that way. The Golden Dawn linked it to Gemini, the twins, which gives us the concept of possibilities. The idea of a requirement to choose goes back to the Marseille image, which shows a young man between two women, seemingly deciding which he will choose for a partner. Above him, Cupid prepares to shoot an arrow, as if to inspire him with love.

L'INNAMORATO   LES AMANTS   VI   THE LOVERS   EL ENAMORADO

DIE LIEBENDEN   DE GELIEFDEN

It often strikes me that people miss the implications of the arrow. Love, it reminds us, takes the choice from our hands, or at least a rational choice, the kind where you consider both options and decide which makes the most sense.

The image of union is primarily modern. Arthur Edward Waite kept the basic structure of the Marseille image but changed it in significant ways. Instead of a young man between two women, all in proper dress, we see a single man and woman, both naked and unashamed, and instead of Cupid with his bow, an angel holds a hand over each, as if to bless and unite them, perhaps a marriage without need of church or ritual.

Look at the Rider Lovers alongside the Devil:

> RIDER
*Lovers
&
Devil*

> MARSEILLE
Devil

The Devil appears like a parody of the earlier card. In fact, the Devil is the older image, close to the Marseille "original," above.

In one of their most brilliant designs, Waite and Smith worked backwards from the Devil to create the Lovers, so that card six shows us a perfect relationship, while the Devil becomes a degraded or destructive relationship.

Some decks, especially the Thoth Tarot of Aleister Crowley and Frieda Harris, depict a highly ritualized *hieros gamos*, or sacred marriage. Hermetically, a hieros gamos shows a union of opposites, in which the masculine and feminine become mixed. The World card, often described as a "hermaphrodite," fully embodies the concept of union. The Lovers card points to that complete expression.

The concept of sacred marriage goes back far beyond Hermeticism. In many "Pagan" cultures (I use the word loosely to signify nature-based traditions, especially pre-Christian Europe), the king or chieftain would symbolically marry the Earth Goddess, sometimes enacted by a priestess, a sexual union meant to help fertilize the land. In this sense, the Lovers becomes a culmination of the previous cards, with the Hierophant ritually marrying the Empress (the land) to the Emperor (the king, the social order), who themselves embody the masculine and feminine principles first shown in the Magician and High Priestess.

With the High Priestess, we looked at the Kabbalist idea of the female aspect of God, called the Shekinah, in exile from the male. The Lovers depicts their reunion. In some Kabbalist traditions, humans help bring about this reunion through sexual love. This is one of the great Hermetic/Kabbalist truths: that human beings participate in the divine, that in fact a divided god cannot heal without human involvement.

Do all these ideas belong strictly to the modern version? Consider the Visconti. Cupid wears a blindfold ("Love is blind," we say), but the young man consciously looks up at him, as if eager to receive the spear aimed at his heart. Cupid's Greek name is Eros, god of love. Homeric myth describes Eros as the son of Aphrodite (the Empress). Plato and the Mystery cults saw Eros as the first principle of creation.

Hermetically, Eros—love—suffuses all creation, an idea that perhaps illustrates a difference between science and Hermeticism. In Newtonian physics, a force called gravity defines the attraction that holds Earth in orbit around the sun. Gravity is seen as a mechanical connection, and science cannot explain how this "action-at-a-distance" operates (Einstein created a different version of gravity in his general relativity theory). Hermeticism describes the attraction as one of love, of Eros. The relationship between Earth and the sun is both sexual and sacred. Think of the way an attraction to someone across a room can hold our attention, or we can feel connected to a lover halfway across the world. As above, so below. Newton was, in fact, a Hermeticist, and he may have intended his theory of gravity to contain a secret message.

What do the early interpreters tell us? Once again, we find a surprising mix of ideas, with "choice" being only one strand.

Some Lovers Meanings

Excerpted from *Mystical Origins of the Tarot* by Paul Huson.

Pratesi's Cartomancer (1750): Love.

De Mellet (1781): Love. A man hesitating between Vice and Virtue.

Court de Gébelin (1773-82): Marriage.

Lévi (1855): The Hebrew letter Vau, Vice, and Virtue. Interlacement, lingam (the Hindu term for phallus [author's note: specifically of Shiva], which Levi introduces in his *Doctrine of Transcendental Magic* as a kabbalistic symbol of Venus), entanglement, union, combination, equilibrium.

Christian (1870): Arcanum VI. The Two Roads. The Ordeal. A man standing motionless at a crossroads. Two women stand each with a hand on his shoulder, indicating one of the two roads. The woman on the right personifies virtue, the one on the left, vice. Above and behind, the genius of Justice, borne on a nimbus of blazing light, is drawing his bow and directs the arrow of punishment at Vice. The whole scene expresses the struggle between the passions and conscience.

Mathers (1888): The Lovers. Trials surmounted. REVERSED: Unwise plans, failure when put to the test.

Golden Dawn (1888-96): The Children of the Voice Divine, Oracles of the Mighty Gods. The Lovers. Inspiration, motive power, impulse.

Grand Orient (Waite, 1889, 1909): Lovers. Material union, affection, desire, natural love, harmony, equilibrium.

Waite (1910): The Lovers. Attraction, love, beauty, trials overcome. REVERSED: Failure, foolish designs. Another account [Etteila] speaks of marriage frustrated.

Love is the earliest meaning, from the manuscript discovered by Pratesi. De Mellet says love as well (it seems rather obvious, doesn't it?) but introduces the concept of choice between vice and virtue. Lévi keeps the vice/virtue concept but adds union. Paul Christian emphasizes choice, details it, and—curiously—makes the archer Justice, who, he says, aims the arrow not at the young man about to fall in love, but at Vice. It takes Mathers, then the Golden Dawn, then Waite, to return to the seemingly obvious idea that the Lovers means lovers. Waite especially emphasizes attraction and union.

Notice that choice does not mean the need to decide between two equally valid options, such as what to wear to a party, or what job to take, or even whom to marry. Instead, it means moral choice, good and bad, Vice and Virtue. Medieval and Rennaisance imagery often allegorized this choice as two women, one blond, one dark-haired. Blonds in those days did not have more fun, and no one thought of them as dumb. Instead, their light coloring made them appear pure to people who polarized light and darkness. Dark hair and complexion appeared more earthly, more tempting because it was more physical.

We might give a modern slant to the idea of choice and sexuality. In the early cards of the Fool's progress, we see him encountering various aspects of life that he must understand and assimilate—principles in the Magician and High Priestess, nature and social rules as well as mother and father in the Empress and Emperor, education and tradition in the Hierophant. These all involve learning about things essentially outside of us. The Lovers shows a personal experience, that of sexuality. When we become adolescents, we begin to make our first independent choices. Often our parents will disapprove. And the choices do not involve only love and sex. We begin to think for ourselves, to question our parents' and society's beliefs. We begin to become independent people.

As well as pushing us to become people in our own right, sexuality teaches a vital metaphysical lesson, the power of mind. Because it happens to all of us, we don't notice how strange this is, but we can just look at someone, or a picture, or simply think about a person or a situation, and our bodies become physically aroused without ever being touched.

From the Marseille-inspired themes of choice, sexuality, and adolescence, we return to the Rider tradition. The naked man and woman, symbol of fulfilled relationships, are Adam and Eve. The flamelike leaves behind Adam represent the Tree of Life, while behind Eve the serpent winds around the tree of knowledge of good and evil. But something is very different here from the Bible story. There, Adam and Eve commit a disastrous act by eating the fruit. God expels them from the garden, placing a seraph (a kind of angel) with a flaming sword to prevent their return. In the Lovers card, the angel blesses the union. The picture becomes subversive in that it supports knowledge and desire.

The Hebrew word translated as "knowledge" is Da'ath, which also appears as a kind of hidden sephirah on the Tree of Life, in the gap between the top three sephiroth and the bottom seven. Da'ath carries connotations of sexuality, as in the famous line "He knew her in the biblical sense." We can look at the Lovers card as symbolic of Tantra and other sexual practices designed to awaken kundalini energy and move us towards enlightenment. Again, we might contrast this card with the Devil. There sex becomes its own end, physical release without either spirituality or real emotional connection. Of course, sometimes this is just what we want. Like all Tarot cards, the Devil has its place.

In the Rider picture, the man looks to the woman and the woman looks to the angel, whose blessing connects them, like closing a circuit so that energy can move. This too is subversive. Western culture, especially in the Middle Ages but even today in some places, has described men as rational and women as emotional, with the further idea that rational men are closer to God, who is pure reason, while women are closer to animals. Therefore, women were not to speak in church but let their husbands speak for them. Here the man, in a sense, goes through the woman to see the angel. Since these are not people but symbols, we can say that the masculine must go through the feminine to reach the divine.

This does not so much reverse the roles as reverse their significance. In other words, the rational masculine can serve us well in certain aspects of life, but to reach spiritual consciousness it must go through feminine instinct. Yang must embrace yin to experience Tao. To put it another way, the conscious self must travel through the unconscious to reach superconsciousness, the divine self. In the three-line structure of the Major Arcana, the first line represents the challenges of consciousness, of our place in the world. The second shows a journey through unconscious to initiation, death, and rebirth. The third takes us into the realm of spirit, called superconsciousness. The Lovers card codifies this as the relationship between the man, the woman, and the angel.

It also can show us a picture of ourselves, with our own conscious, unconscious, and higher consciousness brought together and flowing with dynamic energy. If you use the Rider deck or one of its variants, it is worth taking this card out and studying it, writing about it, meditating with it. It holds powerful mysteries.

The Rider deck contains three angels, seen in the Lovers, Temperance, and Judgement. Opinions vary, but I see them as Lovers/Raphael, Temperance/Michael, and Judgement/Gabriel. Raphael means "healing power of God." Love heals. (Since there are four archangels, where is the fourth, Uriel? We will answer this later, but for now see if you can find another Major card with a winged figure standing above two lower ones.)

The Lovers card represents one of Waite's major changes from the Marseille. Until the Golden Dawn version was published, people assumed that the Rider came from the Hermetic Order. In fact, the Golden Dawn shows a very different picture, the Greek hero Perseus rescuing the maiden Andromeda from a sea monster.

The Shining Tribe Lovers comes from a meditation I did with the Rider version. When I entered the picture (for this technique, see the Readings chapter), Adam and Eve were having a picnic. There they were, naked, with the angel above them, but now behind a redwood table with potato salad and barbecue. When I went to join them, however, the angel swooped me up into the sky for a passionate kiss. After I drew the picture, two things struck me. One was that in most versions of the card, the figures do not actually touch each other. They present a formal arrangement. The Shining Tribe version lets us see the way love transforms us, lifts us. We often think of sex as tawdry, or funny, or just exciting, but sex can give us a glimpse of divine union.

The second thing the picture does is open up the genders of the two figures. Most versions show a man and a woman (or a man and two women). Some lesbian feminist decks depict two women; very few decks show two men. In the Shining Tribe, because the bodies embrace, we cannot identify their gender. They go beyond limited identities.

Shortly after I finished the Shining Tribe deck, I attended a myth and theatre festival in France that was dedicated to Aphrodite. As part of my contribution, I did a Shining Tribe reading. The first card was the Lovers! Looking at it, I realized that it teaches a lesson of self-love, of the human and the divine inside of us joining together as lovers. When we feel most human—weak, vulnerable, struggling—we must embrace our own divinity. When we feel most angelic and powerful, wise, archetypal, we should make sure we embrace our humanity. And these two aspects do not simply join together, they love each other. This too is the message of the card.

The Lovers in any deck heads up one of the most powerful of triads. The sixth position includes Lovers, Death, and Judgement—love, death, and resurrection. Love is like death in that it takes us beyond ego. No matter how much we might work at being great lovers, how much we might try to project an image, in the act of love we must let go of self, at least for a moment. In the Middle Ages, people called orgasm "the little death." The idea actually came from a belief that a man shortened his life by six or seven seconds every time he climaxed. This belief came from a too-literal understanding of esoteric practices of withholding orgasm to transform energy. But even with such a negative idea, men still pursued sex, still surrendered to love.

And the connection to Judgement, the resurrection card? Love heals.

What do we say when this card appears in readings? First of all, it signals love, so that we often welcome it joyously. Obviously, this meaning becomes strongest when we have asked about a possible relationship, but even in a reading about, say, a new job, the Lovers can mean meeting someone, especially if other cards support this idea, such as the Two of Cups. If the Hierophant and/or the Four of Cups appears with the Lovers, the combination hints at marriage.

At the same time, other traditional meanings may apply, especially a choice. The querent may have to make some difficult choice, maybe between a temptation and what the person knows he or she should do. Vice and virtue. Or especially with a Marseille deck, the Lovers card can mean a choice between possible partners.

In business readings, the card can signal a good and fruitful partnership, or again a significant choice to be made.

Another possible meaning is adolescence, or a person coming to a new level of themselves. Finally, it can mean a person in harmony with her or his various levels.

Reversed, it means, first of all, *not* love. If someone asks, "Will I meet a partner at this event (new job, etc.)?" or "Will this relationship become serious?" or "Will I meet my soul mate in the next six months?" the reversed Lovers card says, "Probably not. Not this time."

The Lovers upside down also can indicate a hard choice or someone who avoids such a choice. It may indicate someone not in touch with some aspect of her- or himself, or, in the case of a young person, a troubled adolescence.

A Lovers Reading

1. How have I experienced love in my life?

2. What has it done?

3. What do I desire?

4. What holds me back?

5. What does love ask of me?

6. What can love give me?

LE CHAR   IL CARRO

THE CHARIOT   VII   DER WAGEN
EL CARRO   DE ZEGEWAGEN

Chariot: 7

Astrological correspondence:
Cancer

Kabbalistic letter: ח Cheth

Path on Tree of Life: Binah
(Understanding) to
Gevurah (Power)

VII

THE CHARIOT.

Chariot cards from
VISCONTI,
MARSEILLE,
RIDER, GOLDEN
DAWN RITUAL,
EGYPTIAN &
SHINING TRIBE

The Chariot

CARD SEVEN COMPLETES the first line of the Major Arcana and thus signals the achievement, or triumph, of the first level. The word *triumph*, in Italian *trionf*, is the original name for all the trumps (a word that itself means "triumph"). The cards were called *Trionfii* before they received the name *Tarocchi. Trionf* also meant a display in a kind of parade, similar to the decorated floats with people in costumes that we see today in Halloween or Mardi Gras parades. The *trionf* displays traveled in carts or actual chariots. Thus, card seven reflects some of the oldest levels of Tarot itself.

Though *triumph* originally meant a set piece in a procession, it now, of course, means victory, and victory is one of the primary meanings of the Chariot card. The idea of a victory procession with a hero in a bedecked chariot takes us back at least to ancient Rome and up to the present day, with heroes like astronauts or football champions driven in limousines to receive the cheers of people lined up in the streets or leaning out of windows. The Kennedy assassination happened in such a procession, ending the practice for politicians, but it still occurs for sports heroes. In fact, I am writing this the day after such an event honoring the New York Giants for their win in the Superbowl.

It wasn't just heroes the Romans carried in triumphal processions. Each year, a chariot pulled by trained lions carried a black stone through the Roman streets. The stone symbolized the goddess Cybele, whom the Romans called "Magna Mater," or Great Mother, of the gods. In the Tarot, the Great Mother is the Empress, but we will look closer at the image of a woman and a lion in the next card, Strength.

Let's take a look at what the early interpreters say about this card.

Some Chariot Meanings

Excerpted from *Mystical Origins of the Tarot* by Paul Huson.

Pratesi's Cartomancer (1750): Journey.

De Mellet (1781): Chariot of War. Crimes of the Iron Age.

Court de Gébelin (1773-82): Osiris Triumphant.

Lévi (1855): The Hebrew letter Zayin, the Cubic Chariot. Weapon, sword, cherubic sword of fire, the sacred septenary, triumph, royalty, priesthood.

Christian (1870): Arcanum VII. The Chariot of Osiris: Victory. A war chariot, square in shape, surmounted by a starred baldaquin upheld by four columns. An armed conqueror advances carrying a scepter and a sword in his hands. He is crowned with a fillet of gold ornamented at five points by three pentagrams or golden stars. The square chariot symbolizes the work accomplished by the will, which has overcome all obstacles, the four columns supporting the starry canopy, the four conquered elements. The lifted sword is the sign of victory. The two sphinxes, one white, one black, symbolize Good and Evil—the one conquered, the other vanquished—both having become the servants of the Magus who has triumphed over his ordeals.

Mathers (1888): The Chariot. Triumph, victory, overcoming obstacles. REVERSED: Overthrown, conquered by obstacles at the last moment.

Golden Dawn (1888-96): Child of the Power of the Waters, Lord of the Triumph of Light. The Chariot. Triumph, victory, health, success, though sometimes not enduring.

Grand Orient (Waite, 1889, 1909): Chariot. Triumph of reason. Success, the right prevailing, conquest.

Waite (1910): The Chariot. Providence, war, triumph, presumption, vengeance. REVERSED: Riot, dispute, litigation, defeat.

Notice Pratesi's one word, "Journey." This meaning has become common with contemporary readers, and here we find it as the "original" interpretation. Also interesting, Lévi introduces the concept of the metaphysical cube here in the Chariot, not the Emperor. This is more striking when we realize that the Marseille Tarot, the only one Lévi knew, did not show a cubic Chariot.

The Rider version, in fact, gives the Chariot a cube shape, so much so that it resembles a concrete block, creating the sense of someone set in his ways. In fact, the way the Rider chariot sits on the ground suggests an inability to move, with the charioteer almost embedded in it. We need the Fool here to get us to leave our triumph, the successful completion of the challenges of stage one, and begin a whole new journey with Strength and the Hermit.

Notice that in the Marseille the wheels curiously point in opposite directions. We find something similar in other versions, notably the Thoth cards of Crowley and Harris, as if the Chariot is not actually meant to go anywhere.

Lévi reminds us of the warrior aspect of a charioteer, even though the Marseille figure holds a scepter rather than a sword or spear. Lévi says "weapon," and "sword," but then introduces a metaphysical, even mythic, level of "cherubic sword of fire," an image that recalls the seraph with the four-sided flaming sword who bars Adam and Eve (and us) from returning to Eden. Because we cannot go back, we must go forward until we find a fuller sense of paradise in card twenty-one, the World.

Lévi also introduces the "sacred septenary," reminding us of the importance of the number seven. We can recall the seven planetary spheres, the seven musical notes, seven chakras, seven colors of the rainbow—but also the seven openings in the male body, so that the Chariot becomes a particularly masculine card. Strength, by contrast, shows us a feminine kind of power, just as the female body contains eight openings.

Paul Christian elaborates on the "square" chariot and the four columns. This double use of four indicates manifestation, that is, the idea of accomplishments in the physical world. For Christian, this means "the four conquered elements," the idea that the magus or initiate must overcome the natural world as a series of trials.

Christian also introduces the idea of sphinxes instead of horses, something we see in the Rider version. Whether horses or sphinxes, the one black and the other white represent duality and all the contradictions and difficulties of our lives. Plato described the mind as a chariot pulled by a black-and-white horse. Christian names the sphinxes Good and Evil, and where the young man in the Lovers must choose between Vice and Virtue, the Charioteer must overcome both—"the one conquered, the other vanquished." Because he has "triumphed over his ordeals," the magus makes duality itself his "servant."

This introduces the theme of *will*, for many the primary quality of the Chariot. But what do we mean by will? We also describe the Magician with this term, so are they the same? In my view, the Magician demonstrates the principle, or ideal, of focused will, and the Chariot shows us the person who has learned to use the will to deal with the challenges of life. Waite uses such terms as "success…conquest…war, triumph, presumption, vengeance."

By strength of will, the Charioteer makes his way in the world. By strength of will, he holds together the contradictions of his life. In most versions of the card, there are no reins; by will alone he keeps the horses or sphinxes from going off in opposite directions and pulling apart everything he has built.

This is one view. My friend and fellow Tarotist Zoe Matoff sees the Chariot as a vehicle for *divine* will. The Charioteer does not need to take charge or hold the reins, because he makes *himself* the vehicle for what needs to happen. "Not my will but Yours" becomes his motto.

Whichever way we see the Chariot—as magus, as success in the outer realms of life, as agent of divine will—it shows a triumph that comes from absorbing the lessons of the previous cards. We can see this symbolically in the Rider image. He holds a long rod like a Magician's wand—though held low, under his control, not raised high. The High Priestess comes through in the black-and-white sphinxes, the Empress in the canopy of stars above his head, the Emperor in the stonelike cube of the Chariot itself. The position of the sphinxes recalls the Hierophant's disciples, while the Lovers subtly comes through in the winged circle (like the angel over Adam and Eve) above the image like a nut and bolt. This is called a lingam and yoni, lingam being the phallus of the Hindu god Shiva, yoni being the womb of Shiva's female half, Shakti. Hindus often represent Shiva by actual standing stones, the same kind of stones that signified Hermes in ancient Greece.

While the original inspiration for the Chariot may have come from medieval processions, we can cite a more esoteric image: Ezekiel's vision of the heavenly chariot (Ezekiel 1: 1–28). It's incredibly detailed, with images of four-sided figures, including the characters we see in the corners of the Wheel of Fortune and the World. The Chariot, called in Hebrew *merkavah*, became the basis of mystical practices two thousand years ago that later evolved into Kabbalah. These practices, called *ma'aseh merkavah*, the "work of the chariot," involved intense meditations in which participants traveled to the seven *hekhaloth*, or heavenly palaces. Seven, of course, is the Chariot card, as well as the seven spheres and the seven lower sephiroth on the Tree of Life. In the Shining Tribe Chariot, the driver reaches both hands up, as a gesture of transformation and triumph but also to reach into the river of divine energy. Above him, the circles within circles suggest Ezekiel's vision.

Once, in a class in New York City, I led people in a meditation to visualize their own Chariot, the vehicle to carry them through life. Though I did not base this on the merkavah (in fact, the meditation was inspired by a myth of Shiva), a young woman came up to me afterward, and from her description I understood that she had seen a vision of the heavenly Chariot. Very different from what I had laid out, she saw it fill the sky and descend to her in a great light that filled her with awe. As we work with the cards and the very ancient images embedded in them, we should remember that they are not arbitrary, or random, inventions.

Chariots figure in the myth of Persephone, kidnapped by Hades to become his Queen of the Dead. At the beginning, the ground opens up as the maiden kneels to pluck a narcissus flower. Death charges out of the depths in a great chariot, grabs the terrified girl, and thunders across the world before going back down into darkness. Later in the story, when Zeus (the Emperor) decides Persephone (the Star) must return to her mother Demeter (the Empress), he sends Hermes (the Magician) to bring back Persephone—in a chariot. Finally, when Demeter rewards humanity with the gift of agriculture, she sends a prince named Triptolemus across the world in a divine chariot to teach people this basis of civilization.

The sphinxes first suggested by Paul Christian evoke still another vital myth, that of Oedipus. In the story, Oedipus flees his home because the Oracle at Delphi (see the Magician for the contrasts between oracles and divination) has told him he will kill his father and marry his mother. At a place "where three roads meet," he encounters an arrogant man in a chariot, and kills him. Oedipus continues into the city of Thebes to find the people in great distress. A sphinx—a creature half-woman, half-lion—has settled in the town square, demanding that any passerby answer her riddle. When they fail, the sphinx devours them. The king, in fact, has left the city to go to Delphi for help, but he has not returned, and the people are desperate.

This is the most famous riddle in all of literature, and it goes like this: what creature walks on four legs in the morning, two in the afternoon, and three in the evening? Oedipus answers correctly—man, who crawls on all fours as a baby, walks upright as an adult, and uses a cane in old age. Furious, the sphinx kills herself, and the Thebans, overjoyed, tell the savior that since the king has not returned from his mission, they want Oedipus to rule over them. After all, he is the wisest of men, he knows what a human being is. To give the stranger legitimacy, the people suggest he marry their queen.

By now, those readers who do not know the story will have guessed the secret. The man he killed on the road was his father, the king; the queen is his mother. Oedipus does not know the most crucial mystery of all, his own origin. This is the paradox of card seven, the Chariot—to be successful, to have met the challenges of the previous cards, to be admired and proud, but to know nothing at all about the ultimate truth of oneself and the cosmos. In the second level, the Fool will in fact come to know him- or herself, and in the third, gnosis—knowledge—will extend to reality itself.

In readings, the Chariot means first of all success, especially success achieved through exerting your will on the world. The Chariot implies what used to be called "the good life": success, deserved pride, admiration from others, comfort. These material things can extend to success in love, for of course the card follows the Lovers.

If the reading concerns a specific project, the Chariot becomes a good omen—that is, a card that indicates a positive result, without need to interpret it further. The message becomes stronger when other successful cards appear, especially the World, the Six of Wands, or the Kings, in particular the King of Pentacles.

The Chariot contains a masculine quality, emphasized if it appears with the Magician, the Emperor, or some of the Wands cards. If the Tower shows up, forcefulness can slide into aggression or violence—alternatively, the person's plans can fail or the structure he or she has created might fall apart. The Tower is 16, and 1+6=7, creating a relationship between the two cards.

We do not need to take an extreme view of the Chariot's dark or hidden side. Instead, we simply can say that a strong will creates a persona, a kind of mask (the word *persona* means the masks Greek performers wore to portray the gods—*persona* actually derives from Persephone). This mask may hold up, or it may crack. In the Shining Tribe Tarot, the front of the chariot is a mask, but it's cracking open to reveal another world inside.

On a very simple level, the Chariot may indicate travel or even getting a new car.

Reversed does not necessarily indicate failure. It suggests that willpower is lacking, the person doubts him- or herself. Once in a reading a woman asked why she could not lose weight. She expected some awful, repressed secret to show up, but instead the Chariot reversed came out, and I said to her, "You lack willpower." Surprised, she said, "That's it?" Sometimes the Tarot speaks to us very directly.

The Chariot reversed may appear when a person has maintained a situation through willpower and can no longer do this or just does not want to continue. For example, if someone has stayed in a job she dislikes because she thinks she must, and does so by force of will, the Chariot reversed may tell her she cannot keep doing this. The other cards in the reading may indicate whether she fails or comes to an understanding that she wants something different in life.

This is the paradox of the Chariot upside down. The will fails, it may be painful, especially if that Tower appears, but it may be the best thing for the person. If Strength appears after the reversed Chariot, it shows the person finding the inner strength to change. If cards of relationship or cooperation appear, such as the Lovers or the Three of Cups, then the person gets help from others or learns to communicate more.

And of course a reversed Chariot may mean a canceled trip or car trouble.

A Chariot Reading

This is one of my favorite spreads, because the positions are based on the first eight cards of the Major Arcana. If a card comes up in its own position—say, the Emperor in position 4—its power is emphasized.

It is possible to use two decks for this reading: one to lay out the positions, another to shuffle the cards and set them on top of the position cards.

0. (Fool) What am I leaping into at this time in my life?

1. (Magician) Where is the energy, the magic?

2. (High Priestess) What is secret or hidden or unspoken?

3. (Empress) What is my passion?

4. (Emperor) What are the rules (possibly hidden or unconscious)?

5. (Hierophant) What is the path laid out for me?

6. (Lovers) How do I express my passion?

7. (Chariot) Where is it all heading?

The purpose of this reading is to help you become more conscious, so that you can take the reins of the chariot that is your life.

THE CHARIOT.

Strength: 8
Astrological correspondence: Leo
Kabbalistic letter: ט Teth
Path on Tree of Life: Chesed
(Mercy) to Gevurah
(Power)

Strength cards from
VISCONTI,
MARSEILLE,
RIDER, GOLDEN
DAWN RITUAL,
EGYPTIAN &
SHINING TRIBE

Strength

The first thing to say about Strength is that for many people it does not belong here at all. In the Tarot of Marseille, and for many modern Tarotists, card eight is Justice and Strength is card eleven. The Golden Dawn reversed the order, largely because Leo (the lion) seemed to go with Strength and Libra (scales) with Justice. In the order of the signs, Leo comes before Libra, with Virgo (a good choice for the Hermit) coming between them. Waite, a Golden Dawn leader at one point, followed this order, so that most people now think of Strength as eight.

For myself, I find it valuable to see Strength as the initiator of the second level and Justice as the midpoint, not just of the line, but of the entire Major

Arcana. In my approach to Tarot, meaning counts more—trumps, we might say—than systems. While I find the Golden Dawn order most meaningful, I also see value in the older tradition. If we see cards eight through fourteen as a search for our true selves, then Justice can symbolize the desire that moves us to begin, Strength the quality we need in the middle of this process. On the other hand, while the desire for truth may motivate us, we need a great deal of inner strength to begin such a process. We turn away from the Chariot's willpower and find the courage to look inward. After the initial explorations, we come to the center of looking at our lives and balance the scales.

In the Middle Ages and Renaissance, Strength, also called Force, or Fortitude, meant one of the four cardinal virtues. In medieval thought, this meant subduing or overcoming the passions, especially sexual desire. The lion symbolized "animal" desires. We might think of someone who struggles with some unacceptable urge—to have an affair, maybe, or to steal, or give in to an addiction—and contains this desire through self-discipline. Some older versions of Fortitude showed the hero Hercules clubbing a lion to death (the first of his twelve labors). The image of the woman who closes the lion's mouth (some people say she opens it, others that she gets the lion to speak) shows us a different way to subdue the passions, through trust. Still, the goal remains the same: overcoming desire. Aleister Crowley challenged this idea by naming his Strength card "Lust" and showing the woman riding the lion, her nude body exultant.

We should recognize that people in the Middle Ages sometimes saw lions in a much more positive sense. As the "king of beasts," and golden like the sun, the lion symbolized Christ, the golden light of existence for Christian mystics. At least two modern fantasies use this kind of imagery. C. S. Lewis's children's book *The Lion, the Witch, and the Wardrobe* has a Christlike lion king who dies and is resurrected. Charles Williams, author of the Tarot novel *The Greater Trumps*, used the lion for the archetype of majesty in his mystical thriller *The Place of the Lion*. In Williams's novel, the world becomes endangered when a powerful meditation unwittingly allows the Platonic Ideals to take physical existence in the bodies of animals escaped from a circus. At the end, the hero takes on the role of Adam, the archetypal human, and names the beasts, causing the archetypes to retreat. The human overcomes the lion with the power of speech, an image of Strength.

We might think of this card as the quality of naming, and thus understanding, nature. Older generations might have seen it as a symbol of agriculture and civilization, taming the wilderness. Today we might think of it more as ecology, in which the human and the natural worlds exist harmoniously. Notice in the Rider version the way the flower belt on the woman extends gently around the lion's neck.

So much of this symbolism accepts the idea of Strength as subduing desire. For many people, the picture shows a simpler quality, the appreciation of your own strength, self-confidence. We can talk of inner strength, believing in yourself without having to control or dominate others. And since I do not see passion as something dangerous (or sinful!), I used the image of an untamed lioness in my own version of this card. The Shining Tribe Strength comes from a Persian medallion of a griffin, a winged lion. While some have seen the posture as defensive, I tend to think of the lioness reaching for the future while looking to the past. She is rooted in the earth but can move into the unknown.

Because people's ideas of Strength vary so much (both the quality and the card), I decided to poll various Tarotists for their views. To my surprise, quite a few kept the idea of subduing or conquering desire. Avigayil Landsman, who writes about the spiritual and divinatory meanings of the Hebrew letters, quoted the line, "Who is strong? He who is in control of his passions." Johanna Gargiulo-Sherman, creator of the Sacred Rose Tarot, said that the spiritual prevails over the physical, and the animal instincts give way to doing "the right thing."

The question is, how do we know what is right if it goes against our instincts? The Hierophant might tell us to follow his doctrines, the Emperor to obey his rules. But if we see the Tarot overall as a model for self-development, the question becomes trickier—and tricks put us in the realm of the Magician. Maybe we could think of merging with our desires, or our desires raised up, so that right action, personal will, and divine will become the same.

Megan Williams, a Tarotist from Australia, takes what I think of as a more modern approach. Strength is an inner quality, feminine, built of self-love and trust. In readings, she thinks of building trust, showing love. Numerologist Carey Croft describes it as the quality that allows you to do something not easy but necessary, in alignment with your higher self. It can signify strength of mind, of spirit, and the ability to focus. Joan Pantesco, who also goes by the name of Purple, focused on the lion, or rather the relationship between the male lion and the woman. Strength for her is androgyny, a blend of masculine and feminine.

Avigayil Landsman, mentioned above, took a fascinating view of the lion, describing the woman as a midwife and the lion a cervix the woman helps to open. Feminine Strength becomes the power of women to give birth. This idea might help explain a very ancient connection of goddesses and lions. One of the earliest carvings, some eight thousand years old, shows a powerfully built woman seated in a chair, with the "crown" of a baby emerging from between her legs. Female lions, or leopards, crouch on either side of her. Various Middle Eastern goddesses were shown with lions, and in the Chariot we described how the Romans celebrated Cybele, Great Mother of the gods, by having her black meteorite carried in a chariot drawn by lions. Cybele came from the same area in western Turkey, Anatolia, as that seated goddess thousands of years earlier.

Laura Triana stressed the esoteric tradition around Strength. The Hebrew letter Teth means a snake, and thus the kundalini energy that rests like a coiled snake at the base of the spine. Usually we experience kundalini as sexual, but it can travel up the spine and transform to spiritual enlightenment.

The snake also represents the life force, which occultists recognized as spiraling energy long before the discovery of DNA as a double helix. Her number 8 can look like a spiral.

Artist and Tarot reader Paige Vinson said to her the card meant closeness to animals. Zoe Matoff took that a step further to suggest animal communicators, people who use knowledge and psychic connections to find what specific animals need to say to the humans around them. Or it could mean listening to your own animal nature.

Now that we have seen what people today think of Strength, what about early cartomancers?

Some Strength Meanings

Excerpted from *Mystical Origins of the Tarot* by Paul Huson.

Pratesi's Cartomancer (1750): Violence.

De Mellet (1781): Fortitude, who comes to the aid of Prudence by vanquishing the lion, the wild, uncultivated land.

Court de Gébelin (1773-82): Force or Strength.

Lévi (1855): The Hebrew letter Kaph, Strength. The hand in the act of grasping and holding.

Christian (1870): Arcanum XI. The Tamed Lion: Strength. In the divine world, the Principle of all strength, spiritual or material; in the intellectual world moral Force; in the physical world organic Force.

Mathers (1888): Strength, or Fortitude. Power, might, force. REVERSED: Abuse of power, overbearingness, want of Fortitude.

Golden Dawn (1888-96): Daughter of the Flaming Sword, Leader of the Lion. Fortitude, courage, strength, power not arrested in the act of judgment, but passing on to further action, sometimes obstinacy.

Grand Orient (Waite, 1889, 1909): Fortitude, or Strength. Courage, vitality, tenacity of things, high endurance.

Waite (1910): Fortitude. Power, energy, action, courage, magnanimity, success and honors. REVERSED: Despotism, abuse of power, weakness, discord or disgrace.

Pratesi begins with violence, possibly in response to that image of Hercules clubbing a lion. De Mellet sees the woman "vanquishing" the lion, who symbolizes wild nature. Paul Christian, Mathers, and the Golden Dawn all stress power. So does Waite, as both Grand Orient and himself.

So where does that idea of gentleness come in, of feminine passion? Maybe it literally comes from women, and modern women at that, the many who have helped shape Tarot interpretation over the last three or four decades. One of the earliest of these modern interpreters was Eden Gray, author of several Tarot books in the late 1960s and early '70s. Here is what she says about Strength:

> Force of character, spiritual power overcoming material power, love triumphing over hate, the higher nature over carnal desires. Reversed: Domination of the material. Discord, lack of moral force, fear of the unknown in ourselves, abuse of power.

With all these possibilities, what should we say when Strength shows up in a reading? More than most other cards, it can depend on what the quality means to the querent. When you look at this card—and make sure you really look at it—think of how you understand strength, and if you are reading for someone else, ask that person.

Is it the power to withstand life's struggles? Overcoming your animal nature? Working *with* your animal self? A person who literally works with animals—a vet, a trainer, or an animal communicator? Does the lion mean desire or sexuality, and if so, what is the woman's relationship to it?

My own first meaning for this card calls for people to realize their own strength, especially in situations where they believe themselves inadequate. Depending on the question and the other cards, it can indicate a need for strength. In my experience, the Tarot does not just say "This would be a good idea." If a card appears as something a person needs, it also says the person can find this in herself.

Strength does not necessarily recommend any particular action. Sometimes it means the strength to do nothing. The other cards may indicate what, if anything, needs to be done. Strength tells you that you have the ability to do what is needed.

Reversed might mean the desires unchecked, giving in to temptation, especially sexual. Is that necessarily a bad thing? Past generations thought so. Now opinions differ. But if the other cards show some danger from reckless behavior, then we might worry about unchecked desire.

In my experience with Strength reversed, I think first of weakness, or a person who doubts her or his own strength. If someone faces a difficult task or is involved in a longstanding, difficult situation, upside-down Strength can show a feeling of "I can't do this." The other cards may indicate that the person actually does have more resources than she or he knew, more inner courage or resolve. But maybe not. Maybe "weakness" is not a judgment but a description of the situation. Reversed Strength may warn us against trying to do something that cannot be done.

And is weakness necessarily a bad thing? Too often we endure bad conditions just because we can—because we can take it or because someone else is weak and we need to be strong. Once in a reading we asked, "What is the best thing the person can do right now?" We were surprised to see Strength reversed appear. After a moment, I realized it told the person, "Let yourself be weak. Let someone else carry the burden."

1. How am I strong?

2. How am I weak?

3. When do I need to be strong?

4. When do I need to be weak?

5. What strengthens me?

6. What weakens me?

Hermit: 9

Astrological correspondence:
  Virgo

Kabbalistic letter: ʼ Yod

Path on Tree of Life: Tipheret
  (Beauty) to Netzach
  (Victory)

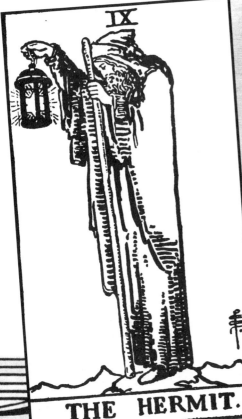

Hermit cards from
  VISCONTI,
  MARSEILLE,
  RIDER, GOLDEN
  DAWN RITUAL,
  EGYPTIAN &
  SHINING TRIBE

THE HERMIT

The Hermit

LET'S STATE THE obvious first: the Hermit means being alone. Whether by choice or circumstance, a person goes through a period either literally alone or emotionally apart.

What does alone mean? People sometimes make a distinction between "aloneness" and "loneliness." Presumably we choose the former and suffer the latter, and hope that the choice will always be ours. Almost anyone in a long relationship will enjoy occasional times when their partner goes away and they can do whatever they want—make noise at all hours, eat things the partner hates,

or simply rediscover who they are outside the relationship. Very few, however, would want to give up the relationship entirely for the sake of permanent "alone time."

When I travel, I happily can go entire days without talking to anyone. At home I enjoy seeing friends. I know someone who will spend days in the house, not answering the phone or even listening to the messages, but she gets frustrated on planes if she sits next to a person who doesn't want to talk.

If someone asks the cards, "Will I find my soul mate this year?" and the Hermit appears, disappointment will be the likely result. But if a person asks, "What do I need in my life right now?" the Hermit may excite with its possibilities. And even if the question becomes, "What do I need to find my soul mate?" the Hermit may suggest a useful quest for self-acceptance.

But is this all the Hermit means, to be alone? The image, and its history, reveals a web of ideas.

When I was a child, I read everything, but I loved fairy tales best of all. In college, where I needed to specialize in some aspect of literature, I chose King Arthur, for didn't those stories resemble fairy tales, with knights and wizards, and castles that vanished in the morning, and a golden chalice that healed the sick? I soon noticed an interesting literary device. Merlin acted as Arthur's tutor (though often playing tricks on him, a playful Hermes as much as a magus Hermes), but when someone else—Lancelot, for example—needed instruction or magical information, a "hermit" would appear to reveal the necessary truth. I began to imagine the Arthurian woods filled with wise old hermits dressed in long, ragged robes and carrying stout staves. They were always old and always wise.

Where did this image come from? To some extent, actual models existed—people who abandoned ordinary social involvement to devote themselves to meditation and prayer. Most went to monasteries, but a few probably took their chances on their own. At the same time, the *image*, the idea of a hermit, exists across many cultures. The Hindu god Shiva lives in a dark cave until the time comes to destroy the universe. Shamans go off for long periods to draw visions to themselves. A great Eskimo shaman named Igjugarjuk told the explorer Knud Rasmussen that he would go on the ice for days without food or shelter because "solitude and suffering open the human mind."

Is this, then, the Hermit, a shaman on a vision quest? Since he holds up a lantern, we could say that he has found his vision and now uses his knowledge to light the way for others. When the Hermit appears in a reading, we need to ask if he signifies the querent or someone who will serve as a teacher, a guide.

In our culture, people will sometimes experience the Hermit through therapy. A person separates from normal daily concerns—at least for an hour or two a week—to discover his or her true self. But the Hermit also appears in the therapist, the wise figure who (we hope) has gone through the process of self-discovery before us and now can help light the way.

An older model for these experiences comes through initiation. Again, the Hermit can show the candidate who leaves behind normal society or the teacher/master/guru who leads the way. Both the Hierophant and the Hermit signify teachers. The Hierophant directs the learning that we all can find in doctrines, books, ceremonies. The Hermit reveals mysteries that we must experience directly. Does this mean that whenever the Hermit appears we *must* find a teacher/guru/shaman/therapist? No, for remember, the card can indicate our own personal quest or just time alone.

When I first encountered the term "Hermeticism," I thought it might derive from *hermit*, and in fact we might think of the wise old man as Hermes Trismegistus. Both the Fool and the Hermit give us versions of Hermes, the trickster/thief and the great teacher. Maybe we can only understand Hermes if we think of the two together.

Just by his example, the Hermit shows that enlightenment is possible. The Marseille Hermit holds up a closed lantern, but Waite designed the Rider version open, so we can see the light in the form of a six-pointed star. He does not hold it for himself but for others. Waite describes his basic lesson as "Where I am, there you also may be."

The Wise Old Man who appears at crucial moments—all those hermits in the King Arthur tales—embodies what psychologist Carl Jung termed an "archetype," an image ingrained in the human psyche (and possibly physically in the brain) so that it spontaneously appears in myths and fairy tales of many cultures but also in people's dreams or in the way they interact with such figures in their lives as teachers—or Jungian analysts. Coming out of a patriarchal society, Jung saw these figures as male, just as the classic Tarot decks do. Some modern Tarots portray Crones, Wise Women, or Witches in the role of card nine.

Anonymous, in *Tarot Meditations*, evokes the Hermit as that which leads or inspires us, and sees him in archetypal terms. "It is the venerable and mysterious Hermit, who was master of the most intimate and cherished dreams of my youth, as moreover he is the master of dreams for all youth in every country who seek the narrow gate and the hard way to the divine. Name for me a country or a time for which the youth...has not had its imagination haunted by the figure of a wise and good father, a spiritual father, a hermit."

The radical philosopher Friedrich Nietzsche gave us a modern version of the archetype in his book *Thus Spake Zarathustra*. The character's name actually comes from a much more ancient Wise Old Man, the Persian prophet Zoroaster, founder of monotheism. In the book's prologue, we read that Zarathustra has spent thirty-five years in a cave and now has returned to teach humanity—the classic Hermit.

People mistakenly believe that Nietzsche considered himself the *Ubermensch*, or Overman (a much better term than Superman, for obvious cultural reasons). In fact, Zarathustra makes clear that he is not the Overman but one who will clear the way for this new being to emerge. He will teach and open the path. Unfortunately, humanity soon disgusts him, for they cling to their old morality, their Hierophant rules of good and evil, their subservience and selfless-ness, which Zarathustra considers a sickness.

What characterizes this Overman? He (or she, though Nietzsche's sense of women seems limited) lives for life, not service or piety; believes in health, not morality; and finds truth within his own being, rather than in priestly rules.

The Hermit shines a light for us, but only if we climb high enough to see him. For he dwells on a mountaintop, and we need the commitment and courage of Strength to reach a level where we can even see the Hermit's lantern. The Shining Tribe Tarot shows the Hermit himself on the path. He has left the ordinary world behind and mounted the hill of medita-tion, where he will step through a dark doorway. On the other side, he will find a lantern left by previous Hermits. We make the commitment in the darkness of our ignorance, and only when we do so will we discover that the light is waiting for us.

There's an old Sufi joke that speaks of these issues and the Fool's relationship to the Her-mit. A man walking down the street in ancient Baghdad sees Nasruddin, the Fool of many such tales, searching the ground under a streetlamp. Asked what he is doing, Nasruddin answers, "I lost my keys, and I need them to get into my house." (Remember that many people describe the Tarot cards as "keys," and then consider what a locked house might sym-bolize.)

Bending down to help, the man says, "Where exactly did you drop them?"

"Oh, over on the next street," Nasruddin answers.

"The next street? Then why are you searching here?"

"The light's better."

Maybe the Hermit tells us that before we can search for the keys, we need to climb through darkness to the genuine light.

Have interpreters always seen the card as the Wise Old Man? Here are the various meanings.

Some Hermit Meanings

Excerpted from *Mystical Origins of the Tarot* by Paul Huson.

Pratesi's Cartomancer (1750): The Old Man.

De Mellet (1781): The Hermit. The sage in search of justice.

Court de Gébelin (1773-82): The Sage, or seeker after truth.

Lévi (1855): The Hebrew letter Teth, the Hermit or Capuchin monk. Goodness, revulsion from evil, morality, wisdom.

Christian (1870): Arcanum IX. The Veiled Lamp: Prudence. Arcanum IX is represented by an old man who walks leaning on a stick, holding in front of him a lighted lantern half hidden by his cloak. He personifies experience acquired in the labors of life. The lighted lantern signifies the light of the mind, which should illuminate the past, the present, and the future. The cloak that half conceals it signifies discretion. The stick symbolizes the support given by Prudence to the man who does not reveal his purpose.

Mathers (1888): The Hermit. Prudence, caution, deliberation. REVERSED: Overprudence, timorousness, fear.

Golden Dawn (1888-96): The Magus of the Voice of Light, the Prophet of the Gods. The Hermit, or Prophet. Wisdom sought for and obtained from above. In the mystical titles, this with the Hierophant and the Magician are the three Magi.

Grand Orient (Waite, 1889, 1909): Hermit. Caution, safety, protection, detachment, Prudence, sagacity, search after truth.

Waite (1910): The Hermit. Prudence, circumspection. Also treason, roguery, corruption. REVERSED: Concealment, disguise, fear, unreasoned caution.

We will look at Pratesi's "Old Man" in a moment, but first notice that de Mellet and Court de Gébelin introduce the idea of the Sage. And yet, he seeks truth, or justice, but he has not yet found it—and since in the Marseille deck Justice comes just before the Hermit, maybe de Mellet's sage missed it and needs to go back a step. We do not find the full archetype until the Golden Dawn, with its "The Prophet of the Gods."

Paul Christian calls the Hermit "Prudence," an idea followed by Mathers and Waite. Prudence, like Strength's Fortitude, is one of the cardinal virtues. Some modern Tarot historians, who reject the idea of any esoteric meanings for the first Tarot, see prudence as the original interpretation, but this strikes me as unlikely, especially since no one suggested it before 1870.

Pratesi's "Old Man" might simply represent maturity, and this has become a modern meaning. However, look at the Visconti version of the card. He holds an hourglass, not a lamp, and thus becomes a symbol of time and the limits of mortality. We still see this image in our culture—every December, in fact, as the old year, gray and worn out and limping toward rebirth as baby January. If we consider that the Wheel of Fortune follows, and some see it as the turning year, then the Old Man becomes more significant.

The image carries a wider meaning, that of the planet Saturn. As the outermost visible planet and the slowest moving (from our perspective here on Earth, watching its progress), Saturn has always represented limitations and mortality. The Golden Dawn linked Saturn to the World card—final planet, final card. Some modern Tarotists believe Saturn should go with the Hermit. The astrologer Liz Greene used the Hermit on the cover of her book about Saturn.

We might think of the Hermit as part of a series leading up to Death. The Hermit symbolizes endings through the number nine, the last single digit. But nine is also the number of new life, for the nine months of pregnancy.

In the second triad, the Hermit comes between the High Priestess above and the Tower below. The Hermit keeps everything within, silent, undefined. The Tower explodes everything outward, breaking down separations and categories. The Hermit's wisdom and dedication hold these forces together.

Here is a Hermit story from the very source of the archetype in Western culture, the Desert Fathers of early Christianity—the word *hermit* comes from a Greek term that means "one who lives in the desert," for this is exactly where these first monks set up their retreats. Annie Dillard tells this story in her amazing book *For the Time Being.*

> Abbot Lot came to Abbot Joseph and said:
>
> Father, according as I am able, I keep my little rules, and my little fast, my prayer, meditation, and contemplative silence. And according as I am able, I strive to cleanse my heart of thoughts. Now what more should I do?
>
> The elder rose up in reply and stretched out his hands to Heaven, and his fingers became like ten lamps of fire. He said: Why not be totally changed into fire?

Unless we hold the light of love and passion, all our attempts at knowledge, or meditation, or sacred truth become a lantern that gives off no illumination, no warmth on that lonely mountaintop. We must *become* the images, we must turn ourselves into fire.

In the Golden Dawn version shown here, he stands in the circle of the ouroboros snake biting its own tail, a symbol of eternity. The Hebrew letter shines within the lantern and also from his head. Yod is the first letter of the Tetragrammaton, Yod-Heh-Vav-Heh, and assigned by the Golden Dawn to the element of fire. *Why not be totally changed into fire?*

As a figure of Hermes himself, the Hermit carries a complex light in his lantern. But what meanings does he bring us when he appears in a reading? First of all, aloneness, separation, withdrawal. If you're looking for love, you probably don't want to see this card (unless, perhaps, you've fallen love with your meditation teacher). But even if we might not want it, we might need it, for many of us need to learn we can live and enjoy life without a partner to "complete" it. For people in a relationship, especially a difficult one, the Hermit might reveal a desire to end it. It may hint that that tensions come from an unacknowledged desire to pursue your own interests alone.

The second most significant meaning is the Wise Old Man archetype—a teacher, a mentor, a therapist or spiritual leader. Depending on the position in the reading, the card may signify the need for such a figure, or that he or she already exists and will soon appear—and of course, the querent him/herself may be the wise figure. Sometimes other people will project the Hermit (or some other archetype) on someone they know. Any Tarot card can represent such a projection, but those that show relationship or authority—the Hermit, the Lovers, the Devil, the Empress, and the Emperor—seem more susceptible.

The Hermit can mean maturity and the wisdom that comes with age. If it appears in some way in opposition to the Fool, we might look at the other cards to see which approach works better—carefree youth or cautious maturity. Remember, though, that both cards show aspects of Hermes. The question is not which is right or wrong, but what helps us in the current situation.

And reversed? This is not a time to be alone. It might indicate more involvement with other people, or an end to loneliness, or success in seeking a relationship. It also might mean a *fear* of loneliness. The Celtic Cross spread contains a position for "hopes and fears." Some people fear being alone at the same time that they desire it.

The Hermit reversed can mean the lack of a teacher or guide and so the need to find your own way. It also may signify a "Peter Pan complex," someone who doesn't want to grow up. But maybe the person needs some Peter Pan fun. Consider once more the Rider Hermit and Fool. We see them both in high places, but where the Hermit stands stiffly, wrapped in gray with a white beard, the young Fool dances freely. Which attitude does the person really need right now?

> RIDER
Hermit
&
Fool

THE HERMIT.

THE FOOL.

A *Hermit Wisdom Reading*

1. What is the Hermit's secret?

2. What is the Hermit's light?

3. What does it reveal?

4. What questions does the Hermit want us to ask?
    - A.
    - B.
    - C.

A *Hermit Personal Reading*

1. What do I need to do on my own?

2. Where will I find my light?

3. What will it illuminate?

4. What does the Hermit want me to see?

5. What or who is my secret teacher?

6. What can I learn?

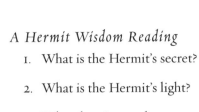

Wheel of Fortune: 10

Astrological correspondence: Jupiter

Kabbalistic letter: ⟁ Kaph

Path on Tree of Life: Chesed (Mercy) to Netzach (Victory)

Wheel of Fortune cards from VISCONTI, MARSEILLE, RIDER, GOLDEN DAWN RITUAL, EGYPTIAN & SHINING TRIBE

THE WHEEL OF FORTUNE 2

Wheel of Fortune

IN THE KING Arthur stories, so many of whose images have found their way into Tarot, there comes a moment before the final battle that will destroy the hope of a world where might doesn't make right, but serves it. The time is night, and the next day Arthur will face his incestuous bastard son Mordred. For now, he dreams and sees a great wheel, and on top of it a bearded king on his throne, strong and magnificent. Then the wheel turns, and because the king has attached himself to it, when he gets to the bottom, it crushes him. Arthur wakes up with a realization of doom.

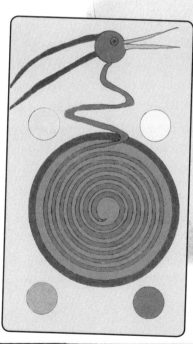

For medieval audiences, this scene taught a moral lesson, one we will see again in Death. No matter your wealth or power, old age, sickness, and death will destroy you the same as everyone else. So, do not attach yourself to the changing fortunes of this world, but cling instead to the eternal truths.

And yet—as we've seen so often, deeper meanings may lie behind this sermon of an image. Ever since Sir James Frazer's magnificent work *The Golden Bough*, people have argued over the concept of the sacrificed king, whether Pagan Europe did this or modern mythographers have made it up. The concept goes like this: the king represents the year, though usually longer cycles of, say, seven years. "Represents" here does not mean an intellectual metaphor. In old ways of thinking, the symbol is real, a genuine identity.

The king is the year, but the goddess is the land. In spring and summer (or the early part of the seven-year cycle), the king is young and healthy, the land fertile. But in autumn and winter (the end of the cycle), the king ages and the land grows barren. To restore a potent partner to the goddess, the people sacrifice the king and choose a successor. Think for a moment of American presidents, how they come into the office fresh and vigorous and leave worn and exhausted—no sacrifice is needed, just an amendment forbidding them to run again. Joseph Maxwell, in his book on the Marseille Tarot, links card ten astrologically to the Tropic of Capricorn, when the sun reaches the lowest point of the year—the winter solstice.

We can look at the Wheel of Fortune as being about time, different kinds of time. King Arthur's dream exists in *moral* time and *mortal* time, when the dream of a king's death teaches a lesson. Look beyond the Wheel's mortal time to eternal time, in which God resurrects the dead to live forever. The Tarot shows us the return from death in card twenty, Judgement, where the angel blows the horn and people rise from their graves. The Wheel is ten and Judgement is twenty, as if we go beyond the single reality of mortal time to a higher truth.

The Wheel can symbolize cyclic time. Everything goes around, and what is up turns down and what is down turns up, forever, or at least for the life of the Earth. Modern Pagans and other practitioners of Earth-based religion have adapted the Wheel as a symbol of the year and its seasonal celebrations. Neo-Pagans and Wiccans add four "cross-quarter" days to the equinoxes and solstices to get eight sabbats. The Rider version of the Wheel contains eight spokes, though probably not to represent seasonal sacred days.

At first glance, the Visconti Tarot seems to show something like Arthur's dream. We see an older man on the ground, but without a crown. On one side, a young man goes up; on the other, a perhaps older figure goes down. But what of the figure sitting on top, who seems to be wearing jackass ears? The ears suggest the King of Fools, and therefore carnival time—that is, time outside the normal social rules. Or maybe they just show us the general foolishness of humanity—moral time again. In the center we see a blindfolded angel. We might think of her as Justice, except that in Tarot, Justice usually does not cover her eyes.

The Marseille Wheel shows a crowned figure on top of the Wheel, but it is an animal with wings and a human face—a sphinx carrying a sword, maybe to cut down foolish mortals. On the right side, an animal goes up while another goes down on the left. Joseph Maxwell does not identify either creature but sees their color and posture as keys to their meaning. Red, on the left, symbolizes desire and instinct, which pull us down; while on the right, yellow, the color of intellect, pulls us upward. The animals' right hands symbolize purity of action.

I find this dualistic, perhaps missing the point that a wheel goes round and round. Anonymous, in *Meditations on the Tarot*, identifies the animals as a monkey on the left, a dog on the right. The monkey descends in order to rise again, the dog rises in order to descend. Here we see not just cyclic time in nature but *spiritual* cycles, the movement between matter and spirit.

Another kind of cyclic time is the Hindu and Buddhist idea of the wheel of reincarnation, in which we go through life after life, sometimes higher, sometimes lower. Though the sphinx is, of course, a Greek and Egyptian image (the Greeks probably got it from the Egyptians), we might identify the blindfolded sphinx on the Marseille deck as the laws of karma, acting impartially.

It strikes me as fascinating that the Marseille deck shows a monkey descending, centuries before Darwin's idea of the "descent of man" from the apes. Perhaps it is no surprise, for monkeys resemble humans, only more animal-like, less rational. Why a dog for the ascent? For the values of loyalty, faithfulness, and love?

Notice the crank on the Marseille Wheel. It suggests that the turn of events in our lives, or the seasons, do not just happen, but some unknown hand—God, universal law, karma—spins the Wheel.

The Egyptian Tarot, following Paul Christian's ideas, displays the sphinx as spiritual wisdom while making the creatures on the sides more mythological. The Golden Dawn shows more of a crouching beast, while the Rider restores the sphinx to its Marseille posture but removes the wings. And now the figures along the sides become more explicit. The snake on the left is a form of Typhon, the Greek name for Set, the Egyptian god of destruction and the murderor of Osiris. On the right, we see a jackal-headed man, the god Anubis, Osiris's son, who with Isis and under the direction of Thoth restores Osiris to life. Anubis leads the dead to the hall of Justice (see next card), a role similar to Hermes guiding dead souls, so that Hermeticists sometimes put the two together as Hermanubis. Thus, the Rider shifts us into spiritual time, where the body (inevitably) goes down, but the soul can rise.

This is the basic image, but the Rider expands the number of symbols on the cards to create a sense of mystery, or rather secrets—that is, information that most of us do not know but can learn. On the Wheel itself we see alternating Hebrew and Roman letters. The Hebrew spells the Tetragrammaton, Yod-Heh-Vav-Heh, the all-powerful name usually "translated" as "Lord." Kabbalists see the name as a formula of creation (see also the four suits of the Minor Arcana).

The four Roman letters illustrate how if we see life as a wheel, we get so many more possibilities than if we consider it a straight line. Starting at various points and going in either direction but staying in order, we can find various four-letter words in different languages. Here is a sentence from MacGregor Mathers, co-founder of the Golden Dawn: ROTA TARO ORAT TORA ATOR. The Wheel (Latin *rota*) of Tarot (*taro*) speaks (Latin *orat*) the law (Hebrew *Tora*, usually spelled torah) of Love (from *Ator*, or Hathor, an Egyptian goddess akin to Aphrodite).

Inside the rim and connected to the compass points marked by the Roman letters, we see the alchemical signs for salt, water, sulfur, and mercury. Together, they promise that we can transform the endless cycles and turns of the Wheel.

But what of the four creatures found in the clouds? Because of the influence of the Rider, people assume they belong to the standard imagery, but a quick look at the others will show that Waite and Smith added them—in fact, borrowed them—from the World card.

On the World, we see these realistically; on the Wheel, like cartoons. We are halfway through the Major Arcana, and we have come to a certain level of knowledge and experience,

but much remains hidden, symbolic. At the end we will see clearly. "The myth is the penulti-mate truth," wrote Ananda Coomaraswamy, whereas Paul, in I Corinthians, tells us, "Now we see as through a glass darkly. Then we shall see face to face."

The pictures themselves reveal layers of meaning only an image can convey. The books they hold reveal that they symbolize the "four evangelists": Matthew, Mark, Luke, and John (we should remember that Waite was a Christian, and the Tarot comes from a Christian culture—but we do not need to subscribe to Christian beliefs to comprehend its symbolism). But why would tradition link the four authors of the Gospels to winged creatures? Ezekiel's great vision of the Merkavah, or Chariot (see card seven, the Chariot) described these same four beasts as marking the four corners of the heavenly chariot.

Ezekiel experienced his vision in Babylon. While the Hebrews suffered in exile, they also learned a great deal, in particular astrology. Ultimately, the four creatures represent Aquarius (the human), Scorpio (the eagle), Leo (the lion), and Taurus (the bull). Four thousand years ago, these were the signs of the solstices and equinoxes. As the zodiac shifted, they became known as the four "fixed signs."

This subtle reference to the zodiac directs us to cosmic time, the movements of the stars and planets. But it also is Earth time, for the fixed signs represent the seasons, with Leo as summer, Scorpio as autumn, Aquarius as winter, and Taurus as spring.

And more—the shifting of the zodiac reminds us of what Plato called the Great Year. Due to a wobble in the Earth's axis, the zodiac appears to rotate, very slowly, around the Earth. A physicist friend once explained to me how this works, complete with diagrams. I still didn't get it, but I trust that it happens, and more—that the ancients knew about it and even worked out a number for this Great Year: 25,920 years. Various numbers that appear in myths and esoteric teachings are, in fact, references to this long cycle. The Babylonians used the number sixty as a base number for astrology; 25,920 divided by 60 is 432. Hindu cosmology describes four ages, or *yugas*, of existence, each one 432,000 years, and when all four have run out, the world will end, only to start up again after a great period of rest—a truly cosmic framework for the Wheel of Fortune (see also card twenty, Judgement).

The number 432 suggests an inverted pyramid. If we complete it by adding one (for the totality of existence), we get:

$$x \ x \ x \ x$$
$$x \ x \ x$$
$$x \ x$$
$$x$$

Turn the number around, and we get 1+2+3+4=10, the Wheel of Fortune. The wheel of our existence consists of the sum of the first four cards, the archetypal figures of the Magician, the High Priestess, the Empress, and the Emperor.

Watch what happens if we add two cards. Add five, the Hierophant, keeper of doctrines, orthodoxy, and strict moral codes, and we get fifteen, the Devil. If we then add love to all this doctrine—card six, the Lovers, follows the Hierophant—we get 1+2+3+4+5+6=21, the World card, the image of fulfillment and liberation, which we now have seen looks like the Wheel of Fortune but with the symbols made clear.

The third triad consists of the Empress, the Wheel of Fortune, and the Star. We have seen how the Empress shows us Demeter, goddess of growing things, and the mother in the myth of Persephone. We will find in the Star the daughter herself, Persephone, abducted by Death to become his bride, who now spends part of each year among the living and part among the dead. In between, we find the Wheel of the seasons, the fruitful times and the barren times that mark Persephone's movements between life and death. Seasonal time and mythic time join together.

The Wheel also stands in the middle of a numerological triad: 19 reduces to 10 (1+9=10), which further reduces to 1 (1+0=1). This gives us Magician, Wheel of Fortune, Sun.

The Shining Tribe version shows a different image, along with a different title, Spiral of Fortune. Inspired by a Native American rock art painting, it shows a spiral enclosed by a circle. The turns of the spiral represent the seeming cycles of our lives, especially the way we believe we go round and round in circles, repeating the same actions over and over. In reality, the picture tells us, we move in spirals, and each time we go down, we rise again just a little bit higher, until at last we break free of repetition into a new awareness of life's possibilities.

With such powerful symbolism, we might assume the card has always contained such messages. I have saved the historical meanings for the end this time, to demonstrate how meanings change and evolve through the many turns of the Wheel of Tarot tradition.

Some Wheel of Fortune Meanings

Excerpted from *Mystical Origins of the Tarot* by Paul Huson.

De Mellet (1781): The Wheel of Fortune. The injustice of the fickle goddess.

Court de Gébelin (1773-82): The Wheel of Fortune.

Lévi (1855): The Hebrew letter Yod, the Wheel of Fortune. Principle, manifestation, praise, manly honor, phallus, virile fecundity, paternal sceptre.

Christian (1870): Arcanum X. The Sphinx: Fortune. A wheel suspended by its axle between two columns. On the right Hermanubis [the Greco-Egyptian god composed of Hermes and dog-headed Anubis], the Spirit of Good, strives to climb to the top of the wheel. On the left Typhon [the Greco-Egyptian Set], the Spirit of Evil, is cast down. The Sphinx, balanced on the top of this wheel, holds a sword in its lion's paws, personifying Destiny ever ready to strike left or right. According to the direction in which it turns the wheel, the humblest rises and the highest is cast down.

Mathers (1888): The Wheel of Fortune. Good fortune, success, unexpected luck. REVERSED: Failure, unexpected good luck.

Golden Dawn (1888-96): The Lord of the Forces of Life. Wheel of Fortune. Good fortune and qualified happiness.

Grand Orient (Waite, 1889, 1909): Wheel of Fortune. Mutation, revolution, the external side of fortune.

Waite (1910): Wheel of Fortune. Fortune, success, elevation, luck, happiness. REVERSED: Increase, abundance, superfluity.

One of the first things we notice is the gender variance between de Mellet (fickle goddess) and Lévi (manly honor, phallus...paternal sceptre). Paul Christian first introduces some of the concepts and symbols that later became standard. After that, however, we discover a shift away from esoteric ideas to the more exoteric meaning of luck—fortune in the most literal sense of the word.

One final symbol, the central symbol, that is the literal center of a wheel—everything on a wheel turns constantly up or down, nothing ever stays the same, except the hub. Our true center remains constant. Juliet Sharman-Burke, designer of the Sharman-Caselli Tarot, calls the center of the Wheel "the core of our being." A wheel mounts on an axle, and in order to do that, the center must be empty. Lao-tzu writes in the Tao Te Ching, "Thirty spokes unite in the hub of a wheel. A wheel is useful because its center is empty." The events of our lives, the many turns of the Wheel, radiate from a center that is not any *thing* but has all that Fool possibility of Nothingness. The number 10 consists of 1, the Magician, and 0, the Fool.

What a rich card, what powerful images. And we can delve into these deeper truths when the card comes up in readings. And yet, the primary sense that often emerges is simple—the Wheel turns, life changes, and something new will emerge. Dame Fortune takes hold of that crank and gives it a turn. What will emerge we cannot really say, and often that is the point.

We can take heart that tradition seems to assume the Wheel turns for the better. Increased fortune, unexpected good luck.

If the Wheel appears with cards of addiction or recklessness—the Devil, the Seven of Swords, Temperance reversed, the Eight of Swords—it may indicate compulsive gambling. The Wheel of Fortune, after all, is a gambling device. If the Wheel appears with cards of self-examination, especially Justice and/or the Hermit (11 and 9 to the Wheel's 10), it may call on us to look within events, to seek that unmoving center where we can find the true self.

When the Wheel comes out reversed, some see it as a bad turn, on the logical assumption it just goes the other way. I suspect, however, that we might see this as one of the cards, like the Sun and the Four of Wands, where the meaning remains essentially the same right-side up or reversed—a change of circumstances that we cannot logically predict or control, but maybe of lesser consequence.

The reversed may show someone beginning to recover from a gambling addiction (look at the other cards before assuming this). It also may show someone who begins the difficult process of self-examination, of learning to stop blaming bad luck for whatever disaster his or her life has begun.

A Wheel of Fortune Reading

1. What turns the Wheel?

2. What outer change will come?

3. What inner change is possible?

4. What new situation will I face?

5. What rises?

6. What falls?

7. What is at the center?

Alternative

The Wheel of the Year with one card for each month. Set out in clock fashion, with January at the top and June at the bottom, February at 1 o'clock, March at 2 o'clock, etc. Begin with current month and set all cards facedown before turning any over. In other words, if the month is October, the first card goes at the 9 o'clock position and will be the first card turned over after all cards are placed facedown on the table. The second card goes at 10 o'clock, for November, and so on, until September is set down at the 8 o'clock position. Then the reading begins by turning over the October card and going round until September is revealed. This reading is good for birthdays, or anniversaries, or beginnings.

WHEEL of FORTUNE.

Justice: II

Astrological correspondence:
 Libra

Kabbalistic letter: ל Lamed

Path on Tree of Life: Gevurah
 (Power) to Tipheret
 (Beauty)

Justice cards from
VISCONTI,
MARSEILLE,
RIDER, GOLDEN
DAWN RITUAL,
EGYPTIAN &
SHINING TRIBE

11

JUSTICE

Justice

"Justice, justice, shall you pursue, that you may thrive
and occupy the land the Eternal (YHVH), your God,
is giving to you." (Deut. 16:20)

IN THE TRADITIONAL (Marseille) sequence of the
trumps, Justice appears as card eight and Strength
as eleven. Justice as eight suggests a commitment
to truth in preparation for the withdrawal of the
Hermit. In the Golden Dawn numbering, Justice
comes exactly in the middle of the Fool's Progress, with ten cards before it and ten after it. This
match is one of the many pairs symbolized in the
perfectly balanced scales shown in most versions
of the card. Here are some of the others:

LA GIUSTIZIA VIII JUSTICE
LA JUSTICE   LA JUSTICIA

GERECHTIGKEIT   GERECHTIGHEID

Past	Future
Others	Self
Above	Below
Within	Without
Unconscious	Conscious
Emotion	Reason
Altruism	Self-needs
Potential	Realization
Means	Ends

The standard imagery for Tarot Justice—a seated woman holding a sword and scales—resembles the figure in many courthouse statues. They derive from a Greek goddess named Themis, also known as Astraea. The resemblance of "Astraea" to "astral," as in the astral plane of spiritual principles, indicates that Justice is not just an earthly concern or a human invention with no meaning outside the arbitrary rules and decisions of the legal system.

Legal Justice, especially in America, often wears a blindfold to indicate impartiality. The scales, however, tilt since the courts must decide for one side or the other. In Tarot, Justice sees clearly, with all blindfolds of prejudice, conditioning, indoctrination, and fear removed. The scales are balanced for harmony and unification of the physical and the spiritual.

By "spiritual" here, I do not mean any particular religion, tradition, or doctrine, or even a belief in a supreme being. Instead, there is a kind of awareness of a sacred dimension of existence that the Tarot teaches can emerge in each one of us. Nevertheless (to give the Hierophant his due), particular traditions can help awaken that awareness. We will look at two particular traditions, one Hebrew, the other Egyptian. The Hebrew comes from my own experience.

Some years ago, I needed to go to the courts for a restraining order against someone. I will not say who it was or the circumstances, except that it was difficult and frightening to do, but very necessary—and also that New York State terms such a document "an order of protection."

The order required that the person not communicate with me in any way, including telephone calls or messages. The day after it was issued, my answering machine filled up so many times, almost nonstop, that I finally unplugged the phone. Now I needed to make a decision. The counselors who had helped me through this process had told me that the most important thing about an order of protection was follow-up—report all violations. Should I go to the police with the thirteen messages I'd preserved (there were many more I'd erased)?

I decided to ask the cards, using the Greenwood Tarot of Chesca Potter, a marvelous deck now sadly out of print. I can't say why I chose that one, it just caught my eye. When I picked up the deck and turned it over, Justice faced me from the bottom of the deck. I shuffled, cut the deck, put it back together, and the first card was Justice. Justice twice. The next card was the Four of Stones. The Greenwood is one of those that contains a theme word on each card. The theme for the Four of Stones is "protection."

The next morning was Saturday, and I decided to go to the Woodstock Jewish Congregation before making a final decision. The Bible passage from that morning included the passage quoted above, "Justice, justice shall you pursue." Justice twice. The commentary said that if we cannot resolve a conflict peacefully between people, we have no choice but to go to the courts. So I went to the police with the tape, and it actually resolved the issue peacefully. It's my experience that when we really need to know something, the Tarot speaks to us with absolute clarity. In this case, so did bibliomancy, looking in a book for the answers to questions.

The Torah (the five books of Moses, of which Deuteronomy is the last) almost never repeats words. Repetition signals great emphasis. Some see that as the message. The pursuit of justice is so vital we must pursue it with passion, with doubled effort. Tarotist Zoe Matoff reminds me of a saying attributed to St. Augustine: "When God wants us to hear something, He says it twice." She also comments that repetition calls something into being, like a spell.

I find that repetition says something else as well, meaningful to the Tarot card. There are two kinds of justice, and we must pursue both with equal energy, for one cannot exist without the other. In human justice, we treat people honestly and with respect, struggle to create a just world. People often weary of the pursuit of justice. Every victory or advance seems overwhelmed by a hundred setbacks, and how much can we do? And yet, we must continue, for ourselves as much as whatever effect we can have. Justice stands at the center of our lives as well as at the center of the Major Arcana. Justice is who we are, our basic nature.

Along with justice in the world, we must pursue spiritual justice. This includes self-awareness, a deep and honest look at who we are and what we have done or not done, whether we've stayed true to our nature or betrayed our innermost being. Spiritual justice calls on us to examine our relationship to the divine. The Hierophants of the world sometimes describe this relation as a set of rules. Follow the commandments, don't sin, make your offerings, burn the right incense, say the right words at the right time, and God or Goddess will reward you, usually when you die. These lists of rules speak to me of a deep pessimism about human behavior—that if doctrines and churches did not control people, we all would do despicable things. But justice comes from deep in ourselves as well as from any heavenly source. As above, so below. As within, so without. If it exists in the sacred world, it exists in the human. One of the things I admire about modern Paganism is its essential optimism. "Do as you will and harm none," it tells us, and that says, to me, that if we follow our genuine inmost nature, if we truly trust who we are, we will not seek to harm other people or nature.

Aleister Crowley went further (as he so often did) and described "Do as thou wilt" as the only command. This speaks of an even more powerful optimism, one perhaps shared with Nietzsche and Ralph Waldo Emerson in his much-misunderstood essay "Self-Reliance." If we follow our nature, look inside ourselves, we will discover our own divinity. This is a difficult path, and the Devil waits just a few cards away. But the Devil is not the final card.

Remember the words above the entrance to the Delphic Oracle—not "Know the future" but "Know yourself." This willingness to genuinely know ourselves opens the way to spiritual justice. Delphi was one of the inspirations for the Shining Tribe Justice. We enter an inner place where the truth speaks. The picture shows a primordial goddess with hard, piercing eyes. In the Rider deck, too, the eyes stare out at us intently, a challenge to look at who we are and what we have done, to balance the scales.

Coming in the middle of the Major Arcana, Justice forms the midpoint of our lives, no matter when we might experience it. In Justice, we balance the past and the future. Through self-examination, any amends we need to make with others, forgiveness of those who have hurt us, and forgiveness of our own mistakes, we free ourselves from the past and create a genuine future.

People sometimes ask, "If the cards can predict the future, does that mean free will does not exist?" First of all, the cards do not predict events, and they certainly do not cause them (as some people fear). Instead, they show us trends and likelihoods. But what makes something likely? The answer lies in our lack of self-knowledge. As long as we do not truly know ourselves, we will follow patterns, act from fear or shame or unacknowledged desires. We will respond to life in predictable ways. We all possess free will but we rarely use it, for genuine freedom requires self-knowledge. We must meet the staring eyes of Justice and balance the scales.

Justice, justice, shall you pursue, that you may thrive and occupy the land the Eternal, your God, is giving to you. We cannot live without justice. This sounds like an abstract ideal, but think of the stunted lives and early deaths of abused children, or the survivors of genocide. We really do need justice to live. And we need to pursue justice. The child's cry of "That's not fair!" reveals an inner sense of how the world should work. The parent's answer, "Life isn't fair," describes how things are, but justice is an ideal, something to pursue as passionately as wealth, love, and adventure.

What might we mean by "occupy the land"? This is not a place outside us, a piece of geography, but the land of our true being, a sacred land so complete that the final card of the Major Arcana simply calls it the World. To enter it, we must pursue justice—justice, for the longing for justice comes from our deepest selves. The sentence describes Y-H-V-H as "your God," not a remote, detached figure on a throne far away, but a part of us. And notice the verb tense is *giving*. Our pursuit of justice never ends, just as the sacred land of our true selves is a constant gift.

What, then, of the Egyptian story? The version of Justice in the Egyptian Tarot above shows a scene from the Book of the Dead (whose actual title, Pert Em Hru, means "coming forth into light"). When a person dies, the god Anubis (see the previous card, Wheel of Fortune) leads the soul to the goddess Ma'at, with our old friend Thoth standing alongside to write down what happens. The goddess, whose name means "truth," takes the person's heart and places it on one side of a scale; on the other side lies an ostrich feather. If the scales balance, the person moves on to the next life, in a higher spiritual realm. All souls bore the name Osiris, for they seek to mimic the god who died and came back to life. If, however, the heart weighs down the scales, a monster named Ammit devours the unlucky "Osiris."

On an exoteric level, the story serves, like so many others, to scare people into obedience to a moral and religious code, for as well as truth, Ma'at meant correct behavior, the sort of list of do's and don'ts considered necessary by those who do not trust the human spirit to "do as you will and harm none." But is that all that is going on?

If you've ever held an ostrich feather, you will know that it weighs next to nothing. A human heart weighs about half a kilo. Clearly, we have entered the realm of symbol. Expressions such as "heart to heart," "the heart of the matter," or "a good heart" (vaguely) recognize something the Egyptians, and later the Sufis, understood in detail: that the heart is more than a pump; it is the center of our being, the place of knowing and truth. The heart chakra stands at the mid-point of our bodies, with three chakras of physicality below and three of awareness above, just as Justice stands at the midpoint of the Major Arcana. The heart forms the border, the place where Above and Below join together. What weighs down the heart—when we seek to "come forth into light"—is guilt, and fear, and shame. What opens the heart, makes it weightless, is Justice. *Justice, justice shall you pursue, that you may thrive.*

Paul Christian and Maurice Otto Wegener (whose images followed Christian's ideas and are the source of the Egyptian Tarot used here) first aligned the card of Justice with Ma'at and the feather. Here is what Christian and the other early interpreters said about this card:

Some Justice Meanings

Excerpted from *Mystical Origins of the Tarot* by Paul Huson.

De Mellet (1781): Justice.

Court de Gébelin (1773-82): Justice.

Lévi (1855): The Hebrew letter Cheth, Justice. Balance, attraction and repulsion, life, terror, promise and threat.

Christian (1870): Arcanum VIII. Themis: Equlibrium. The ancient symbol of Justice weighs in the balance the deeds of men, and as a counterweight, opposing evil with the sword of expiation. The eyes of Justice are covered with a bandage to show that she weighs and strikes without taking into account the conventional differences established by men.

Mathers (1888): Themis, or Justice. Equilibrium, balance, justice. REVERSED: Bigotry, want of balance, abuse of justice, overseverity, bias.

Golden Dawn (1888-96): Daughter of the Lord of Truth, Holder of the Balances. Justice. Strength arrested in the act of judgment. Legal proceedings, a court of law, a trial by law.

Grand Orient (Waite, 1889, 1909): Justice. Equilibrium on the mental side rather than the sensuous; under certain circumstances, law and its decisions; also occult science.

Waite (1910): Justice. Equity, probity, vindication. REVERSED: Law in all departments, legal complications, bigotry, bias, excessive severity.

Christian actually combines Themis and Ma'at, and emphasizes an outer force that weighs our actions and at the same time opposes evil. In Wegener's original version, Justice wears a blindfold to illustrate Christian's idea that she "weighs and strikes" without concern for social convention. Does Justice exist outside humans? Is there an actual goddess? Maybe a principle exists beyond the rules of any particular social order.

Mathers stresses balance; reversed, the bigotry, bias, and overseverity that arise when we lose our inner balance. The Golden Dawn brings in, for the first time (!), legal justice and the law. Waite follows this idea, but only "under certain circumstances" or when the card appears reversed. And reversed also includes "bigotry, bias, overseverity."

As the center of the middle line, Justice forms a vital test. If we can meet her eyes with a heart that will not weigh down an ostrich feather, we can move forward with grace and ease. The Hanged Man will mean surrender and initiation. If we have closed our hearts so that we cannot look Justice in the eye, the Hanged Man will become a place of suffering.

As the central card of the fourth triad, with the Emperor above and the Moon below, Justice balances structure and mystery, law and wilderness. The number eleven (in the Golden Dawn/Rider sequence I have chosen to follow) also implies another triad, since it reduces to two, but so does twenty. Thus, we get High Priestess-Justice-Judgement. The High Priestess keeps silent, not trying to analyze or explain. By contrast, the angel in Judgement blows the horn so that we must rise up and respond. A student in a class (I regret I do not remember her name) once said that in Judgement we give our final answer to the question asked in Justice. She did not specify the question, so I will suggest one: *Who are you?*

In most versions of the card, the sword points straight up, a symbol of commitment to truth. In the Rider, only three cards contain upright swords; all the others tilt. They are Justice, the Ace of Swords, and the Queen of Swords.

When Justice appears in a reading, what "special circumstances" (to quote Waite) may lead us to see it as the law? Most simply, when we know that the reading concerns a legal question, in particular a trial or lawsuit. Justice right-side up indicates a fair and just result, which, of course, might not mean the person gets the result he or she is hoping for. If we do a reading in a court case, we should shuffle the cards so that some become reversed. If Justice upright points to a just result, reversed can mean an unjust one, with suggestions of bias somewhere in the system. If the other cards strongly suggest this at the beginning of a case, the person might reconsider. If the card does not appear in the spread, look through the deck until you find it. Does it stand right-side up or upside down? And what cards appear on either side of it? They can show issues in the situation.

More widely, the card means self-examination, a time to weigh things in the balance as you assess your life. You might face a moral choice of some kind and need to examine your motives. Be careful of blaming others, or—the other extreme—of believing that everything is your fault. Balance the scales.

Another kind of balance—awareness and action. The sword reminds us of the requirement to pursue Justice, possibly with a specific action. Does some situation require a response? The other cards can suggest whether we might need to act, and if so, where—in the community, in a relationship, in work, or elsewhere.

Reversed indicates the possibility of unjust or unfair conditions. If cards such as the Tower, some of the Swords, or reversed court cards appear, it may warn us to be careful. But reversed Justice also may indicate an unwillingness to look at yourself or your own part in some difficult situation. What do you need to do to bring Justice right-side up again? Do you need to protect yourself or take action?

A Justice Reading
(in the shape of scales)

1. What is outer Justice?

2. What is the wisdom of pursuing it?

3. What action is best?

4. What is inner Justice?

5. What part do I play?

6. How will Justice come about?

7. What is the link between inner and outer Justice?

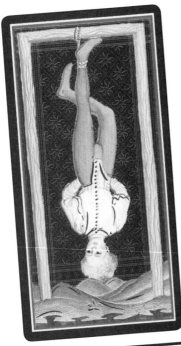

Hanged Man: 12

Astrological correspondence:
  Neptune

Kabbalistic letter: מ Mem

Path on Tree of Life: Gevurah
  (Power) to Hod
  (Glory)

*Hanged Man cards
  from* Visconti,
Marseille,
Rider, Golden
Dawn Ritual,
Egyptian &
Shining Tribe

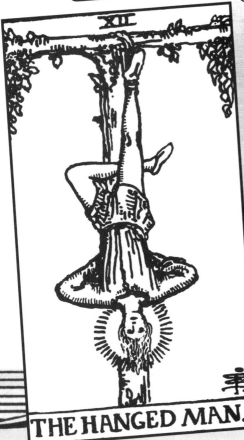

The Hanged Man

THE FIRST THING we might notice about this card is the title.

Well, no. The *first* thing people see is that he's upside down. Give a Tarot deck to people new to the cards, and let them leaf through it. When they get to card twelve, they usually will turn it around. This, then, becomes a fundamental meaning of the Hanged Man—to seem, at least, upside down, the wrong way around. To give others the irresistible urge to turn us around so that we look and think and act like everyone else.

THE HANGED MAN.

XII

THE HANGED MAN · XII · EL COLGADO
DER GEHÄNGTE · DE GEHANGENE

LE PENDU

L'APPESO

> RIDER &
  MARSEILLE
  *Hanged Man
  reversed*

⌄ RIDER &
  MARSEILLE
  World reversed

THE WORLD.

XXI

THE WORLD · XXI · EL MUNDO
DIE WELT · DE WERELD

LE MONDE

IL MONDO

We can understand this in terms of social conformity. The person who refuses to devote himself to a career and instead works at a minimum-pay job might be a Hanged Man. But there are deeper meanings. The Hanged Man's entire viewpoint, his perception of reality, may vary 180 degrees from those around him. If others see reality only as what we can touch or see, or perhaps as a struggle between body and soul, and you perceive a constant flow, even a love, between matter and spirit, you may seem wrong to everyone else. The more you can hold on to your truth and not worry about other people's beliefs about them, the more you will discover the Hanged Man's serene attachment.

But what about the title? The usual past tense of hang is hung. Hanged is used only for executions. Coming just before Death, the Hanged Man might suggest punishment. In Italy, traitors were sometimes executed upside down, hanging by the feet. When the Italian people turned against Mussolini for pulling them into a disastrous war, a mob seized him and his wife and hanged them upside down. And in fact, many Italian decks call card twelve the Traitor. Some early decks show a man hanging upside down from a gallows tree, body all askew, face distorted, with coins or small bags of money falling from his pockets. This suggests Judas Iscariot, who supposedly betrayed Christ for thirty pieces of silver.

Over the years, I've noticed that many modern Tarot readers assume a negative meaning for the Hanged Man—not treason so much as being stuck, hung up, a painful sacrifice. To be honest, this surprises me, for I've always seen this card as a kind of liberation of the spirit.

Look at the oldest known version, the Visconti. Notice the relaxed posture and serene expression. We find the same quality in the Marseille and especially the Rider, where the face is surrounded by a halo of light that appears on no other card, including the three angels of the Lovers, Temperance, and Judgement.

If we reverse the Hanged Man's number, 12, we get 21. Look what happens when we turn the Hanged Man around (not to "correct" him but to more clearly see his posture) and place him alongside the World.

Clearly something is going on here besides treason, execution, suffering, or sacrifice. The Hanged Man so closely resembles the World because it shows us at a stage where we can glimpse the great truths. We begin to understand, not just conceptually, but with genuine knowing, what the Greeks called *gnosis* and the Kabbalists *Da'ath*. Where the World dances freely, outside ordinary reality, arms out, the Hanged Man maintains the state of knowing by staying upside down—opposite to everyone else and not trying to do anything. Thus the arms remain tied behind the back in most versions.

The occult tradition sees the Hanged Man's arms as a triangle, for the idea of trinity (threeness, not a particular religious threesome), and the crossed leg as the number four, for quaternity. Three and four, spirit and matter. If we just add the two numbers—that is, simply add spiritual concepts to material practices—we get seven, the Chariot, in control of self and the outer circumstances of life. But if we multiply three times four, we get twelve, the Hanged Man.

> RIDER
*Hanged Man
reversed
&
a Tree of Life*

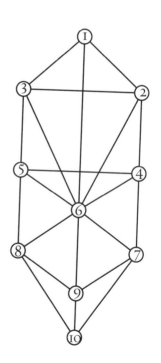

With the High Priestess, we saw how the Tree of Life hid behind her body, one of the "secrets" in the card. The Hanged Man becomes the tree. Look at the pattern again, slightly adjusted, alongside the Hanged Man's body (again, turned around for easier reference).

The top of the head is sephirah 1, the Crown (literally); the shoulders are 2 and 3, the elbows are 4 and 5, the center of the body is 6, the knee and foot of the crossed leg are 7 and 8, the knee of the vertical leg is 9, and the foot is 10. But remember that the figure on the card is upside down, so that the body of the Hanged Man is a reversed tree.

Many Kabbalists describe the sephiroth as just that, a tree that grows upside down, with its roots in Heaven and its branches reaching to earth. Thus, the seemingly backward Hanged Man depicts the true state of reality, and what we consider normal—in which matter is real and spirit just an idea—represents the actual reverse of the truth.

Do you remember learning about the eye in high-school biology? The retina receives images upside down, and then the brain switches our perceptions so that we can move about. We quite literally see the entire world the wrong way around.

Many readers will know of the chakra system, seven energy centers in the human body. They bear different colors, for the life energy known as kundalini transforms as it moves up the spine. The order of the colors, from the base of the spine to the top of the head—called the crown, same as the Tree of Life—runs as follows: red, orange, yellow, green, blue, indigo, violet. Do these sound familiar? They are the colors of the rainbow, in exactly the same order, except in the rainbow, red appears at the top and violet at the bottom. The body matches the rainbow, but only when the body is upside down.

Two views of the Hanged Man—suffering or enlightenment. What do the early commentators say?

Some Hanged Man Meanings

Excerpted from *Mystical Origins of the Tarot* by Paul Huson.

Pratesi's Cartomancer (1750): The Traitor, betrayal.

De Mellet (1781): The Hanged Man. Prudence.

Court de Gébelin (1773-82): Prudence.

Lévi (1855): The Hebrew letter Lamed, a man hanging by one foot. Example, instruction, public teaching.

Christian (1870): Arcanum XII. The Sacrifice: Violent Death. Arcanum XII expresses in the divine world the revelation of the law; in the intellectual world the teaching of duty; in the physical world sacrifice.

Mathers (1888): The Hanged Man. Self-sacrifice, sacrifice, devotion, that which is bound. REVERSED: Selfishness, that which is unbound.

Golden Dawn (1888-96): The Spirit of the Mighty Waters. Hanged Man or Drowned Man. Enforced sacrifice, punishment, loss, suffering.

Grand Orient (Waite, 1889, 1909): Hanged Man. Renunciation, for whatever cause and whatever motive.

Waite (1910): The Hanged Man. Wisdom, circumspection, discernment, trials, sacrifice, intuition, divination, prophecy. REVERSED: Selfishness, the crowd, the body politic.

The hand-marked manuscript discovered by Pratesi says "Traitor," and then the idea seems to disappear until very recently. Then we find "Prudence," the same cardinal virtue that Christian and Mathers assigned to the Hermit. Christian also introduces that idea of sacrifice, even violence, but only in the physical world. Waite includes sacrifice, but also such qualities as wisdom, intuition, even divination and prophecy.

The Golden Dawn introduces an alternative title, the Drowned Man, to match the description "The Spirit of the Mighty Waters." The Hebrew letter Mem they give to the Hanged Man is one of three "mother letters" that compare to the elements Fire, Water, and Air. The Fool is Aleph, for Air; Judgement is Shin, for Fire; and Mem, which literally means "water," is Water. In Water, all things that seemed fixed and rigid dissolve, including the ego and its assumptions about reality. To "drown" can mean to surrender, to release the self. In *The Waste Land*, the modern epic poem based on the Grail legend, T. S. Eliot has his Tarot reader, Madame Sosostris, say, "Here is your card, the drowned Phoenician Sailor...I do not find the Hanged Man. Fear death by water."

The Hanged Man is an archetype of initiation. Consider some examples. Christian tradition describes Peter as crucified upside down. The reason—that he would not want to compete with Christ—seems so absurd we can suspect a hidden meaning. Yogis literally stand on their heads as a way to move kundalini. R. J. Stewart, in the book for his Merlin Tarot, tells a wonderful story about Merlin predicting three separate deaths for the same person—death by falling from a high place, by hanging, and by drowning. In the story's climax, the young man falls off a cliff, gets his foot caught in branches, and ends up with his head in a river. He dies three times, and his body forms the Hanged Man (and the Drowned Man as well). Stewart describes this as an initiation, dying to be reborn.

In Norse myth, Odin, or Wodan—whom the Romans identified with Hermes-Mercury—hangs himself on the World Tree, called Yggdrasil, to make himself worthy to receive the magical alphabet of the runes. He pierces his side and sacrifices his right eye (right is the side of ego) to Mimir, guardian of the dark well where the runes hide. Finally, after nine days and nights (the number of the Hermit, and Odin wanders the world disguised as an old man leaning on a staff), he reaches down and seizes the letters.

Now back still further. A tale in the Talmud, some two thousand years old, tells of two angels, Shemhazai and Azazel, who scorn humanity for its constant failure to resist temptation. Easy for you to say, God tells them. If you walked on the earth, you would do the same. The angels laugh at such absurdity.

So God clothes the angels in human bodies and places them on Earth. And there they encounter human women, and immediately their good intentions vanish like smoke in a sharp wind. Azazel grabs hold of the woman he desires, and when she resists, he rapes her.

Shemhazai, however, retains some decency, or at least pride. He walks up to the woman he wants and tells her, "Sleep with me. I'm an angel."

The woman, whose name is Istahar, says "Oh, please. I've heard that one before."

"No, really," he says, "I'm an angel."

"If you were an angel, you'd know the secret name of God."

"Well, of course I know that."

"Then tell it to me."

Shemhazai laughs. "I can't tell you," he says. "You're just a woman."

"And you're just like all the other men," Istahar says. "Talk big and got nothing to show."

Furious now, Shemhazai blurts out the name, and as soon as she hears it, Istahar repeats it, using its power to escape into the sky. Then God transforms her into a star, for that is what "Istahar" means.

Now, too late, Shemhazai cries out and begs forgiveness. Because of this, God suspends him upside down between Heaven and Earth, an eternal bridge between matter and spirit. And Azazel? God suspends him over the Abyss, the terrible darkness that the Greeks call Tantalos and the Christians Hell ("Darkness visible," John Milton called Hell).

We are all suspended, not one fixed state or another, a constant flux at every moment. We just don't know it. Maybe if we could hang by one foot from a vibrant tree, we might remember. Poet Kathryn Good-Schiff says that we believe we stand upright on the earth, but since gravity holds us by our feet and we stick out from Earth's body, we all hang upside down—and just don't know it.

I wrote the above passages about the archetypal roots of the Hanged Man while on the train to New York City, going to an exhibit at the Metropolitan Museum on African "Reliquaries," sacred objects buried with the dead. The exhibit included a short film on initation among the Mitsogho people. The ceremony involves a bowed wooden harp, called a *ngombi*, played while the leader tells the ancient mysteries. The film describes the ngombi's creation. A Pygmy climbed a high tree, and then he fell. Before he could hit the ground, his foot became tangled in branches. A Hanged Man. But his insides spilled out, and his intestines scattered over the land. They became the strings of the ngombi, which is death, and its song is death, for all things must die, and as long as we pretend otherwise, we do ourselves great harm. After the Hanged Man comes Death, but after that? Temperance, perhaps Shemhazai set free, each of us set free.

And after Temperance? The Devil, for maybe the time will come to release Azazel from his bondage. But we can look at that later. Right now, let us enjoy the serenity of the Hanged Man, for after all, when you're tied upside down to a tree, what else is there to do but enjoy it?

How we see the Hanged Man might depend on the card before it. If we can pass the "test" of Justice—if we can look at ourselves and our lives with open eyes, and open the heart so that it will not weigh more than an ostrich feather—then the Hanged Man becomes a card of joyous surrender, of becoming the tree, the rainbow. But if we get stuck at Justice, the Hanged Man may represent being stuck in our lives, fearing what will happen, facing some painful sacrifice.

In the fifth triad, the Hanged Man comes between the Hierophant and the Sun. He reverses the way of knowing, from the Hierophant's outer teachings to the Sun's direct revelation. Or we can say that he plants his feet in doctrine and tradition and then grows into the light of truth.

The number 12, like 21, combines 1 and 2, the Magician and the High Priestess. And both reduce to 3, the Empress, mother of never-ending life. The ultimate Hanged Man image comes in the first initiation: birth. Babies emerge from the enclosed universe of their mother's bodies into a world wide open and wondrous. And they emerge headfirst—"crowning," it's called. In older cultures, before women lay on beds attended by doctors, women squatted, and the babies came into the world upside down, headfirst and tied to their origins by a cord from the center of their bodies.

Do you want to experience the Hanged Man? You don't need to sacrifice yourself or do elaborate rituals, or even stand on your head (though it may help). Open your eyes and look. Look as a baby looks. Here is the Jesuit scientist and mystic Teilhard de Chardin: "Throughout my whole life, during every moment of it, the world has become gradually lighting up, and blazing before my eyes until it has come to surround me entirely, lit up from within." This is the light of the Hanged Man's halo, the light that fills the world.

As the above implies, interpretations of the Hanged Man vary a great deal. For some, it can mean being stuck, facing a painful sacrifice. For me, it speaks of attachment to values. I see it as joyous though self-contained, perhaps misunderstood by other people. In the Shining Tribe Tarot, I made the "Hanged Woman" playful, childlike, to make clear I intended it as wondrous and not painful. The querent who receives the Hanged Man may be an outsider, or with different attitudes than other people, with no push to convince others, and no need to seek others' approval. Being tied to the tree means being connected to something beyond yourself, and thus able to withstand the winds of society or other people's opinions. For people on a spiritual path, it may signal a moment of illumination or an actual initiation experience.

Reversed depends on the different approaches. If the card primarily means being hung up, reversed can signify movement—getting unstuck, or the end of a difficult sacrifice. For me, it tends to mean conformity, allowing other people's opinions, or society's attitudes, to take over from your own. Waite says "the crowd, the body politic." You've made yourself the supposed right way around—the same as everyone else. But at what cost?

Hanged Man Reading
(shape of spread based on the Rider Hanged Man)

1. Past

2. Future

3. Attachment now

4. Core truth

5. What is surrendered

6. Comfort, calm

7. What is given

8. What is received

9. What is revealed, understood, learned

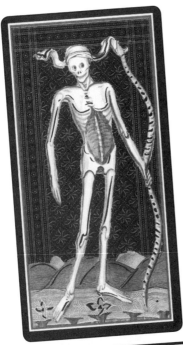

Death: 13

Astrological correspondence:
  Scorpio

Kabbalistic letter: נ Nun

Path on Tree of Life: Tipheret
  (Beauty) to Netzach
  (Victory)

Death cards from
VISCONTI,
MARSEILLE,
RIDER, GOLDEN
DAWN RITUAL,
EGYPTIAN &
SHINING TRIBE

Death

Thou knowest 'tis common, all that live must die,
Passing through nature to eternity.
Hamlet

THE DEATH CARD has become something of a cliché in Tarot, or rather two clichés, the first in popular culture, the second among Tarot readers. In movies, the Tarot tends to appear in thrillers that want a touch of the supernatural. A reader will set out the cards for a frightened client, and sure enough, there comes Death, with swelling music and (the producers hope) a gasp from the audience. A few years ago, a serial killer—the "DC sniper"—left a Marseille Death card near one or two of his murders. Maybe he hoped Hollywood would make a movie about him.

For Tarot readers, the cliché goes in the opposite direction. As soon as the card appears on the table, we say something like, "This card does not mean anybody's about to die. It means the end of something, with the chance for something new to emerge." It's probably good to say this. Most times, the Death card does not mean an unexpected death, and even if we accept that it might, do we really want to predict that? What effect might it have? And suppose you were wrong? What suffering might you cause for the sake of a dramatic moment in a reading? Sometimes, as Tarot readers, we can fall into the trap of wanting our predictions to come out, no matter the disaster in people's lives. It excites us to think, "He said he was healthy, but I saw death in his cards, and two weeks later, *bam*, he keeled over with a heart attack." We would prefer the story run, "I told him to get to the doctor, and the doctor detected an aneurysm. They got it just in time." A happy ending is best, but either way we can hold our heads high as psychics. And yet, most modern readers consider it better not to go there at all. And so we tell our querents, and ourselves, that Death does not mean death.

Let's see what the tradition says.

Some Death Meanings

Excerpted from *Mystical Origins of the Tarot* by Paul Huson.

Pratesi's Cartomancer (1750): Death.

De Mellet (1781): Death.

Court de Gébelin (1773-82): Death.

(Do we begin to see a pattern here?)

Lévi (1855): The Hebrew letter Mem. Death. The Heaven of Jupiter and Mars, domination and force, new birth, creation and destruction.

Christian (1870): Arcanum XIII. The Scythe: Transformation. In the divine world, the perpetual moment of creation, destruction and renewal; in the intellectual world the ascent of the Spirit into the divine spheres; in the physical world death, that is, the transformation of human nature on reaching the end of its organic period.

Mathers (1888): Death, change, transformation, alteration for the worse. REVERSED: Death just escaped, partial change, alteration for the better.

Golden Dawn (1888-96): The Child of the Great Transformers, Lord of the Gates of Death. Death, time, transformation, change, sometimes destruction, but only if borne out by the cards with it.

Grand Orient (Waite, 1889, 1909): Death, transforming force, destruction.

Waite (1910): Death. End, mortality, destruction, corruption. Also, for a man, the loss of a benefactor; for a woman, many obstacles; for an unmarried woman, failure of marriage prospects. Reversed: Inertia, sleep, lethargy, petrification, hope destroyed.

Lévi introduces the idea of "new birth," but it's not really until Paul Christian and MacGregor Mathers that we see the concept of "transformation." And even then, it still means actual death. And notice how Waite, usually the one who brings in subtle and spiritual meanings, sounds the direct note: "Death. End, mortality, destruction, corruption."

So, should Tarot readers return to the Death card as prediction of someone dying? I still think of this as a bad practice to follow generally, but I also think we need to respect the long-held opinion of tradition. If the card and your own psychic sense tell you that this is what it means, see if the cards around it give you further clues, and then see how you can speak about it in a way that supports what the person will go through. If you are uncertain, or if you think it's death but have no idea who or when, it's better not to bring it up. In that case, it's better to stay with the theme of endings and change, and perhaps talk about death as part of that theme.

Sometimes the card points to death as an issue in people's lives. If the querent's relative or friend has recently died or is terminally ill, or if the querent works in a hospice or (as happened in a reading once) is working on treatments for a deadly disease, then the Death card will mean the significance of death, and the other cards can help guide the person toward a better understanding of it.

Moving away from the literal—it may mean the death of a marriage, or a job, or a long-held belief. It is not always sad, for it can lead to liberation or new beginnings—but don't assume it's easy. In an earlier book, using the therapy model for the middle line of the Major Arcana, I gave the example of someone who enters therapy to change a lifelong habit. Often, people will understand the issues fairly early, after six months or so, and yet they continue in their old patterns for much longer. They fear death. I originally thought of this because of a friend who was trying to lose weight. "I've been a fat person all my life," she said. "If I lose weight, I won't exist." This is death not of the body but of the ego, the definition of who and what we are. And even when we desire it, it's not easy. For of course she was right. The person she was—whom she knew how to be—would no longer exist.

We all fear death, we all resist it from deep in our psyches. Our very cells want to live. Never underestimate how instinctively we fight death. We can understand this in evolutionary terms. Early humans who did not fear death probably got killed before they had a chance to reproduce and pass on those fearless genes. Those with a deep fear of death avoided it long enough to have children. And yet, if we want to grow, especially spiritually, there comes a time when we must get past that ingrained fear. For one thing, we will all die sooner or later. Thalassa, organizer of the Bay Area Tarot Symposium, laughs when she reads of the "death rate" going up or down. "The death rate's the same as it's always been," she says, "one per person."

There is another reason to get past the fear of dying. Fear narrows our ability to open to existence itself, to open the heart and see the wonders of existence.

The fear of death surrounds the Death card with superstition (including those movies with dire fortune tellers). The card almost always bears the number thirteen, but in most older decks it has no title, as if to name it might invite it.

Why is thirteen, especially Friday the thirteenth, so unlucky? I used to think it a Christian tradition—Christ was crucified on a Friday, with Judas the thirteenth person at the Last Supper. Apparently, Rome in general executed people on Fridays. Consider also that there are twelve signs in the zodiac (and twelve gods on Mt. Olympus), and so thirteen goes beyond the ordered, known universe. And what might lie beyond the twelve signs? Death.

While the fear may go back thousands of years, some give it a more recent origin: Friday, October 13, 1307. On that day, the church and the King of France destroyed the Knights Templars and arrested their leader, Jacques de Molay.

But thirteen goes to something deeper. A lunar cycle lasts approximately 28–29 days, which is also the length of time of most women's menstrual cycle. This creates thirteen months in a year. Thirteen therefore signifies mysteries of the moon, lunacy, the feminine. The Inquisition identified the moon with witchcraft and identified thirteen with supposed orgies of witches and demons. Some modern witches take a much more positive view of the link of thirteen and witches, requiring thirteen members for a traditional coven.

The moon's thirteen cycles remind us of death and rebirth. Unlike the steady, dependable sun, the moon dies, goes through three days of darkness, and is born again, only to become old and weak once more and fade until finally, once again, it dies.

Death comes in the middle of what is possibly the most powerful triad, Lovers-Death-Judgement. Love, death, and resurrection, the great story. We give ourselves to love in this world, and if we are lucky it is received, but what really matters is that we give love with passion and commitment. And then death comes and ends everything. But if we can hear the trumpet blast of the angel within us, we can understand that love extends beyond all our limited perceptions. In my structure of the Major Arcana, the sixth position shows us a powerful experience we get when we make our way through the challenges of the middle group of three cards. The Wheel of Fortune showed us a vision of fate, or karma, or any of the other names for the essential mystery of events and the turns of our lives. In Justice, we open ourselves to truly look at who we are to balance the scales. And in the Hanged Man, we attach ourselves to the ever-flowing Tree of Life. What comes next is Death.

Death is always what comes next. Somehow we need to accept this, not just intellectually but within our being. We die so that other creatures may come to life. Literally. Dead creatures feed the living, and the remains fertilize the earth. And further...if we could perpetually clone ourselves—make identical copies, like amoebae, who reproduce by splitting into two genetic replicas of the original—we would never end. But nothing new would ever emerge either.

Death came into the world with sex. When organisms became male and female and reproduced sexually, they could mix their genes to create offspring that were like their parents but not the same as them. And so the parents died, unlike the amoebae who live forever as long as they can keep splitting into two copies. Sex and death are really one thing. And resurrection—of one kind or another—comes into the world with death. For how can you be reborn if you don't die?

Representations of Demeter and Persephone show them almost exactly alike, the daughter a copy of the mother. When Death—Hades—comes in his chariot, driven by sexual desire, everything changes. Among other things, we get the death and rebirth of nature in the turning of the seasons, and plant life, which dies and comes back to life.

Who knows what really happens after death? Hierophants of all sorts assure us they know, but the details always vary. Why believe any of them? Have they died and sent back messages? The great magician Harry Houdini told his friends he would do everything he could to contact them on Halloween, some Halloween, after his death. By all accounts, it hasn't happened yet. Maybe next October 31. Maybe with you.

Some traditions urge us not to concern ourselves with death. The Torah, the five books of Moses, remarkably contains no concept of an afterlife. The idea of a "world to come" does not emerge until the prophets. Zen Buddhism suggests we pay attention to "right now" and not worry about "later on." And yet we cannot escape death, just as we cannot escape the fear of it, and so the Mystery rituals and tribal initiations confront their candidates with death so that they may "die before they die" and discover their eternal selves. Temperance, the card after Death, gives us a vision of that eternal self in the image of a calm angel.

The Marseille Death shows a skeleton with a scythe, reaping a harvest of heads and hands and feet—the head for the ego, the limbs for our activity in the physical world. In most versions, the heads wear crowns, for like the medieval Wheel of Fortune crushing a proud king, the image conveys the idea that even kings must die. The Visconti Death carries a bow instead of a scythe, as if he strikes from afar, a possible reference to the Plague that had wiped out one-third of the European population in the century before.

Dr. Waite radically changed the image, so that we see Death like a knight in black armor carrying a white rose banner, symbol of the Rosicrucian Mystery tradition. Four people confront the figure. A king, symbol of the proud and resistant ego, lies dead. A bishop stands in prayer, held up by doctrine and faith. A maiden turns away her face, for in adolescence we become self-aware, and the ego begins to fear its destruction. A child, symbol of openness, greets Death with flowers instead of fear. Paul Foster Case criticized Waite for this card, for a particular reason. The bishop's mitre, shaped like the mouth of a fish, links the card to the Age of Pisces, the astrological symbol of the fish. In our time, however, we have begun to shift into a "new age," or Aeon, the Age of Aquarius (for more on this idea, see the Wheel of Fortune and Judgement). The mysteries of Death, Case argues, carry through all ages.

Death is the final card to have a numerological triad (along with the Wheel, Justice, and the Hanged Man). If we consider the Fool as card 22, then 2+2=4, and 1+3 also equals 4. Thus we get the Emperor and the Fool, power and innocence, with Death between them.

We have already considered the difficult moments when Death turns up in a reading. Does it predict actual death? Probably not, though we need to consider death as an issue, especially if someone has died or is dying, or if the person works with death in some way. Some of the

Swords cards might emphasize death, especially (in the Rider deck) the Three, the Four, the Six, the Nine, or the Ten. Traditionally the Ten of Pentacles can mean an inheritance, so the combination of that card and Death might indicate the death of a relative.

Very often Death means the end of something—a marriage that has run its course, a job the person needs to quit, a long project that comes to an end. What matters is what we do with this situation. Do we resist, deny, accept? If the Tower appears as well, the change might happen very abruptly, with possibilities of violence.

Sometimes in a reading we want to make a person feel better. We say that the Death card means rebirth, or change, or a new beginning. Actually, it means death. Something ends, and one way or another, it will feel like dying. Good things may come, but first we need to accept the end of what had existed. Even if something unpleasant dies, such as a painful relationship, we still may grieve for the loss of what we have known, how we have defined ourselves.

Death reversed can mean the holding back of death. If someone has been sick a long time, with fear of not surviving, the upside-down Death may say that the person will not die soon or in the immediate future. It does not, however, promise recovery, just that life continues. The reversed Death card may indicate resistance to change, inertia. Things do not die, they simply go on. This, too, can bring a reassurance if not a resolution.

A Death Wisdom Reading

1. What is Death?

2. Where does it come from?

3. What causes it?

4. Why do we have to die?

5. What comes from Death?

6. What will come after?

7. What does it mean in a reading?

1. What is my attitude to Death?

2. How am I okay with it?

3. How do I have trouble with it?

4. What needs to die in my life?

5. How do I let it die?

6. What needs to live?

7. How do I help it live?

Temperance: 14

Astrological correspondence:
  Sagittarius

Kabbalistic letter: ‏ס‎ Samekh

Path on Tree of Life: Tipheret
  (Beauty) to Yesod
  (Foundation)

*Temperance cards
  from* VISCONTI,
  MARSEILLE,
  RIDER, GOLDEN
  DAWN RITUAL,
  EGYPTIAN &
  SHINING TRIBE

TEMPERANCE

TEMPERANCE

Temperance

A CONFESSION: TEMPERANCE has never been one of my favorite cards. I do not dislike it, I just do not find it exciting. Temperance is one of the cardinal virtues, along with Fortitude (Strength card) and Prudence (Hermit or Hanged Man). As a virtue, Temperance speaks of calm and balance, combining different energies, walking a middle way. All very worthwhile, but not thrilling. The number, fourteen, reduces to five (1+4=5), the Hierophant, while the four in fourteen reminds us of the Emperor. Three of my least-favorite cards in one package.

Temperance became more significant for me when I observed three of its dynamic features.

169

First, in most versions the angel stands with one foot on land, the other in water, suggestive of a mingling of the inner life and action (something that often concerns writers). Temperance allows us to do things without losing our personal sense of balance. Action without ego.

The second feature goes back to the Tarot of Marseille as well as the Rider, and is implied in the Visconti. This is the angle at which the angel (or the woman in the Visconti) pours the water. Quite simply, you can't do that. Water won't pour at any angle but straight down. Thus, the card shows us a figure who calmly and gracefully does the impossible. Both this quality and that action without ego remind me of a famous expression from the Tao Te Ching—"Do nothing, and nothing will be left undone." And this might be a motto of the Fool, so that these two cards that seem so opposite—the Fool says that "He who hesitates is lost," Temperance tells us to "Look before you leap"—actually come together. Rather than stopping us, Temperance shows us how to act magically while seeming to do nothing. Aleister Crowley retitled this card Art, by which he meant the art of alchemy, transformation through the combining of energies at the highest level.

The third quality comes from the Rider, though I borrowed it for my own version in the Shining Tribe Tarot. The wings are too big, too powerful, for the picture to contain them. This gives the picture a vibrancy that belies its calm.

Culturally, we've come to think of angels as gentle, soothing, and loving, but only in "pure," nonemotional, nonsexual ways. This is not how people saw angels in earlier centuries. The word means "messenger," and angels acted as God's agents. They were often fierce, such as the seraph who guards the entrance to Eden with a flaming sword. And they can be passionate, even destructive, as shown in the story of Shemhazai and Azazel, recounted in the Hanged Man and the following card, the Devil.

People differ on the identities of the three angels in the Rider Tarot. I follow the tradition that sees the angel of the Lovers as Raphael, Judgement as Gabriel, and Temperance as Michael. Micha-El means "who is like unto God." Many people add a question mark in their minds, with the assumed answer of "No one." But if we take it as a statement, then it describes Michael as just that, like unto—with the qualities of—God. When we pass through the trials of the second level of the Major Arcana, we discover our own divine nature.

Look closely at the Rider angel, just below the collar. You will see the four Hebrew letters of the Tetragrammaton worked into the stitching (see the Wheel of Fortune and the Minor

Arcana for more on these letters). Below that we find a golden triangle in a white square—the fire of spirit within purified earthly matter.

Card seven represented a victory over the outer challenges of life. Card fourteen shows us a victory over the ego and its fearful grasp on external structures, the things we cling to in fear of Death, the things that keep us from discovering that if we give up fear, we, too, can become "like unto God."

In Christian mythology, Michael heads up God's armies against the arrogant rebellion of Lucifer, the "light-bringer" who becomes Satan, the "adversary." It is Michael who grabs Lucifer by the left ankle and flings him into the dark abyss of Hell.

Let's look at what the early interpreters have said about this card.

Some Temperance Meanings

Excerpted from *Mystical Origins of the Tarot* by Paul Huson.

Pratesi's Cartomancer (1750): Time.

De Mellet (1781): Temperance. An angel instructs Man on the avoidance of Death.

Court de Gébelin (1773-82): Temperance.

Etteila (1785-1807): Temperance. The Angel of the Apocalypse. REVERSED: Convictions. The services of a priest, for whatever sacramental reasons determined by the other cards.

Lévi (1855): The Hebrew letter Nun. Temperance: the Heaven of the Sun, climates, seasons, motion, changes of life, which is ever new yet ever the same.

Christian (1870): Arcanum XIV. The Solar Spirit: Initiative. In the divine world, the perpetual motion of life; in the intellectual world, the combination of ideas that create morality; in the physical world, the combination of natural forces.

Mathers (1888): Temperance. Combination, conformation, uniting. REVERSED: Ill-advised combinations, clashing interests.

Golden Dawn (1888-96): Daughter of the Reconcilers, the Bringer Forth of Life. Temperance. Combination.

Grand Orient (Waite, 1889, 1909): Temperance. New blood, combination, admixture.

Waite (1910): Temperance. Household economy, moderation, frugality, management, accomodation. REVERSED: Things connected with churches, religions, sects, the priesthood, sometimes even the priest who will marry the inquirer. Also disunion, unfortunate combinations, competing interests.

Both Pratesi and Lévi follow the "temp" of Temperance and see time—time itself for Pratesi and the changes of life for Lévi. Paul Christian continues this idea with what he calls the "perpetual motion of life," but in the divine world. For the intellectual and physical, he introduces the concept of combinations, which continues through all the others.

The idea of combining qualities comes partly from the image of poured water. Nothing is spilled or wasted (hence Waite's idea of "moderation, frugality," which are basic qualities of the virtue of Temperance), yet the energies of left and right mingle. Some decks vary the picture by showing one wing as golden, the other silver, for solar and lunar energies.

One old meaning of the word *temperance* involves mixing water with wine to lessen the alcohol content. From this we get the modern idea of temperance as abstention. In the late nineteenth century, the Women's Christian Temperance Union battled alcoholism, sometimes directly going into bars with axes to smash all the bottles and kegs. Maybe they drew on the warrior qualities of the archangel Michael. While this may seem an extreme interpretation, remember that the next card, the Devil, shows us the archetype of addiction, one of the ways we "fall" from the balance of Temperance.

Medieval science taught that the body contains "humors," or "tempers." A healthy person balances these, lets energy flow between them. "Lose your temper" means losing the balance and the ability to combine different qualities.

The modern Golden Dawn interpretation shown here, created by Sandra Tabatha Cicero, gives us two versions of Temperance. In one, a female angel stands on a tightrope and mixes fire and water. In the other version, energy streams into or out of a kind of witch's-cauldron, with a red lion to the right and a white eagle to the left, both chained to her waist, and a scorpion and goat lurking behind her. The lion and goat are Leo and Capricorn, while the eagle and scorpion symbolize different levels of Scorpio. These animals link the card to Strength (Leo), and then Death (Scorpio) before it and the Devil (Capricorn) after it. The Golden Dawn gave two versions because they considered one an "earlier" form that linked Sagittarius to other correspondences and the "later" to signify Sagittarius alone.

In some modern decks, such as the BOTA, designed by Paul Foster Case and drawn by Jesse Burns Parke, a rainbow appears behind the angel. As well as the idea of combining colors and chakra energies, the rainbow identifies the card with Iris, the Greek goddess of the rainbow. Iris presided over oaths taken by the gods themselves, which they swore on water from the River Styx, the river of death. Therefore, the card can symbolize an unbreakable oath or commitment, and can be used to make such an oath—that is, before swearing such a commitment, set out the Temperance card.

Iris holds the cup of the waters of death. The Grail, symbol of restored life, is of course also a cup. Thus, we might see the two cups of Temperance as life and death.

Temperance follows the card of Death and shows us an exalted state, belied, almost hidden, in the calm image. We have found our angelic selves, the essence that transcends the limits of ordinary life, the part "like unto God." But this is also a dangerous state, for we can easily lose the moderation that should mark it. The ego may lie low, pretend to have vanished, while it whispers to us, "*Like* unto God? You *are* God. Whatever you do is perfect."

We all know stories of great spiritual leaders who misuse their power over their followers, amassing great fortunes, sexually abusing their acolytes, sometimes even sanctioning murder of their opponents. It's easy to label them as fake, for after all, how could someone on a spiritual plane do such things? But the answer may be more complex. Maybe their own spiritual beauty seduces *them* before anyone else. Those on the highest level fall the farthest. Remember, the Devil is the next card.

Here is a story a friend told me some twenty-five years ago. He said he had traveled a long time in Asia, and in Thailand took up residence in a monastery. There he meditated and followed the daily practices, and at a certain point he attained the wonder of enlightenment—or so he thought. For a time he basked in the sense of oneness, of divine energy flowing through him and everything around without separation. But one day the thought came to him that he had not visited the West in some time, and he missed his friends and everything he knew there. But what of his enlightenment? Would he lose it if he left the monastery? Of course not! Enlightenment does not require a place or a set pattern of behavior. So he traveled to Amsterdam and found his old friends and his old life. Within two weeks, he said, he'd become involved in drugs, conflicts, and excess of all kinds—and at the moment that he felt the last sense of enlightenment slip away from him, lost completely, he heard a small voice in his head. It said, "Gotcha."

In readings, Temperance speaks primarily of that middle way, of calm. It can be extremely valuable in crisis situations, especially when other people give way to hysteria, anger, excessive reactions. Temperance tells us to stay balanced in the midst of all this. Like any card,

Temperance not only recommends such an attitude, it assures us we ourselves are capable of acting and feeling from such a state. In other words, it does not just say, "Temperance would be good for you right now," it says, "You can do this." And because it gives us an image, not just an abstract idea, it helps us create it. If we look at the picture of Temperance and let it enter into us, not as a concept but as an experience, it will change our actual state of mind and behavior.

I once did a reading for myself during a period when I could not seem to stop myself from over-reacting to everything and everyone around me. I could watch myself doing it but could not control it. Most of the cards reflected this extreme state (Five of Swords, for example), but in the position of "possible outcome" in the Celtic Cross stood Temperance. It said to me, "You can do this instead." So over the next days, whenever I would find myself spinning out of control, I visualized Temperance. Slowly, it became real for me, and the cycle stopped.

We also can use Temperance as a tool to overcome addiction. The card in a reading does not necessarily mean battling compulsions (like Michael fighting Satan), but if the other cards indicate that issue—and the person describes it as a problem—then we might look at Temperance as a part of the solution.

Temperance combines energies. Despite my personal negative reaction, the card is magical, dynamic, and so can indicate creative problem-solving. It may indicate that a solution to some longstanding issue lies in combining different people's approaches, talents, or ideas.

Reversed, we become intemperate, extreme, given to excessive behavior. This becomes strongest alongside the Devil right-side up, as if the angel has failed to control the "evil" impulses. Something may have gotten out of balance. This meaning becomes stronger with Justice reversed or the reversed Six of Pentacles in the Rider deck, for both figures carry balanced scales. The Ten of Swords with Temperance reversed might suggest acupuncture to re-set the person's energies, or "tempers."

Sometimes, reversed Temperance becomes a recommendation, for some situations call for extreme reactions, the way a parent might take risks to protect a child. In less dramatic situations, Temperance reversed may call on us to relax our guard, go wild, take a chance on something. This becomes stronger with the Fool right-side up.

A *Temperance Reading*

Can be used for people facing a difficult choice or in situations with extreme contradictions or contrasts.

1. Current situation

2. Alternative

3. Possible middle way

4. Needed approach

5. How to let energy flow

6. What commitment is needed

Devil: 15

Astrological correspondence:
  Capricorn

Kabbalistic letter: ע Ayin

Path on Tree of Life: Tipheret
  (Beauty) to Hod
  (Glory)

Note: The Visconti
  Tarot does not have
  a Devil card

Devil cards from
  MARSEILLE,
  RIDER, GOLDEN
  DAWN RITUAL,
  EGYPTIAN &
  SHINING TRIBE

THE DEVIL .

The Devil

EVIL. THE SHADOW. Proud rebel against God. Addictions. Really bad relationships. Hidden power. Darkness. Wild sex. Drunkenness. Guardian at the threshold. Temptation. Indulgence. The Serpent of the Goddess. The true hero of Eden. The way of knowledge. The fall from a great height. The prince of this world. Obsession. Black magic. The glory of the morning star. Satanic rituals. The inventor of Tarot.

People have said all this and more about card fifteen. Like the Death card, the Devil often shows up in lurid movies. The simple fact that such a card exists encourages Fundamentalist fantasies of the entire Tarot as being literally invented by Satan to lead people away from the true religion.

Beyond such simplistic ideas, the Devil invites different points of view because of our varied attitudes to darkness, power, desire. The final row of the Major Arcana, which begins with the Devil, may seem the most complex, but it also is the simplest, for it tells a story of the liberation of light. In many decks, the Devil is the only card with a completely black background. Then we see lightning in the Tower, then Starlight, Moonlight, and Sunlight, ever-increasing light and clarity. The last two cards, Judgement and the World, show us what I call the light of the spirit and the light of the self. But does all this happen because we somehow conquer the Devil's darkness? Or does the darkness in fact contain the light?

Before we dive further into the Devil's possibilities, let's see what the early interpreters said about it.

Some Devil Meanings

Excerpted from *Mystical Origins of the Tarot* by Paul Huson.

Pratesi's Cartomancer (1750): Anger.

De Mellet (1781): The Devil. Typhon. Human nature defiled and enslaved.

Court de Gébelin (1773-82): Typhon.

Lévi (1855): The Hebrew letter Samekh. The Devil. The Heaven of Mercury, occult science, magic, commerce, eloquence, mystery, moral force.

Christian (1870): Arcanum XV. Typhon: Fate. In the divine world predestination; in the intellectual world Mystery; in the physical world the Unforseen, Fatality. Typhon, the spirit of catastrophes, who rises out of a flaming abyss and brandishes a torch above the heads of two men chained at his feet.

Mathers (1888): The Devil. Fatality for good. REVERSED: Fatality for evil.

Golden Dawn (1888-96): Lord of the Gates of Matter, Child of the Forces of Time. Devil. Material Force. Temptation, obsession, especially with the Lovers.

Grand Orient (Waite, 1889, 1909): The Devil, or Typhon. Fatality, evil, the false spirit; can indicate also the good working through evil.

Waite (1910): The Devil. Violence, vehemence, fatality. What is predestined, but not for this reason evil. REVERSED: Evil fatality, weakness, blindness.

> RIDER
> *Lovers*
> *&*
> *Devil*

To some extent, these meanings take the Devil at face value, as a symbol of evil. Fatality also appears, whatever is beyond our control, which we may experience as evil. People used to consider disasters like earthquakes the work of the Devil, because, after all, God would not want us to suffer. Waite makes the point that such things "are not for this reason evil."

When the interpreters consider what evil is, they tend to fall back on the dualism of much Hermetic doctrine, that the physical world exists as a prison, or "husk," for the true spiritual light. The goal—the "Great Work," to borrow a term from alchemy—becomes to liberate the imprisoned spirit. Rather than see that such liberation can occur through the physical world by embracing the beauty of nature or the power of sexuality, some say we must reject these and become pure mind, disembodied divine love. Waite says about the Devil, "There is no correspondence in that world [spirit] with things that are of the Brute." No correspondence?

When the Emerald Tablet tells us "That which is above is like that which is below," does it exclude the harshness of physicality?

The Devil is 15, and 1+5=6, the Lovers. In the Rider deck of Waite's design, the Devil appears as a crude parody of the Lovers.

If the Lovers symbolizes fulfillment through love and relationship, the Devil can indicate love perverted, when sex exists only for itself. We should not dismiss this idea as old-fashioned Puritanism, for sex can become an addiction without satisfaction, but there is something of the prude about it. And we should remember that in fact the Devil is the older design. Waite redesigned the Lovers card so that it would seem like a purified version of the Devil.

If the physical world is in some way an imprisonment, then the physical world can become the means of our liberation. Through the body, through sexual practices such as Tantra or modern sex magick, we can awaken the kundalini energy and transform ourselves. It has long struck me that the Song of Songs may in fact be a disguised description of such practices.

The Lovers and the Devil. Maybe the Lovers shows sexual magic done with spiritual intent and the Devil sexual rites that become their own end and so leave us trapped in darkness. The Devil in a reading can mean bondage or other forms of sexual "deviancy." Before we dismiss such things, consider that shamans are often tied up before they go into a trance. If the Lovers become too pure, too proper, we might find the path to greater consciousness lies through the Devil.

In the Rider tradition, the deck contains three angels: on the Lovers, Temperance, and Judgement (the Marseille shows Cupid on the Lovers). We've identified these three as Raphael, Michael, and Gabriel, but what of Uriel, whose name means "Light of God"? Tarot teachers Wald and Ruth Ann Amberstone see him in the fourth winged figure, the Devil, who rises above the demons exactly as Raphael rises above Adam and Eve in the Lovers.

Where does the image of the Devil come from? The traditional Tarot Devil is a kind of monster with large bat wings, horns, and a tail. Renaissance accusations of witchcraft often included the idea that women engaged in orgiastic sex with the Devil, who was pictured much that way. Consider this—in stories, men make contracts with the Devil by signing a contract in blood, but women give themselves through their sexual fluids.

Devil images are often projections of fear. The *Malleus Maleficarum*, or Witches' Hammer, a guide for witch-hunting inquisitors, includes extreme fantasies of women's sexual power over men, including supposed baskets of actual penises stolen from men's bodies. Here we see the Devil as obsession and terror projected by men onto women. Because the masculine rulers of culture did not overcome their own devil of fear, millions of women died horrible deaths.

The Visconti deck contains no Devil or Tower cards. Neither does the other surviving early deck by the same artist, a deck called Cary-Yale Visconti. While the same two cards may have gotten lost in both decks (we have just one copy of each), maybe those cards simply did not exist until later. Maybe no one saw a need for cards of evil and destruction until the time of the Marseille deck, when the witch craze had taken hold of European imagination.

We should recognize that there may have been actual witches, but they were Pagans, not servants of evil, and any sexual rites were a celebration of nature, not supernatural perversions. Looked at this way, the Devil can be a joyous figure, a playful card, and in fact the modern Hermetic tradition describes its "esoteric function" as mirth: the Devil as the card of the stand-up comic.

The Golden Dawn version of the card introduces the goat-headed figure we often think of as the standard Devil and that other assumed icon of the card, the five-pointed star. In our sample, this pentagram, in fact, only appears in the Golden Dawn and the Rider, and upside down only in the Rider. Among its other meanings, the pentagram evokes the human body, for if you stand with arms out and legs apart, you form a five-pointed star. Right-side up, it means nature and physicality, and has been adapted as the symbol of Wicca. Upside down, it suggests the genitals above the head, desire overcoming reason. But we see this image in only that one version and its many modern imitators.

The Shining Tribe shows a Devil seemingly trapped in layers of doorways, with jagged energy all around. The body becomes hypersexual, seductive at the same time that repression confines it. But there are no actual doors. Belief holds us back more than actual oppression. We find a similar idea in the Marseille and Rider, where the ropes or chains are loose enough for the people to remove them and walk away. People in great danger face very real problems. But even in terrible circumstances, the spirit can recognize its ultimate freedom.

There is another way to look at the Shining Tribe Devil in his doorway. We can say that he guards the entrance, and we must find a way through that doorway to explore the rest of the cards, which lie beyond it. And further, that the only way to reach those cards is through the Devil's doorway.

In the triad of the Magician-Strength-Devil, we see lemniscates (infinity signs) above the heads of the first two, and the pentagram above the Devil. In the Rider and other versions, the Devil squats on a rectangular block of stone, a half-cube. As we saw with the Emperor, occultists sometimes see the cube as a symbol of existence—the "cube of space," as Paul Foster Case terms it. A half-cube symbolizes one-half of the truth. This is the belief that only matter exists, and there is no spiritual dimension to life.

The Hierophant is five, the Devil fifteen. Hierophants sometimes use fearful images of devils to frighten people into obedience. If we add the numbers of all the cards up to the Hierophant—0+1+2+3+4+5—we get fifteen, the Devil.

Some see the Devil image as Baphomet, a supposed god worshipped by the Knights Templar, that ill-fated order destroyed on Friday, October 13, 1307. And Baphomet seems to be derived from the image of Pan, a Greek god who was half-goat, who led humans in wild sexual rites. Pan's pipes drove people to "panic," which perhaps originally meant not fear but reckless, insane, or just sensual behavior.

According to some sources, Pan was the son of Hermes, patron god of the Tarot. Hermes, as the Magician, heads up the triad, with the Devil at the bottom. We may insist that good, or "white" magic has nothing to do with evil, but there may be complex shifts of energy between the Magician and Devil, with Strength needed in the middle to hold, or mediate, the energy. Other stories describe Pan as older than the Olympians, a power of nature and the earth, and even the god who taught prophecy to Apollo.

Pan occupies a special place in Christian myth. An odd story from the first years of the Christian era tells how a sailor named Thamus heard a voice order him: "When you get to Palodes, proclaim 'The great god Pan is dead.'" When Christians heard of this, they saw it as proof that Christ had replaced the Pagan deities. In fact, the worship of Pan continued in the Greek world for some time, and modern Pagans have seen him as a symbol of earthiness, sexuality, desire, and play. A number of modern decks have changed card fifteen to "Pan."

Pan and a group of satyrs were pictured as half-human, half-goat, and highly sexual. The image survives not just in the Devil's supposed cloven hooves but in the common expression "an old goat" for a man who pursues younger women. The Golden Dawn assigned Capricorn, sign of the goat, to the Devil.

Pan and Baphomet are the most direct mythological sources, but there are others. In the Hanged Man, we learned of the two angels who descended to Earth and lusted after human women. The angel who refused to repent after raping the woman who rejected him was named Azazel. For the Jews, and thus many Kabbalists, Azazel became a Devil-like figure, similar to the Christian Satan, ruler of the *yester hara*, or evil impulse, which many Kabbalists identify with the physical universe and sexuality.

The name Azazel appears in the Bible, but not in the passage that gave rise to the story of the two angels. That passage simply says, "The sons of heaven came down and mingled with the daughters of Men." Azazel appears in the instructions for the Day of Atonement, where Israelites are told to take a goat (that same animal) and transfer all the evil deeds of the people onto him, and then send him into the wilderness—"to Azazel." The Hebrew equivalent of "Go to Hell" is "Go to Azazel."

There is a further twist with Tarot connections. In the legend of the two angels, the archangel who binds fallen Azazel in the dark abyss is Raphael, the very angel who blesses Adam and Eve in the Rider Lovers.

And more—the myth names the two women in the story. The one whom Azazel rapes is called Na'amah, sometimes identified as a demon herself, the sister of Lilith. But the other, who escapes Shemhazai (he who becomes a Hanged Man) and flies into the sky to become a star, is named Istahar. "Istahar" is a variant of the Babylonian Ishtar, one of the queens of heaven whom we looked at in the Empress.

Ishtar is, in fact, the planet Venus, that beautiful morning or evening star (depending on the time of year). Just as the Empress in many modern decks bears the symbol of Venus on her shield, so we also might identify Venus with the card called the Star, the figure of a beautiful woman who pours out her waters of replenishment. Istahar, having escaped the desires of the Devil and the violence of the Tower, cards 15 and 16, emerges as card 17, the Star.

But Venus brings us right back to the Devil as well, for Christian myth describes Satan (the word means "adversary") as originally an angel, the most radiant of all the sons of heaven. His name was Lucifer Morningstar. Lucifer means "light-bringer," while Morningstar identifies him as the planet Venus.

Do you see? Everything is connected.

The astrological patterns of the planets do not depend on their actual elliptical orbits around the sun. We do not live on the sun, we live on Earth, where we observe the planets' "apparent motion," the movements in the sky above our heads. Long ago, people tracked these movements and their repetitious patterns. Mercury, for example, the planet of the Magician (Mercury, remember, is Hermes' Roman name), traces a series of loops within the larger circle it makes over a period of time. When people say that Mercury has "gone retrograde," they refer to the seemingly backward motion of the loops (draw a loop on a piece of paper, and you will see that part of it goes backwards). Now here is the remarkable part: there are twenty-two of these loops, the same number as the letters of the Hebrew alphabet and the cards in the Major Arcana.

Venus traces an even more remarkable pattern. Over some eight years, it forms a perfect five-pointed star in the sky. Thus the pentagram, depicted in movies as a mark of Satan, in fact represents Venus, the goddess of love. But as we have seen, it also is the human body. And in a very vital way, it embodies the plant world as well. Cut an apple in half horizontally and you will discover a five-pointed star in each half. A pomegranate, the fruit of Persephone and Demeter, will do the same thing. Wild roses and many other flowers contain five, or multiples of five, petals in their blossoms. Thus, the pentagram unites Heaven and Earth, with the human body as a link or a bridge. As above, so below, in one powerful image.

But why have the pentagram with the Devil? How did Lucifer Morningstar (Venus) become Satan? Historians will give various theories (such as a misreading of a passage in Isaiah), but I would like to suggest a mythic, or symbolic, one that gives insight into the last line of the Major Arcana. For part of the year, Venus disappears from the sky. In ancient times this coincided with winter, and thus barrenness. Venus's return in spring announced the return of fertility. This is the Venus of the Star card. The Devil is Venus in darkness, the light in exile from itself, an illusion of barrenness and despair.

Psychologically, our light can vanish at any time, any season, when the awfulness of life, or weakness, or fear, or desire for what will hurt or even destroy us can overwhelm our belief in love. We feel ourselves in chains, and slaves of a force of destruction. But the chains can come off, just as Venus will always return to the sky.

In the Golden Dawn ordering of the cards, the Hebrew letter Ayin belongs to the Devil. *Ayin* means "eye," and people usually take it here as the materialist claim that what you see—the physical world—is all you get. But *seeing* can liberate us when we learn how to look. Like Aleph, the letter of the Fool, Ayin is silent, and there is an important pun in Genesis that connects them. Before Adam and Eve leave Eden, we read that "God made them garments of skin to protect them." People assume this means animal skins to keep them warm in the harsh world outside paradise. But the word for skin, *ohr*, is also the word for light, just spelled differently. The skin that God gives them is their own bodies, a fixed physical form that contains the eternal light of their true being. Our bodies protect us. As long as we live in the illusion of duality, the world of the ego, our own light will overwhelm us. Look at the figures on the Rider Devil card, and see how comfortable they look. The Devil, in a sense, holds us safe until we are ready to go through the doorway (look again at the Shining Tribe card) to the final cards of the Major Arcana, where we will "heal the world" by rediscovering our true selves.

Does all this mean that evil does not exist? Pick up any newspaper and you can read horrendous stories of human cruelty, from the murder of children to genocide. On the very day I was writing this, the *New York Times* reported that in some places in Africa, where civil war and famine have overwhelmed people, parents are deciding that their children are witches, and are either turning them out in the street or torturing them to drive out the demons. You can find similar horrors in almost any country, almost any day.

What do we make of such things? Do we turn around and say that all the esoteric discoveries above are meaningless? Do we decide that the Devil—Satan, Azazel, Iblis—exists after all, dragging his cloven goat foot through the world, slithering his forked tongue at us, and offering contracts in blood as well as hot sex in midnight rituals? To me, that simply leads to the *Malleus Malificarum* and women burnt alive for witchcraft. Do we say, like some of the Gnostics, that the whole world is simply a brutal illusion, and we need to free ourselves from our bodies? Having lived sixty-two years in wonder at the beauty of life, at a world where the path of the planet Venus, and roses and apples, and the human body with its arms and legs out all form the same image, I find such rejection of the world both too negative and too easy. Maybe as Tarot readers, and just as people, we need to accept what is, all the pain we see around us, and at the same time look beyond and within for the realization of our deeper selves.

Here is a statement from a Hasidic master, quoted by Annie Dillard in *For the Time Being*. Dillard (and I) see it as a response to those Kabbalists who reject the physical world and everyday life as "husks" imprisoning the light:

> When you walk across the field with your mind pure and holy, then from all the stones, and all growing things, and all animals, the sparks of their souls come out and cling to you, and thus they are purified and become a holy fire within you.

What a complicated journey this has been, one of the Fool's strangest tours in his progress from innocence to the liberated light of the World. What, then, do we say when the Scowling Horned Guy turns up in a reading? With all the cards, we look at the range of meanings and see what works best in the context of the reading. Nowhere is this more important than with card fifteen.

This *seeing* must always take into account how the querent reacts to the card. Years ago, my partner, a superb Tarot reader, used to do weekly readings for a friend. One week she couldn't do it, so I volunteered. The Devil came up as the very first card. I was staring at it, thinking of such matters as obsession,when the woman said, "My favorite card!" To her it simply meant party time. Recently, I asked some friends what card might signify jokes. We agreed on the Devil.

At the other extreme would be the concept of evil or someone acting in an evil way. This not-so-common interpretation might become stronger with aggressive or painful cards, such as some of the Swords or some reversed court cards.

More commonly, the Devil means oppression of some sort, or addiction, whatever chains us. Often, these things have a quality of illusion about them, due to that image of the ropes or chains being big enough to come off. The Devil can mean illusions of any kind, mistakes, errors, clinging to values or situations or people that can harm you. The Magician carries a secret tradition of trickery, but the Devil's games and lies can bring real harm.

With Cups cards, the Devil may mean alcoholism, and we might extend this to the other suits. The Devil with Swords (needles) might indicate drug addiction; Wands, sexual obsessions; and Pentacles, problems around money, maybe a gambling addiction. Tarotist Carey Croft suggests another idea. If the Devil means chains, then if it appears next to a Minor card, that card may suggest the issue. For example, next to the Two of Cups, the Devil might indicate a relationship problem; around various Pentacles, a problem at work.

Reversed, the Devil often means liberation. Someone realizes he or she is not chained in some way, that he or she can free him- or herself and walk away. It can mean seeing through an illusion or a turn to the spiritual in life. Sometimes it can mean being serious and responsible rather than frivolous. Or a relationship that was primarily sexual becomes more emotionally serious. This becomes stronger if the Lovers appears, especially if there is a time sequence—that is, the reversed Devil first and then the Lovers.

A Devil Reading
(in the shape of a pentagram)

1. What have I lost?

2. What blocks me from returning?

3. What illusory chains hold me?

4. What reality holds me?

5. How can I free myself?

6. What will happen?

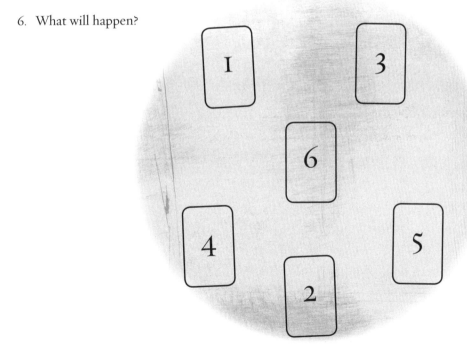

A Devil Wisdom Reading
(in the shape of horns)

1. What is evil?

2. Why does it exist?

3. Where does it originate?

4. How should we respond to it?

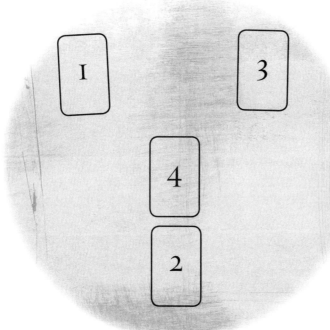

Note: The Visconti Tarot does not have a Tower card

Tower: 16

Astrological correspondence: Mars

Kabbalistic letter: פ Peh

Path on Tree of Life: Netzach (Victory) to Hod (Glory)

Tower cards from MARSEILLE, RIDER, GOLDEN DAWN RITUAL, EGYPTIAN & SHINING TRIBE

The Tower

EVEN MORE THAN the Devil (the previous card), the Tower may cause people to wince when it turns up in a reading. We associate it with upheavals, extreme situations, even violence. A woman came to me once. She had met a man and begun a wonderful relationship, but as soon as he'd told her he loved her, he became increasingly jealous and erratic. (In Tarot terms, we might describe this as the Lovers, card 6, changing into the Devil, card 15; 1+5=6.) Finally, when he became violent, she called the police and got a restraining order. Still, she could not let go of how good it had seemed, and so she asked the cards if there was any way it could work.

191

The reading showed various images of trouble and aggression. It indicated that his violence came from within, and if she took him back, the same thing would likely happen. The "outcome" card (the last card in the traditional Celtic Cross spread) was the Tower. Immediately she said, "Can we do it again?" Normally I would not do that, for it trivializes the reading, but it seemed worthwhile to see if the cards might offer a different approach that could help the situation. So we did them again, and once more the Tower came up as the outcome.

Is that the Tower's disturbing side? We'll make it more so. On September 11, 2001, terrorists flew planes into buildings in New York City known as the Twin Towers. The towers burst into flame and people jumped from the windows, preferring that death to being burned alive. Except for the doubled towers, this is the exact image of card sixteen, a tower struck and on fire and people leaping from the windows. After that terrible day, Tarot readers all over the world reported that the Tower card had appeared frequently in the weeks before. One woman in Melbourne, Australia, who makes her living as a reader, said that the Tower had shown up in every reading for two weeks, no matter the subject. Did any of these Tarot readers try to warn the U.S. government or New York City? Not as far as I know. They might have guessed that the Tower's constant appearance signaled some large event in the world, but only something like a psychic vision could have told them what actually might happen. Such are the limits of divination.

Should we gasp when the Tower comes up, or see it only as upheaval—whether personal or cultural? Absolutely not. For one thing, it can indicate a liberation—a Devil situation overthrown. The Tower might indicate a blow-up at work that frees you to leave a bad job. In the relationship described above, if the man had not lost control early on, if the woman had not been forced to call the police, she might have ended up a terrified emotional captive or even dead somewhere down the line. The Tower can mean shocking news, stunning revelations that can radically change your understanding of something or shake you loose of old habits.

Not all that reassuring, is it? Let's look a little deeper. If the Devil represents the imprisonment of light, the Tower shows us its release. If the Devil's "materialism" indicates our limited perceptions, the Tower shows us the moment when we (re)discover the great truths of our own spiritual nature. Even more radically than the Hanged Man, what we believed was reality gets turned upside down—which is why in many versions the people fly out headfirst. In its most extreme and most joyous form, the Tower symbolizes the great breakthrough known as enlightenment, when the soul opens up and all existence fills with light.

Let's look at some images of this experience—for it is, in fact, an experience and not just a concept or metaphor. In yoga (the spiritual tradition, not just the exercise program), meditation and other practices arouse the life energy of kundalini that lies coiled like a sleeping snake at the base of the spine. This kundalini travels through the chakras like an electric fire until it opens out of the top of the head, the crown chakra.

Kabbalah tells us that creation descends down the Tree of Life, from the first sephirah of pure being to the final sephirah, the tenth, which is the physical world. The path of descent resembles a serpent or a lightning bolt. We live in that bottom sephirah, the density of matter, but if we wish and can concentrate our intention, we can ascend, through study and meditation, until we may enter—return—to the oneness of that highest sephirah, called Kether, which means "crown," the same term as in yoga.

Here is the lightning on the Tree of Life; this is the lightning that strikes the Tower.

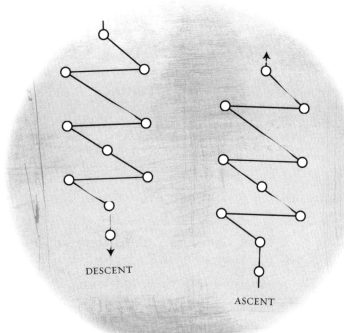

DESCENT

ASCENT

The Buddha is said to have experienced enlightenment while sitting at the base of an ancient tree. Christian tradition tells how Saul of Tarsus, a persecutor of the early Christians, was on his way to Damascus when lightning struck him, and he emerged as St. Paul, who would spread the doctrine of divine love.

In a curious bit of Tarot history, some old decks title this card La Maison de Dieu, the House of God. Interpreters do not seem to know what to make of this. Some assume it a misprint for Maison du *Diable*, House of the Devil. Paul Huson compares the card to medieval images of Satan holding souls in prison in a tower, and describes the card as the Harrowing of Hell, when Christ descended to the Underworld to release the righteous souls who had suffered the bad luck of being born before the birth of Jesus. Thus, the House of the Devil becomes transformed into the House of God. However, in most versions of the card, people do not look happy.

To me, "House of God" suggests the ancient Temple of Solomon, whose image is central to Freemasonry and the occult Tarot. We saw its entrance veiled in the High Priestess, top card of the second triad, which runs High Priestess-Hermit-Tower. The lightning in the Tower shows us the moment when the veil is opened and we see the truth—of ourselves and of the cosmos. The card appears so drastic because the experience can be shattering, overwhelming. In between the mystery of the High Priestess and the revelation of the Tower, the Hermit holds up a lantern of truth into the darkness.

The temple in Jerusalem was an actual building, but it is also a myth, just as the Tarot is a myth as well as a pack of brightly colored cards. The lightning of the Tower destroys the illusion of duality, or separation. Part of that illusion is the supposed distinction between history and myth, between "reality" and imagination.

In Kabbalistic lore, the Shekinah, the feminine aspect of God, lived within the actual temple, in the Ark of the Covenant (remember the movie *Raiders of the Lost Ark?*). When the Romans destroyed the temple, in 70 CE, the Shekinah went into exile with humanity, for the connection had broken between Above and Below. We can describe Tarot as a myth of exile and return, of a broken world and its healing. We also can call it a blueprint of restoration. The High Priestess shows us the Shekinah veiled, the World card shows her restored and no longer hidden. The most important thing to realize is this: the Shekinah is us.

The most obvious biblical reference to the Tower is probably the Tower of Babel, and in fact a number of modern decks have shown a ziggurat-style building, on the assumption that Babel comes from Babylon, where the Israelites lived in exile from their homeland (after the Babylonians destroyed the first, or original, temple; the Romans destroyed the second one). It was in Babylon that Ezekiel saw his vision of the chariot that inspired the early mystical tradition that would become Kabbalah. In Tarot, the Tower is 16, and 1+6=7, the Chariot.

In the theme of exile, myth and history become entwined. The Babylonians destroyed the first temple, the Romans the second, and once again, large numbers of Judaeans were driven from their homeland. But we are all in exile, and our homeland is our knowledge of our true being. In a wonderful Welsh myth of destruction and restoration, a man named Gwion Bach goes through a terrible dismemberment, only to be reborn as a magical babe who can sing poetry and answer any question. The peasants who discover him take him to the king, who asks, "Who are you, and where do you come from?" "My name is Taliesin," he answers, "and my home is the region of the summer stars." Taliesin is us.

Centuries after the destruction of the temple, many Jews migrated to Iberia (Spain and Portugal), where along with the dominant Moorish culture they experienced a great flowering that lasted some five hundred years. This golden age ended with another mass exile, the expulsion of all Jews and Muslims by the newly dominant Christian rulers in 1492. Some of the money stolen from the expelled people was used to finance Columbus.

Several decades later, in Cairo, a young genius rabbi named Isaac Luria read the Zohar, itself a great myth of exile and return. Inspired, Luria traveled to join a small community of Kabbalists in the mountains of Galilee, the same place where Jesus had taught in the years before the Romans destroyed the temple. It was Luria who first fully developed the links of the Hebrew letters to the pathways on the Tree of Life, a tradition Éliphas Lévi would much later extend to the Major Arcana. And it was Luria who taught that we lived in a broken universe, and that we must devote ourselves to *tikkun olam*, the restoration of the world. Seen one way, the Tower shows the breaking, what Luria called the "shattering of the vessels." But seen another way, it shows the revelation of true knowledge—*gnosis* in Greek, *Da'ath* in Hebrew—necessary to begin the restoration.

Consider again the story of the Tower of Babel, its possible historical source and its mythic meaning, and its relation to Tarot. Babylon was one of the earliest civilizations, the people who first formulated Western astrology. The Israelites learned a great deal in Babylon, but they also may have worked as forced labor on the mighty ziggurat towers. And they encountered people from all over the Middle Eastern world, with their dazzling multiplicity of languages.

In the myth, humanity originally all spoke one language, and they all came together to build a great tower that would rise all the way to Heaven itself. However—this part is not in the Bible but in later versions—they used corrupt magic, taught to them by none other than Shemhazai and Azazel, the two fallen angels whose story we have seen in the Hanged Man and the Devil, and will find in the Star as well. Everything is connected. God looks at this and says, in effect, this is what they do when they all speak one language, and so scrambles human speech and scatters the people all across the earth.

Clearly, this story "explains" why humans speak so many thousands of languages. It also teaches a moral lesson about the danger of using occult power for the sake of ego. We can look at the sequence Temperance-Devil-Tower as a pathway of self-destruction. A person who studies, becomes initiated, and goes through a death and a rebirth achieves a high level of knowledge and power. But if he or she believes they have left the world behind, they may misuse that power, become lost in a dark arrogance until some kind of disaster happens. Waite describes the Tower as the chastisement of pride in the attempt to penetrate divine mysteries.

That gives us a neat moral lesson, doesn't it? Let's go deeper. The Kabbalist letter for the Tower, Peh, means "mouth," the organ of language. At the same time, some describe "speech" as the primary quality of the Chariot. Remember, 16 (Tower) becomes 1+6=7 (Chariot). The Chariot shows us *human* speech, the ability to define both the world and the self. The "mouth" of the Tower opens with *divine* speech, the overwhelming power of experience that is beyond language and consciousness. The lightning flash. An old comics fan like me might think of *Captain Marvel*, in which a homeless orphan (humanity in exile) passes through a dark tunnel lined with images of the classic vices until he meets a wizard named Shazam. When Billy says the wizard's name—the power of speech, of a sacred name—lightning strikes him, and he becomes Captain Marvel, endowed with the power of six different gods.

Christians teach of Pentecost, when "the Spirit descended" into the populace and people spoke in strange sounds or varied languages. God filled them, and they could speak wonders beyond human consciousness. Babel is one side of the Tower, Pentecost is the other. And Captain Marvel flies between them.

What do the original interpreters say? Will we find hints of what I call the esoteric Tower, the lightning that tears away the veil of the High Priestess? Or will it be all violence and destruction?

Some Tower Meanings

Excerpted from *Mystical Origins of the Tarot* by Paul Huson.

De Mellet (1781): The Tower. The House of God. The earthly paradise from which man and woman are expelled by a comet and hailstorm, or a fiery sword.

Court de Gébelin (1773-82): House of God, or the Castle of Plutus.

Etteila (1785-1807): The Lightning-Struck Temple. The Capitol. Poverty. REVERSED: Prison. Unjust calumny.

Lévi (1855): The Hebrew letter Ayin. Tower: The Heaven of the Moon, alterations, subversions, changes, failings.

Christian (1870): Arcanum XVI. The Lightning-Struck Tower: Ruin. In the divine world, the punishment of pride; in the intellectual world, the downfall of the Spirit that attempts to discover the mystery of God; in the physical world, reversals of fortune. Material forces that can crush great and small alike. Rivalries which only end in ruin for all concerned. Frustrated plans, hopes that fade away, ruined ambitions and catastrophic deaths.

Mathers (1888): The Lightning-Struck Tower. Ruin, disruption, loss, bankruptcy. REVERSED: These in a partial degree.

Golden Dawn (1888-96): Lord of the Hosts of the Mighty. Tower. Ambition, fighting, courage. In certain combinations (or reversed), destruction, danger, fall.

Grand Orient (Waite, 1889, 1909): Ruined Tower. Destruction, confusion, judgment; also the idea of divine wrath.

Waite (1910): The Tower. Misery, indigence, adversity, calamity, disgrace, deception, unforeseen catastrophe. REVERSED: According to one account [Mathers again], the same in a lesser degree. Also imprisonment, tyranny.

THE LOVERS.

JUDGEMENT.

> RIDER
Lovers
&
Judgement

∨ RIDER
Devil
&
Tower

THE DEVIL.

THE TOWER.

De Mellet describes it as the "earthly paradise," that is, Eden. "Man and woman" here implies Adam and Eve expelled into the harsh world. For many, expulsion from paradise means the "descent" into an earthly body. Zoe Matoff points out that since the lightning strikes *down* and the people plummet to the rocks, it can mean the entrance into the unhappy state of matter rather than the flash of enlightenment that releases us. The Tarot is never simple, is it? Genuine symbols resist a single, fixed meaning.

Court de Gébelin's term "the Castle of Plutus" returns us to the story of Persephone that seems to run through the cards. Plutus was another name for Hades, the Lord of the Underworld who abducts Persephone, taking her from the Empress's bright nurturing into the darkness of death. We will pick up this story again in the next card, the Star.

Paul Christian introduces the modern interpretation that culminates in Waite's "misery, calamity, disgrace, catastrophe." We see some relief from these themes in the Golden Dawn's idea of ambition and courage, with destruction only from "certain combinations," or reversed. Mathers and then Waite bring in the intriguing idea that the reversed card can mean "the same in a lesser degree." More about this in a moment.

Here is something I discovered only recently in the Rider deck. The symbolism of duality usually places the man, or the light, on the right side of the picture, and the woman, or darkness, on the left. We see this in the pillars of the High Priestess, and then more specifically in the Lovers. For many years, I assumed this carried through all the way to Judgement. In class one day I confidently stated that there too we see the man on the right. But when we looked, I discovered I had let my expectation cloud my vision, for in fact the man and woman have switched sides.

When we looked closer, we saw that the change occurred in the Tower. In the Devil, the man and woman are in the same place as the Lovers. They change sides when flung from the Tower. It's as if something that began as a vibrant idea gets worn out by the time we get to the Devil. It has reached its limit, and now we need to drastically change our perceptions. Or maybe we can say that with the force of enlightenment, we no longer look on the images from outside but enter them, become the symbols, so that right and left get turned around.

We have already seen much of what people say when this card appears in a reading. The most common meanings are upheaval, sudden change, a blowup. This can lead to a liberation. The situation is not always so drastic. Once, in a day reading for myself, I could not see what the Tower represented or why it said I needed to avoid a Chariot approach and take a Seven of Swords approach (three "seven" cards). Later that day, I took my dog for a walk on a country road, where two ferocious dogs charged us. I managed to yell at them and hold them off, and we got away from their property. But we still had to get back to my car. I was going to try to just charge past when I remembered the reading. The two dogs threatening disaster were the Tower. Don't charge past like the Chariot, the reading said, sneak by like the man on tiptoe in the Seven of Swords. And in fact we waited awhile, then quietly went past without rousing them.

A very literal meaning of the card would warn us against lightning. We might think of this if the card came up for someone about to venture into an area with a storm about to occur.

Rather than an event or an action, the Tower may signal information, some shocking news that turns our view of a situation upside down. We might think of a woman discovering that her husband is having an affair. We should not leap to such an interpretation without other cards supporting it.

For reversed, we can think of Mathers and Waite's idea of "same in a lesser degree." There is still an upheaval but not as drastic. Fights do not go all the way, people hold back, or a situation that seemed disastrous turns out not as extreme as the person thought. However, we also need to consider the possibility that things just continue, and there is no release or liberation. There might be a sense of denial or holding on to something that needs to be released. If the Tower can mean a revelation of some sort, then reversed can indicate information or an idea not fully revealed.

A Tower Reading

1. What structure have I had in my life?

2. How has it confined me?

3. How has it supported me?

4. What breaks it apart?

5. How are others affected? (can draw a card for each specific person)

6. What can emerge?

7. What do I have to do?

A Tower (Maison de Dieu) Wisdom Reading

1. Who lives in the House of God?

2. What destroys it?

3. What is liberated?

4. What happens after destruction?

5. What begins?

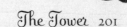

Star: 17

Astrological correspondence:
   Aquarius

Kabbalistic letter: צ Tzaddi

Path on Tree of Life: Netzach
   (Victory) to Yesod
   (Foundation)

Star cards from
   VISCONTI,
   MARSEILLE,
   RIDER, GOLDEN
   DAWN RITUAL,
   EGYPTIAN &
   SHINING TRIBE

The Star

WHAT A LOVELY image. Most decks follow the Marseille and Rider, showing a nude woman on one knee, pouring water from two gourds, one onto land, one into a pool of water. A small bird often appears in a tree, while stars shine in a clear sky. Most often, beginning with the Visconti, the main star contains eight points. The Golden Dawn identified this card with Aquarius, so that it becomes the card of the New Age, or Aeon. It also works historically, for images of Aquarius often show a masculine version of the star maiden.

The Visconti (the oldest version) shows a different picture than the Marseille—still a woman, and still graceful, but clothed, with a dress that may contain stars. She resembles the figure of

> VISCONTI
Temperance
&
Star

Temperance, who holds two ornate cups, so that at first glance we might think *she* represented the Star.

Both women stand high above a landscape, at a cliff edge, with hills or mountains dwarfed behind them. The imagery suggests the Queen of Heaven, a title Christians give to Mary but that goes back to a series of goddesses, such as Babylonian Ishtar, Hebrew Astarte, and Greek Aphrodite. The English word *star* probably derives from Ishtar/Astarte. Istahar, from the story of the fallen angels (see Hanged Man, Devil, and Tower) is a version of Ishtar. All these figures, these Queens of Heaven, refer to that beautiful light, brightest after the sun and moon, yet soft and seemingly sensuous, the planet Venus. The morning star. And in Tarot, the term recalls the Empress, top of the third triad, with the Star at the bottom.

And, as we saw with the Devil card, the ancients identified another figure with Venus, Lucifer—Light-bringer—Morningstar. As a rebel against the divine, Lucifer was cast into darkness to become Satan (an action by Michael, the angel of Temperance). When we ourselves lose our understanding that we are part of the divine, that in fact no separation exists, we cast ourselves into darkness and sometimes despair. We believe ourselves chained. The Tower liberates us with its revelations, but the Star returns us to ourselves.

Astronomically, the Devil signifies the time of year when Venus—planet but also goddess of love—is missing from the sky. When it returns in the Star, it brings hope and restoration. We have not so much escaped from the Devil, or overthrown it, as liberated the light.

Not everyone accepts the definition of the Star as Venus. Some Tarot interpreters see it as Sirius, a star whose appearance every year coincided with the flooding of the Nile that made life possible in the otherwise desert country of Egypt. Both Venus and Sirius disappear—get lost in darkness—and return, so that both symbolize hope and restoration. Another candidate is the Star of Bethlehem that the *magi*—a Persian word, plural of magus, from which, of course, we get magician—followed to find the Christ child, yet another symbol of hope and salvation. The Star of the Magi shone at the beginning of the old Aeon, the Age of Pisces. The new Aeon belongs to Aquarius—the Star card.

When we look at the old meanings, we discover, in fact, that Sirius goes back to the very beginnings of the Tarot's occult tradition, with the magi not far behind.

Some Star Meanings

Excerpted from *Mystical Origins of the Tarot* by Paul Huson.

Pratesi's Cartomancer (1750): Gift.

De Mellet (1781): The Star. The creation of the stars and fishes.

Court de Gébelin (1773-82): Sirius the Dog Star with Isis.

Lévi (1855): The Hebrew letter Peh. The Blazing Star. Heaven of the soul, outpouring of thought, moral influence of idea on form, immortality.

Christian (1870): Arcanum XVII. The Star of the Magi: Hope. In the divine world, Immortality; in the intellectual world, the Inner Light that illuminates the Spirit; in the physical world, Hope.

Mathers (1888): The Star. Hope, expectation, bright promises. REVERSED: Hopes not fulfilled, or only in a minor degree.

Golden Dawn (1888-96): Daughter of the Firmament, Dweller between the Waters. Star. Hope, faith, unexpected help. REVERSED: Deceived hope.

Grand Orient (Waite, 1889, 1909): Star. Light descending, hope; the symbol of immortality.

Waite (1910): The Star. Loss, theft, abandonment; another reading says hope and bright prospects. REVERSED: Arrogance, haughtiness, impotence.

Court de Gébelin says Sirius, but no one seems to have followed his lead, at least for divinatory meanings. His friend, Comte de Mellet, seems to identify the card with the fifth day of biblical creation, though Genesis describes the sun and moon as the fourth day, and fish (and birds and animals) on the fifth. Genesis doesn't mention stars.

Paul Christian introduced both the idea of the "star of the magi" and the theme of hope that has become the dominant way to look at the card. Waite includes hope, but only as "another reading." He prefers the far more negative ideas of "loss, theft, abandonment," the opposite of Pratesi's single word, "gift."

To be fair, Waite's "outer method of the oracles" attempts to capture the card's divinatory tradition. He often says something different in "The Doctrine Behind the Veil" (the more in-depth part of his book *The Pictorial Key to the Tarot*). On the Star, he in fact dismisses the hope interpretation but goes on to say how "prepared minds" will see her as "Truth unveiled, glorious." He identifies her with the Great Mother, Binah, or Understanding, on the Tree of Life (third sephirah). For myself, I think of "Truth unveiled" as the previous card, the Tower, in the same triad as the High Priestess, who sits before the veiled entry to the temple. And I tend to see the Mother in the Empress, card three, same number as Binah.

Though Waite disdains "hope" as "the sum of several tawdry explanations," it has become the message of the card to modern readers. If we think of the Tower as some extreme situation that blasts open what was repressed or painful, then afterwards comes peace, a feeling of being cleaned out, liberated, holding nothing back. Hope. Thinking now about this lovely card, I wonder if hope might be the most precious thing we have, even more than love, for if we love but cannot hope, we live in a bleak world.

The figure I personally identify most with the Star is not Ishtar/Venus or Isis, but Persephone. Not the mother, but the daughter. It was this identification, rather than the more traditional link of the Empress to Demeter or the pomegranates on the High Priestess, that led me to see how we can trace the myth of Persephone's abduction and return in the Major Arcana's images of life, darkness, and restoration.

In the fall of 1990, I traveled to Greece as part of a series of sacred journeys for my book *The Body of the Goddess*. The Mysteries, with their nine-day ritual of loss and recovery, emerged as the book's theme. On the ninth day, after the initiates, the Mystai, had seen the great revelations, they would pour water from two vessels into cracks in the earth, crying out "Hye! Kye!" which means "Rain! Conceive!"

I arrived in Eleusis, the site of the Mysteries, on the actual first day of the ritual as it would have been performed in the two thousand years before 496 CE, when the Sacred Precinct was destroyed. Nine days later I was in Crete, the place where tradition said the Mysteries originated. I had planned to visit a prehistoric cemetery, but when I climbed the steep path, two ferocious dogs barred the way, like the three-headed dog, Cerberus, who barred the entrance to Hades in Greek myth. It struck me that the day of Persephone's return was not one to play tourist in the Underworld, so I took two bottles of water and walked along a cliff until I found a small cave opening. Eleusis contains such a cave, and the ancients saw it as an entrance to the Land of the Dead. "Hye, kye!" I called out in the goddess's honor and poured out my spring water, one bottle into the cave, the other into the chasm over the cliff edge. Just as I finished, a hawk spiraled up from the land below, clockwise—or deosil, as the Wiccans say—into the sun.

The Alexandrians, with their synthesis of Greek and Egyptian traditions that flowed into the Hermetica, would have recognized the hawk as Horus, the son of Isis. For me, the image of a goddess who returns from darkness, and the pouring of water from two vessels, exactly evoked the the Tower and the Star. I designed the Star card in the Shining Tribe Tarot (see next page) to illustrate Persephone's return as the bringer of hope.

Isis/Sirius brings regeneration through the flooding of the Nile. In the Rider, it is Isis who sits before the veiled temple of the High Priestess. It is Isis who brings Osiris back from the dead so that he, like Persephone and Christ, can open the way beyond death, or *through* death, to a new life.

An odd little bird appears on the Marseille Star and many later versions. Tradition sees it as an ibis, the bird sacred to Thoth.

> Shining
Tribe &
Marseille
Star

The third triad contains the Empress, the Wheel of Fortune, and the Star. The Empress embodies both Venus and Demeter. Two cards below, we see Demeter's daughter, Persephone, but we can identify the Star itself with Venus. In between, the Wheel signifies the turning year, including the Season of the Snake, when Persephone goes down into darkness, and the time of her return, when the bleak earth once more comes alive with hope and new life.

The actual star in the card often has eight points (double eight in the Marseille shown above), an evocation of the compass, and by extension another candidate for just what star it is—Polaris, the North Star. Because Polaris shines above the North Pole, it never moves, and so people have used it as a focal point for navigation for many centuries. For modern Pagans and Wiccans, the eight-pointed star evokes the eight sabbats, or seasonal holidays. The eight points also recall the Wheel of Fortune, the middle card of the triad.

And another meaning for the eight points: the Greeks and others posed a mathematical problem called "squaring the circle." This meant creating a square with the same internal area as a circle. A square represents the material world, with its four directions and four solar points of the year (for a listing of all the fours in our physical universe, see card four, the Emperor, and the introduction to the Minor Arcana). A circle represents the heavens, for the only circles we encounter in our experience are the sun, the full moon, and the pupil of the eye, which allows us to look up and wonder. So, squaring the circle would mean to bring Heaven and Earth together.

The thing is, it cannot be done. If you remember your high-school geometry class, the area of a square depends on pi (Greek letter π, pronounced "pie"), a so-called irrational number represented in the fraction 22/7—numbers vital to the Major Arcana. Since pi does not come into play to find the area of a square, they can never be reconciled. We cannot create a perfect replica of the spiritual world in the physical. But maybe we can find an image halfway, an intermediary point. An eight-sided figure, an octagon, fulfills that idea, as if a square had morphed halfway into a circle.

> SQUARE,
OCTAGON,
CIRCLE

An eight-pointed star, with its evocation of heavenly light shining down as an eternal gift, suggests the constant presence of spirit within ordinary lives. In various traditions, the Queen of Heaven, so often identified with the planet Venus, descends into the world. One of the most ancient poems known to us, from Sumer, describes how Inanna (forerunner of Ishtar/Istahar) descends from the Great Above, first to take on a human body and experience the physical world, and then to descend further, down to the Great Below of death, where her sister, ruler of the Underworld, imprisons her until she summons her husband to take her place. He thus becomes the dying and resurrecting god, along with Osiris, Adonis, Dionysus, and of course Christ, though there the Queen of Heaven becomes his mother. In Kabbalist myth, the Shekinah leaves the heavenly realm of detached spirit to follow humanity into exile, the Star shining over us to give us hope.

Often these stories carry a strong sexual element, for the relation between earth and sky, matter and spirit, is erotic, not indifferent and certainly not hostile. The Tower and Star portray a hidden sexuality, the Tower as male orgasm, the Star as female. If this surprises you, look at the pictures. Another way to look at it—the Devil shows us the attraction of sex, the Tower the wild heat, and the Star the relaxed aftermath. And if we might carry this further, the Moon shows us the strangeness and uncertainty that can come after people have had sex for the first time, and the Sun when they realize their relationship has emerged stronger and more joyous.

One more thing: the Star pouring out her waters gives us a powerful image of healing. Isis brings Osiris back to life. Persephone leads the dead to a new life. Here's a version we all know from childhood—in the story of Rapunzel, a sorceress imprisons the girl in a tower without a door. When the sorceress discovers the girl with a man, she furiously throws them out the window into a wilderness. This is the image of the Tower (not to mention Adam and Eve). Brambles scratch out the prince's eyes, so that he wanders for years until at last he hears the voice of his beloved. She holds him, like Mary holding Jesus, and when her tears fall on his face, his eyes do not just heal, they regenerate. Modern occult tradition teaches that a deep study of the Tarot and the Tree of Life will not just change our consciousness, it will change our very cell structure, transforming us into different beings.

In Temperance, the angel pours water back and forth between the two cups. The Star holds nothing back, kneeling gracefully rather than standing. And she is human, not idealized, for if we wish to transform ourselves, we must do it through the body as well as the mind.

In readings, the Star gives hope, a quality especially valuable in hard situations, which is mostly what causes people to consult the cards. It also can mean a relaxed, open attitude, joy, and relief. Sometimes this comes after an explosion or extreme experience. It also can be a card of healing and regeneration. The Star would be valuable in any reading that involved sickness, chronic conditions, or a long period of convalescence.

The Star can mean someone who feels good in her or his body. It can be sexual pleasure or simply sensuality.

There is another meaning, suggested by the title. What does it mean to be a star? Is it recognition, privileges, pressure, attention? You don't have to be a movie or rock star to experience these things. There are subtler ways that people become stars, such as in their families or careers. The card can mean that role or just a moment when someone gets to shine brightly.

Reversed, the Star most commonly means a lack of hope. Negativity. The most extreme state is despair, but we don't need to go that far. It can simply mean doubt or pessimism. Another possibility is a false hope. Something we have counted on or believed in may not come to pass. If the reading concerns healing, it may take longer than expected, or some particular approach or method may turn out less effective than what a person hoped.

In regard to the idea of someone as a star, the reversed Star card can mean a shy person, not ready to show herself to the world, who keeps her light hidden. Sometimes a person needs to do this, either because of a hostile environment at home or at work, or because she or he has not fully developed what they will share with people. An artist may not want to show paintings that are not ready, a scientist may avoid publicity until the work truly is complete.

The founder of the Jewish Hasidic movement acted the role of a simpleton until the time came to reveal himself. The Golden Dawn's letter for the Star, Tzaddi, begins the word *tzaddik*, a holy person. The model for such a person is that hidden Star, known as the Master of the Good Name. I imagine that Tarot readings for him when he was young might have shown the Fool and the Star reversed. If those two cards come up, it may hint that someone is more than he or she seems.

The reversed card might suggest some problem with body image, such as anorexia or sexual guilt. Such possibilities can become stronger if the Star reversed appears with the Devil, the Five of Swords, or the Eight of Swords.

A Star Reading

Looking at themes of the Star card, mix the deck in your usual way, and choose one card for each of the following:

1. Hope

2. Guidance

3. Peace

4. Healing

THE STAR.

Moon: 18

Astrological correspondence:
   Cancer

Kabbalistic letter: ק Koof

Path on Tree of Life: Netzach
   (Victory) to Malkuth
   (Kingdom)

Moon cards from
VISCONTI,
MARSEILLE,
RIDER, GOLDEN
DAWN RITUAL,
EGYPTIAN &
SHINING TRIBE

The Moon

ATTITUDES TOWARD THIS card, if not its meaning, have changed more than any other, except for the Fool. And the Fool, remember, was originally linked to the moon as a lunatic, living in the lunar half-light of insanity. The occult tradition has tended to see the moon negatively—madness, animal instincts, reflected rather than true light. The resurgence of feminine spirituality, as well as Wicca and Neo-Paganism, has challenged all this. What has happened with the Moon card is even stranger than what we find with the Fool and the Magician. In those two, the actual meaning changed. In the Moon, the concepts remain but the understanding of them has altered. To some extent, our culture has moved in recent decades from a solar to

a lunar consciousness, from an emphasis on rationalism, clarity, and masculine forcefulness to intuition, mystery, and subtlety.

Let's take a look at the historical development.

Some Moon Meanings

Excerpted from *Mystical Origins of the Tarot* by Paul Huson.

Pratesi's Cartomancer (1750): Night.

De Mellet (1781): The Moon. Creation of the Moon and terrestrial animals. The wolf and the dog represent wild and domesticated animals.

Court de Gébelin (1773-82): The Moon.

Lévi (1855): The Hebrew letter Tzaddi. The Moon. The elements, the visible world, reflected light, material forms, symbolism.

Christian (1870): Arcanum XVIII. Twilight: Deceptions. In the divine world, the abuses of the Infinite; in the intellectual world, the darkness that cloaks the Spirit when it submits itself to the power of the instincts; in the physical world, deceptions and hidden enemies.

Mathers (1888): The Moon. Twilight, deception, error. REVERSED: Slight deceptions, trifling mistakes.

Golden Dawn (1888-96): Ruler of Flux and Reflux, Child of the Sons of the Mighty. Moon. Dissatisfaction, voluntary change (as opposed to XIII, Death). REVERSED: Error, lying, falsity, deception.

Grand Orient (Waite, 1889, 1909): Moon. Half-light, mutation, intellectual uncertainty, region of illusion; false-seeming.

Waite (1910): The Moon. Hidden enemies, danger, calumny, darkness, terror, deception, occult forces, error. REVERSED: Instability, inconstancy, silence, lesser degrees of deception and error.

Pratesi and Court de Gébelin keep it simple—"night" and "Moon." What does that mean? That something will happen at night or when the moon is shining? Or does it mean the qualities of those things, the dark or mysterious, the unknown? Lévi introduces the idea of reflected light, but it is Paul Christian who takes the interpretation in a negative direction. "The abuses of the Infinite" strikes an ominous note. Notice his meaning for the intellectual world: "the darkness that cloaks the Spirit when it submits itself to the power of the instincts." We see again the dualism that has run through so much of occult commentary, the valuing of intellect over instinct. This attitude continues, becoming strongest in Waite, with his "danger...darkness...terror." And yet, it seems to me that the Moon, especially in the Marseille and Waite's own Rider version, shows us a way beyond sharp splits of positive and negative. We see two pillars, like the columns of the High Priestess, the black and white horses/sphinxes of the Chariot, or the chained demons of the Devil. But now the pillars, or towers, have become gray, as if they've lost their power or just their sharp distinctions, and a path winds between them from the waters of the unconscious to the mountains of higher consciousness.

Seen in the context of the final line of the Major Arcana, the Moon, the middle card, represents a kind of test, just as the Emperor and Justice, the cards above it. The line begins with the darkness of the Devil, then the Tower lightning tears it open, and we experience the peacefulness of the Star. Now we must return to the world, and from such a deep interior place. The path travels through the strange half-light of animal instincts, dreams, and myth. The Moon card shows us that journey, one of the most difficult in the Fool's progress.

There are some who would prefer to stay in the inner world of marvels, who might mistake mystical wonder for genuine liberation. Spiritual literature abounds with stories and teachings warning us against this. It is, in fact, one reason why the moon is said to evoke insanity—luna-cy—because if we do not travel through the experiences, back to daily life, we can lose our true selves. Celtic myth tells of mortals who enter the faerie world under the light of the full moon. They stay for what seems a day, but return to find that so many years have passed, everyone they know has died.

In Ovid's *Metamorphoses,* we read of a young man named Actaeon, a hunter who stumbled upon the bathing place of the moon goddess Artemis/Diana. Instead of looking quickly and leaving, he stands and stares until the goddess discovers him. She turns him into a stag so that his own dogs tear him to pieces. The Moon card contains no stags, but most versions do not show any humans either. Where people might stand—structurally, it resembles such pictures as the Lovers, the Devil, and Judgement—we see a dog and a wolf, with a crab or crayfish between them.

A Zen proverb puts it this way: What does one do before enlightenment? Chop wood and carry water. What does one do after enlightenment? Chop wood and carry water.

As Lévi noted, the moon does not shine on its own but reflects the sun. Thus we can see it as half-truth. The Golden Dawn relates it to the Hebrew letter Koof (also spelled Qoph), which can refer to the back of the head, whereas the letter for the Sun, Resh, refers to the front of the head, the cerebral cortex, the part of the brain that governs rational thought. The back contains the brain stem, the oldest part of the brain, that we share with lizards and dinosaurs.

But this is theory. Consider the effect the moon can have. While statisticians insist that emergency rooms and police stations do not really see extra activity during a full moon, cops and nurses will tell you they do. A nurse once told me that it was not so much *more* cases as really strange cases.

Do dogs and wolves actually howl at the moon? I don't know, I've never encountered it, though I live in the country with a dog (no wolves in Rhinebeck), but others tell me they have. Have you ever felt a strange sensation, a kind of primal, undefined fear, usually at night? This is lunar, whatever phase the actual moon might be in. And when you wake up from a dream with a weird energy in your body so that you lie there with your mouth open, that too is the moon. But so is the inexplicable thrill we get when we hear a myth or a fairy tale that we cannot reduce to a simple allegory. "The myth is the penultimate truth" wrote Ananda Coomaraswamy, and while some attempt to get to the *ultimate* as soon as possible, others may choose to enjoy the passage through myth. Here is a great secret—we ourselves are myth, we ourselves are stories. Not light imprisoned in gross, dense bodies, but light shaped into stories. A Hasidic proverb runs, "Why did God make humans? Because God loves stories." And this, from contemporary essayist Callan Williams: "From the moment we are born, our bodies begin to die and our stories begin to grow."

As well as its connection to the letter Koof, the moon is a "planet," and therefore goes with a sephirah on the Tree of Life—in this case nine, called Yesod, or Foundation. Non-Tarot Kabbalists also identify this sephirah with the moon, myth, and dreams.

In the Golden Dawn version of the tree, three lines run from the bottom sephirah called Malkuth, where we find the everyday world of the senses. This gives us three ways to enter the higher levels, through Yesod, but also through Hod on the left, dedicated to Mercury and therefore mind, or Netzach on the right, dedicated to Venus, planet of love, emotion, and sensuality. However, in the most famous pre-Golden Dawn tree, the version of Isaac Luria, only one path connects everyday Malkuth to the rest of the tree, and that is Yesod.

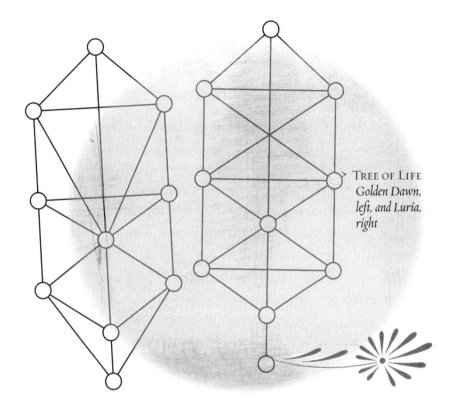

In this older image, if we wish to go beyond the material to "higher" truths, we must travel through the lunar realm of myth and dream and intuition. This is the gateway. It also means that all those higher truths come down to us filtered through the moon's half-light.

The resurgence of Goddess spirituality in the 1970s has greatly changed how modern Tarotists view the moon. Women's special connection to the moon comes from one of the most striking facts of our existence, that the human menstrual cycle lasts the same length of time as the lunar month. Many women will ovulate on the full moon—the Mother part of the Triple Goddess—and bleed on the new, the time of the Maiden. In isolated communities, most if not all the non-pregnant women will follow this pattern together. As we saw in the High Priestess, we can look at this link as an interesting coincidence or we can see it as the most powerful demonstration of "As above, so below."

Many polytheistic cultures have identified the moon as female and the sun as male. We think of men as being solar—forceful, direct, sometimes overpowering, and women as lunar—

subtle and changeable. If we make this a rule, and expect all humans to follow these patterns, we fall into crude dualism. The Moon challenges us to go beyond these limitations, to pass through the gateway of the two towers. Nevertheless, the revival of the divine feminine has allowed us to celebrate and explore moon qualities long considered negative or disturbing.

An interesting detail: one of the rare cultures to see the moon as male was Egypt, and one of the gods who represented the moon was none other than Thoth, supposed creator of the Tarot itself and teacher of the doctrine "As above, so below."

The Pagan movement and the revival of shaman traditions have allowed us to appreciate another aspect of the Moon card, the arousal of animal instincts. Western tradition has taught us that humans are halfway between the angels and the beasts, and we must try to suppress the beast and raise up the angel. Why should we split ourselves this way, why try to detach from our bodies—as if anyone could do such a thing?

The Marseille version shows "moondrops" of colored light in the sky. In the Rider, these take on the shape of the Yods, the tenth letter of the Hebrew alphabet and first letter of the divine name YHVH (see also the Wheel of Fortune and the Minor Arcana). The Yods symbolize the soothing of the troubled spirit, as if the Moon first arouses deep reactions in us, then calms us, so long as we accept what is happening and do not try to fight or deny it.

In most decks, beginning with the Marseille, the animals look up at the moon. In the Golden Dawn, the one on our left turns to the waters and the crayfish. The crayfish, a kind of freshwater lobster, symbolizes sensations, fears, instincts from those oldest parts of the brain, before even the evolution of mammals—to use Waite's great phrase, "that which lies deeper than the savage beast." In most versions, the crayfish has only half emerged, like a primal fear that creeps up in us but never becomes fully conscious, for it does not belong to the conscious brain.

Some decks leave out the animals but include the crayfish. The Visconti, the earliest version, shows none of these things but instead gives us the moon goddess Artemis/Diana. My own Shining Tribe version emphasizes the heavens—the crescent moon as Artemis's bow, stars as the string, and lightning as the arrow—set against a triple mountain formation that represents the Winged Goddess. A few decks change the crayfish to a crab, the animal of the lunar sign of Cancer. A crab is not a freshwater creature, and so most decks keep the crayfish, as if to emphasize that these deep sensations do not come from some vast, all-encompassing source but from intimate parts of ourselves.

The pool of water reminds us that the moon governs the tides (an effect of gravity). The tides rising and falling, along with the moon's change from new to waxing to full to waning to dark, tells us that the Moon card symbolizes cycles.

And when the Moon comes up in readings? I have seen cases where it meant literal lunacy, madness. But these were situations where insanity was an issue and where the querent need-ed to look seriously at that question. On a lesser scale of lunacy, the Moon might indicate a difficult passage in someone's life, when powerful emotions or fears get stirred up.

Traditional meanings also include half-truths and deceptions, and we should not overlook this possibility, especially where other cards support it. More positively, we can see the Moon as dreams, intuition, and psychic development. It also means subtlety and sensitivity. We should call on these qualities in any reading, but especially when the Moon appears.

The Moon card can indicate situations that are cyclical or repetitive. The other cards, as well as the querent's situation, can indicate where in the cycle the person finds her- or him-self. More simply, right-side up could mean waxing or advancing, while reversed suggests a waning situation.

In a health reading for a woman, the Moon might hint at issues around menstrual cycles or reproductive organs. Health readings are always tricky, and we should approach them with caution.

Reversed, the Moon can indicate that idea of something waning or on the way out. For people given to mood swings, it might mean depression or simply a time to be quiet, with-drawn. This becomes stronger when the Moon appears with the Hermit or the High Priest-ess, both connected to the moon. The High Priestess often wears a lunar headdress, while the Moon's number, 18, reduces to 9, the Hermit (1+8=9). The Golden Dawn's astrological correspondence for the High Priestess is, in fact, the moon.

Sometimes, the reversed card strengthens its more problematic aspects, such as disturb-ing dreams, difficulty accepting emotions, or psychic abilities out of control. But the reversed Moon also can indicate a lunar time coming to an end. How can we know the difference? The other cards, along with intuition, should help us. If we see the upside-down Moon and then such cards as the Sun or the Ace of Wands, we can say that a lunar phase is ending.

A Moon Reading

1. What lies in the deep?

2. What stirs it awake?

3. What will it reveal?

4. What will be the effect?

5. How can we use this energy?

6. What will calm it?

7. What light does the Moon reflect?

Bonus: The moon appears in more songs than any other heavenly body. Try doing this reading while playing "Moon River" or "The Old Devil Moon."

LE SOLEIL   IL SOLE

THE SUN
EL SOL   XIX   DIE SONNE
                             DE ZON

Sun: 19

Astrological correspondence: Sun

Kabbalistic letter: ר Resh

Path on Tree of Life: Hod
(Glory) to Yesod
(Foundation)

Sun cards from
VISCONTI,
MARSEILLE,
RIDER, GOLDEN
DAWN RITUAL,
EGYPTIAN &
SHINING TRIBE

XIX

THE SUN .

The Sun

IN THE STORY of Rapunzel, after her tears have healed the prince's eyes (see the Star card), he beholds an amazing sight. They have children! A boy and a girl stand together, conceived in the tower and born in the wilderness, in exile. Tarotists used to the Rider version of the Sun, which shows a single child riding on a horse, may not realize that the prince's discovery forms the classic image of the Marseille Sun card.

According to Paul Huson, Waite took his cue from a number of seventeenth- and eighteenth-century Tarots "of the Belgian pattern." Or possibly it was Lévi's description of this card as "a naked child mounted on a white horse and displaying a scarlet standard." For Waite, the horse represented

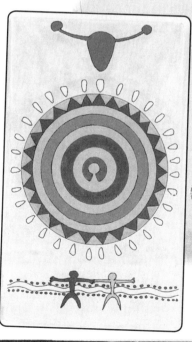

225

the animal side of our nature "in complete harmony" with spirit. The image of riding away from a stone wall also gives a feeling of liberation, a theme we often find in the Rider deck.

So why, then, should we look to the older, the Marseille, image? I would say the answer lies in going past dualism. Throughout the previous cards, we have seen images of separation, of masculine and feminine, light and dark. It starts in the High Priestess, or even earlier if we think of the Fool's innocent androgyny separated into the male and female of the Magician and the High Priestess. In the Devil, the separation seems to reach its limit and become a chain of limitations. The Tower blasts this open, and the waters of liberation pour forth in the Star. We need to make our way back to our daily lives, traveling through the shadow duality of the Moon's towers, and the dog and wolf, until we reach the Sun of clear consciousness.

Then why not the single, joyous child? Because that image jumps ahead to Judgement and the World. Here is how I see it: in the Sun, we see a boy and girl holding hands. They symbolize the two principles that have stayed apart through the previous cards. In the Marseille Sun, the two come together, and we see young figures, renewed. Then, in Judgement, the two have matured, and we see a baby between them. It stands with its back to us, for it represents something new and unknown, even to itself. Finally, in the World card, a single figure, often described as hermaphroditic, faces us as she dances in space. For the Sun to show a baby riding towards us seems to me to confuse the symbolism.

In the Shining Tribe Sun card, we see abstract figures, one light, one dark, joined at the bottom of the card. The same two had appeared at the bottom of the Magician, far apart. The dotted path between them symbolizes the road of consciousness the Fool travels to bring together the two principles.

I make no claim for absolute truth in this description of the final cards. We Tarotists too often allow a special insight to seduce us into believing we've found the clue to complete understanding, not just of Tarot but of "life, the universe, and everything" (to quote Douglas Adams' satire on the quest for ultimate truth).

One problem with my schematic structure is that not all Marseille or other early versions show a boy and a girl. Some show two boys. In the version here, they are androgynous, making it hard to say. However, they do symbolize the joining of opposites, for the one on the right wears a red cloth, the one on the left a blue. The rays of the sun itself alternate between blue, red, and yellow. In occult tradition, yellow is the color of the mind as well, of course, as the color of the sun itself.

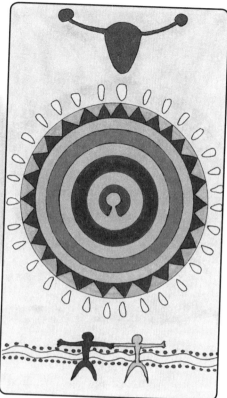

Alexandra Genetti, in her Wheel of Change Tarot, identifies the children as Castor and Pollux, Greek twin sons of Leda and the Swan and thus brothers of Helen of Troy. Castor and Pollux form the sign of Gemini, usually linked to the Lovers card. For Genetti, they represent the birth of both the solar child and his shadow on the winter solstice. For the first half of the year, the light grows, the bright child reigns, only to be sacrificed as the Hanged Man on the summer solstice. For the next half-year, as the days grow shorter and shorter, the dark child, the Devil, takes over, until the winter solstice when the twins once more are reborn. Genetti bases her interpretation on the Pagan imagery of the Wheel of the Year, and it involves a re-ordering of the number of the cards. Re-ordering is certainly no obstacle. We don't even know the original pre-Marseille sequence, and the Golden Dawn famously switched the numbers of Strength and Justice.

Let's look at the older interpretations.

Some Sun Meanings

Excerpted from *Mystical Origins of the Tarot* by Paul Huson.

Pratesi's Cartomancer (1750): Day.

De Mellet (1781): The Sun. The Creation of the Sun and the union of man and woman.

Court de Gébelin (1773-82): The Sun.

Lévi (1855): The Hebrew letter Kaph. A radiant Sun: composites, the head, apex, prince of heaven.

Christian (1870): Arcanum XIX. The Blazing Light: earthly happiness. In the divine world, the supreme Heaven; in the intellectual world, sacred Truth; in the physical world, peaceful Happiness.

Mathers (1888): The Sun. Happiness, contentment, joy. REVERSED: These in minor degree.

Golden Dawn (1888-96): Lord of the Fire of the World. Sun. Glory, gain, riches, sometimes also arrogance. REVERSED OR WHEN WITH EVIL CARDS: Display, vanity.

Grand Orient (Waite, 1889, 1909): Sun. Full light, intellectual and material, earthly happiness, but not attained individually.

Waite (1910): The Sun. Material happiness, fortunate marriage, contentment. REVERSED: The same in a lesser sense.

Pratesi says "day" to match the Moon's "night," and as with the previous card, we can ask what the single word means in a reading. De Mellet says man and woman united, but others do not seem to follow this. Lévi says "prince of heaven," an idea we will look at in a moment, but this too does not seem to have inspired others. Instead, the meanings veer toward the simple interpretation of happiness: contentment, riches, and a good marriage.

When the sun shines, the world is happy. Doesn't that make sense? Don't you feel better when the sun is out? In desert countries, the sun can bring drought, even death. But in northern climates, the sun means summer, flourishing crops, pleasure.

And clarity. Though the list does not show this concept, it has become part of the Sun's modern meanings and something else we know from our lives. "Shine a light on it," we say, and "It'll all be clear in the morning." What seems strange in the dim, reflected light of the Moon becomes simple and direct in the Sun. In the Golden Dawn system, the Hebrew letter for this card, Resh, means "head," and tradition considers it the *front* of the head, seat of the cerebral cortex, whose function is reason.

The Greeks linked the sun to Apollo, god of reason, balance, civilization. Apollo played the lyre, instrument of calm and mathematical proportions, compared to the wild pipes of Pan (for more on these instruments, see the Magician and the Devil). Nietzsche coined the term "Apollonian" for philosophy or art that is measured and rational, compared to the abandon of Dionysus. But if we rely too much on this view of Apollo, we may miss subtler aspects of the Sun card. Apollo was the god of poetry and prophecy, and through his son Aesclepius, the god of shamanic dream healing.

The many cultures that identify the moon as female usually see the sun as male. The Greeks made them sister and brother, Artemis and Apollo. The later Christians did away with the idea of a moon goddess but associated the sun with Christ, the prince of heaven, as compared to Satan, who was "prince of this world." This seems to go back to dualism: the heavens belong to God, the physical world to Satan. The sun shines both above and below.

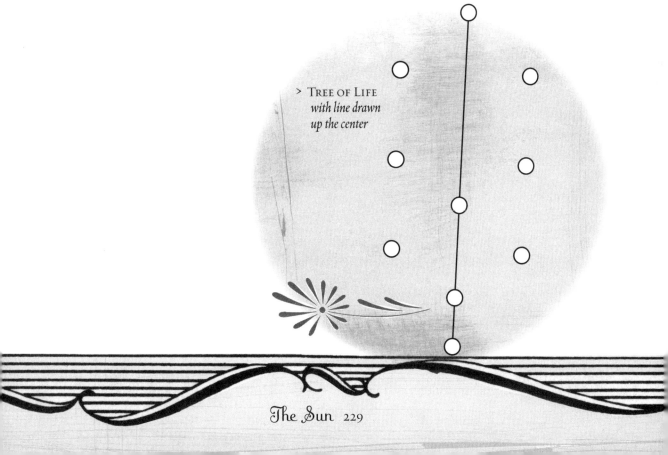

> TREE OF LIFE
*with line drawn
up the center*

The Golden Dawn placed the Sun at the center of the Tree of Life, in the sephirah of Tipheret, or Beauty. They associated the Sun with dying and resurrecting gods who are often seen as figures of great beauty, like the Norse god Balder or Aphrodite's lover Adonis.

The central column of the tree forms a direct line from ordinary life in Malkuth at the bottom to the perfect awareness of Kether at the top. Like the third row of the Major Arcana, this path is simple in its core. From the physical world of Malkuth, we go to the myth and dream world of the Moon in Yesod, and then go to the Sun in Tipheret. From that light, we take the longest journey of the tree, directly up the middle to Kether.

The Sun's number gives us another image of simplicity: 19 reduces to 10 (1+9), the Wheel of Fortune, but 10 then further reduces to 1, the Magician. It all goes back to the basics. The Sun shines on the turning wheel of our lives, but within these events lies magic. The Sun is the first of three cards (four, if we count the Fool as card 22) that relate numerologically to two other cards, but only the Sun does so directly. That is, Judgement, card 20, reduces to 2, the High Priestess, and so does Justice, card 11. Both 21 and 12 reduce to 3. But 20 and 11 have no direct connection, and neither do 21 and 12; 19 directly goes to 10 and then 1.

The fifth triad consists of the Hierophant, the Hanged Man, and the Sun. On the first level, we need teachings and tradition to guide us. Here in the third level, we experience direct light and beauty, like joyous children. In between comes the Hanged Man's surrender and reversal. In the Rider, the halo around the Hanged Man's face shines into the card below it—or we might say that the Sun's light shines up into the Hanged Man's face.

In readings, the Sun card brings happiness. It shows a joyous time, a moment that is simple and fulfilling. Simplicity is one of its hallmarks, and while the traditional meanings include prosperity, it is not so much great riches as enjoying life without worry.

In health readings, it specifies general good health. If a person has been sick or in danger, the Sun indicates recovery and happiness. And on a very literal level, the Sun is the card you want if you are about to go on vacation or do something outdoors.

The Sun also can mean clarity, especially when something has been confused. If some truth has been concealed or lies have been told, the Sun can mean that hidden matters come to light.

In Tarot symbolism, lunar means inward, reflective, and quiet, while solar means outward, bright, and exuberant. If both cards appear (or others that relate to them, such as the Hermit or High Priestess for the Moon, and the Magician or the Four of Wands for the Sun), look to see if the cards indicate a shift from one energy to the other.

When the Sun comes up reversed, I think of Waite's expression, "the same in a lesser degree." It's as if the Sun carries such a positive energy, it does not turn around or negate itself just because the card turns upside down. "Lesser degree" makes me think of clouds obscuring the sun—the light still shines and warms us, but it is not as bright. Happiness becomes mixed with some sadness, or some idea or issue is not as clear.

If the Sun reversed appears with the Moon right-side up, the person shifts from a solar to a lunar state.

A Sun Reading

1. What is clear in my life (or a specific issue, such as relationship or work)?

2. What is cloudy?

3. What helps me see clearly?

4. What confuses me?

5. How can I simplify my life (situation)?

Judgement: 20

Astrological correspondence:
   Pluto

Kabbalistic letter: שׁ Shin

Path on Tree of Life: Hod
   (Glory) to Malkuth
   (Kingdom)

*Judgement cards
   from* VISCONTI,
MARSEILLE,
RIDER, GOLDEN
DAWN RITUAL,
EGYPTIAN &
SHINING TRIBE

JUDGEMENT

Judgement

I HAVE ALWAYS liked this card, always been delighted when it appears in a reading. I see it as great and positive change, a new start. In the past few years, however, I've discovered that many people look at it quite differently. They see the word and assume that someone, usually themselves, will be judged, usually harshly. Add to this the scene of an angel blowing a horn and the dead rising up, and some may remember fearsome sermons about the fires of Hell.

We can understand why people might react this way. The picture in fact bears that title because it comes from the Christian myth of what will happen at the end of the world. The angel will summon us, and we will rise physically from our graves

to receive God's judgment. Artists have done this scene as a triptych: the central panel will show the risen dead, the left a small, joyous group marching up a flowery path to Heaven, while on the right a larger group, arms across their faces in fear or shame, walk toward a fiery cave—the entrance to Hell, where demons wait with pitchforks. Strong stuff.

But now look at the Tarot picture, whether the Visconti (for once, similar to later versions), the Marseille, the Rider, and so on. Nobody is being judged. No one is being sent anywhere. The dead rise up in celebration. In his extended description of this card, Waite writes, "all the figures are as one in...wonder, adoration, and ecstasy." And, "Let the card continue to depict, for those who can see no further, the Last Judgment and the resurrection in the natural body; but let those who have inward eyes look and discover."

In the Shining Tribe, to make clear that no judging takes place, I titled the card Awakening. Waite's design added a second set of people in the background, a change criticized by Paul Foster Case, who considered the primary man, woman, and child sufficient for the symbolism. To me, this change suggests that the shift in awareness does not affect only the person but others as well. I made this point in my version by setting the scene in a modern city. And here's a bit of Tarot art magic: I drew the picture freehand, and afterwards, when I counted some of the details, I discovered twenty-two windows in the building and twenty-two rays of light around the Spirit's head.

The idea of waking up, as if we live in a dream, has fascinated esotericism for a long time. The Taoist master Chuang Tzu famously dreamed of a butterfly dreaming he was a man and wondered which might be the reality. In modern times, Gurdjieff made waking up one of his primary teachings. If we truly wake up, will the world fall away and a wholly different reality emerge, as when we awake from a dream? Maybe so. In my book *Forest of Souls,* I suggested that Einstein's special theory of relativity describes light as the true reality, with such seeming absolutes as physical dimensions and time really being just relative to light.

And maybe the card addresses a waking up of consciousness. We believe that we act deliberately in our lives, but so often we do things for unconscious reasons or just habit, like robots or sleepwalkers. When we awaken, we fully claim our free will.

Something I've always loved about Judgement is a sense that great change has already happened in a person (or a situation)—that the angel does not summon us so much as make us aware. Waite again: "What is that within us which does sound a trumpet and all that is lower in our nature rises in response?" More than any other card, Judgement does not just recommend a change, it indicates that things have already shifted, and the person needs to recognize this.

What do the historical commentators say?

Some Judgement Meanings

Excerpted from *Mystical Origins of the Tarot* by Paul Huson.

Pratesi's Cartomancer (1750): Angel, wedding, and settlement.

De Mellet (1781): The Angel. The creation of man. Men and women formed from the earth, summoned by Osiris.

Court de Gébelin (1773-82): Creation, or the Last Judgment.

Lévi (1855): The Hebrew letter Resh. The Judgment. Vegetative principle, generative virtue of the earth, eternal life.

Christian (1870): Arcanum XX. The Awakening of the Dead: Renewal. Represents the passage from life on earth to the life of the future. The sign of the change that is the end of all things, of Good as well as of Evil.

Mathers (1888): The Last Judgment. Renewal, result, determination of a matter. REVERSED: Postponement of result, delay, matter reopened later.

Golden Dawn (1888-96): The Spirit of the Primal Fire. Judgment. Final decision. Sentence. REVERSED: Determination of matter without appeal on its plane.

Grand Orient (Waite, 1889, 1909): The Last Judgment. Resurrection, summons to new things, a change in the face of everything.

Waite (1910): The Last Judgment. Change of position, renewal, outcome. Another account specifies total loss through a lawsuit. REVERSED: Weakness, cowardice, simplicity; also deliberation, decision, sentence.

As we've seen before, Waite's meanings do not reflect his spiritual views, though he writes more seriously as "Grand Orient." De Mellet continues his creation story and adds that Osiris—who presides over resurrection—summons the man and woman created from the earth, a nice mix of Hebrew and Egyptian myth. Once again, Paul Christian introduces the themes that will later become central—awakening, renewal. Good will end as well as Evil, for instead of judging us on the basis of human moral codes, card twenty takes us beyond dualism.

Mathers and the Golden Dawn give fortune-telling meanings such as "determination of a matter." The Golden Dawn picture, however, emphasizes that the postures of the three people form the letter Shin that goes with the card:

With its three upward prongs like flames, the Shin represents the element of fire, just as the Aleph (Fool) is Air and Mem (Hanged Man) is water. The Hebrew word for Heaven, *sh/mayim*, consists of the word for "water," *mayim*, with a Shin added. Fire and water joined together = divine consciousness.

Consider the connection between Judgement and Justice. The earlier card tells us to look at the truth of who we are, to balance the scales of our lives. In this joyous later card, we learn that our existence goes beyond balance, beyond what economists call a zero-sum game—if someone wins, someone else must lose—to a dynamic belief in liberation, and more, that all existence is something to embrace.

Here is a slightly different view. As mentioned above, a student in one of my classes said that in Judgement we answer the final question of Justice, and only when we can do that will we rise up from whatever has held us back. The numbers of Justice and Judgement bind them as much as their names: 11 and 20 both reduce to 2, the High Priestess. Part of her secret knowledge rests in the connection of the two higher cards.

Judgement comes below Death in the sixth triad: Love, Death, and Resurrection.

We love and we die. This is the truth of our lives. If we cannot accept death, we may not allow ourselves to love. But the Tarot tells us that love and death are not the whole truth. We can open our eyes to eternity—and maybe our ears, for "that which sounds within us" indicates a listening to some inner music that only we can hear.

The standard image shows a man, woman, and child. In the Rider Tower, we saw how the man and woman switched sides from where they were on the Lovers and the Devil. Polarity turned inside out. Here we can recognize the fundamental trinity of Mother, Father, Child. In most decks, we see the child only from the back. He/she represents a new thing that emerges from the old dualism. In the system of Éliphas Lévi, the Fool comes between Judgement and the World. I like to think of it as going in both places, before all the others and just before

LES AMANTS — GLI AMANTI

THE LOVERS — DIE LIEBENDEN
EL ENAMORADO — DE GELIEFDEN
VI

LA MORT — LA MORTE

DEATH — DER TOD
LA MUERTE — DE DOOD
XIII

> MARSEILLE
Lovers,
Death
&
Judgement

LE JUGEMENT — IL GIUDIZIO

JUDGEMENT — GERICHT
EL JUICIO — HET OORDEEL
XX

the end. Maybe the child shows us the rebirth of the Fool as the child of the Magician and the High Priestess.

Aleister Crowley renamed this card Aeon, taking it beyond the personal to the concept of a New Age. An aeon (or eon) is a precise measurement of time, 2,160 years, one-twelfth of the Great Year that runs 25,920 years.

What does this mean for the Tarot? The cards are not just about our own lives and events but are a mirror of the world. Astrology is a part of that mirror. The zodiac rotates, and the zodiac contains twelve signs. The quality of an age, or aeon, comes from the sign that the sun enters on the spring equinox, the moment when light and dark are balanced, like the scales of Justice, with a movement from greater darkness to greater light. Around the time of Jesus, the sun entered Pisces on the equinox, a shift from Aries and, before that, Taurus. So, the world has seen an age marked by earthly Taurus, then fiery Aries, then watery Pisces, and now we come to a new time with the quality of Aquarius, an Air sign. For Crowley, the Piscean Aeon was the time of sacrificed gods, of suffering and resurrection. The New Age, which he saw as dedicated to Horus, son of Isis and Osiris, will show us greater cooperation, harmony, and inventiveness.

Look again at that sequence of light in the final cards of the Major Arcana:

Darkness	Lightning	Starlight	Moonlight	Sunlight	Light of Spirit
Devil	Tower	Star	Moon	Sun	Judgement

And the final card, the World? We can call that the Light of the Self.

In readings, card twenty indicates a fresh start. I do not recall seeing any reworkings of this card that emphasize anyone, human or divine, judging anyone else. Instead, we see various forms of rising up. With this card, I often think that at some level, usually within a person but sometimes in outer circumstances, change has already happened, and the challenge is to acknowledge it. A person who has stayed a long time in a job she hates realizes that she has already committed herself emotionally to quitting, no matter what will happen. A blocked writer goes back to an unfinished novel and knows that something has called him to it. An alcoholic buys a bottle of whiskey, looks at it, and throws it away.

All these examples involve liberation. We also might see Judgement when a couple revive their marriage, or someone disillusioned with spiritual experience rediscovers hope or the power of belief. What matters most is the sense of dynamic change.

Judgement reversed suggests denial, fear, or doubt. We still hear that trumpet call within us, summoning us to embrace a new existence, but we don't trust it. Perhaps we simply do not know how to recognize what has happened or do not know what to do next. Or we do not want to hurt someone's feelings or embarrass ourselves. I knew a woman who realized just before her wedding that she did not love her fiancé and did not want to marry him. But she could not bear the humiliation of canceling the wedding, telling people not to come, disappointing the man or her parents. So she married him and suffered for many years. Sometimes Judgement reversed can warn us of getting stuck in something because we fail to hear "that which sounds within us," telling us to move on.

A Judgement/Awakening Reading

1. What is the hidden question of Justice?

2. How can I answer it?

3. What calls me to rise up/become something new?

4. What can I become?

5. How can my life change?

6. What/who will change around me?

7. How am I called to answer?

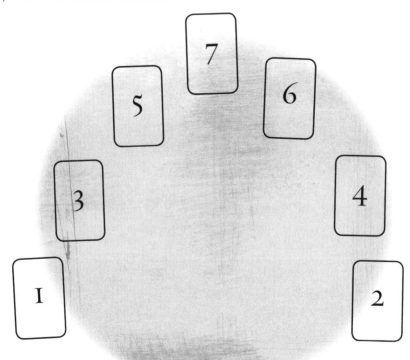

A Judgement/Awakening Wisdom Reading

1. Who is the angel?

2. What truth does it reveal?

World: 21

Astrological correspondence: Saturn

Kabbalistic letter: ת Tav

Path on Tree of Life: Yesod (Foundation) to Malkuth (Kingdom)

World cards from VISCONTI, MARSEILLE, RIDER, GOLDEN DAWN RITUAL, EGYPTIAN & SHINING TRIBE

THE UNIVERSE

The World

WHAT A WONDERFUL image! A joyous dancer, free, graceful in the cosmos. This image of fulfillment appears in several cultures. The Hindu god Shiva sometimes is seen that way, and so is the goddess Kali. Kabbalists have pictured creation as originally a single perfect man named Adam Kadmon, not shown on one leg but still pictured with arms out to the sides.

Years ago, I visited the Church of the Holy Sepulcher in Jerusalem, built on the spot where tradition says Christ rose from the dead. A small shrine stood inside, with a low doorway to enter. Above

the door hung a picture of Christ, and except that it was a man instead of a woman, it was the same picture as the World dancer, complete with sash around the groin and winding into the sky.

Some Tarot historians cite this iconographic image as the actual source of the World, saying that originally the card showed Christ. What now appears as a wreath in modern decks was a mandorla, an almond-shaped figure formed by the intersection of two circles.

The circles symbolize the intersection of Heaven and Earth, while the mandorla between them represents the womb of Mary.

If, in fact, the World originated as an image of Christ's resurrection, how did it appear on a playing card? And how did it change gender? The World card seems to me one of the challenges to the view that Tarot originated just as a game, for it seems a game of spiritual meaning. As for the second question, one theory claims that crude printing made an originally masculine figure appear to have small breasts, and so later printers assumed it was female. Does this mean they would not have recognized a standard image of the Christian God? Maybe. Human error has produced powerful symbols before. In a sense, the whole brilliant tradition of occult Tarot begins with the mistaken belief that the cards come from ancient Egypt.

For our purposes, the exact origin doesn't matter. Anyone who has read any significant portion of this book will understand that I do not consider the Tarot bound by its historical origins or the intentions of the original designers. We also might notice that the oldest version, the Visconti, looks nothing like the image we know from the Marseille. I once came across the idea that the Tarot de Marseille is in fact the true Tarot, and any earlier decks, including the Visconti, are precursors. I can see this point, but why stop at the Marseille? Why not describe the "true" Tarot as the Rider, or the Thoth, or the Shining Tribe, or any other modern deck? Maybe the title of this final trump card, the World, can remind us that Tarot really consists of the totality of all the decks and all the interpretations. The only "genuine" Tarot would have to include the entire world, would become the world.

With the Magician, we saw how an early historical meaning became turned around in the occult approach, yet both are meaningful. With the World, we see different interpretations just within the esoteric tradition. The Golden Dawn placed the card on the final pathway of the tree, from Yesod down to Malkuth, from the lunar realm to the earthly. This places the card at the lowest point, furthest from the spiritual.

Clearly, I disagree with this. To me, the World represents the culmination, full consciousness unlimited by dualism or ignorance. I prefer the view of Éliphas Lévi, who sees it not as the lowest *path* but the highest *sephirah*, Kether, the sephirah of pure light that contains all existence.

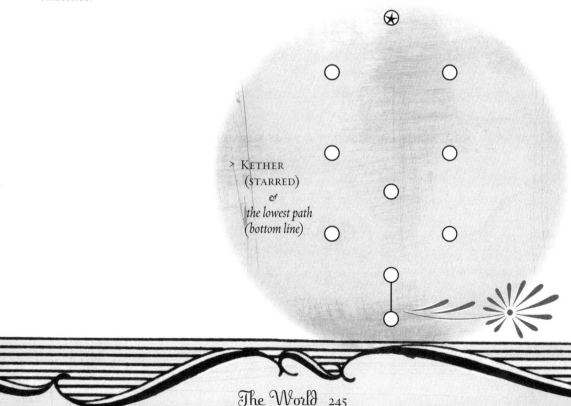

> KETHER
(STARRED)
&
*the lowest path
(bottom line)*

Astrologically, the Golden Dawn attributes Saturn to the World card. Saturn is the far-thest planet visible without a telescope. Just in the order of things, it makes sense that the last card should get the last planet (Uranus, Neptune, and Pluto were not included in the original Golden Dawn system, but they are included in a later revision). Saturn means limitations, mortality. We saw how the Hermit card probably derived from the image of Saturn as an old man holding an hourglass. People who work with this system see the dancer as an image of overcoming limitations, the way an actual dancer uses discipline to seemingly liberate the body from gravity (my thanks to Laura Triana for this image).

To me, the World card doesn't just overcome limits, it transcends them to show us a vision of fully realized existence. What would I do with it astrologically? Perhaps the cosmos rather than any single part of it. But that would mean reordering at least part of the structure, some-thing I will not try to do here. In the Shining Tribe version of the World, I tried to convey that sense of a cosmic figure. Her face radiates circles of energy, and her body contains images of myths, animals, and sacred human constructions. Instead of four animals in the corners, we see waves of color, a suggestion of mysteries beyond creation.

What do the historical commentators say about this card?

Some World Meanings

Excerpted from *Mystical Origins of the Tarot* by Paul Huson.

Pratesi's Cartomancer (1750): Long journey.

De Mellet (1781): The World. The universe, represented by Isis and the four seasons.

Court de Gébelin (1773-82): Time, or the World.

Lévi (1855): The Hebrew letter Tau. Kether or the kabbalistic Crown: in the middle of the Crown is Truth holding a rod in each hand. The microcosm, the sum of it all.

Christian (1870): Arcanum XXI. The Crown of the Magi: the Reward. This, the supreme Arcanum of Magism, is represented by a garland of golden roses surrounding a star and placed in a circle around which are set at equal distances the heads of a man, a bull, a lion, and an eagle. This is the sign with which the Magus decorates himself when he has reached the highest degree of initiation and has thus acquired a power limited only by his own intelligence and wisdom.

Mathers (1888): The Universe. Completion, good reward. REVERSED: Evil reward, or recompense.

Golden Dawn (1888-96): The Great One of the Night of Time. Universe. The matter itself. Synthesis. World. Kingdom. Usually denotes the actual subject of the question, and it therefore depends entirely on the accompanying cards.

Grand Orient (Waite, 1889, 1909): The World. The glory thereof under the powers of the highest providence, the sum of manifest things; conclusion on any subject.

Waite (1910): The World. One of the worst explanations concerning it is that the figure symbolizes the Magus when he has reached the highest degree of initiation. [!] Assured success, recompense, voyage, route, emigration, flight, change of place. REVERSED: Inertia, fixity, stagnation, permanence.

After Pratesi's "long journey"—around the world?—we discover that, for once, the mystical meaning of the card runs throughout. De Mellet uses a term Aleister Crowley will later title the card, "the universe," as if to make clear that "world" means everything and not just our own planet. He also links the dancer to Isis, supreme goddess in the Hermetic tradition, and connects the figures in the corners to the seasons (see the Wheel of Fortune for the sources and astrological meanings of the four).

Lévi associates the World with Kether and "the sum of it all," but also the microcosm, the single being who contains the cosmos, Adam Kadmon of the Kabbalists. Paul Christian calls it "the supreme Arcanum" and sees this as the Magus's personal achievement, for to Christian the Major Arcana can be seen as the development of the Magus. With his usual scorn, Waite calls this idea "one of the worst explanations," without explaining why.

Mathers introduces the most common fortune-telling theme, "good reward," or success along with "completion." Under his own name, Waite also writes of success, and in a fascinating unconscious nod to Pratesi's anonymous cartomancer (unknown in Waite's time), he includes travel. As Grand Orient, Waite gives profounder meanings, paraphrasing Lévi with "the sum of manifest things," an idea that is actually much more limited than "*all* things."

We sometimes find a split in the Tarot world between spirituality and readings—another kind of dualism, and one that weakens both sides, for if your "meanings" do not derive from the truth of the symbols, what do they really tell you? And if that truth stays apart from the practice of Tarot, how can we find it in our lives? Much of modern Tarot attempts to heal this split. Such healing, *tikkun olam* to use the Kabbalistic phrase, brings the World to life.

Some people identify the dancer with the alchemical idea of the divine hermaphrodite. If male and female signify the fundamental duality, then a being who embodies both becomes completion. This is a very ancient idea, found, among other sources, in both Greek and Hebrew myth. The word "hermaphrodite" combines Hermes and Aphrodite, Greek models of male and female sexuality but also mind and emotion, sephiroth seven and eight on the Tree of Life.

Plato speaks of human beings as originally two people joined together, sometimes a man and a woman, but also sometimes two men and sometimes two women (it's really the doubleness that matters, not the genders). Because this made humans self-sufficient and therefore independent of the gods, Zeus split them apart, and now each of us searches for the missing half, our "soul mate," to use a current expression.

In Kabbalah, we learn how that original being, Adam Kadmon, was hermaphroditic, and so was God, from the phrase in Genesis "male and female, He created them," in which "male and female" refers to God as well as humans. When this original human ate from the tree of knowledge of good and evil, which is dualism, a split occurred—not just in humanity but in God. Thus the Shekinah, the female aspect of the divine, becomes separated from the King, the male aspect, and goes into exile with humans. As above, so below. To "heal the world," we must become whole beings. We might describe this as the quest of the Fool. Some see the World dancer as the Shekinah herself, but—or *and*—we can see her as the divine female and male reunited.

There is another way to look at the idea of a primordial split in consciousness. A single being cannot fully know itself and so splits into male and female to experience dialog. Similarly, spirit does not "fall" into matter but willingly enters it. In the Rider image, the Fool steps off the cliff to learn about life and pass through all the different steps to the World, with an awareness not known before. (For more on these ideas, see my book *The Forest of Souls*, which includes the result when I asked the cards, "Show me the reading you gave God to create the universe.")

Though the usual image shows a woman, subtle symbolism implies the hermaphrodite. The number 21 combines 2 and 1, the High Priestess and the Magician. In the Marseille and the Rider, the dancer holds the Magician's wand, the male symbol, but two of them, like the female pillars of the High Priestess.

THE HANGED MAN.

THE WORLD.

> RIDER
> *Hanged Man*
> *&*
> *World*

∨ MARSEILLE
Hanged Man
&
World

LE PENDU   L'APPESO

THE HANGED MAN **XII** DER GEHÄNGTE
EL COLGADO   DE GEHANGENE

LE MONDE   IL MONDO

THE WORLD **XXI** DIE WELT
EL MUNDO   DE WERELD

The number 21 is 12 reversed, or upside down. Turn card twelve, the Hanged Man, around, and you get almost the same image as the World.

Both figures contain the Tree of Life on their bodies. For the World, we find Kether, 1, in the face; Hokhmah and Binah, 2 and 3, in the shoulders; Chesed and Geburah, 4 and 5, in the hands; Tipheret, 6, in the center of the body; Netzach and Hod, 7 and 8, in the knee and foot of the horizontal left leg; Yesod, 9, in the right knee; and Malkuth, 10, in the right foot.

What, then, is the difference between the Hanged Man and the World? Where the Hanged Man must turn conventional thinking on its head, the World sees reality clearly. Where the Hanged Man must bind himself to spiritual values, the World dances freely.

And 21, like 12, reduces to 3 (2+1=3). Card three, the Empress, showed us Nature as the Great Mother. The words "mother" and "matter" both come from the Latin *mater*. In the World, we ourselves become a union of spirit and matter, Above and Below.

Put another way—with the Empress, we looked at the perception that the world, with all its billions of creatures, its rivers and mountains, sky and stars, was originally a goddess who in some way was broken apart to form reality. This is not simply a story to explain the variety and complexity of nature. It comes from an unconscious awareness of unity. In the World, we might describe that original being as restored, but in fact the restoration occurs within us, when we can make what was unconscious fully conscious.

The triad of 7, 14, and 21—the Chariot, Temperance, and the World—symbolizes three "victories": the first over the challenges of life, the second over our fears and limitations, especially the fear of death, and finally the victory for everyone that occurs when any person achieves genuine spiritual understanding. In Buddhist tradition, when Gautama became enlightened under the Bodhi tree, all of nature and all the gods celebrated. In the World, self gives way finally to Self, a sense of all existence as a single radiant being.

Do we need to give up such powerful ideas when the card comes up in readings? Certainly, there are very few readings where we would tell the querent, "You will become a cosmic being and restore a broken universe." At the same time, we do not need to reduce the card to "recompense, voyage," the way Waite does. Can we evoke the perfection of the card while addressing subjects such as prosperity and relationships?

I always rejoice when the World card appears in a reading. Whatever the question, it promises a wonderful result. And it may suggest a breakthrough, some powerful understanding that leads to wholeness and freedom. Sometimes, the card can indicate recognition, as in the world taking notice of someone. Mostly, it promises success.

Some people see the World as the completion of a cycle, to begin again with the Fool. Here, too, the card would show satisfaction and a feeling of fulfillment.

Reversed, the World card does not mean disaster or failure but simply stagnation. Happiness or satisfaction becomes delayed. It also can mean a firm structure, as if situations remain the same rather than transform or give way to something new. Not everyone sees this negatively. Years ago, a friend of mine was going through a very unstable time in her life, in just about every area. She liked the World card reversed because it promised stability. She'd found her world turned inside-out enough that she didn't want any more surprises.

A World Reading

This can be done as a Wisdom Reading or a personal reading.

It is based on cards chosen in a random shuffle from the Shining Tribe Tarot. The cards listed below are not the *answers* but the questions. Since the World card theoretically contains all the others, it seemed fitting to shuffle the deck, choose a few cards, and see what questions they suggested.

1. High Priestess
   What is the inner truth?

2. Star
   What hope does it promise?

3. Moon
   What journey must we take?

4. Awakening
   What great thing awakens?

5. Gift of Rivers
   What is the gift?

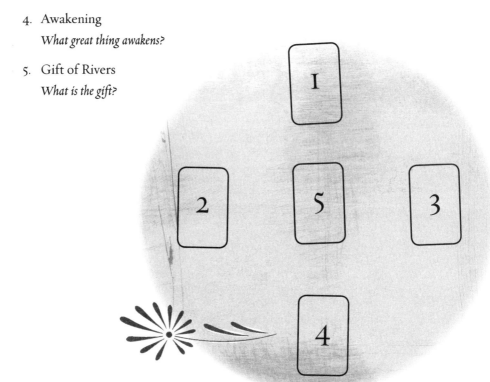

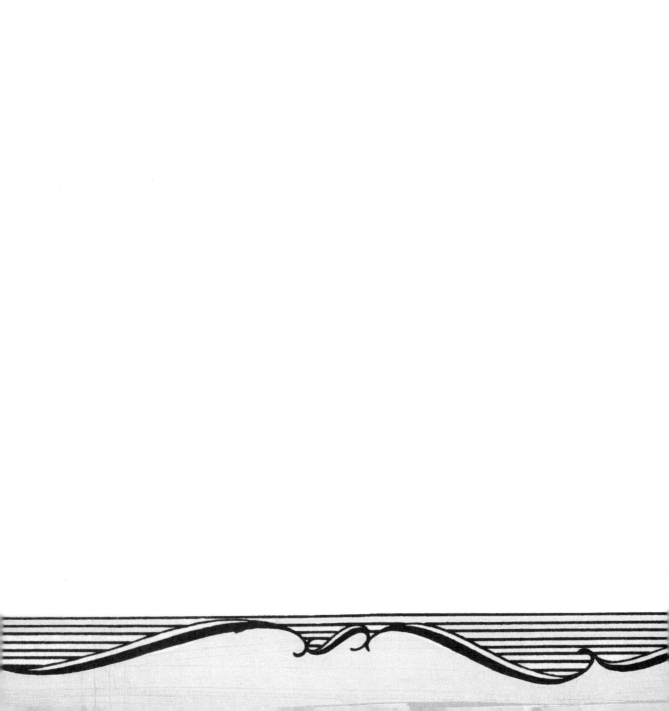

The Minor Arcana

WHERE THE MAJOR Arcana shows us a map of spiritual evolution—what I call "the Fool's progress"—the Minor shows us cycles. Four suits, each with the same structure yet colored by the special quality of the suit. Ten numbers and four court cards. Consider card games. In most games, it doesn't really matter which suit it is—a Four of Clubs is basically the same as a Four of Spades. In Tarot, however, the Four of Wands is quite different from the Four of Swords. They share what we call "fourness," but the suit energy changes them. And the Major and Minor differ in another way. The twenty-two trump cards show us large themes—nature, liberty, light and darkness—and the fifty-six Minor cards give us scenes and characters from our lives.

The Minor cards actually consist of two different sets, the "pips," or numbered cards, ace–ten, and the court cards, page, knight, queen, and king. Most books look at them as a whole, separated by suits—for example, Ace through King of Wands. Lately I find it valuable to look at them separately, for the numbers indicate events and situations, while the courts evoke people—either actual persons, such as the famous "tall dark stranger" of fortunetellers, or character traits.

The qualities of each suit belong to both groups. Just as the Four of Wands combines four-ness with Wands, so the Queen of Wands shows us the qualities of the queen in the confident world of fiery Wands.

The Suits

Before we look at either the numbers or the courts, let's look at what they have in common: the suits. We can look at a whole range of meanings and backgrounds for these four, from history to Kabbalah to modern psychological descriptions. From all of them, we can get a sense of how each suit's specialness weaves in and out of all the others.

First, of course, is the number: four of them. In the section on the Emperor, we looked at this number and its great significance in nature and tradition. Without repeating all the many examples, we can remember the most important point: that it is not an arbitrary choice. We find four in the most basic structures of our lives, from the four points needed to form the most simple solid structure, to our four limbs, to the four directions of before, behind, right, and left, to the four earthly directions caused by Earth rotating on an axis (North and South Poles, sun rising in the east, setting in the west), to the four seasons marked by the solstices and equinoxes. None of these are human inventions.

Let's look at a bit of history. Card historians believe the suits came directly from the Mam-luk playing cards originally brought from North Africa (unlike the Major Arcana, which appear to have been invented in Europe). If you look at early decks, the Swords and Batons (an old name for Wands) look very different than what we see in most contemporary decks.

The Swords are scimitars, double-handled, it seems, while the Wands are, in fact, polo sticks. Polo was an aristocratic game, and its stick appears on a number of Mamluk family crests. The Europeans copied the designs on the early cards with apparently not much concern for what they actually were. The French called the polo sticks Batons, and the English called them Staves. Much later, the Hermetic Order of the Golden Dawn gave them the more magical name of Wands, for the Golden Dawn described the four suit objects as magical "weapons." And over time the complicated game sticks became more like a peasant's club, while the elegant scimitar became the European broadsword. (This is actually an oversimplification, for indeed some early European decks show straight Swords and elegant straight sticks for Wands.)

< MARSEILLE
Six of Wands
(l)
&
Six of Swords
(r)

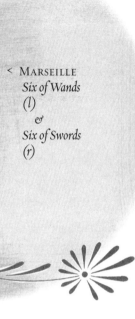

The Cups have always been just that: cups. Pentacles, on the other hand, have gone through a complex transformation. Originally the suit showed disks identified as Coins. Éliphas Lévi suggested changing the name to "Pantacles," by which (according to Paul Huson) he likely meant a magical talisman. Macgregor Mathers changed this to Pentacle, a five-pointed star (called a pentagram) in a circle. This became the name of the suit for the Golden Dawn (though in fact the cards show a cross, not a star, in a disk) and then the Rider deck, and through the Rider to many modern versions. Aleister Crowley called them Disks, while some modern decks, especially in Europe, continue to call them Coins. Hermann Haindl, in his Haindl Tarot, named the suit Stones, an example I followed in my Shining Tribe Tarot. In the Shining Tribe, I actually changed all the emblems from human-made objects to aspects of nature—Trees for Wands, Rivers for Cups, Birds for Swords, and Stones for Pentacles.

One view of the suits describes them as representative of the medieval classes. Wands signify the peasant class, Cups the priesthood (for the chalices used in communion), Swords the aristocracy, and Coins the merchant class. This works well except for the elegant polo sticks that preceded the clublike Wands. Here is a modern version: Wands can represent working people, Cups the arts and social services (including religious figures), Swords the military and police but also law and government, and Pentacles businesspeople and managers.

In the late eighteenth and early twentieth century, people saw mythology in the suits. For some, they suggested the four Grail "hallows," to use the term in Caitlin and John Matthews' Arthurian Tarot. Cups are the Grail itself, the supposed chalice used by Christ to introduce communion at the Last Supper ("This is my blood..."), then used to collect his actual blood when he hung on the cross. The other suits derive from a spear, a sword, and a disk that appear in the Grail stories. However, the Grail stories are not that consistent, some with more objects, some with fewer, and even the Grail itself sometimes appears in early stories as a magical stone, like the philosopher's stone of the alchemists.

Another mythological theory sees the suits as four magical "talismans" of Celtic gods and goddesses—the Spear of Lugh, the Cauldron of Dagda, the Sword of Nuade, and the Stone of Fal. Some see these, in fact, as the original Grail objects that later became Christianized when the Pagan Celts converted. As with so much else in Tarot, this particular cultural tradition fits so nicely, it almost doesn't matter that we know the cards come from a different part of the world. What works, works.

Éliphas Lévi saw biblical origins for the suits. The Wands came from the "flowering rod of Aaron," Moses' brother and high priest. In the story, his wooden staff flowered as a sign that God favored him and his descendants. Lévi identified the Sword with King David and the Coin with the gold shekel of ancient Israel (the weakest connection, it seems to me). The Cup he gave to Joseph (the one from Genesis, not Jesus's human father). In a passage that seems to me of meaning for Tarot readers, a servant says, "This is the cup from which my lord drinks, and which he uses for divination." I sometimes speak of diviners as "the tribe of Joseph."

Biblical figures spoke to Lévi, who after all took on the tribal name of the Hebrew priest-hood—Aaron and his descendants were Levites. The modern Pagan revival, along with the occult interest in the Mysteries, have brought back Greek, Egyptian, and other gods and goddesses into our consciousness. My personal interest (maybe loyalty would be a better word) lies with the Greeks, and here too I think we can find almost perfect matches. Wands belong to Hermes, god of magic, swiftness, and change, and wielder of the caduceus, the ultimate magic wand. Cups, so often seen as the suit of love, give us Aphrodite, goddess of love, beauty, and sensuality. The "element" (see below) for Cups is water, and Aphrodite was born out of the sea. Swords go with Apollo, for this is the suit of mind, and the Greeks saw Apollo as the bringer of civilization and the patron of the arts and healing. But Apollo was also a warrior and conqueror, and so signifies the violent side of Swords. We also might see Swords as Athena, warrior goddess of wisdom and justice (though Swords probably should go with a male figure). Pentacles/Coins, the most earthly and material suit, evokes Gaia, goddess of Earth itself. These are my own associations with Greek gods. You can do something similar with other mythologies.

We also can relate the suits to the first four cards of the Major Arcana. Wands go with the Magician, Cups with the High Priestess, Swords with the Emperor, and Pentacles with the Empress. As with so much else, it does not quite work, for even though both the High Priestess and the suit of Cups belong with the element of water, the Empress embodies the qualities of Cups as much as those of Pentacles.

Gertrude Moakley, a scholar of the Visconti-Sforza Tarot, has identified each suit with one of the cardinal Virtues of the Middle Ages. Wands represent Fortitude, Cups Temperance, Swords Justice, and Pentacles (Coins) Prudence. If these terms sound familiar, we've seen them before—in the Major Arcana cards of Strength, Temperance, Justice, and the Star. If a Virtue "rules" each suit, we can see how the individual cards fulfill or fail that quality. For example, would the Six of Wands show a different side of Fortitude than the Nine? Which one is closer to the Virtue? A Tarotist named Marcia Massino has developed this approach with the Rider deck, though she does not follow Moakley's choices for Cups and Pentacles. She sees Cups as Faith and Pentacles as Charity (giving your money away rather than saving it prudently). She looks at each card as a "triumph," or a "test," of the Virtue. Consider the Six of Pentacles.

At first glance, it may seem the perfect fulfillment of Charity—a man in wealthy clothes giving coins to beggars. But is it really virtuous to have them on their knees? And what of the way he seems to have balanced the scales and gives only a small amount? Massino's approach can be valuable, especially with the Rider or other decks that show action scenes on each card.

△ RIDER
Six of Pentacles

▷ RIDER
Two of Cups
&
Three of Cups

Set out the Swords cards from your deck. Which cards fulfill Justice, and which ones distort or overturn it?

We can create a modern version of the four Virtues by looking at each suit as having a special function. I would say that Wands inspire us to action, Cups serve healing, Swords serve communication and/or conflict, and Pentacles help us understand money and work. Consider the Two and the Three of Cups, again in the Rider.

The Two can help us heal our experiences around romantic relationships, the Three can heal our friendships. This is because both present an ideal image.

Now look at the Seven and Eight of Birds in the Shining Tribe.

< SHINING
TRIBE
Seven of Birds
&
Eight of Birds

The Seven here shows us how to communicate, for we see two figures, each in his own territory, yet they talk—and listen to each other—with great energy. The scene was inspired by the Australian Aborigine practice of tribes meeting each other at a border, and each person literally singing his or her portion of the "songlines," that is, the tribal map, to the person on the other side of the border. The Eight shows an even more basic issue of communication: finding the words and the ideas to express yourself.

By far the most common association with the suits in modern Tarot is the four "elements"—fire, water, air, and earth—first identified by the Greek pre-Socratic philosopher Empedocles. In ancient times, people asked a basic question: What is the world made of? Do all the millions of creatures and rocks and stones and rivers arise out of fundamental qualities? Today we talk of subatomic particles and the ninety-two (natural) elements of the periodic table, but in the past people saw things as outgrowths of the four qualities listed above. Fire and water were primary, with air and earth as more complex levels, almost a second generation. We can see this in their symbols:

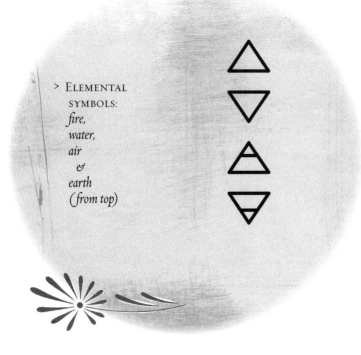

> ELEMENTAL
  SYMBOLS:
  fire,
  water,
  air
  &
  earth
  (from top)

Again we find echoes of the Major Arcana, with the Magician and High Priestess as fundamental principles and the Empress and Emperor as more complex. We also find qualities of male and female—yang and yin, to use the Chinese terms—in the suits, with Wands and Swords as male/yang and Cups and Pentacles as female/yin.

Just as we modernized the four social classes, we can see a new version of the elements. Water, air, and earth become the three common states of matter: liquid, gas, and solid. Fire represents the chemical transformation from one state to another. If we heat ice (the solid form of water), it first melts into water, then boils off into steam (the gaseous form).

While most Tarot people agree on what the elements are, they disagree on which ones go with which suits. As usual, the Golden Dawn forms the standard, which runs as follows: Fire-Wands, Water-Cups, Air-Swords, Earth-Pentacles. Variations include Wands as Air and Swords as Fire (notably in Nigel Jackson's Medieval Enchantment Tarot), or Wands as Earth and Pentacles as Fire, or even Swords as Water and Cups as Air (in the Spanish deck El Grant Tarot Esoterico). Most decks, however, follow the Golden Dawn, and this is the system we will use here.

The Tarot also recognizes a fifth element, called quintessence, or ether. This is the element of spirit, embodied in the Major Arcana. The title "ether" does not refer to the gas used as one of the first anesthetics. Instead, it describes a formless, undetectable substance that supposedly permeates all existence. Ether was thought to be the medium through which light waves traveled through space. An experiment in the late nineteenth century to determine the effects of ether produced the startling result that not only did ether not exist, but light seemed to travel the same speed no matter how you measured it. This led to Einstein's special theory of relativity, which it seems to me could be called one of the great spiritual texts of the twentieth century (for more on this, see my book *The Forest of Souls*). Maybe instead of calling the quintessence ether, we should call it simply light, making the five elements fire, water, air, earth, and light.

Fire represents the first spark of creation, warmth, action, energy, confidence. Water expresses feelings, especially love and relationships, imagination, intuition, family. Air shows us the mind, which, like air, we cannot see but which affects us constantly. We can experience air gently, as in contemplation, or wildly, as in anger like a storm. Because Tarot shows air with a sword, we tend to see its destructive side. One reason I changed the suit to Birds in the Shining Tribe was to show mind as art, prophecy, and vision. The element of earth evokes solidness, stability. The modern emblem, Pentacles, suggests magic, so for many people Pentacles are the magic of nature. Wiccans use the five-pointed star, the pentagram, as the symbol of their religion, based on nature and the body.

Here is a recap of the suits with their various names and qualities:

Wands (Batons, Rods, Staves, Trees): Fire, male, basic; action, optimism, adventure, forcefulness, competition.

Cups (Chalices, Vessels, Rivers): Water, female, basic; emotion, love, relationship, imagination, happiness, sadness, family.

Swords (Blades, Birds): Air, male, more complex; mental activity, conflict, heroism, grief, justice, injustice.

Pentacles (Coins, Disks, Stones): Earth, female, more complex; nature, work, money, possessions, security.

Major Arcana (trumps, keys): Light, androgynous/hermaphroditic, spirituality; Hermetic ideas, exile and return, teachers, liberation.

Here is a simple diagram that shows the suits and basic attributes:

Wands	Cups	Swords	Pentacles
Fire	Water	Air	Earth
Male	Female	Male	Female
Basic		Complex	

None of these qualities exist in isolation but combine, conflict, and move in and out of each other. The primary way we experience this is through readings, where the cards come together in endless variations and patterns.

Wands and Cups both tend to be positive and optimistic, with Swords and Pentacles darker, more difficult. At the same time, Wands and Pentacles deal with action and work, things outside ourselves, while Cups and Swords deal with the intangible qualities of emotion and thought. Notice that in the usual listing, Wands and Pentacles are literally on the outside, with Cups and Swords interior. Think of the four suits as dancers in one of those nineteenth-century ritualized dances, in which couples pair up, then shift, then come back again. No single pair can do the dance alone; it requires all four. And maybe the Major Arcana provides the music.

Before we look at the numbers, we need to consider one more symbol of four that is vital to the Minor Arcana. This is the so-called Tetragrammaton, the four-letter Name of God in Hebrew, usually translated as "Lord" in English Bibles. We have seen this before, in the Major Arcana cards of the Wheel of Fortune and Temperance. Here, again, is what it looks like:

Tradition regards this word as unpronounceable, a mystery rather than a name in the narrow sense of a title. Kabbalists often just spell it out, Yod-Heh-Vav-Heh. The first and third letters, Yod and Vav (Hebrew reads from right to left, so the Yod is on the right), appear somewhat phallic, with the Vav an extension of the Yod and looking like a sword (the word *Vav* actually means "a nail"). The two Hehs, the second and fourth letters, resemble upside-down vessels with an opening at the bottom to pour out what is poured out into it.

Thus, just as the Yod and Vav represent the masculine, so the Hehs give us the feminine.

Wands	Cups	Swords	Pentacles
Fire	Water	Air	Earth
Yod ׳	Heh הׄ	Vav ׳	Heh הׄ
Male	Female	Male	Female

Kabbalists see the Name as a formula of creation, and this concept can help us understand the suits and their relation to each other. Yod—Wands—is the first spark, or desire, to create, coming directly from the Spirit. The first Heh—Cups—receives and germinates the creative urge. Genesis tells us, "There was darkness on the face of the Deep. And God said, Let there be light." The light penetrates the dark deep, Yod enters Heh. Vav—Swords—develops the original spark, the way the letter extends the short, droplike image of Yod. Finally, the second Heh—Pentacles—shows us the finished creation. This pattern holds for the cosmos and also for anything created, from a baby to a painting to a table. We can see the pattern in the form of a triangle.

We will look at the Tetragrammaton again with the court cards.

Numbers

An invocation to the numbers in the Minor Arcana:

One for unity and the movement of power
Two for duality and coming together
Three for creation, whatever is born
Four for structure, the directions of Earth
Five for bodies, and roses, and Venus
Six for the love that moves generations
Seven for spheres and music and color
Eight for infinity and eternal return
Nine for gestation, the moons of our birth
Ten for our fingers and the toes of our feet

The 2,000-year-old Sefer Yetsirah (Book of Formation) tells us that the Creator made the world with ten numbers, not nine and not eleven. Recently, a friend of mine asked me why Jewish tradition requires ten people for a *minyan*, or quorum, to enact a service. He looked startled when I told him it's because we have ten fingers. To me, all spiritual ideas come from actual existence—As below, so above. The numbers twelve and seven represent the heavens—twelve signs, seven visible "planets"—but four and ten, four suits, ten numbered cards, come from our bodies. Our hands, with their ten fingers, enable us to create and build a reality out of our ideas and desires.

The numbers one through ten have fascinated people for millennia. The most important interpretations come from Pythagoras, the founder of one of the first mystical schools known to history, and of course Kabbalah, with its ten sephiroth on the Tree of Life. The two systems do not always match. With Marseille-style decks that have no pictures on the pip cards, readers can choose a system and simply apply it to whatever card comes up. For example, if you decide that two means choice, then the Two of Cups might represent an emotional choice or a choice between two lovers.

Most modern decks, however, follow the Rider, where scenes appear on every card. For better or worse, the Rider established the modern tradition. If you join an email list on Tarot and ask, "What does the Eight of Swords mean in a reading?" almost all the responses will refer to Pamela Smith's vivid scene of a woman tied up and blindfolded. And people will not say, "In Waite and Smith's picture of a blindfolded woman..." but rather "The blindfolded woman in the picture..."

As far as I know, no record exists of how Pamela Colman Smith chose her scenes. A small handful resemble cards from an early and obscure Italian deck known as the Sola-Busca that Smith might have seen in the British Museum.

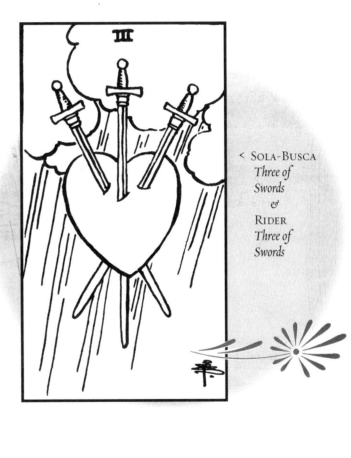

< SOLA-BUSCA
Three of Swords
&
RIDER
Three of Swords

Once Smith painted her pictures, they transcended the formulaic descriptions given as their meanings. These formulas came from various sources, in particular the meanings described by an eighteenth-century French fortuneteller and Tarot designer named Eteilla (his original name, Alliete, spelled backwards, presumably to make it more exotic). Waite wrote of Smith's paintings that "the pictures are like doors which open into unexpected chambers, or like a turn in the open road with a wide prospect beyond." And the doors have continued to open for generations of Tarotists. The Tarot has become an organism, evolving constantly as people see new and subtle possibilities.

Though the images in the Shining Tribe Minor Arcana do not resemble the Rider scenes, they often engage in a kind of dialog with them. So, for example, the Five of Pentacles in the Rider shows a kind of misery that at first seems only physical—two injured people limping in poverty in the snow. When we look closer, we see a church with a window but no door that we can see for them to seek sanctuary. Thus the card suggests to many people a spiritual ill-

> RIDER
Five of
Pentacles
&
SHINING
TRIBE
Five of Stones

ness as much as a physical one. The Shining Tribe Five of Stones, inspired by a Native American canyon painting hundreds of years old, shows an intense spiritual healing, with beings coming out of the rock. After I had done the picture, I discovered that contemporary Indians call the original canyon picture "The Ghost Healers." Tarot often seems to reach across space and time.

If the Minor Arcana consisted only of the Rider deck and its descendants, we could devote our study entirely to creative responses to Pixie's drawings. This was the approach I took in my earlier book *Seventy-Eight Degrees of Wisdom, Part Two*. But not only would that deny the Marseille and earlier decks, and the many modern decks with a different approach, it also would deny us the chance to engage the various ways people have understood the meanings of numbers. So, just as we did with the four suits, we will look at a range of ways people have understood one through ten. Hopefully, this will give people the tools to create their own sense of what these cards can mean. You might choose to focus on a particular approach. For example, you might pay special attention to the themes from the Rider cards, given below (and further explored in the individual cards), or the meaning of the numbers in Kabbalah or Pythagoras. A variety of approaches can give you the tools to develop your own interpretations.

Here is an experiment we did in a recent class of mine. You can try it with a small group of your own. Everyone took a sheet of paper and drew three swords in any kind of pattern they liked. Then we interpreted just that, the figures the swords created. No two were the same, and all were suggestive. We discovered that we did not need to see a scene to get a sense of meaning. As a further step, add one symbolic image somewhere in the picture. A rose, a house, a tree, a hand, whatever seems to fit or simply what comes into your mind. You can continue this with all the numbered cards and create your own Minor Arcana.

The "Invocation" above, written especially for this book, describes what I would call basic qualities of these numbers. Some bring in qualities we've found in the Major Arcana, but only because the Majors also involve numbers: the fundamental polarity of one and two; the fact that three evokes mother-father-child; the structural qualities of four; the way five appears in the human body (four limbs plus the head), five-petaled flowers, and the pattern Venus makes in the sky; six as two times three and thus generations; seven as the planetary spheres, colors of the rainbow, and chakras, and the notes in the musical scale; the shape of the number eight as an infinitely returning loop; the nine months of pregnancy; and the ten fingers of our hands that allow us to do such things as write books on the Tarot.

Here is a list of number attributes that combine basic concepts with everyday experience. With each, I will give at least one example of how we might apply it to the interpretation of the Minor Arcana.

1. Whatever is singular, essential. The Ace of Cups might be simple happiness, the Ace of Swords strong, clear thinking.

2. Choices, but also dialog, combinations. The Two of Pentacles could indicate a choice around money or work.

3. Group activities, family, but also triangles, jealousy. Since Swords carry themes of battle, the Three of Swords might signify conflict in a group, while the more harmonious Pentacles would mean people working together (as suggested in the Rider scene).

4. Structure, stability (for why four means structure, see the Emperor and the previous section on the four suits), but also conventionality, conformity (remember the old expression, a "square"?). The Four of Swords would suggest very structured, logical thinking, the Four of Cups a family where everyone has a fixed role.

5. Time, which is to say change, development, growth, and decay. The Five of Pentacles would mean a change in economic or physical conditions, but not necessarily for the worse.

6. Harmony, opposites reconciled, strong relationships. This comes from that six-pointed star as a combination of an upward and downward triangle. The Six of Wands in a work reading would suggest a dynamic environment where people work very well together. The Six of Cups in a love reading would indicate a reconciliation or a couple that seem opposite but function very well as a couple.

7. Creativity, inventiveness, possibilities. The Seven of Swords could suggest new ways of thinking, new plans.

8. Cycles, patterns, or a situation that continues indefinitely. The Eight of Cups might indicate someone who chooses the same sort of partner over and over.

9. Completion, an idea derived from nine as the last single-digit number and the nine months of pregnancy. The Nine of Pentacles suggests the completion of a project.

10. Abundance of the quality of the suit, possibly excess, with a hint of instability, something that doesn't last. The Ten of Pentacles could show prosperity, the Ten of Wands tremendous energy.

Try this for yourself. See if you can come up with a list of associations for the numbers, then think of how they would translate into each suit. You might want to use a Marseille-type deck—without specific action scenes, just the correct number of symbols on each card—to inspire you. As we look at some of the other number systems, the Pythagorean and the Kabbalist, we will similarly pause to consider how the concepts might apply to particular cards.

Rider Themes

And now, by contrast, my own current sense of themes of the Rider cards by number. Since Smith's pictures do not actually follow a distinct system, we cannot easily say, for example, that all threes mean the same thing. But if we lay them out together, that is, all fours, all sevens, and so on, we may find some common threads. I call this my "current sense" because it changes—evolves—over time, through readings and classes. If you have the Rider or one of its variations, you might want to set out each group as you read through this list. See how your own sense of the pictures compares to mine.

All Rider Aces

Aces—a gift of the spirit. In each card, a hand emerges from a cloud and holds out the emblem of the suit, as if we just need to reach out and take it. We see versions of the letter Yod, from Yod-Heh-Vav-Heh (see above, the four suits), as leaves in Wands, drops of water in Cups, sparkles of light in Swords. These symbolize divine grace, the idea that the power of the suit just comes to us at this moment in our lives. There are no Yods in Pentacles because that suit represents solid matter.

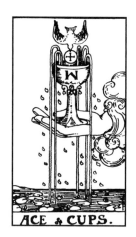

ACE of WANDS. ACE of CUPS. ACE of SWORDS. ACE of PENTACLES

All Rider Twos

Twos—I used to think of this group as relationship issues. But that only applies to the Cups, where we see a man and a woman pledging their love, and paradoxically the Swords, where a woman seems to close herself off from all possibility of relationship. To deny or block something still keeps it as the subject. But what of the Wands and Pentacles? Maybe the twos represent choices or the attempt to find balance.

All Rider Threes

Threes—a flowering, or something created from the energy of the suit. For Wands, this is rootedness and/or new opportunities, for Cups friendship, for Swords heartbreak, for Pentacles masterful work.

  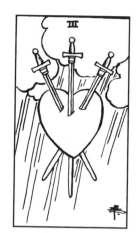 

All Rider Fours

Fours—structure, from the simple bower of Wands (fire does not like to be contained), to Cups' hesitation to try something new, to Swords' retreat into restfulness, to Pentacles' use of money or possessions to protect and define our lives.

All Rider Fives

Fives—life's difficulties. One of the most consistent numbers (see the Kabbalist number meanings below—sephirah five, Gevurah, as the harshest place on the tree). While fiery Wands get energized by conflict, Cups grieve, Swords suffer a humiliating defeat, and that couple in Pentacles find themselves crippled, penniless, and walking barefoot through the snow.

All Rider Sixes

Sixes—unequal relationships. I discovered this in a class recently, when I noticed that in each card one person stands above, and superior to, a single person (Cups), a pair of people (Swords and Pentacles), or a whole group (Wands). I'm not sure just why this should have emerged for the number six, which most people consider a number of harmony, but it seems one of the most consistent themes of any of the numbers.

Tarotist and teacher Ellen Goldberg offers a more generous view, one more aligned with the Kabbalist title of "Beauty" (see below). In fact, for her, generosity is what the Rider sixes are about. The Wands shares his optimism and confidence with those who walk alongside him, the older child in the Cups gives a flower as an expression of the beauty of nature, the man in Swords assists those who are suffering, and the man in the Six of Pentacles has so much money that in order to balance the scales, he must give some of it away.

All Rider Sevens

Sevens—action, or maybe the contemplation or awareness of action. The figure in Wands knows he must stay on top, the Cups fantasizes possibilities, the Swords character enjoys his own cleverness, the Pentacles farmer looks at his garden with satisfaction or concern (depending how you read his expression).

All Rider Eights

Eights—movement. Wands fly through the air, someone leaves Cups behind, in Swords a blindfolded woman needs to discover that nothing actually prevents her from freeing herself, and an artisan develops his skill, creating one Pentacle after another.

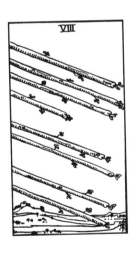   

All Rider Nines

Nines—intensity, the element at a high degree. We see Wands' courage and strength, Cups' enjoyment of life, Swords' grief, and Pentacles in a lush garden.

All Rider Tens

Tens—excess. The responsibilities of Wands bend the back, Cups celebrate family happiness, Swords suffer horribly (the excess in this card leads me often to interpret it as overly dramatic or hysterical), and Pentacles live in splendor but possibly do not see the magic outside their material comfort (the family inside the arch do not look at each other, and none of them notice the mysterious old man sitting outside the gate).

  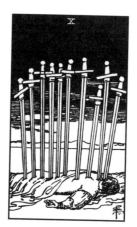 

Pythagoras

From the particular to the principle. The Rider cards work through dramatic scenes, inviting us to speculate about their actions, facial expressions, and body language, as if we can see a brief instant in an unknown play and we are left to invent the plot and characters for ourselves. But let's go back to the numbers. We will look briefly at Pythagorean and Kabbalist ideas and how they might apply to the Minor Arcana.

For this very short description of Pythagoras and numbers, I am indebted to the ideas of numerologist Carey Croft and Tarotist John Opsopaus, creator of the Pythagorean Tarot. All mistakes are mine alone.

Like the anonymous author of the Sefer Yetsirah, Pythagoras believed in the numbers one through ten as the basis for all existence. These numbers could be arranged as a pyramid based on one through four:

```
    *                 * * * *
   * *      or         * * *
  * * *                 * *
 * * * *                  *
```

We will see in a moment that the inverse, 4-3-2-1, is possibly more meaningful than the more obvious 1-2-3-4. Here are the individual numbers. Notice that they include connections to gods and goddesses. Readers of this book will know that I often use this approach. For me, it makes abstract ideas come alive in the image of archetypal beings and stories.

1. MONAD. Here we find unity, first principles. Pythagoras considered one as apart from all the numbers that come after, and we find this reflected in many Tarot decks, where two through ten will show details and complexity, but the aces will display an elegant version of the symbol. The Golden Dawn, too, put the aces in a separate category, leaving the other thirty-six cards (two through nine in each suit) to represent the thirty-six "decans" of the zodiac (see below). As the monad, the aces contain all the qualities of the suit but undifferentiated, that is, everything together. We will find the same idea in the Kabbalist sephirah one, Kether. Pythagoreans identify one with Zeus, father and leader of the gods, whose mind was said to be unfathomable, even to the other gods.

2. DYAD. The principle of separation, which gives the possibility of creation. A gap opens, creating an Above and Below so that a world can emerge. Pythagoreans identify the dyad with Rhea, mother of Zeus. The twos therefore can signify dialog, communication, the potential to create something, with each suit having its own quality.

3. TRIAD. Energy bridges the gap created in the dyad. It restores unity but now in the created world. Pythagoreans identified the three with Artemis, the moon goddess. The moon is the image of the Triple Goddess, Maiden-Mother-Crone, to go with the lunar phases of waxing-full-waning. In Tarot, the Empress, card three of the Major Arcana, embodies the Great Mother (two is actually the card of the lunar feminine).

For an experiment, set out the threes from a Tarot deck, preferably one without scenes, like the Marseille:

Now see if you can imagine them as the mother energy of each suit. What would Mother of Wands be? A source of great energy and optimism? The Mother of Cups might pour forth love. What would you see in the mental Swords and physical Pentacles? The Pentacles, of course, could symbolize actual motherhood, especially if the Empress also appeared.

4. TETRAD. We get a new duality but more complex. Four gives us structure, stability, wholeness. Pythagoras taught that the soul contains four aspects, and here we find a matching idea in Kabbalah, where each person is said to have four souls, aligned with the four worlds and thus the four suits. Maybe the four could designate the soul. What would your Wands soul be like? Your Pentacles soul? How would they be different? (See the Four Worlds reading in the Readings chapter.)

   Four completes that basic structure, 1-2-3-4, which adds up to 10. If we invert the order, and then remove the 1 as a separate category, we get 432. This number is 1/60 of the Great Year, the 25,920 years it takes for the zodiac to make a complete rotation around the Earth. The numbers 432 and 108 (1/4 of 432) appear very frequently in myth and spiritual traditions. The Buddhists will recite 108 prayers, the Hindus tell of four ages, or Yugas, each one lasting 432,000 years. The god here is our friend Hermes, whose four-sided stone pillars, called herms, marked roadways, in particular lining the road into Athens.

5. PENTAD. To the four directions of earth we add a fifth dimension, allowing us to become aware of Above. Five also adds that fifth element, quintessence, to the four physical elements. Thus, with each suit we might see the five as an opening to a higher level of consciousness. This idea stands in contrast to the Kabbalistic sense of five as very harsh.

   Since Pythagoras considered ten the number of perfection, five becomes a demi-god, maybe the ability to glimpse our perfection as immortal beings while still living in the "real" world. Five also shows the human body as the image of the divine, for if we stand with arms and legs out, we form a pentagram.

6. HEXAD. If the fives open a way to higher consciousness or simply new territory, then six defines the territory by establishing directions, including above and below with the four horizontal directions. Six represents harmony (compare Beauty in the Tree of Life). Here is an interesting quality of the numbers: 1+2+3=6. Going to the next group, 4+5+6=15, which reduces to 6 (1+5). At the highest single-digit level, 7+8+9=24, which also reduces to 6. Six represents a recurring harmonic energy. The number six goes with Aphrodite, goddess of love, and as we have seen, the six-pointed star unites masculine fire and feminine water in an image of interpenetration. For each suit, six

might show harmony. What would harmony of Swords be? A mind in peace? Different ideas or mental approaches that work together? Try this for each of the suits.

7. HEPTAD. The Pythagoreans consider seven a second monad, a new energy to be followed by the final numbers 8, 9, and 10, just as 1 is followed by 2, 3, 4 (7+8+9+10=34, which reduces to 7). Seven combines three and four, and we can put this in visual terms as a triangle above a square—spirit above matter.

The ancients linked seven to Athena, warrior goddess of wisdom, who sprang whole from the head of Zeus. Seven adds the center to the six directions, and thus becomes both dynamic and aware. And seven represents the cosmos, both above (the planets) and below (the chakras). The sevens, therefore, would show a dynamic, creative force. In Wands this would be fiery energy, in Cups emotional force, in Swords powerful ideas, and in Pentacles growth and success.

8. OCTAD. Eight is two times four, a double square, and thus the earth, matter. It reestablishes stability after the dynamic seven. John Opsopaus tells us it bears such titles as Safety, Foundation, even Paradise Regained. To the seven planetary spheres we add an eighth, the divine sphere that encloses all the rest. Think of the eights in the Minor Arcana as different kinds of stability. Two was Rhea, mother of the gods as mother of nature, but eight (two to the third power) becomes Rhea as spiritual mother.

9. ENNEAD. Some people may recognize this word from "enneagram," a nine-sided figure said to contain all aspects of life and the self. As the final single digit, nine signifies the end of a process and limitations (like Saturn as the outermost visible planet). But nine also brings birth, for a human pregnancy runs nine lunar months. As 3 x 3, nine symbolizes a third level of completion: 1-3, 4-6, 7-9. Its titles include Fulfillment, Completion, Perfection. If three represents all the trinities, what might three times three indicate? Maybe the trinity of trinities takes us to levels beyond

knowledge. What would the fulfillment of Wands be? (Probably not the somewhat beaten-up looking fellow in the Rider card.) What would unknown levels of Cups look like? (Again, the smug fellow in the Rider Nine of Cups is probably not it.) The Pythagoreans identify nine with Hera, Zeus's sister and wife. Since Zeus is one, and 9+1=10, the following card, the decad, symbolizes the divine marriage between the two great figures.

10. DECAD. This is the supreme number for Pythagoreans, symbolizing higher unity, as if one begins a process of growth that culminates in nine, and then begins again at a higher level with the first double-digit number. What might the greater consciousness of Swords look like? Possibly this might give us a mental awareness of truth beyond logic and empirical knowledge—an opening to the Major Arcana, whose element I've identified as light.

Ten gives us balanced wholeness. Here are some titles from John Opsopaus's description of ten: "Universe ... Heaven. Alliance. Fate ... Eternity...Power." Because it consists of 1+2+3+4, the decad contains all the basic principles. It returns to one, but with the awareness of having gone through all the other numbers. This may remind us of the World card, which returns to the wholeness of the Fool, but with an awareness the Fool found impossible. As well as symbolizing the divine marriage of Zeus and Hera, the decad belongs with the god/dess Hermaphroditus, the child of Hermes and Aphrodite who combines male and female perfection. The World card sometimes bears the title "Divine Hermaphrodite."

Set out the four tens from any deck without specific scenes on the cards, like the Marseille:

If all you have is a deck with illustrated scenes, take four sheets of paper and draw ten Wands on one, ten Cups on the second, and so on. Now consider each one, and see if you can apply some of the ideas about the decad to the suits. What might "Heaven" of Wands be? "Power" of Pentacles? "Eternity" of Swords? "Universe" of Cups?

Kabbalah

And so we come to Kabbalah, probably the main source for number ideas in the modern, Golden Dawn–based Tarot world. It's often seemed to me that one problem with the Tree of Life and Tarot is that the tree actually works better with the Minor cards, or at least makes them seem the more important part of the deck. While the twenty-two lines on the tree, originally designed to match the twenty-two Hebrew letters, fit very well with the twenty-two Major Arcana trump cards (though with arguments over the correct order), the ten sephiroth are clearly the primary symbol. And these go perfectly with the Minor cards. Four worlds with one through ten in each, four suits with ace through ten in each.

We've seen it before, but here it is (see opposite page), with titles for the sephiroth in Hebrew and English, and the cards they go with (remember, Hebrew goes from right to left, and so the higher numbers will be on the left).

The question is, do we go up or down? We've just seen how Pythagoras unquestionably counts from one to ten, with ten as supreme. But Kabbalah tells us that the physical world exists in ten, Malkuth, at the farthest and "densest" distance from divine Kether. This is where we live, and if we wish to advance closer to Spirit, we must climb up the tree. Waite, in his *Pictorial Key to the Tarot*, lists the Minor cards from king to ace. It seems like counting down but, in fact, is going *up* the tree. In my book *Seventy-Eight Degrees of Wisdom,* I followed Waite's approach, but since then I've tended to look at the Minor cards in the usual order, ace to ten and page to king. I think of this as a developmental approach.

Since we have looked at various aspects of the Tree of Life before, I will keep the descriptions of the sephiroth brief. The astrological and color designations come from—where else?—the Golden Dawn.

ACE—KETHER—CROWN: The origin of all things, complete in itself, undifferentiated, pictured as white light, beyond all the distinct parts of creation. Instead of a particular astrological association, Kether is the cosmos. Kether is the source, everything

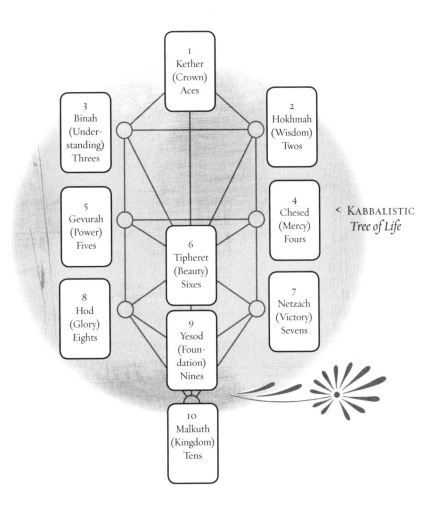

> < KABBALISTIC
> *Tree of Life*

else comes out of it. If the Ace of Cups is the source of Water energy, what might it mean in a reading? How about the Ace of Pentacles as the source of everything earthly? We might describe these cards as powerful, basic, a strong experience of the element.

TWO—HOKHMAH—WISDOM: Here we find a tricky situation. Two is usually the basic feminine number (see the High Priestess), and in fact, Hokhmah, called Sophia in Greece (the word *philosophy* originally meant "the love of wisdom"), appears almost as a goddess in the Bible and other texts. In classic Kabbalah, however, Hokhmah becomes the Father, the head of the masculine pillar on the right of the tree. The

Golden Dawn identified Hokhmah with the entire zodiac and gave it the color gray. Hokhmah represents our highest wisdom. What might the Two of Pentacles mean as the highest wisdom of earth?

THREE—BINAH—UNDERSTANDING: Here we find the Great Mother (the Empress), source of the seven lower sephiroth. If we look at the tree, we see that the top three sephiroth form an upward-pointing triangle, while 4-5-6 and 7-8-9 form downward triangles. This creates a gap between the top three and the lower seven, with 1-2-3 called "supernal," of a higher order than the others. Binah gives birth to those seven lower ones. As the quality of Understanding, it can relate to life experiences and the awareness that comes through them. The color here is black, the planet Saturn. The Three of Swords might embody mental understanding, seeing how the pieces fit together. The Three of Cups would show us emotional understanding.

FOUR—CHESED—MERCY: Four and five, Mercy and Power, form a pair. We also call them Expansion and Contraction. Mercy, on the masculine side of the tree, is loving and generous, a constant outpouring. This contrasts with the usual idea of four as structure and stability, and I'm not sure we can easily combine the two ideas. If you want to try a strictly Kabbalist approach to the Minor Arcana, try the same exercise suggested for the Pythagorean threes. Set out the fours from a deck without specific scenes or draw them on sheets of paper.

Now imagine what a benevolent outpouring of Wands might be, and one of Cups. How would a Chesed of Swords differ from a Chesed of Pentacles?

FIVE—GEVURAH—POWER. If the universe only expanded, if people only acted generously, nothing would sustain itself. We could not learn if our experiences never tested us. And so we find harsh Gevurah, which the Golden Dawn aligns with the planet Mars and the color red. The Kabbalist meaning of five informs the Rider deck images probably more than any other number. We see conflict in Wands, mourning in Cups, defeat in Swords, and poverty and illness in Pentacles. Can you think of alternatives for these choices? Harshness of Wands might mean something burning, of Cups someone shut down emotionally.

SIX—TIPHERET—BEAUTY. At the center of the tree we find Beauty, whose "planet" is the sun and color is yellow. The Jewish Kabbalists associated this sephirah with Jacob, their image of the ideal man (personally, I prefer his son Joseph). The Christian Kabbalists put Christ in the center, while the Golden Dawn opened it to the whole range of dying and resurrecting gods, especially those known for their beauty, like the Norse god Balder. Here in the tree's center, we find a confluence with the Pythagoreans, who see six as Harmony. What would the Beauty of Wands be? Glorious flame? Life energy and health at their most radiant? How about the Beauty of Pentacles? Lush nature, a wondrous oasis?

SEVEN—NETZACH—VICTORY. The title of this card has always struck me as vague. Some call it the Victory of God, but what exactly does that mean? For the most part, the Rider deck shows active images here, a quality I followed in the Shining Tribe. We get a more specific sense of this sephirah from the Golden Dawn's designation of it as the place of the planet Venus, realm of emotion. The color is green. This gives us the vertical line of Wisdom (2), expansive Mercy (4), and emotional Victory (7). What might the emotional Victory of Swords be? Delight in the mind's ability to solve problems? Cups might become extremely emotional, or perhaps the Seven of Cups might indicate a triumph of love.

EIGHT—HOD—GLORY. Just as with Netzach's "Victory," Glory has always sounded abstract to me. And again, the Golden Dawn assignation, this time to Mercury, allows for a clear sense to emerge. In fact, clarity, at least mental clarity, belongs to Mercury, the realm of the mind. And of course, the *god* Mercury is the Roman version of Hermes, the legendary "inventor" of Tarot itself (see the Magician—and numerous others—for more on Hermes). The Greek name for Venus is Aphrodite, so that if we combine eight and seven we get Hermes-Aphrodite, or Hermaphrodite, that complete being we associate with the World card and which Pythagoreans see as the number ten. And if we put seven and eight together, we get seventy-eight, the number of the cards in the Tarot. The order of these planetary realms carries an important truth. If we seek to ascend up the tree from Malkuth, the place of our busy, distracted lives, we pass through Yesod (sephirah nine) and then come to Hod, the place of mind, and after that Netzach, the world of emotion, and only when we have experienced both do we go on to Tipheret, where all the qualities come together in Beauty. Put another way, emotion is higher on the tree than mind. The color for Hod is lavender. If eights signify mind, what would the mind of Pentacles be?

NINE—YESOD—FOUNDATION. Here, too, I value the Golden Dawn's attribution, in this case the moon. We should realize, by the way, that the Hermetic Order did not make their associations arbitrarily or conceptually but simply took the planets in order, beginning with the moon, the closest to Earth (Malkuth, sephirah ten), and moving outwards to Saturn (Binah). As we saw with the Major Arcana card, the Moon rules imagination, instinct, dreams, psychic awareness, intuition. As someone who has tried to champion imagination all my life, I can only agree with the idea of the lunar realm as the "Foundation" of our spiritual existence, the gateway to the rest of the tree, as well as the primary way that spiritual energy spirals down into our daily lives. The color here is silver.

If the primary quality of Yesod is lunar imagination, how might individual nines express this? Maybe some would conflict. For example, the mental approach of Swords or the practical earthiness of Pentacles might be uncomfortable in the realm of the moon. We might get disturbing fantasies, disruptive dreams.

TEN—MALKUTH—KINGDOM. This sephirah represents the "real" world, our daily lives. The planet is Earth itself and the color a mixture of four different quarters. Kabbalists who think in hierarchical terms may describe Malkuth as "dense," or "gross matter." However, as Isabel Radow Kliegman says in her book *Tarot and the Tree of Life*, if we want to change something, ourselves or the world, we have to do it in Malkuth, for that is where everything happens. And if we want to ascend the tree to higher consciousness, we cannot just choose which one we like as a starting point. We must begin where we are, in Malkuth. Thus the ten should signify the solid reality of each suit, and here the Rider images, by far the best known, work well with the feminine suits of Cups and Pentacles. The latter, in fact, shows the Pentacles as a Tree of Life overlaying the scene. We see simple happiness in the Cups and prosperity in the Pentacles. By contrast, Wands and Swords show us oppression and mental anguish (not violent death, despite the picture).

 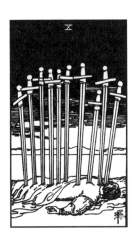  

Trumps and the Minor Cards

Let's go back to something simpler. Consider the numbers in the Major Arcana. If we set aside the Fool, 0, and the World, 21, as both containing the totality of experience, we get twenty cards, two times ten. Thus, we can link each Minor card to two Majors. Here is one more chart:

Aces	Twos	Threes	Fours	Fives	Sixes	Sevens	Eights	Nines	Tens
I.	2.	3.	4.	5.	6.	7.	8.	9.	10.
Magi-cian	High Priestess	Empress	Emperor	Hiero-phant	Lovers	Chariot	Strength	Hermit	Wheel
II.	12.	13.	14.	15.	16.	17.	18.	19.	20.
Justice	Hanged Man	Death	Temper-ance	Devil	Tower	Star	Moon	Sun	Judge-ment

Decans

Before going on to the individual cards, we need to consider one more system modern Tarotists sometimes use for the numbered minors, at least two through nine in each suit. As described above, if we set aside the aces as the basic element, we get thirty-six cards. Since the zodiac contains 360 degrees, this gives us ten degrees for each card. Put another way, there are twelve signs and thus thirty degrees for each (360 divided by 12=30). For example, Wands are fire, and the three fire signs are Aries, Leo, and Sagittarius. Thus the Two of Wands becomes 1–10 degrees of Aries, the three is 11–20 degrees of Aries, and the four 21–30. Leo goes with cards five, six, and seven, while Sagittarius with eight, nine, and ten. Each decan—each card—is ruled by a planet. Paul Huson traces this system and its meanings to a fourteenth-century Arabic text, translated into Latin, called *Picatrix* (wonderful name), which not only listed the decans but gave meanings for each one. Although these meanings are often far from what we think of for the cards today (and were not in fact originally connected to Tarot cards but used only for astrology and magical talismans), they may have influenced the Golden Dawn's interpretations for the Minor Arcana. Huson says that the Golden Dawn papers originally contained a text titled *The Magical Images of the Decans*, which seems to be an English translation from the Latin version of *Picatrix*.

This has been a long and extended summary of the varied influences and possibilities of the Minor Arcana. I have sought here to show the many ways we can view these cards, all valid in their own way, and maybe especially to "liberate" us from over-reliance on any one approach, especially Pamela Colman Smith's compelling scenes for the Rider, or the Kabbalah. For one thing, we notice that these two often do not match up; that is, the Rider pictures often seem to have no relation to the Kabbalist theme for that number. Smith's Six of Swords would not suggest "Beauty" of air to many people (and here is a curious fact of the Rider Swords cards: six of the ten cards show water).

I also have tried to suggest rather than dictate ideas; for example, asking with the Ten of Wands what "Heaven" of Wands might be rather than just giving my own suggestions. In the individual card listings below, I hope people will use the information and suggestions to come up with their own interpretations.

Wands

Element: Fire, basic male energy, yang

Kabbalistic World: Atzilut (Emanation), highest, closest to Spirit

Magical "Weapon": The Magician's wand

Social Class: Peasants, symbolized by the flowering stick (modern: working people)

Biblical Object: The flowering rod of Aaron, high priest

"Ruling" God: Hermes, god of magic, masculine creative energy, guide to souls, trickster

Primary Major Arcana card: Magician

Medieval Virtue: Fortitude, Courage

Wands are active, strong-minded, courageous, optimistic, energetic, adventurous. They can show great confidence but also people's tendency to take on too much or have unrealistic expectations, of themselves as well as others. The main problem of Wands may be a tendency to burn out or recognize only the aggressive way of dealing with problems. The presence of Cups may soften their influence and bring in emotional qualities. Swords allows the Wands energy to think things through more carefully, while Pentacles can make them more practical. Seen another way, however, Water (Cups) may drown the Fire, Air (Swords) may fan the aggressive flames with conflict, and Earth/dirt (Pentacles) can smother the optimistic Fire.

Element: Fire

Sephirah: Kether (Crown), sephirah one in Atzilut (Emanation)

Pythagorean: Monad, unity

Major Arcana: Magician, Justice

Rider Theme: Gift of elemental fire

Ace of Wands cards from Golden Dawn, Marseille, Rider, Sola-Busca, Shining Tribe & Visconti

Ace of Wands

The ace is the primary card, the purest. With fiery Wands, this means great energy, happiness, optimism. If we think of climbing up the tree from ten, then the ace is the culmination, a return to the essence of fire in the world of Atzilut, which means a sense of pure, undiluted spiritual flame. But if we see the cards as a progress from ace to ten, then the Ace of Wands is a beginning, the first card of the Minor Arcana. In the Shining Tribe card, we see a fetus whose umbilical cord becomes a tree reaching into the stars, so that the child is fed by the cosmos.

The leaves falling from the Wand in the Rider image are in the shape of Yods, the first letter of the sacred Name, Yod-Heh-Vav-Heh, and also the first letter in Yeshua, the Hebrew word for Jesus. The Ace of Wands is the gift of life itself.

Aces are singular, essential. The monad, undifferentiated and thus also undeveloped. Its two Major Arcana cards signify creative power: the Magician, but also the need to direct that power in the cause of Justice.

READINGS—Energy, life, health, courage, forcefulness, simplicity, the very beginning of something exciting, enthusiasm.

REVERSED—Hesitation, setbacks, doubt. It simply may not be the time to begin something new.

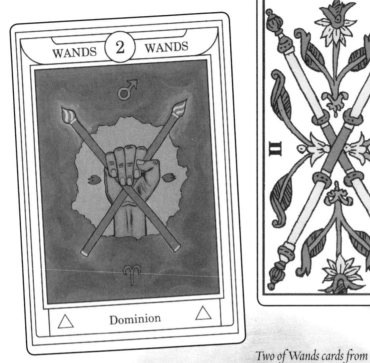

Element: Fire

Sephirah: Hokhmah (Wisdom), sephirah two in Atzilut (Emanation)

Pythagorean: Dyad, separation, dialog

Major Arcana: High Priestess, Hanged Man

Rider Theme: Choices, balance

Golden Dawn Title: Dominion

Decan: 1–10 degrees Aries, ruled by Mars

Picatrix: Boldness, fierceness, resolution, shamelessness

Two of Wands cards from GOLDEN DAWN, MARSEILLE, RIDER, SOLA-BUSCA, SHINING TRIBE & VISCONTI

Two of Wands

With the two, we get the possibility of mirroring, of energy separated to allow something to emerge. The Rider image here does not seem to reflect the two very well, except that it seems to show someone trying to balance two desires or maybe making a decision about them. The first is to stay in his secure castle, the second is to leave and seek adventure in the manner of Wands' fire energy. Fire does not like to be contained, for then it would go out; it needs new experiences to sustain it.

What is the wisdom of fire? If there were two pure flames, what would they say to each other? Or would they feed each other? Perhaps there would be a conflict, as with the backfires that forest rangers use to stop forest fires. That is, two energies would go against each other. The element of fire might not be suitable for dialog and might need other elemental energies truly to balance it. Twos can be choice. What kind of choices does fire make? Here is where wisdom becomes necessary, so that the energy of Wands does not simply go wherever it can but can choose with consciousness (some Swords energy would help). The two Major Arcana cards are both still, so that they seem to help balance that forceful fire.

READINGS—Choice, especially between security and adventure. Seeking the wisdom inherent in fiery energy.

REVERSED—A choice or decision is made, and the person moves into new experience. There may be adventure but also insecurity.

WANDS 3 WANDS

△ Established Strength △

Element: Fire

Sephirah: Binah (Understanding), sephirah three in Atzilut (Emanation)

Pythagorean: Triad, unity restored, but in the created world

Major Arcana: Empress, Death

Rider Theme: A flowering, something created from the energy of the suit

Golden Dawn Title: Established Strength

Decan: 11–20 degrees Aries, ruled by the sun

Picatrix: Pride, nobility, wealth, rule

Three of Wands cards from
GOLDEN DAWN,
MARSEILLE, RIDER,
SOLA-BUSCA,
SHINING TRIBE &
VISCONTI

Three of Wands

The Kabbalist word *Binah* means "understanding," and in this card we might expect to find the idea of understanding fire—finding meaning in it, realizing how to use it. When this card comes up, you might ask yourself how you understand fire—life energy—in your own experience or in the situation of the reading. And maybe the Rider image, showing a man on a hilltop looking out over a river or a bay, indicates someone who has come to understand what the fire of ambition and energy has meant in his life.

Binah also is the Great Mother, the goddess from whom the world comes. What might the mother of fire be? If you can imagine a goddess of flames, you might get a sense of what this card can mean. The Pythagorean idea stresses renewed energy, restored unity in the creative world. This suggests that something has come out of the fire, something has been born. The fetus in the Shining Tribe Ace has changed to three joyous spirits that are actually manifested in the world. The image here is based on *manitokanac*, scarecrow-like effigies that the Salteaux Indians of Canada make to invite guardians to inhabit physical objects and protect the home.

My own general theme for three is group activities, family, but possibly triangles. Thus the Three of Wands could be people sharing creative activities. The Major Arcana cards actually show us the beauty and limitations of outpourings of energy. The Empress emphasizes the idea of the mother of fire. Death, however, reminds us that it will come to an end.

READINGS—Energy manifested, coming to an understanding of what creative energy has meant in your life. Exciting group actions.

REVERSED—A cartomantic tradition from Etteila to Waite describes this card as the "end of adversity," a valuable meaning to keep in mind for any reading. Possibly competition in a group.

WANDS (4) WANDS

Perfected Work

Element: Fire

Sephirah: Chesed (Mercy), sephirah four in Atzilut (Emanation)

Pythagorean: Tetrad, wholeness

Major Arcana: Emperor, Temperance

Rider Theme: Structure

Golden Dawn Title: Perfected Work

Decan: 21-30 Aries, ruled by Venus

Picatrix: Subtlety, beauty, vice

Four of Wands cards from
GOLDEN DAWN,
MARSEILLE, RIDER,
SOLA-BUSCA,
SHINING TRIBE &
VISCONTI

Four of Wands

For most people, and most traditions, the number four means structure, matter, the stability of the physical world. This would seem at odds with the Kabbalistic meaning of Chesed, the generous outpouring, the loving, benevolent father energy. Still, it is worth asking—especially if you wanted to emphasize a Kabbalist approach to the Minor Arcana—what would be the generous outpouring of fire? Maybe it would involve giving energy to every activity, every person who needed help or just wanted attention. There could be a danger of overwhelming people or else a need for some Gevurah pulling back.

The Rider card here strikes me as a strong image—a simple bower made of four poles and a canopy of flowers. Fire becomes structured, but in an open way and in service of celebration. Behind them, the walled city shows the more confining sort of structure that defines our normal lives—responsibility, work, rules. Because the bower resembles a wedding canopy (particularly for Jews, who create such structures for a bride and groom to stand under during the ceremony), some people see this card as an indicator of marriage.

If, as both Pythagoras and Kabbalah say, the soul has four parts (or we have four souls), then four is the number of the soul. What would the soul of fire be? What would your soul of fire be?

READINGS—Simple structures, life-energy defined and given shape. Finding goals. People celebrating together. An outpouring of excitement and energy. Possibly marriage.

REVERSED—This is one of several cards Waite describes as basically the same reversed, maybe to a lesser degree—clouds over the joyous party. Another meaning might be that our enthusiasm overwhelms our attempts to contain and direct it. The modern idea of "attention deficit disorder" might apply here.

WANDS (5) WANDS

Strife

Element: Fire

Sephirah: Gevurah (Power), sephirah five in Atzilut (Emanation)

Pythagorean: Pentad, higher consciousness, demigod

Major Arcana: Hierophant, Devil

Rider Theme: Life's difficulties

Golden Dawn Title: Strife

Decan: 1–10 degrees Leo, ruled by Saturn

Picatrix: Boldness, liberality, victory, cruelty, lust, violence

Five of Wands cards from
GOLDEN DAWN,
MARSEILLE, RIDER,
SOLA-BUSCA,
SHINING TRIBE &
VISCONTI

Five of Wands

As described above, the Rider theme for the number five is one of the most consistent and most closely based on Kabbalah. Gevurah is the harsh place on the tree, the place of contraction and adversity. Because Wands is so optimistic, the Rider image shows some boys or young men clashing sticks but not really hurting each other. Competition energizes rather than hurts. If we get away from this image and just consider the theme of Gevurah, we might think of a flame that burns away what is old and weak.

My own theme for five is time and change. This might mean a shift in someone's energy, a new interest or sense of purpose, or, more pessimistically, the end of something that had burned brightly for a while but cannot sustain itself.

The Pythagorean concept of five is more exalted—demigod and the opening to higher consciousness. We might understand this best if we see the head as the fifth point in the five-pointed star of the body. Five of the element of fire might open to a powerful sense of life's possibilities.

The two Major Arcana cards suggest a struggle of ideas, especially good and evil. The Pope (Hierophant) versus the Devil! Both, it seems to me, try to confine fire or control it, but the element escapes all doctrines.

READINGS—These depend partly on whether you lean towards the Rider, which features competition and the excitement of being out in the world, or the Pythagorean: a glimpse of life's fiery possibilities. Or maybe it's simply change, energy moving in a new direction.

REVERSED—With Rider-themed versions, competition turning nasty, people who don't follow understood rules. Beyond that specific version, it can mean a narrowing of beliefs in life possibilities, or else a fire, a passion, that burns steadily, without highs but also without danger of going out.

Victory

Element: Fire

Sephirah: Tipheret (Beauty), sephirah six in Atzilut (Emanation)

Pythagorean: Hexad, harmony, above and below, masculine and feminine

Major Arcana: Lovers, Tower

Rider Theme: Unequal relationships/ generosity

Golden Dawn Title: Victory

Decan: 11–20 degrees Leo, ruled by Jupiter

Picatrix: Quarreling, ignorance, pretended knowledge, wrangling, victory over the low and base, drawing swords

Six of Wands cards from GOLDEN DAWN, MARSEILLE, RIDER, SOLA-BUSCA, SHINING TRIBE & VISCONTI

Six of Wands

Taken alone, without other suits, especially Cups for water, Wands fire can be overwhelming. In the six we automatically add water, even without any Cups cards around it, because the image of the six-pointed star consists of interpenetrating fire and water triangles. So there is a sense of harmony, the harmony of fire, and what might that look like?

You can answer this question just through your own sense of it, or you can try asking the cards. Take your deck and set the Six of Wands on the table. Then shuffle it with three questions in mind: (1) What is the harmony of fire? (2) What supports this? and (3) What undermines it? You can do this with any issue—what is it, and what supports and what undermines it.

One answer—without doing a reading—would emphasize that for fire, the joining of masculine and feminine is passion. Thus, the Six of Wands might indicate a passionate relationship, or just a passion for life. Here the Major Arcana cards go nicely, with not only the Lovers but the Tower, sometimes described as a card of orgasm. All this makes the Six of Wands a card you might want to get for a new relationship. Besides the sexual energy, it indicates people who share excitement and enthusiasm.

The Rider theme of unequal relationships shows a figure on a horse, with a wreath of victory, surrounded by others on foot. They are unequal only in that he is their leader. His con-

fidence inspires them, and this is how he (or the card?) expresses the generosity of the suit. The Shining Tribe image shows a cartoon-like woman walking jauntily through a strange landscape. The decan of Leo, the roaring lion, ruled by expansive Jupiter supports the idea of confidence. The Picatrix meanings, on the other hand, seem far too negative for this card.

READINGS—Passion, romantic, or shared enthusiasm. Situations that are exciting and harmonious at the same time. Confidence and optimism, the ability to inspire others.

REVERSED—Difficulties in a passionate relationship. Lack of shared interests. Pessimism and doubt that can lead to isolation. Possibly looking under the surface for deeper meaning.

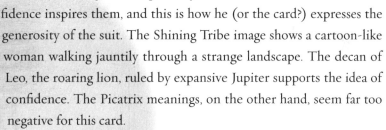

Element: Fire

Sephirah: Netzach (Victory), sephirah seven in Atzilut (Emanation)

Pythagorean: Heptad, dynamic aware energy, the cosmos

Major Arcana: Chariot, Star

Rider Theme: Contemplation or awareness of action

Golden Dawn Title: Valor

Decan: 21-30 degrees Leo, ruled by Mars

Picatrix: Love, pleasure, society, avoiding of quarrels, carefulness in parting with goods

Seven of Wands cards from
GOLDEN DAWN,
MARSEILLE, RIDER,
SOLA-BUSCA,
SHINING TRIBE &
VISCONTI

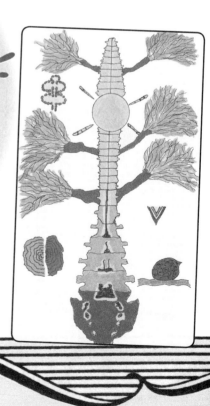

Seven of Wands

The sevens seem to me to represent creativity and inventiveness, an awareness of possibilities after the harmony of the sixes. Fiery Wands would have great creative energy—the force of fire in a dynamic setting. The lower Major Arcana card here, the Chariot, goes well with the suit, having its own forceful energy. The higher card, the Star, brings a gentleness, while at the same time its posture of pouring out water and holding nothing back also goes well with the drive of the card.

The Star also might remind us that seven on the Tree of Life, Netzach, is the realm of Venus, since as we saw in the Major Arcana, one interpretation of "Star" is the morning star, Venus. Thus, we see fire in the emotional world, where it may, in fact, have cross energies—the powerful desires and drive possibly in conflict with feelings.

The Rider image is active, seemingly holding his own against figures from below, though we only see their wands reaching up towards him. The theme of awareness comes in with his knowledge that he must stay on top; he cannot relax. The combination of seven and Wands pushes him into a situation where he has to keep active. The decan of Leo ruled by Mars suggests an aggressive quality, confident Leo made warlike. The Picatrix meanings, on the other hand, seem to go in the opposite direction, avoiding conflict.

The Shining Tribe image shows fire in a different way. We see a spinal column with no head—that is, no ego, as if the life energy is more important than focus on yourself—and the sun shining at the heart chakra. Complete openness allows the fire its full beauty and power. Seven is a number of the cosmos, for the seven planetary spheres, but also of ourselves, for the seven chakras. With fire, we bring Above and Below together by becoming one with the energy.

READINGS—Dynamic, energetic, creative, possibly aggressive. There is a need to open ourselves to fire rather than use it against others, or simply to stay on top.

REVERSED—The energy can become scattered, not as focused as we would like it to be.

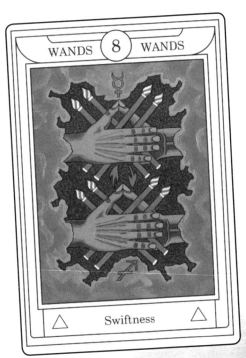

WANDS (8) WANDS

Swiftness

Element: Fire

Sephirah: Hod (Glory), sephirah eight in Atzilut (Emanation)

Pythagorean: Octad, stability, safety, the spiritual mother of the gods

Major Arcana: Strength, Moon

Rider Theme: Movement

Golden Dawn Title: Swiftness

Decan: 1-10 degrees Sagittarius, ruled by Mercury

Picatrix: Boldness, freedom, welfare, liberality, of fields and gardens

Eight of Wands cards from
GOLDEN DAWN,
MARSEILLE, RIDER,
SOLA-BUSCA,
SHINING TRIBE &
VISCONTI

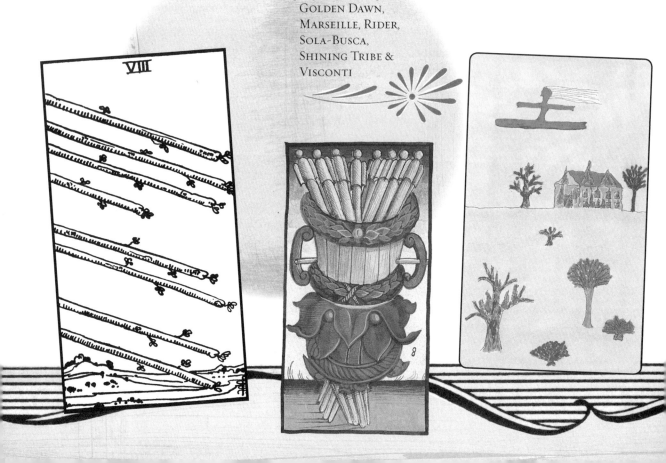

Eight of Wands

The decan here works perfectly with the Kabbalistic meaning, for it shows us high-minded, explorative Sagittarius in Mercury, the mental realm that is the theme of the eighth sephirah. Thus we might expect to find a very mental, principled approach to being a forceful person—someone strong-willed who nevertheless acts only according to carefully thought-out ideals. The Major Arcana card of Strength supports this idea, though the higher card, the Moon, brings in very different qualities—the unconscious, the dream world. These might be needed to balance the forcefulness of Sagittarius/Mercury.

The Pythagorean idea emphasizes both stability and spirituality. How does fire become stable? Maybe it's only by giving it a higher purpose, in service to spirit.

The Rider theme for the eights, movement, is probably at its strongest in Wands, which makes sense, since Wands is the most dynamic suit. It's actually one of Smith's simplest pictures, and the only Minor card in the Rider deck not to show any people (the hands in the aces and the pierced heart in the Three of Swords only have parts of bodies, but the Eight of Wands has nothing of humans at all). Thus, of all the Wands, the Eight is the one that is pure energy. At the same time, the wands in the sky seem angled towards the ground, as if they soon will find the stability that many associate with the number eight. The Shining Tribe card

also shows movement—a woman joyously flying over a burning house, as if she has left some bad situation that cannot be fixed. My own idea for the number eight, based on the shape of the number, is cycles and repeating patterns. What would repeating patterns of fire be? I know that for myself I tend to take on too many projects, just because I find each one exciting and don't like to consider practical limitations.

READINGS—Movement, swiftness, heading towards stability. For an ongoing situation, this card can indicate coming to a conclusion or resolution, usually positive. Possibly, repeating patterns of behavior. Or, acting from ideals and mental constructions of the right thing to do.

REVERSED—Situations remain unresolved, unstable. A person may try to work out mentally what action to take but find this difficult to do. It could mean breaking a pattern.

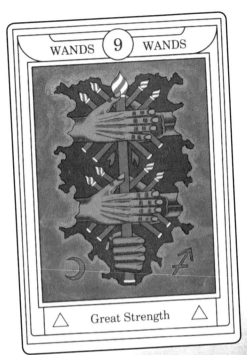

Element: Fire

Sephirah: Yesod (Foundation), sephirah nine in Atzilut (Emanation)

Pythagorean: Ennead, fulfillment, completion, perfection

Major Arcana: Hermit, Sun

Rider Theme: Intensity, the element at a high degree

Golden Dawn Title: Great Strength

Decan: 11-20 degrees Sagittarius, ruled by the moon

Picatrix: Fear, lamentation, grief, anxiety, disturbance

Nine of Wands cards from
GOLDEN DAWN,
MARSEILLE, RIDER,
SOLA-BUSCA,
SHINING TRIBE &
VISCONTI

Nine of Wands

Nine is the number of completion, both because it is the last single digit and because of the nine months of pregnancy. Thus, each nine should show the fulfillment of the suit in some way. The Rider shifts this to simple intensity, and since the qualities of Wands include courage and stalwartness, the Rider figure shows someone who stands very strong and muscular while looking warily over his shoulder at the row of wands lined up behind him. Does he await an attack? Notice his body language (often an important quality in Smith's art): the shoulder hunched up, the arms covering the chest as if to shield the heart and lungs. And notice as well the bandage on the head, the psychic wound of defensiveness. The Rider version of the Nine of Wands could show someone who has had to fight for a long time and now cannot let go or trust people.

But is this really the fulfillment of fire? Might we instead see some result of all that exuberance? Or simply the love of life expressed fully, freed from issues that would hold it back? If we think of the nine as the completion of pregnancy, what would be born out of fire? And what of the lunar aspect of Yesod? If we think of the fire of imagination, the Nine of Wands becomes highly creative and inspired.

READINGS—If you are using the Rider, then the image is of courage and strength in a tense situation. Defensiveness. But if you wish to go beyond these meanings, it becomes a card of fulfillment of energy, creativity, excitement, and inspiration.

REVERSED—Again, with the Rider we get a sense of being overwhelmed, of maybe finding a different way to deal with problems, or of allowing someone to get close to you. Beyond this specific interpretation, the Nine of Wands reversed can mean incompleteness in creative projects—or having finished one thing and going on to something new.

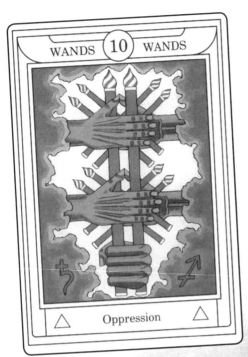

WANDS 10 WANDS

Oppression

Element: Fire

Sephirah: Malkuth (Kingdom), sephirah ten in Atzilut (Emanation)

Pythagorean: Decad, higher unity, greater consciousness

Major Arcana: Wheel of Fortune, Judgement

Rider Theme: Excess

Golden Dawn Title: Oppression

Decan: 21-30 degrees Sagittarius, ruled by Saturn

Picatrix: Ill will, levity, envy, obstinacy, swiftness in all things, deceitful acts

Ten of Wands cards from GOLDEN DAWN, MARSEILLE, RIDER, SOLA-BUSCA, SHINING TRIBE & VISCONTI

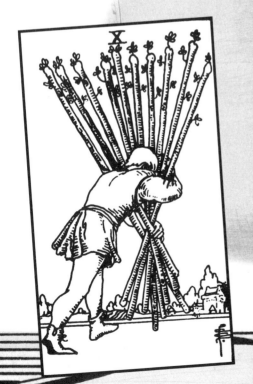

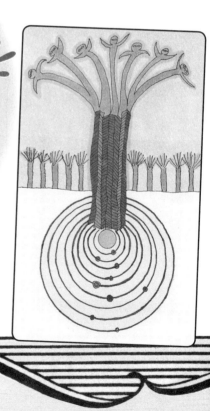

Ten of Wands

With ten, we get the sharpest split between the Kabbalist and Pythagorean traditions. The Kabbalists see it as furthest from the divine, as "gross" matter. Thus, the Golden Dawn titled the card "Oppression," and with the Rider we see the idea of fiery excitement having taken on too many responsibilities or being simply weighed down by the burdens of daily life. And if we think of the kind of person we might associate with fire—someone charismatic, enthusiastic, loving life in all its excitements—then yes, such a person might feel oppressed by the responsibilities that he or she takes on just because they seemed like a good idea at the time.

But what of the idea that this is Atzilut, the world of pure Emanation and spiritual fire? And what of the Pythagorean idea of ten as the highest attainment? What would be the greater consciousness of fire? How would we express unity and awareness in our enthusiasm and love of life? In the Shining Tribe Ten of Trees, I showed a magical tree bursting with new life. The end of each branch becomes a spirit, for in the ten of fire, everything new becomes a branch of consciousness.

READINGS—With the Rider, feeling overburdened by responsibilities. In relationship readings, someone who makes all the effort to keep the relationship going. Outside this frame of reference, it can be a card of new life and greater awareness of the meaning of your actions and enthusiasms.

REVERSED—In the Rider and similar decks, freedom from burdens, release of responsibilities. With relationships, someone who has made all the efforts refuses to do so. In the larger frame of reference, new possibilities remain, but they are not as clear.

A Reading Inspired by the Suit of Wands

1. What is the fire in my life?

2. How am I passionate?

3. How do I burn myself out?

4. How can I direct my fiery energy?

Cups

Element: Water, basic female energy, yin

Kabbalistic World: Beriah (Creation), "primordial soup," world beginning to emerge

Magical "Weapon": The healing chalice, the Grail

Social Class: Clergy, symbolized by the communion chalice (modern: arts, social services, religion)

Biblical Object: The cup of Joseph, the diviner

"Ruling" Goddess: Aphrodite, goddess of love, passion, and sensuality

Primary Major Arcana Card: High Priestess

Medieval Virtue: Temperance, or Faith

Cups are flowing, emotional, complex, and intuitive. They deal with love and relationships but also family, both happiness and sadness as deep feelings (compared to the mental disturbance and grief of some Swords), and imagination. They are the natural companion to the Wands, water to fire, yin to yang. Their primary Major Arcana card, the High Priestess, reveals water as deep, quiet, mysterious, with more below the surface than people are likely to recognize.

Because the Grail is their central symbol, the Cups have a quality of healing. We can use them to heal emotional areas of our lives. If the Two of Cups is about relationships, then we can focus on it, either in an actual ritual or just in a gentle meditation with the picture, to get past our wounds and visualize ourselves in a strong, loving couple. The same goes for other cards in the suit.

Cups can be too passive or too sensitive, even on a psychic level. Wands' fire energy enlivens them, Swords can help them understand all those emotions, and Pentacles can ground them in nature or work.

The Ace of Cups

Element: Water

Sephirah: Kether (Crown), sephirah one in Beriah (Creation)

Pythagorean: Monad, unity

Major Arcana: Magician, Justice

Rider Theme: Gift of elemental water

Ace of Cups from
GOLDEN DAWN,
MARSEILLE, RIDER,
SOLA-BUSCA,
SHINING TRIBE &
VISCONTI

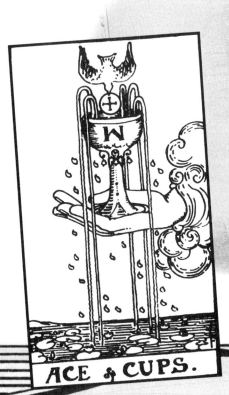

ACE of CUPS.

Ace of Cups

This is the primary card of the suit, and here the Rider is valuable, with its depiction of the Holy Grail. Most decks tend to show an ornate cup with definite suggestions of a sacred chalice (some modern Pagan or Wiccan decks show a cauldron), but the Rider is quite specific, with the dove of the spirit bringing the wafer from above (no one seems quite sure what the W—or upside-down M—is on the cup). This gives the entire suit the quality of healing. The drops of water form the Hebrew letter Yod, symbol of divine grace (see Ace of Wands). The Shining Tribe card shows a woman and an animal coming to nourish themselves at a river flowing from the mouth of a god.

The ace is the crown of the tree, the element in its purest form, the monad. For both the Kabbalists and the Pythagoreans, one is undifferentiated, not separated into parts and details. The two Major cards, the Magician and Justice, remind us that there is magical healing in this card, but just as in the Grail stories, it needs to be aligned with Justice.

READINGS—Pure water energy, love, creative flow, spiritual healing, possible new relationship. Emotional and spiritual nourishment.

REVERSED—Happiness may be blocked, a connection broken. Sometimes the reversed Ace can mean we don't recognize love when it is offered to us. In a stressful situation, you may need to remember to nourish yourself physically, emotionally, or spiritually.

CUPS 2 CUPS

Love

Element: Water

Sephirah: Hokhmah (Wisdom), sephirah two in Beriah (Creation)

Pythagorean: Dyad, separation, dialog

Major Arcana: High Priestess, Hanged Man

Rider Theme: Choices, balance

Golden Dawn Title: Love

Decan: 1-10 degrees Cancer, ruled by Venus

Picatrix: Dominion, science, love, mirth, subtlety, magistracy

Two of Cups from GOLDEN DAWN, MARSEILLE, RIDER, SOLA-BUSCA, SHINING TRIBE & VISCONTI

Two of Cups

The sign for this decan is Cancer, but what is more significant probably is the planet: Venus, the realm of love. We also find the idea of love as at least one of the ideas in the Picatrix. The Rider picture is famously about love and has come to mean a new relationship (compared to the established relationship of the Lovers card). And yet, there is a formality to it, a sense of the balance of male and female that must precede the mingling of their energies. The card has a strong esoteric quality that belies Waite's insistence in *The Pictorial Key to the Tarot* that the Minor cards do not have a deeper meaning. We see the caduceus, the staff of Hermes, with its two snakes wound around a stick, a symbol of male and female entwined, and also of the kundalini energy that lies like a coiled snake at the base of the spine, which when it rises becomes two strands, solar and lunar energy. Usually we would see just wings at the top of the caduceus, but here we find a lion's head between them, an alchemical symbol of transformation. Notice that the Marseille image, derived apparently from the North African Mamluk deck that inspired European cards, also hints at the caduceus.

For once, the various themes seem to merge. We can see the Pythagorean dyad theme of dialog in Smith's picture. The further idea of separation and a gap would seem to be the opposite of love, but it is only because there are two, with a gap between them, that love can flow. And if we ask, what is the wisdom—Hokhmah—of water, isn't the obvious answer love?

READINGS—A relationship, especially a new one, that becomes meaningful. A flow of energies. The possibility to heal old wounds from past relationships.

REVERSED—A relationship may not be as significant as originally thought. Old wounds or scars may interfere with new love.

CUPS 3 CUPS

Abundance

Element: Water

Sephirah: Binah (Understanding), sephirah three in Beriah (Creation)

Pythagorean: Triad, unity restored, but in the created world

Major Arcana: Empress, Death

Rider Theme: A flowering, something created from the energy of the suit

Golden Dawn Title: Abundance

Decan: 11-20 degrees Cancer, ruled by Mercury

Picatrix: Pleasure, mirth, abundance, plenty

Three of Cups from
GOLDEN DAWN,
MARSEILLE, RIDER,
SOLA-BUSCA,
SHINING TRIBE &
VISCONTI

Three of Cups

Three is the Goddess, the Great Mother, and the mother of water is overflowing, loving, joyous. Along with the Three of Pentacles, this card is one of those most aligned with its primary Major Arcana card, the Empress. The higher card, Death, may seem an opposite energy (many of these pairs seem to work that way, such as the Hierophant and the Devil), but since death and life are always mixed together, the Three of Cups teaches us that life flows out of death, and the Great Mother gives birth constantly. Since this is Beriah, Creation, she gives birth to form, to all the possibilities of existence. The decan, with its Mercury ruler, adds a quality of awareness to all this emotional outpouring.

The Rider becomes an image of friendship and of celebration, though not especially of romance. In fact, the only card that clearly is romantic in the Rider Cups is the Two, though we see a happy family in Ten and possibly the loss of relationship in Five and Eight. But then, Waite came out of the late Victorian era, so perhaps we should not expect to see much in the way of sex or romance.

My own theme for three is group activities, and with Cups that becomes emotional bonds, closeness among friends. In the '70s, when some people were experimenting with open relationships, the Three of Cups occasionally came up for people who were trying to follow an ideal of nonpossessiveness or nonjealousy. Today we call this polyamory, and the Three of Cups might apply to this behavior as well.

The healing power of this card would be around friendships.

READINGS—Overflowing emotions, deep bonds between friends or family, possibly overwhelming others emotionally. Simplest— a party.

REVERSED—Strains between friends, possibly the need to be alone for a while or the need to heal a friendship. Plans for some group activity might fall through.

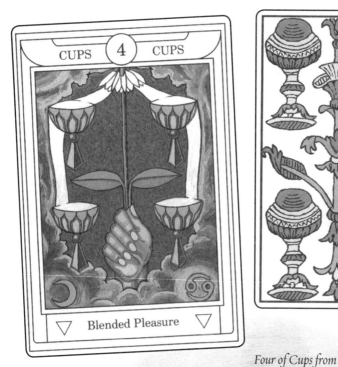

CUPS **4** CUPS

Blended Pleasure

Element: Water

Sephirah: Chesed (Mercy), sephirah four in Beriah (Creation)

Pythagorean: Tetrad, wholeness

Major Arcana: Emperor, Temperance

Rider Theme: Structure

Golden Dawn Title: Blended Pleasure

Decan: 21-30 degrees Cancer, ruled by the moon

Picatrix: Running, hunting, pursuing, acquiring goods by war, contention among men

Four of Cups from
GOLDEN DAWN,
MARSEILLE, RIDER,
SOLA-BUSCA,
SHINING TRIBE &
VISCONTI

Four of Cups

Four is a number where many people agree on the themes—structure, stability, rules, and also the material world. Since Cups is the suit of emotions, this card might indicate a family, or some other social group where people have definite roles. The Emperor as one of the Major Arcana cards suggests a hierarchical structure. The higher card, Temperance, suggests more of blended emotions among people and, in fact, is Gertrude Moakley's suggested Virtue for this suit.

The flowing qualities of water work against structure, and this is how I view the Rider figure, who seems reluctant to reach up and take the new cup offered by the same sort of hand from a cloud as on the Ace. Or perhaps he is just bored or apathetic. Sometimes the Rider Four of Cups indicates someone who has been disappointed in love and now does not look at a new possibility that has come up in his or her life.

The one tradition that does not follow the idea of structure so much is the Kabbalist. Chesed means benevolent outpouring, great generosity on the emotional level.

READINGS—A family or other group where emotions are structured, possibly by everyone having a role. Possibly a benevolent outpouring of feeling, though the person doing it might tend to dominate others (Emperor) and need to hold back (Temperance). For the Rider, apathy and a hesitation about trying something new.

REVERSED—Emotional structures breaking down, people exploring new aspects of existing relationships. Holding back emotionally to give others room to express themselves. With the Rider, the willingness to try something new.

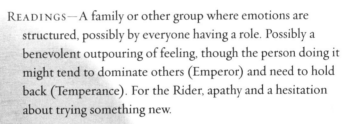

CUPS **5** CUPS

△ Loss in Pleasure △

Element: Water

Sephirah: Gevurah (Power), sephirah five in Beriah (Creation)

Pythagorean: Pentad, higher consciousness, demigod

Major Arcana: Hierophant, Devil

Rider Theme: Life's difficulties

Golden Dawn Title: Loss in Pleasure

Decan: 1-10 degrees Scorpio, ruled by Mars

Picatrix: Strife, sadness, treachery, deceit, destruction, ill will

Five of Cups from
GOLDEN DAWN,
MARSEILLE, RIDER,
SOLA-BUSCA,
SHINING TRIBE &
VISCONTI

Five of Cups

Often, it seems that the Picatrix meanings do not match any of the standard themes for a card. Here we find a conjunction between at least the Kabbalist, Rider, and Picatrix themes, though the Picatrix seems to go further, adding "treachery, deceit, ill will."

Despite Waite's great interest in Kabbalah, his Minor meanings and Smith's pictures do not always match the sephiroth. The Fives, however, do follow the theme of Gevurah, which is life's harshness and the way problems test us. For Cups, this becomes an image of sadness, mourning something that is lost. The picture shows three spilled cups, with two remaining behind the person and a bridge over a river to a house. The scene implies turning around, seeing what remains, picking them up, and crossing the bridge for life to continue. But it is a mistake to try and jump to that idea when this card comes up. We need to experience the sadness before we can move on from it.

The Pythagorean tradition is much more positive: the demigod, halfway to the full realization of ten. With Cups, this gives us a greater understanding of feelings and what they have meant in our lives. The pentad can mean an opening to higher consciousness. Emotions, and perhaps relationships, would be the path to such awareness. The Shining Tribe picture some-

what combines the Pythagorean and Kabbalist pictures in that it symbolizes accepting life's sorrows and finding truth. The fish bend to follow the river, which then becomes the neck and head of a bird.

My own theme for five is time and the changes it brings. The spilled cups of the Rider image is one kind of change, but it is not the only one. Nothing stays the same in this world, including feelings.

READINGS—Possible loss, sadness, but maybe any change in feelings. Neither happiness nor sadness is permanent. Lessons learned and greater consciousness coming from emotional experience.

REVERSED—With the Rider, or cards based on it, the time comes to pick up what is left after a loss and move on. Conversely, if we think of the basic meaning as emotional change, then reversed can mean greater stability, especially in a relationship.

CUPS 6 CUPS

Pleasure

Element: Water

Sephirah: Tipheret (Beauty), sephirah six in Beriah (Creation)

Pythagorean: Hexad, harmony, above and below, masculine and feminine

Major Arcana: Lovers, Tower

Rider Theme: Unequal relationships/generosity

Golden Dawn Title: Pleasure

Decan: 11-20 degrees Scorpio, ruled by the sun

Picatrix: Affronts, detection, strife, stirring up of quarrels, science

Six of Cups from
GOLDEN DAWN,
MARSEILLE, RIDER,
SOLA-BUSCA,
SHINING TRIBE &
VISCONTI

Six of Cups

The Rider imagery of unequal relationships here shows us two figures, possibly children (people disagree), with the larger one—a boy? a fairy-tale character?—offering a cup with a flower to a girl, who seems strangely overdressed. It is an odd scene, usually interpreted as nostalgia, a looking back at the past, especially childhood. Some people see it as having sinister undertones; one woman I know links it to incest and the way such families create false pictures of family happiness and harmony. The idea of generosity takes it much more on face value: he gives her a flower to share with her the beauty of life.

Genuine harmony is really the theme of the card, for both Pythagorean and Kabbalist traditions. Six evokes the six-pointed star, with its merger of masculine and feminine, so that the Six of Cups might mean a love relationship that goes beyond the rather formal Two. Deep feeling in a long-standing marriage would be one theme; this goes well with the Lovers card as the lower Major Arcana connection. The Tower, on the other hand, could threaten such stability, but it also could give it more passion.

The idea of opposites joining could mean a reconciliation or two people who seem very different but form a loving bond.

As the center of the tree, Beauty, the Six of Cups might signify the emotional ideal, a model of how we might experience our feelings and behave in meaningful relationships.

READINGS—While it's difficult to reconcile the Rider imagery of nostalgia with the idea of emotional harmony and perfection in stability, we might need to choose between these possible interpretations.

REVERSED—For the Rider, letting go of the past, possibly a more honest look at family or other relationships. The healing function for this card might be to heal the memories of childhood. Beyond the Rider, a stable, harmonious situation becomes strained. How serious this is should be clear from the other cards.

CUPS 7 CUPS

Illusionary Success

Element: Water

Sephirah: Netzach (Victory), sephirah seven in Beriah (Creation)

Pythagorean: Heptad, dynamic aware energy, the cosmos

Major Arcana: Chariot, Star

Rider Theme: Contemplation or awareness of action

Golden Dawn Title: Illusionary Success

Decan: 21-30 degrees Scorpio, ruled by Venus

Picatrix: War, drunkenness, fornication, wealth, pride, and of rage and violence against women

Seven of Cups from GOLDEN DAWN, MARSEILLE, RIDER, SOLA-BUSCA, SHINING TRIBE & VISCONTI

Seven of Cups

We have included the Picatrix meanings in the Minor Arcana for the sake of completeness, since there is evidence the Golden Dawn may have consulted it. Often it seems very different from how most consider the card, and here it seems quite extreme. Considering how much violence against women exists in the world, it probably is a meaning to keep in the back of your mind if other cards in a reading hint at battering or other kinds of abuse, but that is not how most people see the card.

The Rider image of fantasies, daydreams, and fantastic thoughts also seems not really related to the meaning of seven (though I followed the theme of fantasy for my own Shining Tribe card). It does show us a slightly different side of Cups, that of imagination. Imagination is in some ways the source of human love and relationship. When we fall in love at first sight, it is not a physical reaction but an "imaginal" one (the word, from the philosopher and student of Sufism Henri Corbin, signifies experiences of the imagination that are real and meaningful, compared to the dismissive "imaginary").

If we consider the Kabbalist sephirah as the realm of love and emotion, and the seven as an active number, then we get a great force of love. I have described seven as creative and inventive, so we might see the Seven of Cups as experiencing new feelings. This is a card that might need balancing with other elemental energy. The Wands would spur the person to action, the Swords would allow them to think about all that feeling or fantasy, and the Pentacles to create something real.

READINGS—Great emotion, someone who loves powerfully, who might be driven as much by imagination and fantasies as by actual circumstances. Someone who enjoys the fantasy of love, in love with being in love.

REVERSED—The need to take action on fantasies. Love might not be returned. A choice might have to be made.

CUPS 8 CUPS

Abandoned Success

Element: Water

Sephirah: Hod (Glory), sephirah eight in Beriah (Creation)

Pythagorean: Octad, stability, safety, the spiritual mother of the gods

Major Arcana: Strength, Moon

Rider Theme: Movement

Golden Dawn Title: Abandoned Success

Decan: 1-10 degrees Pisces, ruled by Saturn

Picatrix: Many thoughts, anxiety, journeying from place to place, misery, seeking riches and food

Eight of Cups from GOLDEN DAWN, MARSEILLE, RIDER, SOLA-BUSCA, SHINING TRIBE & VISCONTI

Eight of Cups

Here we find one of the Rider deck's most compelling images, the theme of movement in the emotional suit, shown as someone leaving something behind. We can imagine that the figure from the Seven has been disappointed in love (or other fantasies) and now must move on. The Major Arcana Strength card comes in here, for it often requires emotional strength to leave what we have. Notice that the cups are not knocked over, as in the Five. The person knows it is time to leave. A recent interpretation (recent to me, at least) points out there is a gap in the arrangement of the top row of cups, so perhaps he has left to look for what is missing in his life. A crescent moon shines, but the way the picture is done, it might be an eclipse of the sun—that is, a shift from solar to lunar energy.

All of this is very interesting, but it does not match the usual themes suggested by the number. Above, I commented that I see eight as a number of cycles and repetition (from the infinity-shaped number). This suggests someone who chooses the same sort of partner over and over. More widely, the figure of eight evokes Above and Below joined, so there is a wider harmony here than in the six, which is harmony between opposites. Another kind of harmony comes when we consider the Golden Dawn idea that sephirah eight, Hod, is the realm of Mercury, the mind. This would be harmony between thought and emotion.

READINGS—Several meanings are possible, depending on the symbolic ideas. The Rider gives us leaving something before it has ended because we know it is time to move on. Looking for something that is missing in our current lives. Alternatively, harmony between ideas and feelings, or someone who repeatedly follows the same pattern in emotional relationships. If Cups help us heal from past issues, the Eight could help those who have felt abandoned or who have given up too easily.

REVERSED—For the Rider, this is not the time to leave a situation. A lack of connection between the head and the heart. Breaking a pattern in relationships.

Material Happiness

Element: Water

Sephirah: Yesod (Foundation), sephirah nine in Beriah (Creation)

Pythagorean: Ennead, fulfillment, completion, perfection

Major Arcana: Hermit, Sun

Rider Theme: Intensity, the element at a high degree

Golden Dawn Title: Material Happiness

Decan: 11–20 degrees Pisces, ruled by Jupiter

Picatrix: Self-praise, high mind, seeking after great and high aims

Nine of Cups from
GOLDEN DAWN,
MARSEILLE, RIDER,
SOLA-BUSCA,
SHINING TRIBE &
VISCONTI

Nine of Cups

The Picatrix meaning here seems interestingly at odds with the Rider image, which most people interpret as someone smug, self-satisfied, and interested primarily in pleasure. Waite's key words for the Nine reversed actually evoke the Picatrix "high mind." They include truth, loyalty, and liberty, as if the person abandons his low-level satisfactions and seeks something more out of life. In general, however, I find the Rider choice of picture for the Nine not what we might expect for the number and suit. It might have gone better with Pentacles.

If we see the man in the Rider Eight of Cups as searching for the missing cup, then the Nine is the happy completion of his search. The Shining Tribe Nine of Rivers shows eight broken vessels with water spilling out. They represent whatever is lost and cannot be recovered, while the Grail-like central vessel shows what is longlasting and meaningful.

One further meaning for the Rider card—some see it as a suggestion of alcoholism. This would depend on other cards in that direction, such as the Devil or possibly King of Cups.

Nine, to me, seems mostly about completion and the possible birth of something new. This could be a love fulfilled and the establishment of a strong relationship (marriage if supportive cards appear). Since the nine months of pregnancy end when the woman's "water breaks," we can see the Nine of Cups literally as someone giving birth.

The Pythagorean ennead, three times three, hints at levels beyond ordinary knowledge. What would Cups—water—be if we took it to a level above our ordinary experience? The Kabbalist sephirah, Yesod, is the lunar realm, bringing us back to themes of imagination, dreams, myth. Maybe this card carries power to take us into mythic worlds.

READINGS—Again, a range of possibilities. From the Rider, satisfaction, pleasure, comfort, possibly having found something that was missing. From the Shining Tribe, focusing on what is lasting and meaningful rather than what is lost or impermanent. More generally, something born out of imagination or powerful emotion. Possibly an actual birth.

REVERSED—For the Rider, moving towards deeper concerns, away from physical satisfaction. Something that needs to be "born" from emotional issues but is not ready to emerge.

CUPS **10** CUPS

Perfected Success

Element: Water

Sephirah: Malkuth (Kingdom), sephirah ten in Beriah (Creation)

Pythagorean: Decad, higher unity, greater consciousness

Major Arcana: Wheel of Fortune, Judgement

Rider Theme: Excess

Golden Dawn Title: Perfected Success

Decan: 21-30 degrees Pisces, ruled by Mars

Picatrix: Pleasure, fornication, of quietness and of peacemaking

Ten of Cups from GOLDEN DAWN, MARSEILLE, RIDER, SOLA-BUSCA, SHINING TRIBE & VISCONTI

Ten of Cups

As a number beyond the completion of nine, ten can have the meaning of an excessive degree of the quality of the suit, so that it is likely to change over into something else. We find this idea in the I Ching, the Chinese oracle, that when something reaches its extreme, it is about to change, sometimes into its opposite. The Rider seems to take up this idea with the tens. Hopefully, this is less the case with the Ten of Cups than with any of the others (we probably would want the Ten of Swords to change into its opposite), because this card shows a joyous family. The positive emotional quality of the suit shows us a simple scene. There is no mansion for these people, but also no burdens. The parents are conscious of all they have, holding up their arms to the cups arrayed in the rainbow, while the children dance freely. I followed this idea for my own Ten of Rivers in the Shining Tribe deck, though there the house is drawn realistically, to suggest that the happiness has roots in reality, is not fleeting.

We would expect something joyous from the Pythagorean interpretation as well, for the decad is their highest number, with such titles as "Heaven...Eternity...Power." Since ten is the sum of 1+2+3+4, the decad contains all the elements. At the same time, the Ten of Cups emphasizes water. So we might ask, how would the Ten of Cups show the emotional coming together of different aspects of life?

The Kabbalist idea of ten is almost the opposite of the Pythagorean, stressing that Malkuth, the physical world, is the furthest from the perfection of one, Kether. However, a more positive view looks at ten as the reality number, the place where the qualities of the suit take form in our lives. Here, the Rider seems to go well, with the idea that family happiness is what can emerge in life if Cups fulfills its possibilities.

READINGS—One of the happiest cards in the deck, in pretty much whichever system we use. Emotional connections, fulfillment. It is probably not a card of great wealth but rather of simple pleasures.

REVERSED—There may be something that calls into question or threatens a person's happiness. More likely, it seems to me, the reversed Ten would mean that someone does not recognize what she or he has.

A Reading Inspired by the Suit of Cups

1. How am I emotional?

2. How do I express my feelings to others?

3. How do I hide them?

4. What is my emotional history?

5. How does it affect my life now?

6. How can I find and develop love?

Swords

Element: Air, second-generation male energy, yang

Kabbalistic World: Yetsirah (Formation), the emergence of distinct forms or ideas

Magical "Weapon": Sword of truth

Social Class: Nobility, warriors (modern: military, police, law, government)

Biblical Object: Sword of King David

"Ruling" God: Apollo, god of civilization and reason, conquest, and also art, healing, and prophecy

Primary Major Arcana Card: Emperor

Medieval Virtue: Justice

A sword is the first human artifact created only for the purpose of killing other humans. Other blades, such as knives or axes, serve as tools, or for hunting (spears). But a sword is useless for anything but combat. This gives the suit an aggressive quality, an overlay of sorrow, that we cannot get away from, no matter how high-*minded* we try to make it. A sword also belongs to the aristocracy; for peasants even to own a sword was likely a capital offense. Though today many will see the nobility as oppressive, the word *noble* shows them as symbols of idealism. Waite described the Knight of Swords, not the Knight of Cups, as Sir Galahad, the Knight of the Grail.

Swords represent air, which in turn is the element of mind. Traditionally, Tarotists say that it cuts through illusions and makes fine (*sharp*) distinctions, though I confess I've never found this entirely convincing. For my Shining Tribe Tarot, I made Birds the suit of air—mind as art and prophecy as much as intellect and conflict. Wands gives Swords more optimism, Cups more gentleness and even love, and Pentacles can ground all the mental energy.

The Ace of Swords

Element: Air

Sephirah: Kether (Crown), sephirah one in Yetsirah (Formation)

Pythagorean: Monad, unity

Major Arcana: Magician, Justice

Rider Theme: Gift of elemental air

Ace of Swords from GOLDEN DAWN, MARSEILLE, RIDER, SOLA-BUSCA, SHINING TRIBE & VISCONTI

ACE of SWORDS.

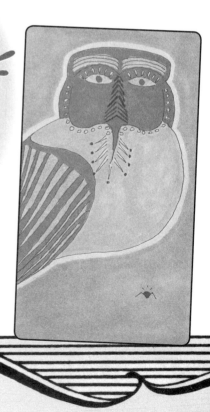

Ace of Swords

Even if the deck usually shows scimitars, the Ace generally is a straight sword, for singleness of purpose. At the same time, such swords are usually double-edged, and the idea that it can cut both ways characterizes the entire suit. There is that quality of intellectual penetration, and then there is the conflict and the pain the sword can cause. In the Golden Dawn and Rider images of the Aces, a hand holds out the suit image, and this idea of a gift of the power of that suit could apply to the Aces in any deck, whether we see an actual hand or not. The Ace stands before us, ready for us to take hold. If so, what exactly is the gift of the Ace of the Swords? We can think of it as a sharp mind that cuts through all the confusions of life, penetrates people's armor and even our own defenses—how easily we can slip into metaphors, not just of cutting but of military action, when we speak of the Swords! A keen mind is indeed a gift, for it can free us from useless guilt, among other weaknesses.

But maybe the Sword's deeper gift is sorrow, an awareness of the suffering of life. *Some gift,* we might think, *can't we just have some chocolates?* And yet, isn't it a gift to be able to see the truth of our existence?

Does the Sword point up or down? This is a key question. If down, it shows the mental energy entering into physical concerns and daily life. If it points up, the Sword shows the

mind's ability to go beyond the distractions of the physical and reach principles of truth. The Magician, the first Major Arcana card for the Ace, moves energy down into manifestation. The higher card, Justice in most modern decks, actually holds a sword, and it too usually points straight up. In the Rider deck, only Justice, the Ace, and the Queen hold swords that do not deviate to either side.

The Virtue of this suit is Justice, and we see, even feel it, in the Ace more than any other. "Justice, justice, shall you pursue," the Bible tells us (see section on the Major Arcana Justice). We must use the power of intellect for justice, not manipulation.

READINGS—Clear thought, spiritual truth, singleness of mind and purpose. We may be called on to speak or act with justice.

REVERSED—Confusion, difficulty thinking clearly, possibly a danger of aggression or manipulation.

SWORDS 2 SWORDS

Peace Restored

Element: Air

Sephirah: Hokhmah (Wisdom). sephirah two in Yetsirah (Formation)

Pythagorean: Dyad, separation, dialog

Major Arcana: High Priestess, Hanged Man

Rider Theme: Choices, balance

Golden Dawn Title: Peace Restored

Decan: 1-10 degrees Libra, ruled by the moon

Picatrix: Justice, aid, truth, and helping the poor

Two of Swords from
GOLDEN DAWN,
MARSEILLE, RIDER,
SOLA-BUSCA,
SHINING TRIBE &
VISCONTI

Two of Swords

For those who know the Rider deck, one of the things that immediately may strike us about this card is how it seems the opposite of most of the themes. Instead of wisdom, or balance, or even "peace restored," we see a blindfolded woman who holds two heavy swords at her shoulders. Unlike the tied-up woman in the Eight, she clearly has done this herself, as if to avoid having to make any choice at all or to look at her surroundings and interact with them. In a class we tried this once; two people brought swords and blindfolds, and we each got to act out the picture. The swords were heavy, and it took a good deal of strength to hold them there for even a short period of time. So she has made a choice to use her energy to keep everything out, as if she deliberately rejects dialog, peace (except the peace of isolation), and the Picatrix call to justice and helping others.

What she does match is the Major Arcana cards. Both the High Priestess and the Hanged Man turn inward, away from social involvement. And it is possible to see the Rider image as a meditation or a martial art, a kind of training to look inward rather than get distracted by the outer world.

If we get away from this compelling picture, what subject might we expect to see in the Two of Mind? Dialog on a high mental plane would be one possibility, dialog between two sharp minds. Or an intellectual collaboration. And what might the wisdom of Swords be? A true awareness of the principles of our lives, the meaning of the suffering of human existence.

READINGS—Intellectual wisdom, dialog on a high level. With the Rider, a deliberate turn away from any outer involvements, either to avoid communication or to awaken inner qualities, as in meditation.

REVERSED—Breakdown in communication, a mental balance upset. With the Rider, becoming involved with others, dropping defenses.

Element: Air

Sephirah: Binah (Understanding), sephirah three in Yetsirah (Formation)

Pythagorean: Triad, unity restored, but in the created world

Major Arcana: Empress, Death

Rider Theme: A flowering, something created from the energy of the suit

Golden Dawn Title: Sorrow

Decan: 11-20 degrees Libra, ruled by Saturn

Picatrix: Quietness, ease, plenty, good life, dance

Three of Swords from GOLDEN DAWN, MARSEILLE, RIDER, SOLA-BUSCA, SHINING TRIBE & VISCONTI

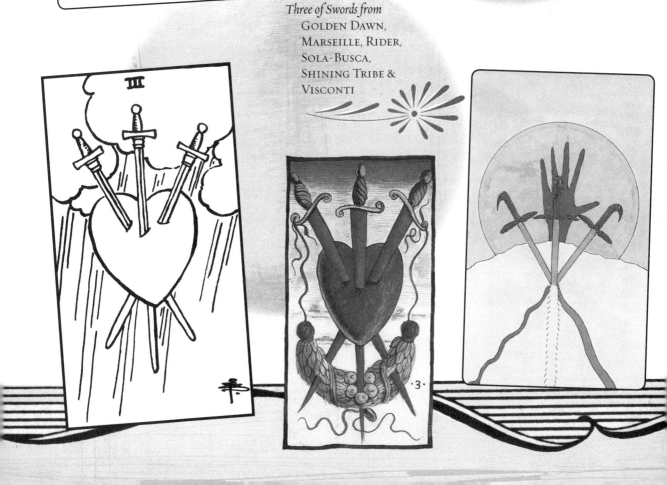

Three of Swords

This card is a great example of how the Golden Dawn used the decan system (you can see the astrological glyphs on the Golden Dawn version) but did not feel bound by the Picatrix descriptions. Instead, they seem to have focused on the sword itself, and the idea that the Great Mother of Swords would evoke pain and sorrow. The Rider deck clearly follows this theme, with its image of a pierced heart. Notice that the swords all point down, the direction of manifestation, while the Golden Dawn version shows the swords up, maybe to go beyond sorrow to understanding, the literal meaning of Binah. And the swords, or at least the center blade, have cut through a rose, symbol of the Rosicrucian movement and sacred to Aphrodite, goddess of love. Sorrow is the destruction of love. The Shining Tribe image borrows from the Rider but shows the ability to heal by accepting the pain, taking hold of it and releasing.

If we separate from the idea of sorrow, what else might the understanding of Swords, or air, be? For the suit symbol, it could be a true understanding of the meaning of sorrow in our lives. For the element, it might indicate an understanding of our own mental processes, different for each person.

My own sense of the number as group or family suggests the possibility that the Three of Swords indicates conflict in a group. This could produce sorrow, but it also could stay at the level of anger.

READINGS—Sorrow, with the hope that by accepting it, we can go beyond the pain. Conflict in a group, such as a family or at work. Understanding the quality of your own mind.

REVERSED—Denial of some pain. Attempts to bring back harmony in a group of people. Not understanding your own thought processes.

SWORDS 4 SWORDS

Rest From Strife

Element: Air

Sephirah: Chesed (Mercy), sephirah four in Yetsirah (Formation)

Pythagorean: Tetrad, wholeness

Major Arcana: Emperor, Temperance

Rider Theme: Structure

Golden Dawn Title: Rest from Strife

Decan: 21-30 degrees Libra, ruled by Jupiter

Picatrix: Ill deeds, yet of singing and mirth and gluttony, sodomy, and following of evil pleasures

Four of Swords from
GOLDEN DAWN,
MARSEILLE, RIDER,
SOLA-BUSCA,
SHINING TRIBE &
VISCONTI

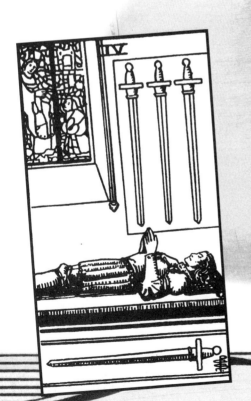

Four of Swords

There is a temptation here to bring together the Picatrix meaning with the Rider image and think of the knight in the picture as sleeping off a hangover. But is he just resting? To some he looks dead, to others it seems not a person at all, but an effigy on top of a stone coffin. I've said that structure is the theme of four in the Rider, but admittedly here it's a bit strained—air resists structure, as anyone knows who has tried to keep the mind focused on a single subject, so structure comes only through a withdrawal from stimulus. The Rider image often seems like a fairy-tale scene to me, a knight under a spell who can only be awakened by the right person. In the Grail stories, the Fisher King lies in a kind of coma until the Grail can heal him. Perceval can do so, simply by asking what is going on when he sees the Grail maidens carrying the sacred objects. Speech would have activated the healing power. Instead, he follows politeness rather than instinct, and the king remains asleep.

The wholeness and stability of tetrad would suggest we look at the Four of Swords as solid, structured thinking, producing results in the physical world. If Swords are conflict, the Four might contain the issues that cause problems, bringing stability (and so perhaps rest).

The theme of Chesed, expansive goodness and mercy, seems to go against the usual view of the Four as structure and stability. It might, however, be a valuable meaning to consider—mercy and generosity in situations of conflict, or the Four of Air can refer to orderly, logical thinking.

The Four of Birds is a key card in the Shining Tribe Tarot. A woman has been climbing a mountain on a vision quest. Only when she stops to rest and allows the mountain to support her can the birds come to her with a vision. The card teaches us that we can allow things to happen rather than always try to control events.

READINGS—Varied possibilities, maybe even more than usual. Rest, withdrawal, peacefulness. Logical, structured thinking. Healing, but maybe the need to respond to someone who is suffering. Mercy and generosity replacing anger. Allowing what we want to come to us instead of chasing after it.

REVERSED—Arousal from rest. Taking a firm position in a conflict. Confusion over whether or not to intervene in a situation. Intuitive thinking rather than logic.

SWORDS **5** SWORDS

Defeat

Element: Air

Sephirah: Gevurah (Power), sephirah five in Yetsirah (Formation)

Pythagorean: Pentad, higher consciousness, demigod

Major Arcana: Hierophant, Devil

Rider Theme: Life's difficulties

Golden Dawn Title: Defeat

Decan: 1-10 degrees Aquarius, ruled by Venus

Picatrix: Poverty, anxiety, grieving after gain, and never resting from labor, loss, and violence

Five of Swords from
GOLDEN DAWN,
MARSEILLE, RIDER,
SOLA-BUSCA,
SHINING TRIBE &
VISCONTI

Five of Swords

In most decks, this is one of the most difficult cards. Actually, many people who look at the Rider picture and do not know what it intends to illustrate see it as positive. This is because they assume the largest figure is the focus character, and so they see the card as triumph and satisfaction. Only if we know it illustrates the theme of defeat do we look primarily to the two figures moving away. This feature of the design presents a challenge sometimes in readings. Do we ask the querent how they see it and simply accept "triumph" as the meaning for the particular reading? Or do we point out the intent of the deck's creators? Some readers make a firm decision. They will say the meaning of any card depends on what the querent sees in it, or the opposite—that the meaning is fixed, and the reader should explain it. I tend to waver on these approaches, depending on the reading.

Notice, by the way, that the Golden Dawn basically repeats the image from the Three, except the two outer hands now hold double-bladed swords. These odd objects come from the Marseille tradition, where in the higher numbers the scimitars become linked together for the even numbers, with the addition of a single straight sword in the odd numbers.

Gevurah is the most difficult place and Swords is the suit of conflict, but also of mind, and they come together to produce not just defeat but a sense of humiliation and shame. In other words, the defeat is as much a mental state as an event. The Picatrix meaning would seem to go more with the Five of Pentacles.

The Kabbalah meaning of the number five does not entirely match the way many people see the number. If we consider five as the number of time, then yes, the passage of time sometimes brings defeat, but it also can produce victory. More simply, there is the change of ideas that can come through time. And the Pythagorean idea of the demigod allows for the idea of a mental state that is partway towards a true higher consciousness.

READINGS—Defeat, shame, and the need to release such states of mind. Warning against engaging in battle with someone who may be too strong. Old ideas or prejudices giving way to new ways of thinking.

REVERSED—Beginning to move past some disturbing loss or defeat. Newfound confidence. Another possibility—fixed ideas that resist change.

Element: Air

Sephirah: Tipheret (Beauty), sephirah six in Yetsirah (Formation)

Pythagorean: Hexad, harmony, above and below, masculine and feminine

Major Arcana: Lovers, Tower

Rider Theme: Unequal relationships/generosity

Golden Dawn Title: Earned Success

Decan: 11-20 degrees Aquarius, ruled by Mercury

Picatrix: Beauty, dominance, conceit, good manners and self-esteem, yet not withstanding modest

Six of Swords from GOLDEN DAWN, MARSEILLE, RIDER, SOLA-BUSCA, SHINING TRIBE & VISCONTI

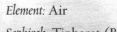

Six of Swords

Here the Picatrix begins with the actual title of the Kabbalah sephirah, Beauty. Clearly, however, it means seeing yourself as beautiful because it includes conceit and dominance. Beauty in Kabbalah is more a sense of harmony and balance, coming in the exact center of the tree. The Golden Dawn title, Earned Success, seems to belong more to Pentacles, with their emphasis on work and practical matters, not to mention their original title, Coins. The connection to air becomes a little clearer if we know that the divinatory description from the Golden Dawn begins "success after anxiety and trouble." Still, it's hard to see just why anxiety (a Swords condition, to be sure) should earn us success.

The Rider image seems to show a group of people in a ferryboat. The man poling the boat clearly controls the situation, as well as the fact that the woman and child (my interpretation of the huddled figures) appear so subdued. An aura of silence pervades the card, as if they carry their pain wherever they go. Ellen Goldberg's idea that the Rider cards show the "beauty" of generosity translates as the ferryman assisting people who must leave something behind.

The Rider meanings might derive from the eighteenth-century French fortuneteller and Tarotist Etteila. His meanings, quite long, include "route…passage, way…voyage, kind attention…" Waite often looked to Etteila as the tradition for the card, though usually he somewhat simplifies it. Here is Waite's actual list: "Journey by water, route, envoy, commissionary, expedient, the voyage will be pleasant." Mathers, too, follows Etteila.

If we look at the theme of harmony and relationship for the card, how might we see that in Swords? One meaning might be people of different backgrounds who share similar ideas and interests. Or it could show the ability to synthesize seemingly opposite ideas or beliefs. This is the Lovers aspect of the number. When the harmony becomes disrupted, the higher number, sixteen, takes over, and we get the Tower.

READINGS—Possibly a literal journey. More often, carrying a problem or secret with you. Keeping silent rather than exposing something. Or shared ideas. Holding different beliefs at the same time.

REVERSED—Speaking up. Disrupting some longstanding situation. Conflict of ideas. Arguments.

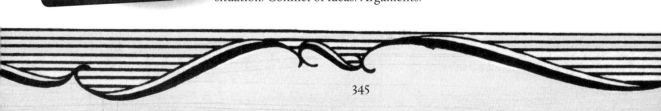

SWORDS 7 SWORDS

Unstable Effort

Element: Air

Sephirah: Netzach (Victory), sephirah seven in Yetsirah (Formation)

Pythagorean: Heptad, dynamic energy, the cosmos

Major Arcana: Chariot, Star

Rider Theme: Contemplation or awareness of action

Golden Dawn Title: Unstable Effort

Decan: 21-30 degrees Aquarius, ruled by the moon

Picatrix: Abundance and compliments, detection and affronts

Seven of Swords from
GOLDEN DAWN,
MARSEILLE, RIDER,
SOLA-BUSCA,
SHINING TRIBE &
VISCONTI

Seven of Swords

In my notes above, I described the sevens as creativeness, inventiveness, possibilities, and suggested that the Seven of Swords could suggest new, innovative ways of thinking or possibly new plans. The first idea, a way of thinking, describes an ongoing state of being, while the second would describe something more specific. Part of the diviner's art is to see which aspect of a card will apply in a particular reading.

The Pythagorean meaning is both broader and larger. Coming after the harmonic Six, and with the suggestion of a new beginning (as One starts the sequence 1, 2, 3, 4, so Seven leads 7, 8, 9, 10), it can mean a genuine breakthrough in a person's thinking. And with its relation to the seven planetary spheres and the seven chakras, that breakthrough could be on large, meaningful issues, especially spiritual awareness.

Paul Huson suggests that the Rider image might derive from the Sola-Busca, for the image shows a young man sneaking off with swords. One big difference is that the Rider character does not carry all of them, giving the sense of an impulsive action that is incomplete or not a real solution. This goes along with the Golden Dawn meaning "unstable effort," leading to "partial success."

To most people, the Rider figure appears smirking, as if very pleased with himself. The sneakiness, and the excited smirk, have led some readers to see it as indicating a secret sexual affair.

The Seven of Birds in the Shining Tribe is one of the most significant cards in the Minor Arcana. Whereas the Rider character seems to consult no one, the two figures in the Birds card engage in intense communication. The dotted line between them shows that each retains his identity yet each speaks passionately. I did not design this with Netzach in mind, but the sephirah evokes Venus, planet of love, and in love we all need to communicate our most powerful emotions. When I asked the cards, "Show me the reading you gave God to create the universe," the Seven of Birds was the first card, suggesting that God needed to create a universe to have someone to talk to. (The entire reading can be found in my book *Forest of Souls.*)

READINGS—Again, various meanings. Dynamic, exciting thinking; intellectual or conceptual breakthroughs, possibly spiritual. Intense communication. Alternatively, an impulsive or clever action that may not solve a problem. Possibly a sexual affair.

REVERSED—For the Rider, willingness to consult with others, to get advice before taking action. More broadly, intellectual frustration or being on the edge of a breakthrough.

Shortened Force

Element: Air

Sephirah: Hod (Glory), sephirah eight in Yetsirah (Formation)

Pythagorean: Octad, stability, safety, the spiritual mother of the gods

Major Arcana: Strength, Moon

Rider Theme: Movement

Golden Dawn Title: Shortened Force

Decan: 1-10 degrees Gemini, ruled by Jupiter

Picatrix: Writing, calculations, giving and receiving money, wisdom in unprofitable things

Eight of Swords from
GOLDEN DAWN,
MARSEILLE, RIDER,
SOLA-BUSCA,
SHINING TRIBE &
VISCONTI

Eight of Swords

The eighth sephirah belongs to Mercury, planet and god of intellect, ideas, and speed, so we might expect these to be reinforced by air, element of mind, and literally "as swift as the wind." In fact, the Picatrix meanings describe areas the ancients associated with Mercury/Hermes—writing, math, and commerce.

Then why does the Golden Dawn call this Shortened Force, and why does the Rider show a woman in bondage (and yes, this card, especially with the Devil, can indicate unusual sexual practices). The odd Golden Dawn title apparently refers to "too much force applied to small things, too much attention to detail, at expense of principle and more important points" (Wang, Golden Dawn Tarot). We might expect that the mental qualities of air would be enhanced in the sephirah of Mercury. Too much of a good thing? (I first typed "too much of a good *think*." Unintentional puns evoke Hermes.)

The Rider theme for eight, movement, appears here as its opposite, a woman tied up and blindfolded. Unlike the woman in the Two, she seems a victim here. Behind her we see a castle, symbol of authority, while a fence of swords surrounds her. Tied up and helpless, she stands in mud, an evocation of shame. However—no one is actually there from the castle, a gap in the swords allows her to leave, and the bonds do not actually go around her legs. All

that stops her is the blindfold, symbol of confusion, isolation, and mental control. The realization that nothing holds her can be very liberating to people who think of themselves as weak or helpless or trapped.

But what of meanings beyond the Rider card? I've suggested that the number eight evokes cycles and patterns; the Eight of Swords might indicate repetitious thinking. Coming after the dynamic Seven, it can symbolize reestablishing stable patterns of thought after a breakthrough.

READINGS—Feelings of helplessness, weakness, being trapped. These may be illusions, more a mental state than actual conditions. Accepting someone else's negative description of you. Alternatively, repetitious thought patterns. Mental stability after an unsettled time.

REVERSED—For the Rider, getting the blindfold off, seeing a situation clearly. Possibly breaking free of repetitious thought patterns. Mental instability.

Element: Air

Sephirah: Yesod (Foundation), sephirah nine in Yetsirah (Formation)

Pythagorean: Ennead, fulfillment, completion, perfection

Major Arcana: Hermit, Sun

Rider Theme: Intensity, the element at a high degree

Golden Dawn Title: Despair and Cruelty

Decan: 21-30 Degrees Gemini, ruled by Mars

Picatrix: Burden, pressure, labor, subtlety, dishonesty

Nine of Swords from
GOLDEN DAWN,
MARSEILLE, RIDER,
SOLA-BUSCA,
SHINING TRIBE &
VISCONTI

Nine of Swords

The Rider picture for this card is probably one of its more famous images, simply because it speaks so strongly. A woman sitting up in bed, covering her weeping face, while behind her rise the swords in a completely black background. The dark night of the soul, to use the philosopher Kierkegaard's famous expression. Even the Ten is not so bleak, for there we see a light at the bottom of the picture (though it might not do much for the man with the ten swords in his back!). I sometimes say of this card that it symbolizes whatever wakes you up in the middle of the night.

There are, however, signs of hope in the image, especially the quilt, with squares of roses and the signs of the zodiac, as if the cosmos and the Goddess of Love protect her. Various people have pointed out that the arrangement of the swords appears like a ladder. Acceptance of truth and our own pain can help us climb out of despair.

It makes sense to associate the Nine of Swords with sorrow and pain. We've seen those themes in the suit, and the final single-digit number should bring them to fulfillment and perfection, the Pythagorean ideas of nine. And if nine means birth, what else would be born from a sword but grief?

But air does not mean only conflict, despite the symbol. What would Yesod—Foundation— of Mind be? Both Yesod and the Kabbalistic world of Yetsirah carry the quality of being one

step away from the physical world that we think of as reality. Thus, the Nine of Swords might represent the ability to create a mental picture of existence—that is, to take all the experiences and information of our lives and construct a framework to understand it. The Tarot itself forms such a framework. Put another way, we can say that the Nine of Swords might show us making sense of our lives, including the pain.

READINGS—Sorrow, grief, what wakes you up in the night. Thus, it can be shocking news or a longstanding pain. Hope through acceptance. Alternatively, the ability to make sense of your life or some major (or shocking) event.

REVERSED—Beginnings of recovery. Climbing out of a low point. Possibly confusion or denial.

Element: Air

Sephirah: Malkuth (Kingdom), sephirah ten in Yetsirah (Formation)

Pythagorean: Decad, higher unity, greater consciousness

Major Arcana: Wheel of Fortune, Judgement

Rider Theme: Excess

Golden Dawn Title: Ruin

Decan: 21-30 degrees Gemini, ruled by the sun

Picatrix: Disdain, mirth, and jollity and of many unprofitable words

Ten of Swords from
GOLDEN DAWN,
MARSEILLE, RIDER,
SOLA-BUSCA,
SHINING TRIBE &
VISCONTI

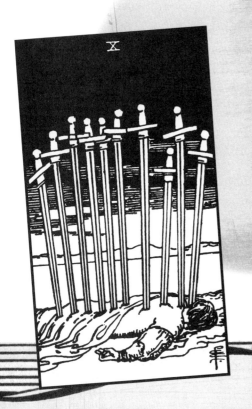

Ten of Swords

We may think that the Golden Dawn came up with the very harsh interpretation of the Ten of Swords, but apparently it goes back all the way. Pratesi includes one word for this card: "Tears." The first published account, from Etteila, says: "Weeping, tears, sobs, groans, sighs, wails…" You get the idea. In modern Tarot, we actually would associate such grief with the Nine of Swords, for the Ten seems to go even further, showing someone murdered.

The Rider Ten of Swords has always seemed to me not quite serious. It only takes one sword to kill someone, and the overkill suggests to me the possibility of hysteria or self-pity. In the Shining Tribe Ten of Birds, I depicted a woman covering her eyes in fear of exaggerated mythic birds. Ten in the suit of air could imply an extreme mental state, separated from reality.

For many, the light in the Rider image suggests hope. Tarotist Ellen Goldberg describes it as an actual picture of the "golden dawn." In direct contrast, Wald Amberstone, of the New York Tarot School, sees the darkness as about to extinguish the remaining light. Another possible sign (literally) of hope—the dead man's fingers form the blessing that we see in the Hierophant/Pope card. Could this mean a sacrifice for the sake of others? Some see the scene as a meditation to overcome the ego or the fear of death.

All these ten approaches belong to the Kabbalistic theme of ten, Malkuth, as furthest from the perfection of one, Kether. Malkuth is the real world, the world of the body, where everything eventually dies, so that Ten of Air can show mental awareness of this great truth.

The Pythagorean view, however, is almost the opposite of the Kabbalist. Ten becomes fulfillment, the wondrous decad. Ten of Swords might mean the ability to perceive a higher reality and how everything fits perfectly together. The marriage of Zeus and Hera.

READINGS—Here we find some of the most extreme variances. Ruin, despair, though possibly exaggerated—hysteria, with things not as bad as they seem. Sacrifice. Alternatively, revelations, the ability to put things together into a brilliant construction.

REVERSED—Relief from suffering, as if the swords literally fall out of the back. Waite describes "advantage" as "not permanent," so that we need to take advantage of the relief and make changes. Possibly being too close to a situation, too caught up in details.

A Reading Inspired by the Suit of Swords

1. What is the shape of my mind?
   (We did this question in a workshop
   with interesting results.)

2. How do I communicate my ideas?

3. How am I able to hear the ideas of others?

4. What do I need to learn?

5. How will I learn it?

Pentacles

Element: Earth, second-generation female energy, yin

Kabbalistic World: Assiyah (Action), the physical world

Magical "Weapon": Pentagram

Social Class: Merchants, from original name, Coins (modern: businesspeople, managerial class)

Biblical Object: Shekel, the coin of ancient Israel

"Ruling" Goddess: Gaia, the Earth itself, most ancient being

Primary Major Arcana Card: Empress

Medieval Virtue: Prudence, or Charity

Pentacles is the suit of the material world. Pentacles involve money, certainly, for that is in fact their origin, as Coins, and so we find both bounty and hardship in their pictures. And they involve work, what we do to get money, though at their best they show us working at our highest level. Issues of health and the body may arise as well, though these are not restricted to this one suit.

By changing the symbol from a Coin to a Pentacle, the Golden Dawn introduced a wider theme, that of magic, for the five-pointed star, the pentagram. It is not magic spells we find in this suit so much as the magic of nature itself, the wonder of existence. As we've seen before, the five-pointed star is the human body with the arms and the legs out (think da Vinci's famous drawing showing the proportions of the body, the Vitruvian Man). It also appears in the center of many plants, in five-petaled flowers, especially roses, and in the path of the planet Venus. The pentacle is not simply a star, it is a star in a circle of light, and so the suit, which takes us into "dense matter," as the Kabbalists say, also reveals the beauty of the body and the world. At the same time, the suit of earth grounds us—in nature, in practicality, in daily life.

The second generation of yin (and the second Heh in Yod-Heh-Vav-Heh) can tend toward inertness. Wands/fire bring greater energy and fresh inspiration towards action. Cups/water create emotional flow, though if we mix too much emotion with practical issues, we can just make it all muddy. Swords/air allow for new ideas and conscious awareness of what we are doing.

PENTACLES · 1 · PENTACLES

The Ace of Pentacles

Element: Earth

Sephirah: Kether (Crown), sephirah one in Assiyah (Action)

Pythagorean: Monad, unity

Major Arcana: Magician, Justice

Rider Theme: Gift of elemental earth

Ace of Pentacles from
GOLDEN DAWN,
MARSEILLE, RIDER,
SOLA-BUSCA,
SHINING TRIBE &
VISCONTI

ACE of PENTACLES.

Ace of Pentacles

Though the Magician is the primary Major card for the suit of Wands, and the Empress for Pentacles, the Magician works very well with this magical suit, and its Ace, with its gifts of nature, work, and money. We also need Justice here, for the history of almost every culture shows us how easily justice gets forgotten as soon as money is involved. The phrase "It's just business" has allowed people to justify many terrible deeds.

In the Rider picture, we see the hand from a cloud in a lush garden, a place of life but also safety. Our word "paradise" comes from Persian *paradeiza*, meaning a garden (technically an enclosed space, because gardens were protected from the outer wilderness). And of course, Eden was a garden. In the picture, we see a gateway shaped like the wreath around the World dancer. At its best, our life in the material world of Assiyah can be like a sanctuary from which we eventually emerge into the wider existence shown in the later cards of the Major Arcana.

There are no Yods in the Rider Ace of Pentacles. Does this mean that the physical world is not a gift of divine grace?

The Pythagorean idea of unity can remind us of the idea we saw in the Empress, that all the myriad bits and pieces of nature are really one being. The Greeks called this original goddess Gaia, the goddess I have called the "ruling" deity for the suit. The Shining Tribe Ace of

Stones depicts a single stone that emerges from darkness and rises to light. Above and Below are connected through the events of our lives.

READINGS—Prosperity, sometimes a new job or an influx of money. The home (or some private place) as a sanctuary.

REVERSED—Problems around money or security. Possibly moving into a new phase of life.

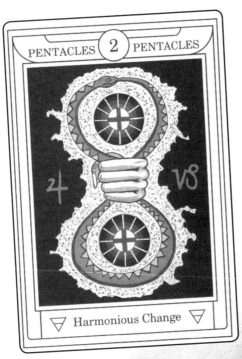

PENTACLES · 2 · PENTACLES

Harmonious Change

Element: Earth

Sephirah: Hokhmah (Wisdom), sephirah two in Assiyah (Action)

Pythagorean: Dyad, separation, dialog

Major Arcana: High Priestess, Hanged Man

Rider Theme: Choices, balance

Golden Dawn Title: Harmonious Change

Decan: 1-10 degrees Capricorn, ruled by Jupiter

Picatrix: Wandering travail, labor and joy, alternate gain and loss, weakness and necessity

Two of Pentacles from
GOLDEN DAWN,
MARSEILLE, RIDER,
SOLA-BUSCA,
SHINING TRIBE &
VISCONTI

Two of Pentacles

In modern playing decks, the signature card, where the publisher gives the name and logo, usually is the Ace of Spades. In older, and traditional, Tarots we find it on the Two of Coins. Sometimes (as in the Marseille version opposite) we see a double loop, like a figure eight, around vertical coins, similar to the Golden Dawn image, though usually not a snake biting its tail. Notice, by the way, that even though the Hermetic Order renamed the suit Pentacles, they do not actually show that symbol but instead display a cross inside a white disk, with twelve white spokes radiating through concentric circles.

The Rider image cleverly shifts the loops sideways to display the infinity sign we see above the heads of the Magician and Strength. The theme of "balance" in this card becomes literal if we take the character as a juggler. He appears to be dancing, while behind him the waves roll in a cheerful motion, giving the whole card a light-hearted quality. Many contemporary people see this card as multi-tasking or as the person who cannot choose priorities.

The card takes on greater meaning if we consider the Kabbalist and Pythagorean ideas. As we have asked with the other suits, what is the wisdom of Pentacles? What higher truths do we learn from nature and money and work? And if two, dyad, means dialog or a mirroring, what kind of conversation can we have with nature? With money? How will they mirror us?

READINGS—Juggling different activities, playfulness in work. Or finding the wisdom in daily life and in nature. Having a dialog with others or yourself over money.

REVERSED—Making mistakes or falling behind in work from taking on too much. Blindness in issues around money.

Element: Earth

Sephirah: Binah (Understanding), sephirah three in Assiyah (Action)

Pythagorean: Triad, unity restored, but in the created world

Major Arcana: Empress, Death

Rider Theme: A flowering, something created from the energy of the suit

Golden Dawn Title: Material Works

Decan: 11-20 degrees Capricorn, ruled by Mars

Picatrix: Ever seeking what cannot be known and what cannot be attained

Three of Pentacles from
GOLDEN DAWN,
MARSEILLE, RIDER,
SOLA-BUSCA,
SHINING TRIBE &
VISCONTI

Three of Pentacles

Compare the Golden Dawn name for this card with the Picatrix. At first they seem completely opposite, the material versus what cannot be known. However, if we seek the unknowable only in the mind, will we really find truth? To seek what cannot be attained within our daily activities and the work we do seems one way to make our lives really meaningful.

The Rider theme of something created from the element shows us an image of such meaningful work. A figure who appears to be a sculptor works in a church, advised by both the architect (holding the building plans) and a monk. Thus, practical knowledge and spiritual awareness help to produce work of the highest level. As described above (in the overview of the numbers), the Rider deck is meant to count *down* to the ace (the highest place on the tree) rather than *up* to the ten. Thus, we see what looks like an apprentice in the Eight and a master here in the Three. In the Shining Tribe image, we see many elements in balance to produce what I call "perfected work."

The Three of the suit of earth does not have to show work at all. As a perfect match for the Major Arcana card, not just of the number but of the entire suit, this card really invokes the Empress, with her lush nature and love of life. Spring and new growth might very well be a theme of this card. The second Major card, Death (thirteen), reminds us that in Assiyah, the world of nature, nothing lasts, and therefore we should appreciate even more the beauty and joy of our lives.

READINGS—Work at a high degree, satisfaction, people working well together. Nature, love of life. Possibly motherhood.

REVERSED—Mediocre work, dissatisfaction, especially from conflicts or lack of opportunity. Failure to recognize the beauty in your daily life. Possibly difficulty becoming pregnant.

PENTACLES **4** PENTACLES

Earthly Power

Element: Earth

Sephirah: Chesed (Mercy),
   sephirah four in Assiyah
   (Action)

Pythagorean: Tetrad, wholeness

Major Arcana: Emperor,
   Temperance

Rider Theme: Structure

Golden Dawn Title: Earthly
   Power

Decan: 21-30 degrees
   Capricorn, ruled by the sun

Picatrix: Covetousness,
   suspicion, careful ordering
   of matters, but with
   discontent

Four of Pentacles from
GOLDEN DAWN,
MARSEILLE, RIDER,
SOLA-BUSCA,
SHINING TRIBE &
VISCONTI

IV

Four of Pentacles

This is a case where the Picatrix description goes well with the Rider, if not with other themes of the number or element. Smith's character is not so much covetous as miserly. The fact that he wears a crown reminds some people of Midas, the king who loved gold so much he wished that everything he touched might turn to the precious metal. He got his wish and was thrilled, at least until he tried to eat or show affection to his daughter. The crown also evokes the basic Major Arcana card for the number, the Emperor. Like the Emperor, the king in the Rider image wants to control his environment—in this case, with money or possessions. The higher number, Temperance, would help him control this need.

The Pythagorean view of structure is more positive—subtlety, wholeness. The Four of Pentacles does not have to mean money; it can refer to our whole way of life as ordered, calm, and enriching.

The theme of structure is quite different than the Golden Dawn's idea of Chesed as benevolent outpourings of mercy. A Four of Pentacles that truly embodied Chesed might show a king who showers help and money on those who need it. Such a picture would fulfill the Virtue of Charity (unlike Smith's miser).

READINGS—Miserliness, using possessions to structure your life or perhaps to shield yourself emotionally. Alternatively, generosity, charity, sharing what you have. The two meanings cannot really be reconciled, for they come from different traditions.

REVERSED—Lack of structure in daily life. Emotional vulnerability. Hesitation about helping others.

PENTACLES **5** PENTACLES

Material Trouble

Element: Earth

Sephirah: Gevurah (Power), sephirah five in Assiyah (Action)

Pythagorean: Pentad, higher consciousness, demigod

Major Arcana: Hierophant, Devil

Rider Theme: Life's difficulties

Golden Dawn Title: Material Trouble

Decan: 1-10 degrees Taurus, ruled by Mercury

Picatrix: Plowing, sowing, building, and earthly wisdom

Five of Pentacles from
GOLDEN DAWN,
MARSEILLE, RIDER,
SOLA-BUSCA,
SHINING TRIBE &
VISCONTI

Five of Pentacles

Now we come to one of those unpleasant fives, at least in the Rider deck, with very different qualities if we step outside of the Golden Dawn Kabbalist tradition. In that tradition, Gevurah is the harsh place on the tree, and so the fives must show struggle of some kind. For Pentacles this means physical hardship, and we see poor and injured people walking through the snow. They pass a church, which should offer sanctuary, and yet the picture contains no door, only a window. Notice, by the way, that the stained-glass pentacles in the window form the top half of the Tree of Life. This is the half furthest from the world of physical reality. Seemingly, it cannot help them. Ironically, perhaps, the first Major Arcana card is the Hierophant, or Pope. The higher number, the Devil, would seem to have taken over. But if they cannot be with others, they have each other. Some see this as a card of a relationship made strong by shared hardship.

The Shining Tribe Five of Stones shows spirits emerging from the rock to bring healing, not just physical but emotional and spiritual. The image was inspired by a very old canyon painting in the American Southwest. After I did the picture, I read that the contemporary Indians who live in the area call the painting "The Ghost Healers."

The meanings open up if we consider less-harsh views of the number five. If we see it simply as time, then it likely would indicate some kind of change in physical circumstances

or economic conditions. The card itself would not say what kind of change, for better or for worse.

The Pythagorean idea of five as the demigod, halfway to ten, indicates the ability to see the meaning in our material lives, to get a sense that there is a reason for it all beyond the endless struggle to stay ahead financially or avoid sickness.

READINGS—For the Rider, physical troubles, whether financial or health. People helping each other, especially if society fails them. Alternatively, change in physical conditions, whether for good or ill. Possibly finding greater meaning in the daily struggles of life.

REVERSED—Relief of suffering. This can lead to strains in a relationship built too much on shared pain. Possibly getting stuck in the small details of daily life.

Element: Earth

Sephirah: Tipheret (Beauty), sephirah six in Assiyah (Action)

Pythagorean: Hexad, harmony, above and below, masculine and feminine

Major Arcana: Lovers, Tower

Rider Theme: Unequal relationships/generosity

Golden Dawn Title: Material Success

Decan: 11-20 degrees Taurus, ruled by the moon

Picatrix: Power, nobility, rule over the people

Six of Pentacles from GOLDEN DAWN, MARSEILLE, RIDER, SOLA-BUSCA, SHINING TRIBE & VISCONTI

Six of Pentacles

Harmony in the physical world. A blending of opposites that allows people to come together and to make something of their conditions. These are the themes if we consider the Pythagorean idea. We might add financial success, especially from an unlikely partnership. Good physical health would be another theme.

The Rider image seems to illustrate both the theme I have stated of unequal relationships and Ellen Goldberg's idea of generosity. Giving charity is the very essence of generosity, and yet what could be more unequal than people on their knees, begging? At first glance, this card seems perfectly to fulfill the Virtue of Charity. Notice, however, how carefully he seems to drop the few coins, how he keeps his scales perfectly balanced. Maybe he attends to Prudence more than Charity.

Waite says something odd about this card in *The Pictorial Key*: "A person in the guise of a merchant..." Why not simply "a merchant?" Bad writing, perhaps, but Tarotist and teacher Edith Katz suggested years ago that "guise" might mean "disguise," and pointed to the scales to suggest it was really Justice giving people what they need, rather than what they want.

The Shining Tribe shifts the meaning to divination. The central figure, derived from Algonkin imagery, is a shaman/seer, who uses physical devices from different cultures—dice,  African cowrie shells, Chinese sticks, a crystal ball—to see the future. Ultimately, however, the rays of light around his face indicate that his visions come as a gift—charity?—from the spirit world. This too represents beauty in Assiyah and the ultimate harmonic blending of opposites, spirit and matter.

READINGS—Partnership, in work and other practical areas. Harmony in the workplace, good health. Charity, but with a mind to what a person can afford. Justice working out in people's lives. Spirituality in daily life.

REVERSED—Lack of harmony at work or in daily life. People acting at cross-purposes. Holding back help from people who need it. People realizing they can help themselves instead of asking for charity.

Element: Earth

Sephirah: Netzach (Victory), sephirah seven in Assiyah (Action)

Pythagorean: Heptad, dynamic aware energy, the cosmos

Major Arcana: Chariot, Star

Rider Theme: Contemplation or awareness of action

Golden Dawn Title: Success Unfulfilled

Decan: 21-30 degrees Taurus, ruled by Saturn

Picatrix: Misery, slavery, necessity, madness, and baseness

Seven of Pentacles from
GOLDEN DAWN,
MARSEILLE, RIDER,
SOLA-BUSCA,
SHINING TRIBE &
VISCONTI

Seven of Pentacles

The Golden Dawn title, and the extended meanings it gave for this card, including "Hope deceived and crushed...Misery...slavery...baseness," would seem to derive from the Picatrix. Paul Huson points out that none of the other traditional cartomancers follow this distressing idea. Etteila says such things as "money, riches...silverware, whiteness, purity...the moon." Quite a collection. Waite's list of meanings includes the rather specific "an improved position for a lady's future husband"!

People who know the Rider image often debate whether the man resting on his hoe looks pleased or dissatisfied. Is he thinking "Good, things are growing nicely, I can rest for a bit," or "Oh my God, there's so much I have to do." In either case, he demonstrates the theme of contemplating action.

The Pythagorean version of seven sees it as dynamic and creative. As the first of the last four numbers—7, 8, 9, 10—it initiates a powerful sequence that leads to the fulfillment of the suit's possibilities. We could see this for Pentacles as new growth leading to success and material happiness. This goes well with the first Major card, the Chariot, while the second, the Star, gives the forceful seven a flowing, hopeful quality.

The Seven of Stones in the Shining Tribe shows an amulet that is given to women giving birth in India. The card therefore means either help in bringing something into the world or else supporting someone else's efforts.

The Kabbalist sephirah, Netzach, means victory, and in this suit that would imply success, maybe the positive completion of a project. If we see the figure in the Rider as satisfied, then we might say that the project is successfully on the way rather than completely done, and this would go with seven as the start of the final group of numbers. Netzach also is the sephirah of Venus, planet of emotion, and so the card can speak of our feelings about the work we do or of nature.

READINGS—Satisfaction with work. The successful and exciting launching of a new and significant project. Contemplation of work done or needing to be done. Enjoyment of nature.

REVERSED—Difficulty launching or finishing a project. Dissatisfaction, especially with material conditions.

PENTACLES 8 PENTACLES

Prudence

Element: Earth

Sephirah: Hod (Glory), sephirah eight in Assiyah (Action)

Pythagorean: Octad, stability, safety, the spiritual mother of the gods

Major Arcana: Strength, Moon

Rider Theme: Movement

Golden Dawn Title: Prudence

Decan: 1-10 degrees Virgo, ruled by the sun

Picatrix: Sowing, plowing, planting herbs, colonization, storing money and food

Eight of Pentacles from
GOLDEN DAWN,
MARSEILLE, RIDER,
SOLA-BUSCA,
SHINING TRIBE &
VISCONTI

Nine of Pentacles

The Rider version of this card has always been one of my favorites, so much so that I based my own Nine of Stones closely on it. Since the Shining Tribe suit is Stones, not Pentacles, I took the opportunity to show stars brought down from Heaven to shine within the rocks—in other words, dreams made a reality through the woman's dedication, work, and discipline. This seems to me the implied sense of the Rider version, that this is a garden of her own making. It also fulfills the idea of nine as something born from the quality of the suit. In the element of earth, that "something" could be a literal baby, though I have not seen any decks that show this. More widely, the "something" becomes a good life, one that we have made ourselves and that we appreciate. This goes beyond the limited idea of "Material Gain" found in the Golden Dawn. But then, I think of the suit of earth as much more than material gains and losses.

The falcon on her wrist is hooded, under her control. I see this as discipline, self-control and training that allow us to develop our full potential. In the first deck I had, there seemed to be a shadow on the left side of her face (right side of the picture). That would mean she has turned away from the sun, which is to say, spontaneity, maybe even relationships. Notice how this combines aspects of both Major Arcana cards, the Hermit and the Sun. She does

not regret the life she has made, but she knows what she has sacrificed. Even though the "official" edition does not show the shadow, I still find that meaning valuable and implied in the fact that she is alone.

The Pythagorean ennead refers to the end of a process but also to the idea of a spiritual mothering. I would describe this card more as a culmination than a conclusion, and the ability to mother yourself, to give birth to a good life for yourself.

READINGS—Self-discipline, achievement, the possibility to create a good life for yourself. May be the completion of a particular project.

REVERSED—Lack of discipline, low regard for yourself, but also choosing spontaneity over long-range goals.

Element: Earth

Sephirah: Malkuth (Kingdom), sephirah ten in Assiyah (Action)

Pythagorean: Decad, higher unity, greater consciousness

Major Arcana: Wheel of Fortune, Judgement

Rider Theme: Excess

Golden Dawn Title: Wealth

Decan: 21-30 degrees Virgo, ruled by Mercury

Picatrix: Old age, slothfulness, loss, depopulation

Wealth

Ten of Pentacles from GOLDEN DAWN, MARSEILLE, RIDER, SOLA-BUSCA, SHINING TRIBE & VISCONTI

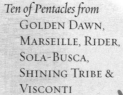

Ten of Pentacles

Here the sephirah and the suit come together very powerfully. This is because even though the Kabbalists see each of the four worlds as having its own Tree of Life, they also sometimes divide the tree into four sections. Atzilut, the world of fire, gets the top triangle (sephiroth 1-2-3), Beriah, the world of water, gets the middle (4-5-6), and Yetsirah, the world of air, gets the bottom triangle (7-8-9). The fourth world, Assiyah, is expressed solely in the tenth sephirah, Malkuth. Thus, the Ten of Pentacles becomes the physical world, what we think of as reality. Dualistic attitudes would see the Ten of Pentacles as therefore "dense," or "gross," or removed from God. Kabbalah teaches that the Shekinah, the female aspect of the divine, dwells in the physical world, in Malkuth in Assiyah. The card for Ten of Earth therefore carries a kind of hidden beauty and spirituality.

The Rider version of the picture actually contains the Tree of Life in the arrangement of the Pentacles. In fact, it's the only place in that deck where we see the full tree (the High Priestess gives us glimpses of it behind her, while both the Hanged Man and the World card embody it). At the same time, notice how the people do not interact with it in any way. In most cards, the people touch, hold, or at least look at the suit objects (see, for example, the Rider Eight of Pentacles or Ten of Cups). Here, it seems to exist apart from them. The

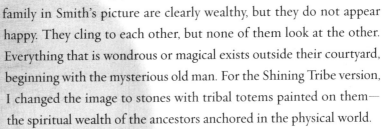

family in Smith's picture are clearly wealthy, but they do not appear happy. They cling to each other, but none of them look at the other. Everything that is wondrous or magical exists outside their courtyard, beginning with the mysterious old man. For the Shining Tribe version, I changed the image to stones with tribal totems painted on them— the spiritual wealth of the ancestors anchored in the physical world.

The Pythagoreans see ten as the highest fulfillment. What fulfills earth? Wealth and comfort, certainly, but also the ability to see the physical world in all its splendor, with its own imperfect perfection.

READINGS—Wealth, comfort, security, but also the enjoyment of these things, the realization of the beauty of life. With the Rider, the choice of security over risk.

REVERSED—Sacrificing security for adventure or new experience. A potential that is not quite realized.

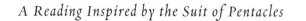

A Reading Inspired by the Suit of Pentacles

1. What is my true work?

2. What helps me to do it?

3. What holds me back?

4. What do I need to do overall?

5. What action do I need to take right now?

The Court Cards

THINK OF THEM as a group of four families. Take the page, knight, queen, and king from each suit (any deck is fine) and set them out on a table. You can lay them down in rows (see below) or maybe just put each in its own area—the Wands court cards off to one side, the Cups somewhere on the bottom, and so on. If you really feel fanciful, you might take four large sheets of paper and draw a crude house on each, big enough to set the court cards from a single suit inside the drawing. Now, using the kings and queens as parents and the knights and pages as children, consider what kind of families they might be. Which parents seem to have a good marriage? Which ones lead their separate lives or have affairs (and with what sort of people)? What are the kids like? Do they listen to their parents? If you think of all the pages as students, how studious are they, and what do they care about? If the knights are teenagers, or in college, what are their priorities (the Knight of Wands might love parties, the Knight of Pentacles might study all the time)?

If you want to try an advanced stage of this exercise, take four more sheets of paper, and for each suit, draw a kind of ideal setting—a city, the beach, mountain climbing, whatever you think.

Then try switching some around. Let's say you drew a peaceful lake for the Cups. Suppose the Cups family left and the Swords people showed up. How would they experience that quiet, watery scene?

Permutations

Possibly the most interesting thing about the court cards is that there are sixteen of them. If four is meaningful and powerful, what of four times four? Since we do not go all the way to ten, we are not in the realm of Pythagorean ideas, or of the Tree of Life, with its ten sephiroth. But we are in the realm of the four worlds, and the four elements, and the four directions, and the four-letter Tetragrammaton, and all the other fours we have talked about. And each one gets magnified by the fact that there are four court cards in four suits.

Without trying to claim a deliberately esoteric origin for the court cards, it's worth remembering that regular playing cards only had three per suit: the page (or knave, valet, or jack), the queen, and the king. Tarot enthusiasts who believe that the Tarot deck predated playing cards sometimes like to imagine that the knight rode off on a quest when regular playing cards were published. Since it now seems much more likely that Tarot cards came *after* the introduction of playing cards into Europe, we might say that the knights rode into the deck. Maybe they came bringing the powerful imagery of four times four.

Here are the sixteen cards as a diagram:

Page of Wands	Knight of Wands	Queen of Wands	King of Wands
Page of Cups	Knight of Cups	Queen of Cups	King of Cups
Page of Swords	Knight of Swords	Queen of Swords	King of Swords
Page of Pentacles	Knight of Pentacles	Queen of Pentacles	King of Pentacles

The usual way to consider these is horizontally—all the characters, page, knight, queen, and king, from each suit. But what of vertically? All the pages go together, all the knights, and so on. And we can go further. One of the early Kabbalist masters, Abraham Abulafia, developed a meditation system based on "permutating" the letters in the sacred names of God. If we permutate the arrangement above, we allow new relationships to develop. Consider—if we go along the diagonals, beginning with the pages, we get:

| Page of Wands | Knight of Cups | Queen of Swords | King of Pentacles |
| Page of Pentacles | Knight of Swords | Queen of Cups | King of Wands |

This leaves an interesting pattern:

	Knight of Wands	Queen of Wands	
Page of Cups			King of Cups
Page of Swords			King of Swords
	Knight of Pentacles	Queen of Pentacles	

By following a simple zig-zag pattern, we can get:

| Page of Cups | Knight of Wands | Queen of Pentacles | King of Swords |

Leaving:

| Page of Swords | Knight of Pentacles | Queen of Wands | King of Cups |

Altogether, we get:

Page of Wands	Knight of Cups	Queen of Swords	King of Pentacles
Page of Pentacles	Knight of Swords	Queen of Cups	King of Wands
Page of Cups	Knight of Wands	Queen of Pentacles	King of Swords
Page of Swords	Knight of Pentacles	Queen of Wands	King of Cups

You can keep doing this, following the same formula (diagonals, zig-zagging for the third line, what's left for the fourth), and get a whole series of permutations. There should be sixteen possible arrangements.

If we ask what the point of this exercise is, it's to discover different relationships. How might the Page of Wands serve the Knight of Cups? What kind of couple would the Queen of Pentacles and the King of Swords make? If we think of knights as dedicated to the service of the lady—a medieval ideal known as courtly love—what kind of dedication might the Queen of Wands receive from the Knight of Pentacles? By playing with different arrangements, we discover the strengths and limitations of each card, each *character* in its suit. We realize that while all pages share what we might call *pageness*, this translates very differently in each suit. As you get to know the court cards more closely—more intimately?—you might want to explore the permutations and see what the different combinations reveal to you. The simplest way to rearrange the cards would be to shuffle the four pages and lay them out in a vertical line, then shuffle the knights and set them in order next to the pages, and on to the queens and kings.

Notice that we can see them as characters, as people. Knight is a role, and Cups is an element. But when we combine them to get Knight of Cups, we move towards a sense of a person. This has been the contemporary approach, pushed by the idea that when they appear in a reading, they represent an actual person in the querent's life. The Major cards signify spiritual qualities and life challenges, the numbered Minor cards situations and experiences, but the court cards show us individual people.

If Court Cards Are People, Who Are They?

It used to be that they were always someone else—not the querent but someone who will *affect* the querent—a husband or wife, a boss, a friend, maybe even a mysterious stranger. This certainly is a valuable way to consider them and should not be overlooked. But how are we supposed to know just what person is being represented? To some extent, reading the court cards in this way requires more of the psychic or intuitive approach than the other cards. We can say that the Star symbolizes hopefulness, or that the Five of Wands indicates a competitive atmosphere, but how are we to know just who the King of Cups might be?

One way to approach this question is through character traits of both the role and the suit—in this case, king and Cups. We might say that the king indicates a person of authority, while Cups suggests—among other things—drinking. Thus the King of Cups could be a boss who gets drunk at lunchtime! There are, of course, many qualities to Cups beside alcohol, and we will look at more subtle interpretations of the King, as well as the other fifteen cards.

To get away from the requirement to identify every court card as a person, modern readers often look at them as aspects of the querent. If the King of Cups appears in your reading, it means that you yourself have been experiencing that card in some way (or may need to, depending on the position in the reading). Tarotist and author Mary Greer says that they always represent an aspect of the querent, even when they also indicate another person. That is, the Queen of Wands may be your mother, but she also is you. This is because we draw to ourselves people who reflect truths about us. To put it another way, what we see in other people comes from who we ourselves are. In other words, you see your mother as the Queen of Wands because you have that quality in yourself. For someone else, such as your mother's boss, your mother might be more the Knight of Pentacles.

Some readers prefer not to try and figure out the riddle of just who a court card might symbolize in the querent's life. Either they avoid such identifications altogether and only talk about the card symbolically, or else they ask the querent what he or she thinks the card looks like. If the Knight of Wands appears on the table, the reader might ask, "How would you describe this person? What does he seem to be doing?" or else, "When you look at this picture, does anyone come into your mind?"

This approach makes a lot of sense and can save a lot of time and guessing games. If the querent responds, "Oh my God! This is Uncle Charlie at that picnic—" and bursts out crying, this is probably much more significant than if you as the reader flounder about with phrases like "This is someone active and energetic," or worse, try to come up with a magical picture in your head of just who it might be and why he or she is important (a knight does not have to be a man, nor a queen a woman—more about gender and the court cards in a moment).

One problem with asking the querent who he or she sees in the card is that it may seem like "cheating." *You're* the Tarot reader, *you're* supposed to know these things. Readers who prefer to work this way will usually inform the querent ahead of time with a statement like, "My readings are interactive. I may ask you what *you* see in the picture." Once I was visiting friends in Oxford, and they very kindly offered to book readings for me during my stay (they themselves read professionally). All the readings went very well until the end of the day, when a woman came who clearly had a magical/psychic idea of what a Tarot reader was supposed to do. When I asked her what a certain scene suggested to her, she got uncomfortable, and when I then asked her how she saw a court card—the Knight of Wands—she jumped up and announced it was unfair, she was "doing all the work." I promptly offered her her money back, and she stormed off. The funny thing was, such fiery impulsive action was really a very Knight of Wands thing to do, thereby demonstrating Mary Greer's point.

Significators

The identification of the court cards with individual people was spurred by the idea that we should begin a reading by choosing a "significator" for the querent, a card to represent the person having the reading. Unlike the other cards, which come out of the usual random shuffle, the significator is a conscious choice of the reader. That is, you come to me for a reading, and I choose a single card to symbolize you. This idea comes from Waite, though it may not have originated with him.

I used to use significators, because that was what I learned to do, but I mostly have abandoned the practice. However, it is worth looking at the process for what it tells us about the court cards. Waite's directions begin with age. He says we should choose a knight for a man forty years or older and a king for a man or boy under that age. If this strikes you as odd that the knight is older than the king, it has to do with Golden Dawn changes, which we will discuss in a moment. Waite then says that we choose a queen for a woman over forty and a page for a young woman or girl.

When I was using significators, I developed my own system for ages. A page for me represented a child of either sex, a knight a young person of either sex, a queen a mature woman, and a king a mature man. This just seemed to make more sense to me.

Waite then goes on to use hair and skin tone for the suits—Wands very fair people with "yellow or auburn" hair and blue eyes, Cups light brown or "dull fair hair" and gray or blue eyes, Swords hazel or gray eyes and dark brown hair and "dull complexion," and Pentacles very dark brown or black hair, dark eyes, and "sallow or swarthy complexions." Now, if you think about this, it really just works for the range of people in England, Waite's own country. In Sweden, most people would be Wands, in Morocco there would be many Pentacles, and people in Tanzania or Vietnam would not be included at all. Still, many readers, who may not even use significators, will use these physical types and ages as a way to try to identify a court card in a reading. In other words, if the Queen of Wands comes up, they might say, "This is an older woman who is significant to you now. She probably has blond hair and blue eyes." Hopefully, they also will use the psychological qualities of the card as well as the physical, and perhaps the spiritual meaning, as suggested by the element and some of those other aspects of the number four. We will look at these in a moment.

Before I simply stopped using significators, I developed my own more direct and, yes, interactive method. I would tell people, "We're having a special today. You can be a page, a knight, a queen, or a king. Which do you prefer?" Most men would choose king or knight, most women queen, but not always, and I've seen a middle-aged man choose page. After the person had chosen, I would lay out the four cards of that level and say, "Which of these do you most see as yourself?" or even "Which one calls to you?"

A more systematic way that people choose a significator is through astrological sign, and this too allows us to glimpse another level of meaning, whether we decide to apply it to significators or not. There are twelve signs and four elements, which gives us three signs for each element. Now, of course, there are sixteen court cards, not twelve, so the Golden Dawn set aside the pages as representing the element itself, rather than a particular sign (this is similar to setting aside the four aces as the elemental root in order to have thirty-six cards for the thirty-six decans—see the numbered Minor Arcana cards). With the pages set aside, the knight, queen, and king of each suit become the three signs of that element. The reader can then ask the querent that classic line from singles bars, "What's your sign?" If the person says, for example, "Leo," then she or he becomes the Queen of Wands. We will list the astrological sign for each court card as we go through them (though, again, the choices are complicated, because the Golden Dawn changed the titles of the cards so that we have to make some adjustments of our own).

Movie Stars, Fairy Tales, Superheroes, and Noble Worthies

Some people get a personal sense of the court cards by imagining them in different settings. They may associate them with their favorite movie or pop stars, or celebrities. To do this, you first need a sense of what each card represents, but once you have that general idea, you can bring it to life by saying, for example, that the Queen of Cups is Marilyn Monroe, or the King of Pentacles is Donald Trump. If the four knights were the Beatles, which ones would they be? (My vote goes to John as the Knight of Wands for his fiery creativity and passion, Paul as the Knight of Cups for emotional appeal, George as the Knight of Swords for his intellectual seriousness as a musician, and Ringo as the Knight of Pentacles for his earthiness.) If you prefer opera, you could do the same sort of thing with the great stars—pages as mezzo-sopranos, knights as tenors, queens as sopranos, and kings as baritones. Or you could do characters from your favorite movies or operas. There have, in fact, been decks published where the artist used traditional figures for the court cards but with the faces of classic movie stars.

You can do the same with books and fairy tales. If the Knight of Wands was a character in a favorite story, who would he be? From the other direction, if you think of a character you love, what court card would symbolize him or her? Tarot enthusiasts often take a particular novel (or movie or TV show) and assign characters. Anything with four distinct groups works especially well. Take, for example, *The Lord of the Rings*. Tolkien describes four "races": the hobbits, elves, humans, and dwarves. Let's say we make the hobbits Wands, the elves Cups, the humans Swords, and the dwarves Pentacles. Now see if you can work out for each group who the page, knight, queen, and king would be. What might it tell you about the King of Swords if you imagine him as Aragorn?

The figures do not have to match the actual title. That is, Aragorn is, in fact, a king, but you could make Frodo the king of hobbits if you think he acts out that role. Sometimes we can do this exercise better if we change the card titles to something that fits the theme (changing the titles of the court cards has become a modern tradition—see below). Comic books often seem to work on an archetypal level, and as a result they can match up nicely with Tarot imagery. For an exercise, I decided to see if I could match the court cards and suits to classic superhero figures. The kings become heroes, the queens partners, the knights enemies, and the pages—of course—sidekicks. One nice side effect here is that "hero" and "partner" are not gender specific, so the hero can be a woman or the partner a man.

Wands: Action, Power, Optimism
> Hero—Superman; Partner—Lois Lane; Enemy—Luthor; Sidekick—Jimmy Olsen

Cups: Love, Gentleness
> Hero—Wonder Woman (according to the story, she was sent by Aphrodite, "ruler" of Cups, to combat war and hate); Partner—her boyfriend Steve, or maybe her mother, the Queen of the Amazons; Enemy—Ares, the god of war; Sidekick—Wonder Girl

Swords: Battle, Powerful Mind, Discipline
> Hero—Batman; Partner—Catwoman; Enemy—Joker; Sidekick—Robin

Pentacles (As Magic Rather Than Earthiness)
> Hero—Dr. Strange, "Master of the Mystic Arts"; Partner—his lover, Clea, or his teacher, the Ancient One; Enemy—The Dread Dormammu (yes, that's really his name); Sidekick—Wong, his faithful servant and a magician in his own right

Do you see how well this works? On a higher cultural level, you could do the same kind of thing with, say, the novels of Jane Austen, or mythological epics such as the *Iliad* or the *Mahabharata*. Catholic saints are another possibility, as are the orishas of West African and African-American religions, and in fact at least one deck has appeared using each of these traditions. It may seem disrespectful to use saints or gods as Tarot court cards, but not if we truly respect the Tarot itself as a spiritual teaching. To see the Queen of Cups as Oshun, orisha of rivers and love, can give the queen much greater meaning than simply a medieval ruler or consort.

If this seems like a modern game, the practice actually goes back to the very beginning of cards in Europe, if not necessarily Tarot cards. Paul Huson, in *Mystical Origins of the Tarot*, describes how Renaissance people assigned historical and mythological characters to the court cards. Because these were done for non-Tarot decks, there are no characters for the knights.

The idea for naming the court cards seems to have come from a popular concept in the decades before playing cards migrated from the Mamluks of Egypt to Europe. In a poem called *Les Voeux du Paon*, "The Vows of the Peacock," the poet Jacques de Longuyon described Nine Worthies, a collection of heroic figures from different times and places in the legendary past. Huson tells us that likenesses of these figures appeared all over Europe, and some found their way onto playing cards, with a few additions to make up the twelve cards (without the knights). The kings were Caesar, Charlemagne, David, and Alexander, to honor the four major empires known to Europeans, the Hebrew, the Greek, the Roman, and the Holy Roman Empire (see the Emperor card). The queens bore the names Rachel, Judith, Pallas, and Argine (unfamiliar names will be explained with the individual cards). The pages (*valets* in the French) were Roland, La Hire, Ogier, and Lancelot.

Wands
  Page—Roland; Queen—Rachel; King—Caesar

Cups
  Page—La Hire; Queen—Judith; King—Charlemagne

Swords
  Page—Ogier; Queen—Pallas; King—David

Pentacles (Coins)
Page—Lancelot; Queen—Argine; King—Alexander

While these historical associations are interesting and can suggest some interesting ideas—the Queen of Swords as Pallas, another name for the goddess Athena, can inspire various ways to get closer to what that card can mean for us—they seem to follow a random method of association. With the Swords, for example, the Page is European, the Queen is Greek, and the King is Hebrew. One interesting historical note, and a personal one. While the French playing cards assigned the Queen of Cups to Judith, the Golden Dawn saw the same biblical figure as the Queen of Swords, a much clearer connection, since biblical Judith is best known for cutting off the head of Nebuchadnezzar's general Holofernes (to be fair, she first got him drunk—a Cups connection). And the personal—in the past, when I've used a significator for myself, I've chosen the Queen of Wands, which, it turns out, the French named as Rachel. Just to add another twist, I used to say that I aspired to become the Queen of Cups, and the French name for that card is Judith, which happens to be the name of my older sister.

Elements

As with the suits for the numbered cards, the most common, and useful, association we can make is with the four elements. The fact that we have four court cards as well as four suits allows us to create a double system. We have seen how the standard association for the suits runs this way: Wands-fire, Cups-water, Swords-air, Pentacles-earth. There are many variations, but this is the most common.

Now here is a parallel list for the court titles: Wands-kings, Cups-queens, Swords-knights, Pentacles-pages. Each court card then becomes two elements; the Queen of Swords, for example, becomes water of air, the Page of Pentacles earth of earth. Since charts work so nicely with the sixteen (4 x 4) court cards, here is one for this system:

	WANDS	CUPS	SWORDS	PENTACLES
KING	fire/fire	fire/water	fire/air	fire/earth
QUEEN	water/fire	water/water	water/air	water/earth
KNIGHT	air/fire	air/water	air/air	air/earth
PAGE	earth/fire	earth/water	earth/air	earth/earth

The first thing we might notice is that there are four "perfect" cards: King of Wands (fire of fire), Queen of Cups (water of water), Knight of Swords (air of air), and Page of Pentacles (earth of earth). This line goes down the diagonal from top left to bottom right. This was the first step in the "permutations" described above. If we go from bottom left to top right (the second step), we get a nice symmetrical pattern: Page of Wands (earth of fire), Knight of Cups (air of water), Queen of Swords (water of air), and King of Pentacles (fire of earth). Notice, by the way, how these two lines run king, queen, knight, page, and page, knight, queen, king.

How do we use this idea in readings or even contemplation of the court cards? For one thing, it helps us get beyond a completely subjective understanding of the cards, on the level of "I really like the Knight of Wands—he seems carefree and happy, the way I feel on vacation. I hate the Queen of Swords—she frowns too much, like me when I have to go back to the office." Now, as the old saying goes, not that there's anything wrong with that. These kinds of responses can tell us a great deal and help us to respond strongly to the cards. But they are limited—usually they apply to a particular deck (the frowning Queen of Swords is in the Rider, for example), the reader and the querent may react very differently to the same picture, and some cards might not trigger any associations at all.

By contrast, if the Page of Pentacles comes up in a reading, and you know that this card equals earth of earth, you can talk about a strong sense of earthiness, concern with nature, or work and money. When the King of Cups appears, you might consider that fire of water can produce either a tension—fire and water are the basic opposites—or a powerful joining of energies. The other cards, and your own feeling for the reading, as well as dialog with the querent, should indicate whether the card reveals tension or harmony.

Name Changes

Since the double element originated (as far as I know) with the Golden Dawn, we need to look at how they changed the names of the court cards. Their sequence runs:

Golden Dawn: Knight   Queen   Prince   Princess

The knight has not actually moved over from where it was, it has replaced the king, which is why Waite describes the knight as a man over forty in terms of choosing a significator, and then, since he has no prince in his more traditional deck, is left with the clumsy device of describing the king as a young male. To my mind, the proper equivalency between the Golden Dawn titles and the standard modern titles should run:

Conventional Tarots: King   Queen   Knight   Page

Golden Dawn: Knight   Queen   Prince   Princess (Please note that in the modern version of the Golden Dawn deck used here, the designer changed the name of the card from Knight to King in order to align the deck with the more standard name for this card.)

One thing we might notice here is that the movement runs from the king down rather than the page up. We saw the same issue with the numbered cards, except in a way it's the opposite. That is, with ten through ace, we begin in the created physical world, Malkuth on the Tree of Life, and climb back up the tree to the first and pure state of existence, the ace, in Kether. However, as I understand the Golden Dawn system, the princess/page is the created world, the element of earth, and therefore the equivalent of the ten. The Golden Dawn knight—king in regular decks—is fire, the direct emanation from the highest level, and so the movement runs like this:

	FIRE	WATER	AIR	EARTH
GOLDEN DAWN:	knight	queen	prince	princess
REGULAR:	king	queen	knight	page

As readers of this book will no doubt realize, I am far from an expert on the Golden Dawn (very far), but I greatly admire two aspects of their work. The first is the vast yet tight web they created of so many strands of knowledge, the second their ability to mythologize the Tarot, as seen in the beautiful titles they give the Minor cards (I also admire the seriousness of their magical practice, but that's another issue). These two qualities come together in a myth of the court cards, as it once was explained to me. The version given here is my understanding, and all mistakes are my own.

The knight (fire) moves into the world from the higher levels and encounters the queen (water). He enters her service and then marries her, becoming, in effect, her king. From their union come the prince (air) and the princess (earth). One thing I like about this is that it invokes the ancient idea that the goddess/queen is eternal and unchanging, and that the king is her consort.

This story is really an evocation of the creation as shown in the Tetragrammaton, Yod-Heh-Vav-Heh. We've already looked at this, so I will just summarize it here, with its relation to the court cards. Yod and the first Heh are fire and water, the purest principles. When they join together, they produce the more complex second level: their children, Vav, the element of air, and the second Heh, earth. The knight joins the queen and from their union come the prince and the princess. Or again, in conventional titles, the king and the queen join together and produce the knight and the page. The prince/knight is mind, consciousness, and the element of air, while the princess/page is physical existence, earth.

Here is my own suggestion of how we might view this movement in elemental, but also mythic, terms. Light, which I suggest as the element for the Major Arcana, sends forth a spark of fire into the waters. The waters, in fact, are older than creation, but they do not really exist until the fire enters them. This is what the Zohar calls a "mystery," not explainable in rational, exoteric terms. However, we can compare it to the idea in quantum physics that particles exist in all possible states until they are observed—at which point they become "real."

When the fire and water unite, genuine creation begins, first with the stirrings of air, and then the fully formed reality of earth. Thus, we might link the court cards to the Major Arcana by saying that out of the Major Arcana comes the king, who enters the queen, and out of her emerges the knight and the page. And maybe we can take it a step further, mythologizing the relationship between the Major and Minor cards *through* the court cards by saying that the entire Minor Arcana lies dormant, asleep in a way, within those uncreated waters—the "darkness on the face of the deep," as Genesis says. When the light—the Major Arcana—sends forth its spark of fire, the waters are awakened, and through the union of fire and water emerges not just the knight and the page, but the four suits as well.

If all this seems a bit confusing, don't worry; it's not essential to understanding the court cards and working with them in readings. For myself, I find the mythic dimensions of Tarot valuable, if not essential, for they give levels of meaning that can underlie the more conventional ways we understand them.

Court Cards on the Tree of Life

The Golden Dawn places the court cards on the Tree of Life in an interesting way. The king (or knight in their system) goes in Hokhmah, sephirah two, which means Wisdom, described by Kabbalists as the father principle (see above, on numbers, for more on the individual sephiroth). The queen goes in Binah, sephirah three, the Great Mother. The card we usually call the knight, which they call the prince, occupies sephirah six, Tipheret, or Beauty, while the page, their princess, goes in Malkuth (Kingdom), sephirah ten, the physical world.

Aligning this image with my own Tarot creation myth above, we might say that the Major Arcana as a whole dwells in Kether, sephirah one, understood as the crown of undifferentiated light. Readers who have followed all this carefully might object that in Tarot tradition the cards of the Major Arcana go on the twenty-two pathways that run between the sephiroth. And of course this is true, but one of the glories of myth is that different ways of seeing things can co-exist at once. Imagine that you are standing in a great open plain. Whichever way you look you see a Tree of Life, vast and beautiful. In one direction, the twenty-two pathways

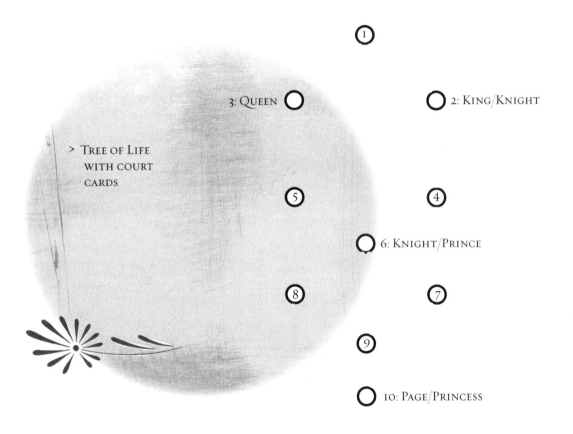

> TREE OF LIFE
  WITH COURT
  CARDS

3: QUEEN ◯

◯ 2: KING/KNIGHT

⑤ ④

◯ 6: KNIGHT/PRINCE

⑧ ⑦

⑨

◯ 10: PAGE/PRINCESS

light up, and you recognize the complexities and wonder of the Major Arcana trump cards. In another, the ten sephiroth shine brilliantly to reveal the Minor cards. And in still another, Kether blazes with the collected light of the entire Major Arcana, while in Hokhmah the king looks lovingly at his queen, whose waters give birth to the knight in Tipheret and the page in Malkuth. Why try to decide which version is the true and correct Tree of Life? Why not accept all of them as true?

And now—to make all this just a little more complicated—remember that there is not just one movement from king to queen to knight to page, there are *four* of them. Four times four. Above, with the suits, we looked at the four Kabbalistic worlds:

Atzilut (Emanation)—Fire

Beriah (Creation)—Water

Yetsirah (Formation)—Air

Assiyah (Action)—Earth

So the process of fire-water-air-earth gets repeated in each world, each element, each suit. There is a fire version of the process, a water version, and so on.

In some ways, the idea of the four worlds works better with the four groups of court cards than the four sets of ace through ten. This is because the Minor cards, at least in modern decks, show very specific kinds of situations, and usually those do not especially match the Kabbalistic world. If you think of Atzilut, the world of pure Emanation, closest to the divine, and then set Ace through Ten of Wands next to it, the cards don't match the concept.

The court cards, however, remain somewhat abstract (except maybe in those decks with movie-star faces). They show us people but not really individual personalities. We play games to make them more accessible—compare them to characters in books, to Uncle Charlie, to psychological traits (adventurous, cautious, arrogant, loving, etc.), but when you really look at them, especially across several decks, they possess almost no individuality. Yes, we give them fortune-telling meanings or label them as personality types. But when you come down to it, the King of Cups is not your drunken boss, or at least not just your drunken boss. He's the ruler of the power of water. Put another way, the King of Cups does not represent your drunken boss—your drunken boss represents the King of Cups.

A Progression of Qualities

We began this survey of the court cards listing them as page, knight, queen, and king. Along the way, we've shifted to king, queen, knight, and page (with a Golden Dawn sidetrack into alternative names). What is the difference? Kabbalistically, it's similar to whether or not we go from ace to ten or ten to ace. If we begin with fire, the king, and progress to earth, the page, we follow the movement of energy from the spark of creation to physical matter. If we begin with earth, the page, and go to fire, the king, there is a sense of returning, or finding the spiritual source and origin.

I would like to suggest a different way to view the movement from page to knight to queen to king, one based on the development of mastery in the suit and its element. The pages are youthful and fresh, though they do not have to be physically young. They represent a beginning state and have an excitement about them. If at the age of sixty you take up sailing, then you are a page (of Cups, for the water, or Swords, for the wind). The knight takes you to a level where it is time to act on your knowledge and experiences. Knights have a job to do—they go on quests, they fight battles and serve justice. Where the page can simply look at something, the knight needs to respond. The knights are still, in a sense, young and vigorous.

The queens and kings are both masters of the element but with a difference due to their relative social roles in the European period that saw the rise of Tarot. Kings were the ones who were in charge and had the responsibility to govern. This does not make the queens inferior—and remember, in my approach to Tarot, a queen card can indicate a man and a king a woman. The queen is, in fact, the true master, the figure who most appreciates the quality of the suit.

Consider the Queen and King of Swords in the Rider deck (see opposite page).

The Queen's sword points straight up, like the Ace and the sword of Justice. This shows the purity and absolute integrity of her thinking. By contrast, the sword of the King tilts slightly to his right (our left), for the need to make decisions and possibly enforce them. Notice also the single bird in the Queen and the two birds in the King. Some say that the King's pair signifies his position on the Tree of Life, in sephirah two, Hokhmah/Wisdom. But then the Queen should have three birds for her place in Binah, sephirah three. To me, the single bird in the Queen is another symbol of intellectual purity, the two in the King another reference to decision-making.

QUEEN of SWORDS.

KING of SWORDS.

< RIDER
Queen of Swords
&
King of Swords

The queens are masters, the kings are rulers. Both are necessary, and in fact they complement each other.

I followed this developmental approach when I designed the equivalent of court cards for the Shining Tribe Tarot. Called vision cards, these run place (page), knower (knight), gift (queen), speaker (king). On the next page is a "diagonal" sample of the vision cards.

The place shows us a place we create or go to in order to experience the quality of the suit. As with the pages, we have no need to do anything more than learn about the element. The knowers show us reaching a stage where we come to a powerful understanding of the suit and its truths. In practice, I have found the knowers more powerful than the knights (but then, it's my deck). The Knight of Cups in the Rider looks deeply into his cup of dreams, or mys-

SHINING TRIBE
Place of Trees,
Knower of Rivers,
Gift of Birds
&
Speaker of Stones

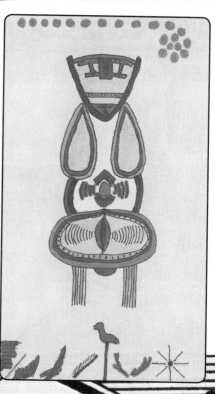

tery. By contrast, the Knower of Rivers has entered into the cave of inner truth and emerged with what I call "radical self-knowledge."

When we experience the place and come to know the element, we receive a gift from the spirit world. This is not a fantasy. Just about anyone who has committed her- or himself to some creative or spiritual path will receive help or spurs at some point, usually in the form of a remarkable coincidence. The gift does not come just for us, but rather to bring us to the level of speaker, where we are required to communicate or share the quality of the suit. The Speaker of Birds (see below) was inspired by a chair I saw in the Royal Ontario Museum. There, of course, the legs were together, so that the person would sit in the bird's lap. After I drew it (with the legs apart in a classical African dance posture) and named it Speaker of Birds, I read that in parts of Africa, the kings would sit on chairs with a bird worked into the back so that the king would speak with the authority of the goddess. The ancient Egyptians did something similar, with the throne shaped as the goddess Isis so that the pharaoh would sit in her lap and rule with her support.

A Further Note on Names

The Golden Dawn and the Shining Tribe Tarot have not been the only ones to change the names of the court cards. In modern times it's become quite common, possibly because the court cards are harder to interpret and people want to come up with something more sugges-tive or simply less feudal. Without going into too many examples, we can cite two early decks in this trend: the Voyager Tarot by James Wanless and Ken Knudson, which gives us child, sage, woman, and man, and the Motherpeace deck of Vicki Noble and Karen Vogel, with daughter, son, priestess, and shaman.

Another interesting example, from the 1980s, is the Haindl Tarot, a deck for which I was privileged to write the book. Hermann Haindl made each set of court cards gods and god-desses from particular cultures, but he also made them a family. The titles, in descending order like the Golden Dawn approach, are mother, father, daughter, son. For Haindl there are two levels of divinity: the oldest, who are the creators and are often remote, and the younger generation, who are more accessible and involved with humanity. This is similar to the Kabbalist idea of the difference between the letters Yod and (the first) Heh, and then the next "generation," the Vav and (second) Heh. For Haindl, however, the female energy is older, more primal, and so he begins the progression with mother and then goes on to father, daughter, and son.

Looking historically, we should realize that at least one card has borne different names over time. This is the page. That term itself seems modern, apparently originating with Waite as a translation of the French *valet*. In playing cards, the more common English term was knave, from which we get the jack of modern decks. Is there a difference between these words? I think of a page as younger than a knave or a valet, and while I may be wrong about medieval classes, it seems to me that pages were part of the nobility, while valets were servants. Knave, by the way, did not originally mean a scoundrel, but a servant. Calling the youngest card a page gives us more of a sense of a cohesive group, a family, and with a clear progression, from page to knight and then queen and king.

Some people find an imbalance in the fact that pages, like knights, are masculine figures. The Golden Dawn addressed this by changing the two to princess and prince, and Waite, in his instructions on choosing a significator, describes the page as a younger female. We also should realize that some of the early Italian decks did show a girl or young woman for this card, with the title *Fantesca*, feminine of *Fante*, which according to an Italian-English dictionary means "foot soldier." Perhaps there is a connection to *infant*, a word which literally means "unable to speak." The pages are non-infants but often appear as children, for example in the first known deck, the Visconti-Sforza.

< VISCONTI
*Knave of
Wands
&
Knave
of Cups*

Rider Court Card Themes and "Ruling" Trumps

For the numbered cards above, I gave my own personal sense of what the themes in the Minor Arcana pictures seemed to be. For the court cards I will do something simpler. A few years ago, I decided to see if I could come up with short theme titles for the Rider court cards. Here is my current version:

Wands

PAGE—Eagerness

KNIGHT—Adventure

QUEEN—Love of life

KING—Confidence/arrogance

Cups

PAGE—Imagination

KNIGHT—Dreams/introspection

QUEEN—Dedication

KING—Channeled creativity

Swords

PAGE—Caution

KNIGHT—Courage

QUEEN—Wisdom/sorrow

KING—Authority

Pentacles

PAGE—Study

KNIGHT—Work

QUEEN—Nature

KING—Wealth

And finally, we can identify a card in each suit with one of the first four numbered cards in the Major Arcana. I call these the trumps' "representatives" in daily life. Here is my own list:

MAGICIAN—King of Wands

HIGH PRIESTESS—Queen of Cups

EMPRESS—Queen of Pentacles

EMPEROR—King of Swords

Notice that the sequence of the suits seems slightly off, at least from the way we've been looking at them. Wands, Cups, Swords, and Pentacles is meant to align with the elemental order of fire, water, air, and earth, which in turn goes with Yod-Heh-Vav-Heh and the rhythm of male/female, male/female. The beginning trumps simply do not follow this pattern. Instead they run male/female, female/male, as if the polarity becomes reversed in the play of nature and mind. Or maybe we could describe the trump sequence as male, female/female, male, with the Magician and Emperor standing guard, in a sense, around the dynamic play of archetypal energy between the High Priestess and Empress.

And remember as well that Wands-Cups-Swords-Pentacles is by no means a universally accepted order.

Now that we have seen the background of the court cards, and several overall ways to look at them, we will meet these people cards one at a time.

THE PRINCESS OF WANDS

VALET DE BATONS   FANTE DI BASTONI

KNAVE OF WANDS   BUBE DER STÄBE
SOTA DE BASTOS   STAVEN SCHILDKNAAP

Element: Fire

Sephirah: Malkuth (Kingdom), sephirah ten in Atzilut (Emanation)

Golden Dawn Title: Princess of Wands, Princess of the Shining Flame, Rose of the Palace of Fire

Elemental Combination: Earth of Fire

Astrological Sign: add?

Rider Physical Quality: A girl or young woman with light hair and blue eyes

Rider Deck Theme: Eagerness

Renaissance Character: Roland

Shining Tribe Title: Place of Trees

Page of Wands from
GOLDEN DAWN,
MARSEILLE, RIDER,
VISCONTI &
SHINING TRIBE

PAGE of WANDS.

Page of Wands

From the Golden Dawn point of view, earth of fire would mean what fiery Wands energy brings into the world, what it produces. If we look at it developmentally, however, as the youngest figure in the court of Wands, we can see it as eager, excited, a card of beginnings. I see the Page of Wands as the first of the court cards (from my developmental approach, the page is the first of each suit, and Wands is the first suit), so that it shares qualities with the Fool and the Ace of Wands.

In the Rider deck, he seems to declare his readiness to do something. The Marseille is older and tougher looking, but the (older) Visconti shows a rather sweet-looking child. The Golden Dawn version we have here, a modern interpretation, shows a young woman warrior for the princess. The Place of Trees is the simplest of the place cards, the idea of a garden or a place to enjoy life, especially with others.

Roland was a popular heroic figure of medieval poetry, the nephew of Charlemagne, and hero of an epic called *Orlando Furioso*, which is Roland Insane. He begins as Orlando Innamorato, Roland in love, but goes mad with passion. Some saw an alternative character for the Valet of Batons, that of Hector, hero of Troy. People in the Middle Ages saw Hector as chivalrous and noble, especially compared to self-centered Achilles, the hero of the *Iliad*.

A Tarot tradition calls the pages messengers. What might the message of fire be? Maybe to enjoy life, to take chances, to begin something. Some people see this card as a "faithful lover."

READINGS—Freshness, enthusiasm, a willingness to begin something. Exciting news, possibly a faithful lover, or even someone "mad" with love, losing all sense through passion. Alternatively, noble and selfless. From the Golden Dawn point of view, something real that comes out of fiery energy.

REVERSED—Uncertainty, hesitancy, caution (especially with the Fool reversed). It may be an unfaithful lover (especially with the Seven of Swords, at least in the Rider version).

THE PRINCE OF WANDS

CHEVALIER DE BATONS   CAVALIERE DI BASTONI

KNIGHT OF WANDS   RITTER DER STÄBE
CABALLO DE BASTOS   STAVEN RIDDER

Element: Fire

Sephirah: Tipheret (Beauty), sephirah six in Atzilut (Emanation)

Golden Dawn Title: Prince of Wands, Prince of the Chariot of Fire

Elemental Combination: Air of Fire

Astrological Sign: Sagittarius

Rider Physical Quality: A boy or young man with light hair and blue eyes

Rider Deck Theme: Adventure

Shining Tribe Title: Knower of Trees

Knight of Wands from
GOLDEN DAWN,
MARSEILLE, RIDER,
VISCONTI &
SHINING TRIBE

KNIGHT of WANDS.

Knight of Wands

What is the essential quality of a knight? It is to leave and return. To go on a quest and then bring back a power, a quality. This is the story that some have suggested around the idea that there are no knights in playing cards. The knight left, but in the Tarot he returns.

So what does the Knight of Wands seek, and what does he discover, and what does he bring back? I would say he seeks adventure above all, an outlet for his fiery energy. If you wanted to identify him as someone in your life, look for the person who is dashing, curious, energetic. He might be ungrounded, have a temper, or simply be impatient with whatever is dull and repetitious. And consider as well that the Knight of Wands might be you, those qualities at work in your life at this time.

There can be a danger of burnout with this knight, for he is air of fire, a recipe for brush-fires. In the Rider, the horse rears up as if he too can hardly contain himself. Those old enough to remember classic television may recall the Lone Ranger on Silver rearing up in just that way. The Knight of Wands can be just that sort of individual hero, not wanting to belong to any group but eager to right wrongs—as long as it's not boring.

In the Rider, the Page, Knight, and King all have salamanders—fire lizards—on their tunics, but only the King's salamanders all have their tails in their mouths, which is to say they are complete. Almost all the Knight's are open, for he has much to experience before he can think of settling down. The Shining Tribe image has a different kind of openness. She spreads her arms beyond the card, as if open to all life.

> READINGS—Adventure, daring, someone energetic and forceful. As a person, he can be very charming, confident. This can be a card of travel.

> REVERSED—Possible delays and interruptions. Over-confidence, as if the knight falls off his horse because he's just not ready for everything he's trying to do. Charm can wear thin.

THE QUEEN OF WANDS

REINE DE BATONS — REGINA DI BASTONI

QUEEN OF WANDS — KÖNIGIN DER STÄBE
REINA DE BASTOS — STAVEN KONINGIN

Element: Fire

Sephirah: Binah (Understanding), sephirah three in Atzilut (Emanation)

Golden Dawn Title: Queen of Wands, Queen of the Thrones of Flame

Elemental Combination: Water of Fire

Astrological Sign: Leo (though some say Aries)

Rider Physical Quality: Older woman with light hair and blue eyes

Rider Deck Theme: Love of life

Renaissance Character: Rachel or Penthisilea

Shining Tribe Title: Gift of Trees

Queen of Wands from
GOLDEN DAWN,
MARSEILLE, RIDER,
VISCONTI &
SHINING TRIBE

QUEEN of WANDS.

Queen of Wands

With the idea of water of fire, we might expect a conflict. In most versions, however, this Queen is confident, strong, happy. In the Rider she holds a simple sunflower, as if plucked from the Sun card's garden. The lions on her throne indicate her connection to Leo. In the Golden Dawn image shown here, the leopard behind her evokes that prehistoric link (going back at least eight thousand years) of fierce goddesses and large cats, especially leopards and lions (see Strength). Despite this Queen's calm and confidence, she can be a powerful warrior. The essential quality of the queen is mastery, and she is the master of fire, the feminine part of complete confidence. Wands are sexual energy, and in the Rider she is famously the most sexual of the queens, for she sits with her legs apart.

The Renaissance identified her as Rachel, wife of Jacob, who was devoted to her husband and her children but also could be unscrupulous. In Jewish Kabbalah, Rachel dwells in Malkuth and Jacob in Tipheret. On Shabbat, she rises to meet him, face to face (an important Kabbalist theme) and they make love—the union (in Hebrew, *yihud*) of the male and female aspects of the divine. The Renaissance identified her alternatively as Penthisilea, a queen of the Amazons, giving the card a hidden warrior quality.

> READINGS—She is confident, life-giving, generous, but sometimes fierce. She can be passionate sexually but impatient with a partner who shows weakness or hesitation. A love of life, a time of ease.

> REVERSED—Generous and good in a crisis, she can become impatient with situations that go on too long. She needs to be around people and in situations that embrace life, and can have trouble understanding limitations.

THE KING OF WANDS

Element: Fire

Sephirah: Hokhmah (Wisdom), sephirah two in Atzilut (Emanation)

Golden Dawn Title: Knight of Wands, Lord of the Flame and the Lightning, King of the Spirits of Fire

Elemental Combination: Fire of Fire

Astrological Sign: Aries (some say Leo)

Rider Physical Quality: Older man with light hair and blue eyes

Rider Deck Theme: Confidence, arrogance

Renaissance Character: Caesar, Emperor of Rome

Shining Tribe Title: Speaker of Trees

King of Wands from
GOLDEN DAWN,
MARSEILLE, RIDER,
VISCONTI &
SHINING TRIBE

KING of WANDS

King of Wands

Just as the queens are mastery and appreciation, the kings are rulers. As the fiery part of each suit, they may seem to dominate the other three, but they can only rule effectively with the queen as partner, the knight as agent, and the page as fresh possibilities. This King, in the elemental world of fire—fire of fire, as the Golden Dawn says—can exude great confidence that can slide into arrogance around people not as powerful or self-assured as he.

While his power seems unified, his role may carry a contradiction. That is, it is the nature of kings to sit on their thrones and be available for governing, laws, and petitioners seeking his help. It is the nature of fire to move, to seek freedom and reject whatever would hold it down. Notice in the Rider image he seems to sit upright rather than lean back on his throne, as if he would like to leave and seek adventure, new experience. He may envy the knight's ability to ride off and look for adventure, or the queen's to enjoy her good life.

Caesar was the model of the emperor, the general who took charge of Rome and had himself crowned its ruler. However, he offended the senate by trying to grab all power, and a group of conspirators killed him. The King of Wands may need to show some caution and respect to those he considers beneath him.

On a more fundamental level, we can identify him as the Magician's "representative," or the link between the Magician's primal yang and the world of the court cards.

> READINGS—A very confident figure, may be a woman as well as a man, for king is a role, not a matter of biology. He may be impatient with those who act or think too slowly, who cannot keep up with him, or face his tendency to take charge. He has no guile, however, or ill will, just a powerful energy.

> REVERSED—Tested or in any way confined, he may react angrily. Conversely, difficult circumstances may cause him to doubt himself, producing something of a crisis for this supremely confident character.

THE PRINCESS OF CUPS

VALET DE COUPES   FANTE DI COPPE

KNAVE OF CHALICES   BUBE DER KELCHE
SOTA DE COPAS   BEKERS SCHILDKNAAP

Element: Water

Sephirah: Malkuth (Kingdom), sephirah ten in Beriah (Creation)

Golden Dawn Title: Princess of Cups, Princess of the Waters, and Lotus of the Palace of the Floods

Elemental Combination: Earth of Water

Rider Physical Quality: A girl or young woman with light brown hair and gray or blue eyes

Rider Deck Theme: Imagination

Renaissance Character: La Hire (supporter of Joan of Arc) or Paris of Troy

Shining Tribe Title: Place of Rivers

Page of Cups from
GOLDEN DAWN,
MARSEILLE, RIDER,
VISCONTI &
SHINING TRIBE

PAGE of CUPS.

Page of Cups

Earth of water makes this card one not very given to movement, at least physically. The image of "still waters run deep" may come to mind, and in fact, the Shining Tribe pictures someone sitting by a deep pool of water, as if in quiet meditation. When we look at the Rider image, we see a young page holding up the cup in what strikes me as a posture of fascination. All the way back to Etteila, this card has carried meanings of "meditation...contemplation."

Something remarkable happens in Smith's image. A fish emerges from the cup, the only cup in the deck where something comes forth besides water. Because his role does not require him to do anything—not ride anywhere, as the knight, or master the element, as the queen, or be in charge, like the king—he can see what most of us would miss, the true products of the imagination.

La Hire—Etienne de Vignoles—was a friend and supporter of Joan of Arc, and by legend the person who invented the French (now also English and American) suit signs. Because of La Hire, this card is the Jack of Hearts in a modern poker deck. The alternative figure, Paris of Troy, is probably the most famous seducer in mythology, luring Helen to leave her husband and thereby starting the Trojan War. Paris gives the card a quality of devotion to love but without principle.

> READINGS—Quiet, meditation, an interest in spiritual or imaginative subjects without any need to do anything with them. Pages can be messengers, and the Page of Cups may bring messages from the subconscious, including psychic information. May be a student of the occult or mythology. Possibly seduction, beauty.

> REVERSED—Troubled by things that come from the imagination or the subconscious. Seduction without principle.

THE PRINCE OF CUPS

CHEVALIER DE COUPES   CAVALIERE DI COPPE

KNIGHT OF CHALICES   RITTER DER KELCHE
CABALLO DE COPAS   BEKERS RIDDER

Element: Water

Sephirah: Tipheret (Beauty), sephirah six in Beriah (Creation)

Golden Dawn Title: Prince of Cups, Prince of the Chariot of the Waters

Elemental Combination: Air of Water

Astrological Sign: Scorpio

Rider Physical Quality: A young man with light brown hair and gray or blue eyes

Rider Deck Theme: Dreams/introspection

Shining Tribe Title: Knower of Rivers

Knight of Cups from
GOLDEN DAWN,
MARSEILLE, RIDER,
VISCONTI &
SHINING TRIBE

KNIGHT of CUPS.

Knight of Cups

This card is an interesting one to show up in relationship readings. One of the hallmarks of the knight is romance. In the courtly love tradition, the knight dedicates his strength, selflessly, to the service and adoration of the lady. And Cups is a romantic suit. Yet even more, Cups represents a dreaminess and a desire to look inwards, a fascination with the self. Thus the card carries a conflict, drawn to love and service but desiring to pursue his own fascinations. Put it next to the Hermit, and the inward quality becomes stronger—next to the Lovers or the Two of Cups, and the romance takes over.

The knights ride out and return. What does the Knight of Cups seek on his quest? Where does he go? What does he bring back, and will it be for others or for himself? He may pursue spiritual beauty or the wonders of fantasy but have trouble doing anything with his discoveries. Some of the old fortuneteller meanings for this card speak of treachery or fraud.

In his book, Waite identifies the Knight of Swords as Sir Galahad, the knight who finds the Holy Grail. But if the Cup is in fact the Grail, then maybe the Knight of Water is the Grail Knight. There is another Grail Knight, Perceval, who disastrously does not speak when the Grail appears before him, and so prevents the healing of the Fisher King. The self-absorption of the Knight of Cups may identify him as Perceval. In the Shining Tribe Knower of Rivers, the figure emerges from his dark cave with renewed sense of purpose and power.

Notice, by the way, the Rider Knight's odd resemblance to Death, below.

Is the Knight a harbinger of great change?

READINGS—Romantic, dreamy, caught up in fantasies, slow moving. Air of water could indicate the mind moving over the unconscious, stirring up deep feelings. He (or she) may be a devoted lover but also may become caught up in his own feelings. He can become in love with love.

REVERSED—Something may stir him to action, or else that inner conflict may become stronger. He may be called on to speak up in some difficult situation or even to make an ethical choice.

THE QUEEN OF CUPS

REINE DE COUPES   REGINA DI COPPE

QUEEN OF CHALICES   KÖNIGIN DER KELCHE
REINA DE COPAS   BEKERS KONINGIN

Element: Water

Sephirah: Binah (Understanding), sephirah three in Beriah (Creation)

Golden Dawn Title: Queen of Cups, Queen of the Thrones of the Waters

Elemental Combination: Water of Water

Astrological Sign: Cancer

Rider Physical Quality: Older woman with light brown hair and gray or blue eyes

Rider Deck Theme: Dedication

Renaissance Character: Judith

Shining Tribe Title: Gift of Rivers

Queen of Cups from
GOLDEN DAWN,
MARSEILLE, RIDER,
VISCONTI &
SHINING TRIBE

QUEEN of CUPS.

Queen of Cups

Water of water; as one of the four "pure" elemental cards, the Queen of Cups carries a special power. She is much closer to the High Priestess than the impatient King of Wands is to the Magician, for the Queen of Cups is intense and deeply committed to her path, which we might call the creative path of love. Waite says of her that "she sees but she also acts, and her activity feeds her dream." In the Rider picture, she stares intently at her elaborate cup, which may be her own creation. It stands out in the deck as unique, the only one decorated and the only one covered. Some have compared it to the vessel that holds the "host," the sacred wafers, or "bread," that turns into the body of Christ in the Catholic mass. With the winged figures on either side, it recalls the Ark of the Covenant from the temple in ancient Israel, which was guarded by two seraphim. The Ark was the dwelling place of the Shekinah, the female presence of the divine. Notice, by the way, how the Queen from the Visconti holds a similar cup, though without the winged figures.

The Rider Queen of Cups has long been one of my favorite cards. Her throne rests on dry land, compared to that of the King, but water swirls all around her and even seems to merge into her dress, so that we can say she blends intense feeling with manifestation. I find the intensity of her gaze symbolic of a strong will, though I know that some Rider devotees find her scowling. In the Shining Tribe deck, the gift of the Gift of Rivers is love. Two streams meet and merge into one, and where they join we see the Holy Grail in the form of a simple bowl.

The Renaissance designation of this Queen as Judith will surprise those who know the Golden Dawn Tarot or the Thoth Tarot of Aleister Crowley and Frieda Harris (based on the Golden Dawn ideas). There we see Judith as the Queen of Swords, holding up the head of Holofernes. Why would the Renaissance link her to Cups? Possibly because she first gets General Holofernes drunk, with a hint that she seduces him, so that he will pass out and not see what she is about to do to him. Since the Queen of Cups fully embodies the feminine element of water, this interpretation suggests a misogynist distrust of women's wiles. A more positive view comes from the description of Judith in the biblical book named for her, as a woman of "good heart." In playing cards, remember, she becomes the Queen of Hearts.

As an image of the Shekinah, the Queen of Cups can be invoked magically for healing and protection. Set her on an altar, light candles around her, or use your own methods to bring her energy alive.

READINGS—Intensity, dedication, love, someone who blends feeling with action. She may represent a creative artist or creativity itself. She also can indicate love, both romantic and love of family. Healing and a sense of protection in some difficult situation.

REVERSED—The unity of vision and action can become ruptured so that she either gets lost in her inner worlds or acts without genuine emotion. One tradition sees her as someone not to be trusted, possibly a connection to the idea of that seductive woman who will cut off a man's ... head.

QUEEN of CUPS.

KING of CUPS.

< RIDER
Queen
&
King of Cups

∨ MARSEILLE
Queen
&
King of Cups

REINE DE COUPES   REGINA DI COPPE

QUEEN OF CHALICES   KÖNIGIN DER KELCHE
REINA DE COPAS   BEKERS KONINGIN

ROI DE COUPES   RE DI COPPE

KING OF CHALICES   KÖNIG DER KELCHE
REY DE COPAS   BEKERS KONING

*Scenes from
a marriage* (SEE PAGE 417)

THE KING OF CUPS

ROI DE COUPES RE DI COPPE

KING OF CHALICES KÖNIG DER KELCHE
REY DE COPAS BEKERS KONING

Element: Water

Sephirah: Hokhmah (Wisdom), sephirah two in Beriah (Creation)

Golden Dawn Title: Knight of Cups, Lord of the Waves and the Waters, King of the Hosts of the Sea

Elemental Combination: Fire of Water

Astrological Sign: Pisces

Rider Physical Quality: Older man with light brown hair and gray or blue eyes

Rider Deck Theme: Channeled creativity

Renaissance Character: Charlemagne

Shining Tribe Title: Speaker of Rivers

King of Cups from
GOLDEN DAWN,
MARSEILLE, RIDER,
VISCONTI &
SHINING TRIBE

KING of CUPS.

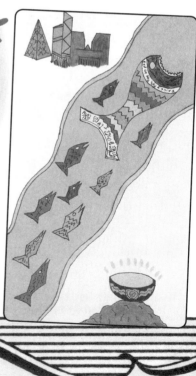

King of Cups

If you set the Queen and King of Cups next to each other, in both the Marseille and Rider decks, you will notice that this married couple look away from each other (see page 415). They show two people who go their separate ways, who possibly have other lovers. The posture and glance of the Marseille King in particular strikes me as having a roving eye and seductive energy. Does this seem a trivial way to interpret the grand figures of the Tarot courts? If gossip was the only way we approached them, it would greatly limit us, but if we want to understand them as *people*, we should consider the human qualities they suggest to us.

We can consider the Queen and King from an elemental viewpoint. Being water of water, the Queen becomes self-sufficient, not needing a partner. The King's fire of water, on the other hand, pushes him to look for accomplishments beyond the Cups realm of the heart. As King, he must rule (or, in modern terms, seek success and establishment in the outer world), where society does not measure value in terms of love or relationship. The King of Cups sometimes strikes me as a very creative, sensitive person, a dreamer like the knight, who has channeled all that sensitivity into business or professional life—say, a poet who becomes a successful lawyer.

In the Rider, his throne floats on the sea, yet the water never touches his feet. Compare this to the Queen, who sits on land and yet allows the water to flow into her dress. The King of Cups may indicate suppressed emotion, someone with deep levels of feeling who does not show this side to others lest it overwhelm him (or her). Charlemagne was a great warrior, but he also championed learning and the arts. Like King Arthur, he was expected to return in the future—in his case, to battle the Antichrist in Armageddon, a possible reference to his having beaten the Muslim invasion of Europe when it tried to cross from Spain into France.

The Shining Tribe Speaker of Rivers is a teacher and a storyteller, the great fish followed literally by the "school" of devotees.

> READINGS—Fire of water suggests alchemical power to transform or channel emotional energy. The King suggests someone successful, maybe with deep emotions or creative impulses that he tends to hide. This may be a card of achievement in the arts. It may indicate someone with a drinking problem who usually covers it up. Sexual affairs are possible.

> REVERSED—One tradition sees the King of Cups as corrupt, who misuses power, and we might find this in the reversed card. The upside-down King can indicate the emotions coming out more, with anger or tears revealing long-hidden feelings. There may be blocked creativity or frustration.

THE PRINCESS OF SWORDS

VALET D'EPEES — FANTE DI SPADE
KNAVE OF SWORDS — BUBE DER SCHWERTER
SOTA DE ESPADAS — ZWAARDEN SCHILDKNAAP

Element: Air

Sephirah: Malkuth (Kingdom), sephirah ten in Yetsirah (Formation)

Golden Dawn Title: Princess of Swords, Princess of the Rushing Winds, Lotus of the Palace of Air

Elemental Combination: Earth of Air

Rider Physical Quality: A girl or young woman with dark brown hair and hazel or gray eyes

Rider Deck Theme: Caution, wariness

Renaissance Character: Ogier

Shining Tribe Title: Place of Birds

Page of Swords from
GOLDEN DAWN,
MARSEILLE, RIDER,
VISCONTI &
SHINING TRIBE

PAGE of SWORDS.

Page of Swords

Earth of air suggests bringing ideas down to earth, and yet in many modern decks, based on the Rider, we see the Page on a hilltop, looking as if the wind might take him into the clouds at any moment. Clearly, the air part is stronger than the earth. He looks back over his shoulder, as does the Marseille figure, though there we see the Knave/Valet/Fante standing among grass. When we see the Marseille card, and even the very feminine Visconti, both with their swords, we may remember that *fante* means "foot soldier." The knights, of course, will be on horseback. Notice, by the way, the elaborate feathered hats worn by the Visconti Page and Knight, seemingly anticipating the Golden Dawn equation of Swords=Air by some 450 years (and the Shining Tribe suit of Birds by 550).

In my view of the court cards as developmental, the pages represent students, or beginners, who do not need to take action but simply appreciate the element and the suit. The Rider Page of Swords is lighter than the other Swords court cards, freer-looking, and yet he looks cautious, even wary, as he holds the heavy sword with one hand and looks back over his shoulder. The sword, remember, is an instrument of battle, and the Page may be someone preparing for a fight. If we switch directions a moment and consider that movement from king down to page, there may be a quality of post-traumatic stress here, the idea of looking nervously back, defensive, long after the danger has ended. By contrast, the Shining Tribe shows the Place of Birds as a literal bird's-eye view. A labyrinth stretches subtly over several mountains, and the only way to see this literal big picture is to get distance, to see as the birds do.

Ogier first battled Charlemagne, then became one of his twelve paladins. Thus he can symbolize the possibility of reconciliation. Ogier's birth was attended by the fairy enchantress Morgan le Fay, who later took him to live in Avalon (with King Arthur), from where he will return when France needs him. This story brings magic into the Swords theme of intellect.

READINGS—Caution, wariness, looking backward, perhaps nervously. The other cards can indicate whether caution is justified. Magic, possibly an apprentice, a student of ideas, bringing ideas down to earth.

REVERSED—Learning to relax, to trust people. Alternatively, the exact opposite, becoming more anxious, more aggressive. This is a quality of reversed cards, that they may let go of the quality of the card or heighten it. Again, the other cards, along with the reader's intuition and the querent's own reaction to the picture, can give a sense of which way it goes.

THE PRINCE OF SWORDS

CHEVALIER D'EPEES   CAVALIERE DI SPADE

KNIGHT OF SWORDS   RITTER DER SCHWERTER
CABALLO DE ESPADAS   ZWAARDEN RIDDER

Element: Air

Sephirah: Tipheret (Beauty), sephirah six in Yetsirah (Formation)

Golden Dawn Title: Prince of Swords, Prince of the Chariots of the Winds

Elemental Combination: Air of Air

Astrological Sign: Aquarius

Rider Physical Quality: A young man with dark brown hair and hazel or gray eyes

Rider Deck Theme: Courage

Shining Tribe Title: Knower of Birds

Knight of Swords from
GOLDEN DAWN,
MARSEILLE, RIDER,
VISCONTI &
SHINING TRIBE

KNIGHT of SWORDS .

Knight of Swords

In the approach of elemental combinations, each suit has a perfect, or unified, card. For Swords it's the knight, whom we might think of as dwelling in the high places of the mind, moving swiftly as only air can, quick-thinking, lofty. If the knights indeed ride off and return, then this knight might bring back great ideas and challenges to conventional thinking. Though most cards show a courageous knight on a rushing steed, few give any sense of the intellect or the high, pure air of ideas.

The Shining Tribe image allows this high realm to enter the human world. Based on a Chinese myth about a sage inventing writing by combining images falling from sky with the tracks of tortoises and birds, it concerns prophecy and divination. After I created it, I learned that the myth indeed involved oracles. The Chinese believed that writing was invented to set down the I Ching. In Tarot tradition, we might think of the Egyptian god Thoth—Hermes Trismegistus—inventor, supposedly, of both writing and Tarot.

Most commonly, the Knight of Swords depicts not intellect but courage. Just as he is "perfect" air of air, he also is the very model of a knight, for what, in fact, does a knight-errant do but fight battles? In the Rider, he sends his horse directly into a storm—the trees bend towards him, and even the horse seems to look back a bit nervously, as if to say, "Are you sure we should do this?"

The Knight of Swords fights fearlessly, but unless he serves higher causes, especially justice, his courage loses all meaning.

> READINGS—Courage, swiftness, daring. Battle can be suggested, and whoever takes up this sword needs to make sure he or she fights for justice. The intellect at a pure level, ideas and principles. A swift mind, brilliant.

> REVERSED—The danger of fighting for its own sake, for the thrill of battle. With all the Swords court cards, the reversed can tend towards corruption, and the knight can become aggressive, overbearing. More simply, he can take on a wild or reckless quality. He may be impatient with people who think more slowly than he does.

THE QUEEN OF SWORDS

REINE D'EPEES — REGINA DI SPADE

QUEEN OF SWORDS — KÖNIGIN DER SCHWERTER
REINA DE ESPADAS — ZWAARDEN KONINGIN

Element: Air

Sephirah: Binah (Understanding),
sephirah three in Yetsirah
(Formation)

Golden Dawn Title: Queen of
Swords, Queen of the
Thrones of Air

Elemental Combination: Water of Air

Astrological Sign: Libra

Rider Physical Quality: Older
woman with dark brown hair
and hazel or gray eyes

Rider Deck Theme: Wisdom, sorrow

Renaissance Character: Pallas
(Athena)

Shining Tribe Title: Gift of Birds

Queen of Swords from
GOLDEN DAWN,
MARSEILLE, RIDER,
VISCONTI &
SHINING TRIBE

QUEEN of SWORDS.

Queen of Swords

Many people see this queen as a figure of sorrow, even a widow. In fact, the tassel hanging from her left hand in the Rider deck may represent a Victorian symbol of widowhood. Butterflies form her crown in Smith's drawing. They can symbolize the transformation of the soul from matter to spirit, through the purity of mind. The Greek word *psyche*, which today means "the mind," originally meant both "soul" and "butterfly."

Staying with the Rider, she appears not happy—she may have seen a good deal of sorrow or pain in her life—but her head rises above the clouds as a symbol of her purity. Her open hand welcomes life and spirit, holding nothing back. She does not tilt the sword as if ready to fight but holds it straight up, like the swords on Justice and the Ace. She knows that without her commitment to truth, she has nothing. One bird flies above her, a further image of her pure mind.

What of other decks, other possibilities? The Golden Dawn image makes it gruesomely clear that they consider this card, not the Queen of Cups, to be Judith, the biblical heroine who beheaded Holofernes. This shows her as a woman of valor and courage but also daring. Another interpretation might see the head as ego and the queen like those Tibetan images of ferocious goddesses holding skulls.

The Renaissance association with Pallas suggests other possibilities. The name was a title of Athena, goddess of wisdom and war, and protector of Athens. Athena famously sprang full-grown from the head of her father, Zeus, and as a result she can symbolize thought unattached to the physical. *Pallas* meant "virgin," for Athena refused any sexual relationship. Instead, she befriended and protected heroes, such as Odysseus. Since Odysseus, in fact, was famous for using intelligence and even trickery rather than just brute force, we might imagine him as the King of this suit, and see the Queen and King not as a married couple, but rather as the goddess and her favorite mortal.

READINGS—Possibly sorrow, even widowhood, or some other difficulty that can leave someone alone, yet wise. Commitment to truth, both in thought and speech. You may not always like what she says but you know she will not lie to you. Some people see her as the image of the intellectual or the writer. The sword becomes the pen (mightier, after all), and the raised hand is her openness to new ideas. As Pallas, she can be remote yet brave and extremely loyal to her friends.

REVERSED—As with the other Swords court cards, reversed can slide towards corruption, that powerful mind and personality turned more towards manipulation and control. Another (happier) interpretation would see her as leaving her high, lonely place and becoming more involved in life, possibly in relationship.

THE KING OF SWORDS

Element: Air

Sephirah: Hokhmah (Wisdom), sephirah two in Yetsirah (Formation)

Golden Dawn Title: Knight of Swords, Lord of the Winds and Breezes, King of the Spirit of Air

Elemental Combination: Fire of Air

Astrological Sign: Gemini

Rider Physical Quality: Older man with dark brown hair and hazel or gray eyes

Rider Deck Theme: Authority

Renaissance Character: David

Shining Tribe Title: Speaker of Birds

King of Swords from
GOLDEN DAWN,
MARSEILLE, RIDER,
VISCONTI &
SHINING TRIBE

KING of SWORDS.

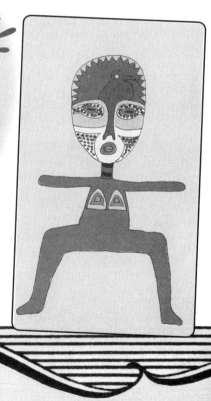

King of Swords

The Renaissance choice of David for this card suggests some interesting possibilities. Many modern people see David primarily as the brave boy who craftily killed the giant Goliath with a stone whipped from a sling. This would seem to suggest the page more than the king. But David actually conveys more complex qualities. He was a great warrior, forming the nation of ancient Israel from what had been a tribal people. And he was a famous poet and harpist, supposed writer of the Psalms. Thus he brings together both aspects of the sword, battle and mind.

Interestingly, some modern decks identify this king with another Israelite: David's son, Solomon. Thus the mind takes precedence, for Solomon was the archetype of the wise man, known in the Middle Ages as the greatest of all magicians, master of the spirits (sometimes called djinn, or genies, or demons), whom he commanded to build the temple where the Shekinah dwelt. And yet, just as with David and Goliath, the image of Solomon in modern times depends on a single story, when two women claimed the same baby, and Solomon craftily offered to divide the child in half, allowing the true mother to reveal herself. Thus, some contemporary decks will show the king holding a sword in one hand and an infant in the other.

This image symbolizes wisdom, for he knew just what to do, but it also invokes a vital quality of this king—that he exercises authority and must make decisions. He is really the very image of a king, and in the Rider deck, he seems to me the most *comfortable* in his role. The Wands King looks like he wants to abdicate, the Cups like he must suppress his water feelings, and the Pentacles King focuses primarily on his wealth. The King of Swords looks out at us with a sense of command. He is very much "the Emperor's representative on Earth."

The Shining Tribe Speaker of Birds also looks directly at us, body open with the power of art.

READINGS—Someone in a position of authority, and more, who is comfortable making decisions, being in command. The French fortuneteller Etteila saw him as an attorney or judge, or in general someone from the professional classes, including doctor, senator, and "legal consultant." Waite (and Mathers) follow Etteila's lead here, with Waite going a step further, to "Whatever arises out of the idea of judgement...Power, command, authority." As well as a person, the King of Swords can signify the very idea of a wise decision, especially for the common good.

REVERSED—A powerful mind and personality serving itself rather than society. Corruption in high places. More benignly, someone uncomfortable with exercising authority.

THE PRINCESS OF PENTACLES

VALET DE DENIERS   FANTE DI DENARI

KNAVE OF PENTACLES   BUBE DER MÜNZEN
SOTA DE OROS   MUNTEN SCHILDKNAAP

Element: Earth

Sephirah: Malkuth (Kingdom), sephirah ten in Assiyah (Action)

Golden Dawn Title: Princess of Pentacles, Princess of the Echoing Hills, Rose of the Palace of Earth

Elemental Combination: Earth of Earth

Rider Physical Quality: A girl or young woman with very dark brown or black hair and dark eyes

Rider Deck Theme: Study

Renaissance Character: Lancelot

Shining Tribe Title: Place of Stones

Page of Pentacles from
GOLDEN DAWN,
MARSEILLE, RIDER,
VISCONTI &
SHINING TRIBE

PAGE of PENTACLES.

Page of Pentacles

This is the "perfect," or unified, card of the suit, earth of earth, and so we might expect to see an image of someone grounded, possibly even slow or physically heavy, what esotericists call "dense." The Shining Tribe version shows a stone circle in the form of a goddess, a picture of the Shekinah brought into the physical world. In the more traditional cards, however, we do not really see an emphasis on material reality. The Golden Dawn version we see here (a contemporary reworking) shows a kind of Amazon warrior, a reminder of that idea of the fante (or fantesca), the foot soldier. The Marseille figure holds up the coin and stares at it, as if uncertain what to do about it.

The Rider Page also looks at the pentacle, but with a much lighter attitude. He seems fascinated, rapt. I think of him as the model of a student, dedicated, caught up in his studies. If pages are messengers, what message would he bring us? Maybe he would tell us what he finds so wonderful in that lightly held pentacle.

The Renaissance character identifies him as one of the greatest heroes of chivalry, Lancelot (remember that these associations do not include the knights, so that heroic figures become the valets). Lancelot epitomized the highest ideals of both the warrior and courtly love—that is, until he fell and became the lover of his king's wife, Guinevere. His dream had been to fulfill the Grail quest, but his surrender to temptation—to the body, to earth—gave that destiny over to his son, Galahad, whom Waite identified as the Knight of Swords, air of air.

There is another possibility here, that of the student of magic—the beginner in occult studies who follows the wonder of the pentacle.

READINGS—A student or beginner in something, in magic or any other area of learning. Fascination with something, without the need to do anything except follow the wonder of it. This idea of study or apprenticeship goes all way back to Etteila, the eighteenth-century diviner. Alternatively, grounding, making something real and solid, earth of earth. Mathers says "household economy, management," qualities that fit the element in a very mundane way.

REVERSED—From Etteila on, the usual meanings speak of luxury, excess, and "prodigality," as if giving in to earth's sensual temptations. A student may have trouble with his studies or feel some outside pressure. Alternatively, it can mean relaxation after intense study or work.

THE PRINCE OF PENTACLES

Element: Earth

Sephirah: Tipheret (Beauty), sephirah six in Assiyah (Action)

Golden Dawn Title: Prince of Pentacles, Prince of the Chariot of Earth

Elemental Combination: Air of Earth

Astrological Sign: Taurus

Rider Physical Quality: A boy or young man with very dark brown or black hair and black eyes

Rider Deck Theme: Work

Shining Tribe Title: Knower of Stones

Knight of Pentacles from
GOLDEN DAWN,
MARSEILLE, RIDER,
VISCONTI &
SHINING TRIBE

KNIGHT of PENTACLES.

Knight of Pentacles

With all the Knights we have looked at their essential nature: to leave and return. Knights go on quests, they slay dragons (a kinetic activity if ever there was one), they return as heroes or with magic or wisdom. If we look at the Rider picture for this card, its most signal feature is the lack of any movement at all. The horse stands squarely on the grass. On the Golden Dawn Prince of Pentacles, the bull has one hoof raised but doesn't look like he's going anywhere fast. In the Shining Tribe Knower of Stones, the figure, inspired by a Native American rock painting in Texas, is filled with energy, so excited by what he knows that his hair stands straight up ("the ultimate bad hair day," someone once called this card). And yet, he too is not going anywhere, his body literally embedded in the stone. In all these examples, air of earth becomes the knight's movement literally brought down to earth.

For many, the Knight of Pentacles is the image of the dedicated worker, not ambitious or given to risk but willing to give all his attention to his duties. This does not necessarily describe someone's personality or lifelong habits. If you face a challenge at work or some other practical area in life—gardening might be a good example—where you need to give it your full attention for a period of time, you might want to invoke the Knight of Pentacles. Whenever you think of something else you'd rather be doing, you can think of the knight solidly on his horse and stay focused on your task.

An alternative image comes to mind for this card—the Green Knight from the medieval story "Sir Gawain and the Green Knight." Without going into details, we can say that the green skin of the mysterious knight identifies him as a nature spirit. In the story, he allows Gawain to cut off his head and then calmly walks off with it tucked under his arm. This gives us the sense of someone without ego through his attachment to the natural world.

READINGS—Hard-working, diligent, devoted to the task at hand, without need for outer rewards or glory. Cautious, not given to wildness or risk. Excited by what you know that is rock-solid, of the body rather than the mind. In the service of nature, without ego.

REVERSED—As is often the case, the reversed can exaggerate any problems with the card or else go in a different direction. Inertia is one possibility, or allowing others to take advantage of you. But the reversed card also can indicate taking more chances or finding other interests.

THE QUEEN OF PENTACLES

REINE DE DENIERS   REGINA DI DENARI

QUEEN OF PENTACLES   KÖNIGIN DER MÜNZEN
REINA DE OROS   MUNTEN KONINGIN

Element: Earth

Sephirah: Binah (Understanding), sephirah three in Assiyah (Action)

Golden Dawn Title: Queen of Pentacles, Queen of the Thrones of Earth

Elemental Combination: Water of Earth

Astrological Sign: Capricorn

Rider Physical Quality: Older woman with very dark brown or black hair and black eyes

Rider Deck Theme: Nature

Renaissance Character: Argine or Argea

Shining Tribe Title: Gift of Stones

Queen of Pentacles from
GOLDEN DAWN,
MARSEILLE, RIDER,
VISCONTI &
SHINING TRIBE

QUEEN of PENTACLES

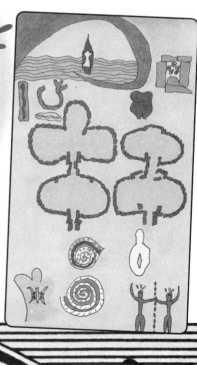

Queen of Pentacles

The Queen of Pentacles embodies the Empress as strongly as the King of Swords takes the role of the Emperor. The two cards occupy very different realms, each one self-sufficient. In the Queen of Pentacles we find a deep love of nature, a joy in whatever grows from the ground. As water of earth, she brings passionate love to the living world. In the Rider deck she sits in nature, with no buildings in sight, compared to the Pentacles King, whose palace stands behind him.

Waite liked this queen. He describes her as "summed up in the idea of greatness of soul" and "the serious cast of intelligence; she contemplates her symbol and may see worlds therein."

In my own developmental view, the queen represents mastery of the suit/element. With Pentacles she is the master of nature, not in the sense of controlling it but in her deep and passionate attachment.

The Shining Tribe Gift of Stones shows two temples from the island country of Malta. Seen from above, the larger one, on the left, forms the outline of a goddess's body. Known as Ggantija, or "female giant," by the local people, the temple may be the world's oldest building, dated at six thousand years. Everything in the picture is doubled—two temples, two spirals, two stick figures—so that the Gift becomes intense joining, with other people and with nature.

The obscure name Argine may have been an anagram of Regina (Latin for "queen"), a reference to various queens, including Marie de Médicis, who came to France from Italy and was so appalled at the wretched food that she imported chefs and taught the French how to cook. The love of good food is certainly part of the Queen of Pentacles. Others say the name is a variant of Argea, who was a queen of the fays, or fairies.

> READINGS—Love of nature, intense involvement with the physical world. Happiness, physical security, possibly wealth, though enjoyment is more central to the meaning. Someone who loves life and is self-sufficient, who prefers nature to cities, who may be a hermit, not because she (or he) dislikes people but just because she doesn't really need them. Alternatively (from the Shining Tribe), someone who bonds powerfully with others but also with the earth.

> REVERSED—The essential connection to nature may be lost or threatened, and she can become irritable, aggressive. There may be too much pressure on a person. The hermit side of this queen can become exaggerated.

THE KING OF PENTACLES

ROI DE DENIERS   RE DI DENARI

KING OF PENTACLES   KÖNIG DER MÜNZEN
REY DE OROS   MUNTEN KONING

Element: Earth

Sephirah: Hokhmah (Wisdom), sephirah two in Assiyah (Action)

Golden Dawn Title: King of Pentacles, Lord of the Wild and Fertile Land, King of the Spirits of Earth

Elemental Combination: Fire of Earth

Astrological Sign: Virgo

Rider Physical Quality: An older man with very dark brown or black hair and black eyes

Rider Deck Theme: Wealth

Renaissance Character: Alexander the Great

Shining Tribe Title: Speaker of Stones

King of Pentacles from
GOLDEN DAWN,
MARSEILLE, RIDER,
VISCONTI &
SHINING TRIBE

KING of PENTACLES.

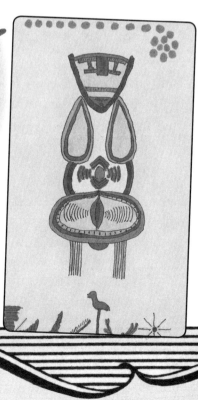

King of Pentacles

This King has truly brought his fire down to earth. He is successful, secure, with wealth and possibly honor, and he likes it that way. Unlike the Rider deck's impatient King of Wands—fire of fire—he does not seem at all uncomfortable on his throne but leans back, fondly holding his golden pentacle. The Marseille figure also sits back relaxed, though he glances off to his left, as if he spots something of interest (a bit like the King of Cups). Even the Visconti King rests his hand on his coin in a similar posture. Notice, by the way, that in the Marseille card, the King wears a hat very similar to that of the Magician and the woman in Strength. Perhaps the Marseille King opens to a deeper level than in other decks.

The Shining Tribe image is the oldest in the deck, carved twenty thousand years ago on a mammoth tusk and uncovered in the twentieth century. Thus, it means to speak, or share, what is oldest and truest in a person's experience. The artist created the image of a goddess from geometric forms, so that in this Speaker abstract concepts become real, grounded in physical experience.

Alexander the Great was the prototypical conqueror. Not only did he overcome all resistance in Egypt, Persia, and Asia Minor, he also ushered in an age of great learning and the world's first truly cosmopolitan culture, the Hellenistic, which mixed Greek and Egyptian ideas and mythologies. Hermes Trismegistus and the Mystery cults, and thus Hermeticism itself, came from this world, so that we might think of the King of Pentacles as the patron of the entire Tarot. The French romances liked to describe Alexander as generous and benevolent, and indeed, there is nothing in the King of Pentacles to suggest that he hoards or keeps secret his wealth and success. If you seek to find a benefactor for a project or to win a grant, you might visualize the King of Pentacles entering your life. This is also a good card to receive if you are looking for a job, because he can mean a friendly boss.

READINGS—Wealth, success, comfort, security. He may focus on material things but more with satisfaction and pride than selfishness or obsession. He can in fact be very generous. A good card in any reading that concerns looking for work or material support from someone. Grounding ideas in solid reality, speaking about what you know from your own experience.

REVERSED—Worries about money or physical insecurity. Dissatisfaction, a feeling that what he has is not enough. Pressures from other people testing the boundaries of generosity. Possibly a turn from material concerns to more abstract or spiritual ideas.

A Reading Inspired by the Court Cards

Though this spread came out of the idea of considering the court cards as distinct families (see the very beginning of this section), it uses the entire deck and is done in the usual manner. I've posed the questions in the present tense, but for people who want to look back at their families when younger, you can do it in the past, changing "Who am I…" to "Who was I…" For simplicity's sake, I have restricted the subjects to self, mother, and father, but of course you could easily add on brothers, sisters, grandparents, etc., depending on your family structure.

1. Who am I in my family?

2. What is my role?

3. Who is my mother?

4. What is her role?

5. Who is my father?

6. What is his role?

For a reading that utilizes the court cards as their own distinct group, see Court Card Confrontation on page 453.

Readings

WHEN YOU COME right down to it, reading Tarot cards is really very simple. You decide on your subject and your questions, you shuffle the cards, and then you turn them over, usually one card per question, and see what they tell you. The trick, really, lies in the seeing.

People sometimes ask if there are any special rules for shuffling or handling the cards, where to sit, what to say. There are, in fact, all sorts of "rules," but should we follow them? Various Tarotists will tell you things you must do or not do, but in my experience you are free to create your own methods—whatever is meaningful to you and will help you get to that place of seeing. Following are some of the rules you may encounter:

1.   *Wrap your cards in silk or place them in a wooden or silver box.*

Supposedly, this protects them from negative influences and people's "vibrations." I've never quite understood just what that term meant in a psychic context, but some people find it important. When I first began my Tarot practice, I used to wrap my decks in brightly colored silk scarves. Since, like many Tarotists, I collect decks, it did not take too long before I discovered I could not remember which set of cards was wrapped in which silk. These days, if I like a deck and plan to use it on a regular basis for readings, I usually will find an attractive bag or box for it, but mostly because that increases the enjoyment of using them. The "magic" of Tarot lies in the images and your own self, not the printed cardboard. If you do like wooden boxes, cigar stores sometimes sell beautiful ones, with no odor, for just a few dollars.

2.   *Do not let anyone else touch your cards.*

This goes with that idea of protecting the cards from vibrations. Again, I have never seen a need for this, and in fact, I would say that it's important for the querent—the actual subject of the reading—to shuffle the cards so that it becomes about her or him, not the reader. However, if you prefer that no one touch your cards but yourself, you can mix them, then spread them on the table and ask the person to point to one, then another, until you have the proper number for the spread.

3.   *You cannot buy a Tarot deck—someone must give it to you,
       or you must steal it.*

I only found out about this bizarre notion a few years ago, when Barbara Moore, the Tarot specialist at Llewellyn, gave a talk on Tarot from the publisher's perspective and said certain size formats were difficult because they were easier to steal, and many people believed they must do that. Since then I have heard it from other sources. This is absolutely not true. I would think that if you got your deck through theft, it might corrupt your ability to use the cards. If you really think you should not buy your deck, take a friend to the store, see which one you like, then give your friend the money and ask her or him to buy it and give it to you.

4.   *You must always sit across from the querent.*

I once saw this rule, described as absolute, in a book of feminist interpretations of Tarot. To my mind, you can sit in whatever arrangement works best for you. I prefer catty-corner at a table, so that it's easy to lay the cards out in a way that we both are seeing them from the same direction.

5. *Always include the possibility of reversed cards*
   (or never use reversed cards).

Reversed cards, of course, mean that the person shuffles them in such a way that some of the cards come out the wrong way around.

When I first began to read cards, I made sure to include reversed meanings, since that was what the few available books said to do. This idea comes, like so much else in Tarot cartomancy, from the eighteenth-century French diviner and occultist, Etteila. Over the years of teaching and writing about Tarot, I have usually included the reversed possibilities just because they are part of the tradition. However, some people never use them, and I often don't myself. I may give the deck to querents with all the cards right-side up, and if they shuffle them in such a way that some get turned around, then we will look at them reversed.

6. *There is one correct way to shuffle the cards.*

Some people love rules and they will insist to you there is only one proper way to mix the deck. This "proper way" usually means whatever they themselves like to do. The only rule I would endorse is that you must shuffle them face down so you cannot know which ones are likely to come out on top. If you want to use reversed meanings, you can shuffle the cards by what I call the mudpie method. Set the deck on the table, then move the cards around with both hands, and finally put them back together in a neat pile. Recently I noticed on television that this is how dealers in casinos shuffle the cards for poker games.

7. *There is one correct way to turn over the cards.*

Again, do it however seems right to you, except that most readers make sure to turn over each card in the same way.

8. *You need to place the cards on a spread cloth*
   rather than directly on the table.

This is another one of those "rules" that come under preference. I find it gives the reading a quality of a special moment to first spread a beautiful cloth on the table top. I sometimes will light a candle as well and set out a small figurine I have of the goddess Persephone. At other times, however, I have done none of this, and the reading has turned out very well.

9. *You have to memorize all the meanings of the cards*
   before you can start reading.

If that was the case, I never would have become a Tarot reader. I began reading right away, with the cards in one hand and a book of meanings in the other. Some of those readings remain among the profoundest I've ever done. There may actually be a drawback to memorizing meanings, a tendency to become rigid in the possibilities of what a card can say in a particular situation. If you learn as you go along, you allow for readings to spark new ideas of what any card might mean. Some of my most valuable interpretations of cards have come out of moments in a reading. I call this "accretion," where you discover a meaning in a particular situation and then realize it can apply in other readings.

10.   *You cannot read for yourself.*

This is a common belief, and yes, it can be difficult, especially if the reading concerns a very emotional situation. We can get too caught up in scary or hopeful cards, and exaggerate the meanings. On the other hand, some people read only for themselves, so no, there is no rule, psychic, karmic, or otherwise. Doing daily short readings for yourself is a good way to get to know the cards, since even if something dire appears, another card will replace it the next day. If you don't trust your own responses at a particular time, you might find a fellow Tarotist and trade readings.

11.   *You should not ask anything about someone*
      who is not there and has not given permission.

On this rule I tend to agree, though not as absolutely as some Tarotists I know. If someone comes to me for a reading and says, "There's a guy at work who I'm really interested in, but I saw him talking to this woman I hate over in accounting. I want to know what he's doing with her," I would tell her I can't do that.

Tarot readers see two problems with this kind of request. One, it's unethical, a kind of spying. Two, if the man is not there to mix the cards and has not asked that the woman mix them for him, it probably won't work. A woman made an appointment with me once, and over the phone said that one of the things she wanted to ask about was her daughter. I said we could do that only with the daughter's authorization that her mother would represent her. The woman said that was no problem, her daughter would be thrilled to get a proxy Tarot reading, but when the appointment happened she said that her daughter had said no.

Will I ever agree to this kind of reading? Yes, if it seems to me the querent needs information to make a life decision of her own. A woman asked once if her husband would leave his girlfriend and return to her. Two years had passed since he'd moved out, and she'd been unable to make any long-range plans. The cards indicated he would not return, but she could make a new life for herself if she accepted that. I saw her a year later, and she told me how she'd gotten a job, made new friends, and basically had started her life over.

12.   *You need to be psychic to read Tarot cards.*

Well, this is the big one, isn't it? Many people confuse Tarot readers with psychics, so when someone asks me for a reading I will usually caution them that I don't try to make psychic predictions. Such material may come up in the reading, but it's not the focus. We look more at self-awareness, understanding, possibilities, spiritual truth within life situations.

Obviously, people do use Tarot cards as psychic tools. The pictures trigger responses in whatever part of themselves gives forth psychic messages. Some who read this way never concern themselves with what the cards mean symbolically, for such knowledge might confuse their inner senses. On the other hand, Johanna Gargiulo-Sherman, creator of the Sacred Rose Tarot and one of the best psychics I know (*New York* magazine once included her in a list of the city's "top five psychics"), is also deeply trained in the Golden Dawn tradition. For her, the two sides of Tarot support each other.

If you wish to develop your psychic, or more intuitive, side in readings, just try it out. When you read for people, let your mind stay open for flashes or images, and more—be willing to express them. If you get an image of a beach and a feeling of sadness, you might say, "Did you go to the beach recently? And did something happen there?" When doing this, tell the person it's just something that's come into your mind, you have no idea what it might mean. It's important not to fall into the trap of accuracy. Tarot is not a trick or a stage performance, and if you worry about making mistakes, you won't dare to say anything.

Here is a thought experiment (to use a concept of Einstein's). Suppose you read cards for strangers, either professionally or at some party or charity event. And suppose a young man sits down, handsome, muscular, with a full beard, and as you lay out the cards the thought suddenly springs into your head *He's pregnant.* What do you do? Almost everyone would think *what the hell was that about* and push it away, or else say something like "Do you have a partner? And is there a chance she might be pregnant?" But your first response may have been right. As I write this, a news story has recently broken of a transgendered man—born female but now living fully as a man, having taken testosterone to masculinize his body—who is pregnant and will soon have a baby. He has appeared on the Oprah Winfrey television show and on the cover of *People* magazine.

13.   The querent should not tell you the question.

Clearly, I do not agree with this at all, since I've written here about the way the questions can help shape the reading. This idea goes with that magical performance expectation people have with Tarot readings. The fact is, if the person doesn't say what concerns them, and you do a general reading, probably the issues will emerge. But you could have gone to a deeper level if you didn't have to play a guessing game. As Tarotist Gail Fairfield has put it, if you go to the doctor and she asks, "What are your symptoms?" you don't answer, "You're the doctor. You tell me." And yet, some readers prefer to let the cards guide them, rather than the querent's questions.

And finally, not a rule but a question:

14.   How does Tarot work?

The answer to this is very simple: no one knows. People will say various things—the person's unconscious or "higher self" guides their hands while shuffling, a mysterious force called "synchronicity" causes the cards to come out in a meaningful pattern (the term comes from Carl Jung and Wolfgang Pauli, and really just means coincidence), the gods bring you messages, the devil brings you messages—but nobody really can say for sure. Some critics of Tarot claim it's all meaningless, or rather it's *too* meaningful. Since every card means something, they just come up in whatever way they will and our own minds create a pattern or message from them. I have no problem with that. As I said, a Tarot reading is not a magic act or a performance. The important thing is not where the message comes from but whether we find any value in it. Personally, my experience tells me that something else is going on, something that more directly shapes the reading, including which cards come out, but in practice I don't think it matters.

Questions and the Querent's Words

Usually, when people set out to do a reading, they have a set pattern of questions, called a spread. These can range from one card to the entire deck (a Tree of Life spread, with one card for significator, seven cards for each on the ten sephiroth, and the extra seven for a "hidden" sephirah called Da'ath, or Knowledge). A few spreads are directed at particular issues—relationship issues, for example, or spiritual development, or work, but most are general, and we adapt them to the situation. So, for example, if the person wants to know about finding a "soul mate" (a current favorite at the beginning of the twenty-first century), and you want to use a simple Past, Present, Future spread, you might adapt the questions as follows:

PAST—What about her past experiences with love has shaped her current state?

PRESENT—What does she need to look at in herself right now in order to open the way for a soul mate? Or, what opportunities for love exist around her right now?

FUTURE—Given who she is right now, what is likely to happen?

Notice that these questions, especially the last, open the way to other issues. If the "future" card seems pessimistic, we might add another question: What can she change to make a full relationship more possible?

Sometimes we need to help the person reframe the question. The soul mate issue often comes out as "When will I meet my soul mate?" This question makes two large assumptions—first, that the reader is magically psychic and can give an exact date and place, and second, that the person her- or himself does not have to do anything to bring about this major change. Rephrasing the issue to something like the questions above will create more space for a productive reading.

There is another way to do a reading, and that is just to use the person's own statements as the "questions." Consider the following, made up for this book but not unlike the kinds of things that people tell a Tarot reader.

> I feel adrift in my life, confused about what I want. I love my work but sometimes I think I should quit my job, and, I don't know, just move to Italy. My husband is very kind, and I think he loves me, but I'm not sure if I love him anymore. My youngest child has just left the home, so I feel like I have a whole new chance in life. Should I go back to school? Paint? Have an affair? Become a nun? I just don't know.

If an actual person said that, I would have her mix the cards and then turn them over, one at a time, for each of these issues:

1. Feeling adrift

2. Confused about what she wants

3. Love work

4. Quit?

5. Move to Italy?

6. Husband kind

7. "Think" he loves her (the exact word is important)

8. Not sure if she loves him anymore

9. Child has left home

10. New chance in life

11. Go back to school?

12. Paint?

13. Affair?

14. Become a nun?

15. Feeling of not knowing

Spreads

Certainly this is the most common way to read Tarot cards. Either we use an all-purpose spread or one specially suited for an issue. There are literally hundreds of spreads, with more invented all the time. People have published entire books containing nothing but Tarot spreads, often grouped under various headings, such as "Work Spreads" or "Relationship Spreads."

The simplest spread would consist of one card, one question: "What do I need to look at right now?" Many people do this on a daily basis, as a way to get to know the cards. As mentioned above, it can take some of the direness out of reading, since no matter what it is, it's just for that day. It's not a bad idea to write down what card it is or leave it out for the day, and then before going to sleep, look at the card again and see if it matches some aspect of your day.

Two-Card Spreads

Two cards can create a mirroring effect or sense of duality, one side versus another. As a result, many people prefer to go to three, for the possibility of synthesis. However, there are several two-card spreads, such as:

You		Someone else
Choice one		Choice two
Past actions		Present results

Three-Card Spreads

Three always feels natural and productive to us, primarily, I think, because we all come from the mixed genes of a mother and a father. Some three-card spreads just add one more to the two. For example, "past actions / present results" easily becomes "past actions / present results / likely future." With two choices, we can first lay a card in the middle. Notice that we don't set the cards out 1, 2, 3 but 2, 1, 3.

To make this easier to visualize, I will place them on separate lines.

CARD 1
(SITUATION)

CARD 2	CARD 3
(CHOICE A)	(CHOICE B)

Here is a reading I find very useful, using the same order of the first card in the middle. It comes from Tarotist Zoe Matoff. I use it as a daily spread, or the first pattern I think of—my "default" reading, to use a computer term.

SITUATION

DON'T DO	DO

Card 1, in the middle, shows us the basic issue. Card 2, on the left, shows a response best avoided. Many of us tend to react with automatic patterns to certain situations. This card can help us become aware of what would not work right now. Card 3, on the right, shows what would likely help.

Here is a three-card spread for relationships where the final card goes in the middle:

1.	2.
PERSON A'S ACTIONS OR ATTITUDE	PERSON B'S ACTIONS OR ATTITUDES

3.
THE RESULTING RELATIONSHIP

Spreads with More Cards

Once we go above three cards, the possibilities become endless (or at least up to seventy-eight, but then, we could always add more decks). As mentioned above, there are books with nothing but spreads, and many more available online (a search as I write this yielded 101,000 hits for "tarot spreads"), so I will give only a few here.

Some spreads are based on themes, some on images. Astrologers will sometimes do a twelve-card spread in the form of a circle, with one card for each of the twelve houses in a chart. You can do something similar for the year, beginning either on January 1 or else on your birthday. Lay out twelve cards as if on the numbers of a clock, with one being the first card.

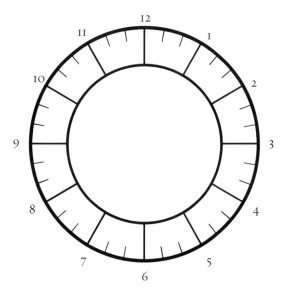

Card one, at one o'clock, will be the first month, card two the second month, and so on for the year. If you wanted to do it for your birthday, and you were born on, say, July 9, then the first card would be July, the second August, ending with June. Essentially this is not really a multi-card reading but a series of twelve one-card readings, though in practice you often can see patterns develop.

The Doorway Spread

I developed this spread originally for my book *Seeker*. Instead of dealing with events, it helps us to get a better sense of who we are at the time of the reading. While it shows both risks and possibilities, it leaves the choice of action up to us. This spread works well for reading your own cards, especially with a sense of self-exploration. It also can be helpful when you face a choice.

Turn over five cards in the following pattern:

1   2

3

4   5

1. **What inspires you?**
What touches you deeply, what calls you to do things, or simply excites you about life?

2. **What challenges you?**
What do you find difficult or frightening? What do you avoid?

3. **What doorway opens for you?**
What opportunities have come into your life? What could be different?

4. **What will you risk?**
Opportunities always carry some element of risk. If your children have grown and you are considering going back to finish your master's degree, you might risk changing the dynamic of your marriage.

5. **What can you discover?**
What might happen if you went through that door? This card can give a kind of snapshot of how your life might look.

The Body Spread

This spread, which uses the human body as the model for setting down the cards and the questions, has been a favorite of mine for years. First developed by a Danish Tarot reader named Anita Jensen, it asks almost nothing about the "future" but a great deal about who we are. In classes and workshops, I will sometimes have a volunteer lie on the floor and place the cards right on their bodies, but in private practice I only do it symbolically (and even then I'm a bit careful with whom I suggest it).

Here is the layout. See if you can visualize the cards actually on your body as you look at the pattern and read the descriptions.

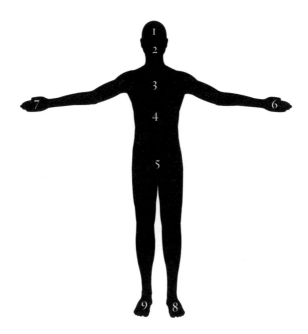

1. Goes on the forehead—What the person is thinking, either current thought patterns in general or about a particular situation (for example, the reading might concern a relationship).

2. Goes over the mouth—What the person is saying. What we say to others, or even to ourselves, might be very different from our inner thoughts.

3. Goes over the heart (actually, I usually place it in the center rather than on the left)—What the person is feeling.

4. Goes over the solar plexus—What the person knows deep down. Gut knowledge.

5. Goes over the groin area—What the person desires. This could be unrealistic, or angry, or something the person does not even dare to hope.

6. Goes on the non-dominant hand (which is the left for right-handed people and the right for left-handed people)—What the person "keeps," or in other words, does not share with a partner or the world.

7. Goes on the dominant hand (the right for right-handed people, the left for left-handed)—What the person shares.

8. Goes on the non-dominant foot—Where the person is coming from, past experience that has helped lead to the current situation.

9. Goes on the dominant foot—Where the person is heading. This can sum up, in a way, the previous cards. It is the only card that involves anything like a "prediction."

The Celtic Cross

Without doubt, the Celtic Cross is the most famous Tarot spread in the world, possibly because it appears in Waite's book, under the (dubious) title "An Ancient Celtic Method of Divination." While the structure is almost always the same, the order varies according to different authors. The order I use comes originally from '60s Tarot author Eden Gray. Because it is so well known—and I want to give what I call an "esoteric" version of it—I will keep the explanations simple. An online search will bring up many variations and subtleties of interpretation.

```
                                          10

                        5
                                              9

            4           1           6

                        2
                                          8

                        3
                                          7
```

CARD 1 goes in the center of the cross. It describes the overall issue or situation. We sometimes call this the "cover card."

CARD 2 goes horizontally across the first. Traditionally people have seen this as "opposition," some force that goes against the first. In fact, the second doesn't always oppose the first; the two may work together. Together, these two cards form what we call the "small cross."

CARD 3 goes below the first two and represents the "root" of the issue. Usually it shows some past experience that influences the present.

CARD 4, on the left side of the small cross, also shows the past, but a more "recent past," without deep roots or long-lasting importance.

Card 5 goes above the small cross. People give different meanings to this position, but I find it helpful to think of it as "possibilities" and see it as the general way things are heading. If the "outcome" card ends up looking very different from the "possibilities," we can look at the other cards to see where the energy shifts.

Card 6 shows the "near future." What will happen next in this situation? We need to remember that this card usually shows a temporary state.

We read the four cards on the right, the "staff," from the bottom to the top.

Card 7 shows "self," some way the questioner, or querent, has contributed to the overall situation.

Card 8 represents "others," the impact of other people on the situation. This card can show the influence of another person or the general environment. In readings about career, I tend to look at this card as the economic situation (say, job prospects) beyond the person's control.

Card 9 concerns "hopes and fears." Often these are the same; we fear the very thing we hope for, and vice versa. It's valuable to remember that it shows the person's attitude, not what is actually happening or will happen.

Card 10 shows the "outcome." This last card doesn't mean a prediction so much as a result of all the previous influences. We can examine what it shows us and try to see just how the root, and the self, and the recent past, and the rest end up moving in this direction. The "outcome" card does not foretell a hard-and-fast event. It just says, "This is the way things are heading." We can use the information in the other cards, as well as our own understanding, to change something we don't like or help along something that appeals to us.

An "Esoteric" Celtic Cross

A few years ago, I came across an interesting passage about a Talmudic injunction against improper questions. As I remember, it reads:

> *Four things you must not ask. What is Above, what is*
> *Below, what came Before, and what will come After.*

At one level, this attacks the very basis of esoteric or even mystical practices or speculations, for Above means what is in Heaven, Below means the Underworld or maybe the state of existence before creation, Before means before you were born, and After means after you die. So maybe the statement intends to suppress such ideas—or maybe it just tells us, as Zen does, to stay mindful of the moment and not send our mind in all directions. The spiritual teacher Ram Dass famously expressed this in the slogan "Be here now."

But when I mentioned the Talmudic injunction to Tarotist Mary Greer, she said, "But that's the Celtic Cross!" And of course it is, the four questions that ring the small cross. So I decided to recast the cross part of the spread as a way to ask these very questions, adding two other questions for the first two cards. The order is slightly different, to follow the order of "forbidden" questions (cards 3-6).

```
                 3

          5      1      6

                 2

                 4
```

1. What is the essence of who you are right now?

2. How do you express this in your life?

3. What is your link to spirit?

4. What is the source and origin of who you are?

5. What has shaped you?

6. What lies beyond your immediate existence?

It should be clear that interpretation of whatever cards come out will not be quick and immediate. You might want to ponder the cards, meditate on them, write in a journal about them, and come back more than once to look at them and think about them.

Two Unusual Spreads

Throughout this book, I have offered spreads inspired by individual cards (the Major Arcana) or the qualities of the suits and court cards. Most of these originated in the Intensive workshops that form the core of this material. Here are two more that came out of the classes and workshops I've taught.

Four Worlds Spread

This reading—actually four short readings done as a group—was inspired by the Kabbalist concept of the four worlds, with their four Trees of Life and the connections to the four suits of the Minor Arcana. You can actually do this reading as a ritual, though it is not required. Here is how to set up the ritual part:

You will need a room with enough space to lay cards out on the floor in four directions and be able to walk easily to each group. Take a deck of Tarot, *not the one you plan to use for the reading*, and separate the four suits. Now take each suit and set it down on the floor in the following pattern.

```
   KING    QUEEN    KNIGHT    PAGE

              ACE

           3     2

           5     4

              6

           8     7

              9

             10
```

The numbered cards, of course, form the Tree of Life pattern, while the court cards act as guardians for the energy. Finally, take the twenty-two Major Arcana cards and set them down in a pile in the center of the room as the source of spiritual being, the element of light. You might want to wrap them in silk, preferably dyed gold or some other radiant color.

Now take the deck you will actually read with and stand in the center (by that set of Majors you have wrapped in silk and put on the floor). Holding the reading deck in your hand, take a moment to center yourself. Breathe deeply. See yourself in the place where all things are possible. Now imagine that your energy is drawn from this place of light to the world of fire, called in Kabbalah Atzilut, or Emanation. Open your eyes and walk to the Wands suit, stopping just at the bottom (so you don't actually step on the cards). Now shuffle the deck in your hands and draw two cards for the following two questions:

1. Who am I in the world of fire?

2. What is my task?

You might want to bring along a small notebook and a pen to write down the cards you receive, because the next step is to return the two cards to the reading deck. Close your eyes once more and imagine your energy returning to that center of light.

Physically return and then face the Cups cards. Once again, see your energy moving, now to the world of water, called Beriah, Creation. Walk to the Cups and ask:

1. Who am I in the world of water?

2. What is my task?

Repeat this process for Swords—the world of air, or Yetsirah/Formation, and finally Pentacles—the world of earth, or Assiyah/Action. At the end of the reading, return to the center and pick up the Major Arcana, then "travel" to each suit and pick up the cards.

Court Card Confrontation

This reading takes advantage of the different qualities of each of the three parts of the deck—the court cards, the Major Arcana, and the numbered suit cards. The court card part of the reading is unusual in that we do not choose the cards without looking at them in the usual manner of shuffling and turning over the cards that end up on top of the pile. Instead, we consciously look at the pictures and choose the three that seem to us to best answer the questions. The other two parts, the Major Arcana and the numbered Minor Arcana, are shuffled and taken from the top in the usual manner.

Begin by separating the deck into three parts: the Major Arcana (trump cards), the Minor Arcana (suit cards, ace-ten), and the court cards (page, knight, queen, and king in the four suits).

Think of a person with whom you have a conflict or some intense issue. Go through the sixteen court cards, looking at each picture, until you find a card that you associate with that person, either by intuition (how the card looks) or what you know of the card's meaning. Set that card on the table, face up.

Now go through the court cards again, looking at the pictures face up, and pick one that represents you in relationship to that person. Who are you around that person? How do you see yourself? Set that card down, face up.

Go through the court cards one more time and pick one that represents you *outside* that relationship. What aspect of yourself does not get expressed when you are around that person?

Set the three cards down in a row: A B C.

Mix the Major Arcana cards. Choosing at random, face down, pick one card for each of the three court cards.

For A, the other person: What kind of archetypal energy do you receive from this person?

For B, yourself in that relationship: What large issues does this person trigger in you?

For C, yourself outside that relationship: What truth is hidden in that situation?

Set these down below the court cards.

A   B   C

1   2   3

Now mix the Minor Arcana cards. You are going to set out three rows underneath cards one, two, and three. The final reading will look like this:

(COURT CARDS) A   B   C

(MAJOR CARDS) 1   2   3

(MINOR CARDS; ROW 1) 1   2   3

(ROW 2) 4   5   6

(ROW 3) 7   8   9

The Minor Arcana cards answer the following questions:

Row 1

1. How this person behaves with you.

2. How you behave in the situation.

3. What you do not do (do not stay calm, or do not express anger, etc).

Row 2

4. What this person triggers in you.

5. How you help create the situation.

6. How you resist change.

Row 3

7. How you can protect yourself within the situation.

8. How you can change the situation.

9. How you can change yourself.

The entire reading contains fifteen cards—three court cards, three Major Arcana cards, and nine Minor Arcana cards.

Wisdom Readings

Throughout this book, especially in the Major Arcana, we have looked at readings that ask questions beyond the personal. In the Introduction, I told how I began this practice, which I now find one of the most exciting parts of my approach to Tarot. I have been doing this for some time—my book *Forest of Souls* is largely based on Wisdom Readings, including one where I asked the cards to "Show me the reading you gave God to create the universe"—and in recent years, some other Tarot teachers and writers have begun to take up the idea, in particular James Wells of Toronto.

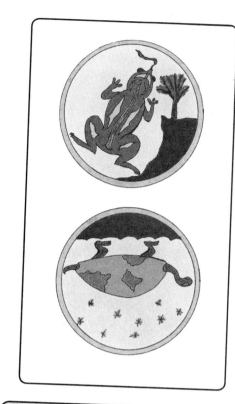

SHINING
TRIBE
*Two of Stones
(top right),
Place of Trees
(left)
&
Three of Trees
(bottom right)*

The idea behind Wisdom Readings is really very simple. If we have this wonderful source of spiritual ideas and images, this Tarot, why should we only ask it personal questions, as if it was some sort of newspaper advice column? (Dear Tarot—I've been without a partner for several years. When will I meet my soul mate? Signed, Lonely in Assiyah) Why not ask it things that really matter?

The process of doing Wisdom Readings is exactly the same as any other. Decide on the questions, mix the cards face down, and then turn over one card for each question. It's only the subjects that are different.

I will end this book with a short Wisdom Reading about the Tarot itself. I decided to ask three questions:

1. What is the soul of Tarot?

2. What does it express openly?

3. What mystery does it contain?

The deck is the Shining Tribe, and the cards are Two of Stones, Place of Trees, and Three of Trees.

1. WHAT IS THE SOUL OF TAROT? *Two of Stones* (Two of Pentacles). This card shows two sides of a coin that might be used to decide between action and non-action, yang and yin. The frog at the top of the picture symbolizes swift movement, taking chances. The turtle at the bottom represents a slow and careful process. The soul of Tarot is really in how it guides us in the essential choices that we face all the time. Do we jump into the unknown, or do we move cautiously?

2. WHAT DOES IT EXPRESS OPENLY? *Place of Trees* (Page of Wands). This picture, inspired by a 3,000-year-old seal from Crete, shows a garden with two women, two trees, and a double axe, the *labrys* symbol of the goddess. The Tarot expresses a joining of two figures, the querent and the reader—or maybe the reader and the cards themselves. This is a joyous place, for Tarot readings are actually exciting experiences. The two trees in the picture evoke the garden of Eden, with its tree of knowledge and tree of life. So Tarot becomes a "place" where we can return to a kind of awareness usually denied us in the confusion of our daily lives.

> SHINING
  TRIBE
  Gift of Birds

3. WHAT MYSTERY DOES IT CONTAIN? *Three of Trees* (Three of Wands). This card
    shows us the Tarot's sense of humor, something I've become more and more aware
    of in recent years. This is because the picture is actually about physical objects that
    contain mystery. In Canada, the Salteaux Indians create scarecrow-like effigies called
    manitokanac. Unlike a scarecrow, which has no meaning except to confuse birds, a
    manitokan becomes a vessel for spirit to guard their households. By creating a physi-
    cal container, the Salteaux give benevolent energy a place to go. The Tarot is like sev-
    enty-eight manitokanac. Together, they create a vessel for Mystery to express itself in
    our lives.

Finally, I decided to turn over one more card, with the question: What gift does Tarot give
us? This time the humor is even more direct, for the very title of the card is a gift, the Gift of
Birds (Queen of Swords).

The message is as direct as the title. In the picture, a flute falls from the sky, the gift of art, while below stands a shaman who has dedicated himself to the bird spirits. He wears a bird-like helmet and carries a banner painted with a bird, and a feathered shield. But if he wishes to use the gift, he will have to drop the banner and the shield, and take off the helmet. He will have to pick up the flute and learn to play it.

The application to Tarot is clear. It offers us a great gift, a way to understand the wonders of life, a form of guidance when events or our own souls trouble us. To receive that gift, we must open ourselves—not just emotionally but also conceptually. And like a flute, the Tarot is something we learn over time so that it can become a more and more profound instrument of help and of wisdom.

Rachel Pollack
RHINEBECK, 2008

Bibliography

Amaral, Geraldine, *Tarot Celebrations* (Red Wheel/ Weiser, 1997).

Amberstone, Ruth Ann, and Wald Amberstone, *The Secret Language of Tarot* (Red Wheel/Weiser, 2008).

Anonymous, *Meditations on the Tarot* (Element, 1985).

Banzhaf, Hajo, *Tarot and the Journey of the Hero* (Samuel Weiser, Inc., 2000).

Boer, Charles, *The Homeric Hymns* (Swallow Press, 1970).

Braden, Nina Lee, *Tarot for Self Discovery* (Llewellyn Publications, 2002).

Butler, Bill, *The Definitive Tarot* (Rider and Company, 1975).

Calasso, Roberto, *The Marriage of Cadmus and Harmony*, trans. Tim Parks (Alfred A. Knopf, 1993).

Calvino, Italo, *The Castle of Crossed Destinies* (Harcourt Brace Jovanovich, 1976).

Case, Paul Foster, *The Tarot: A Key to the Wisdom of the Ages* (Macoy Publishing Company, 1947).

Cavendish, Richard, *The Tarot* (Crescent Books, 1975).

Chatwin, Bruce, *The Songlines* (Penguin, 1987).

Critchlow, Keith, *Time Stands Still* (St. Martin's, 1980).

Crowley, Aleister, *The Book of Thoth* (Samuel Weiser, 1944).

D'Agostino, Joseph, *Tarot: The Royal Path to Wisdom* (Samuel Weiser, 1976).

Decker, Ronald, Thierry De Paulis, and Michael Dummett, *A Wicked Pack of Cards* (St. Martin's, 1996).

Dillard, Annie, *For the Time Being* (Knopf, 1999).

Douglas, Alfred, *The Tarot* (Penguin, 1972).

Dummett, Michael, *The Game of Tarot* (U.S. Games Systems, 1980).

Dummett, Michael, and Ronald Decker, *A History of the Occult Tarot* (Duckworth Publishing, 2002).

Dunn, James David, *Window of the Soul* (Red Wheel/Weiser, 2008).

Eliade, Mircea, *Shamanism* (Princeton University Press, 1964).

Fairfield, Gail, *Choice-Centered Tarot* (Newcastle, 1985).

Gettings, Fred, *Tarot: How to Read the Future* (Chancellor Press, 1993).

Giles, Cynthia, *The Tarot: History, Mystery, and Lore* (Paragon House, 1992).

———, *The Tarot: Methods, Mastery, and More* (Simon & Schuster, 1996).

Gray, Eden, *The Tarot Revealed* (Inspiration House, 1960).

Greer, Mary K., *21 Ways to Read a Tarot Card* (Llewellyn Publications, 2006).

———, *The Complete Book of Tarot Reversals* (Llewellyn Publications, 2002).

———, *Women of the Golden Dawn* (Park Street Press, 1995).

———, *Tarot for Your Self* (Newcastle, 1984).

Guilley, Rosemary Ellen, and Robert M. Place, *The Alchemical Tarot* (Thorsons, 1995).

Haich, Elizabeth, *Wisdom of the Tarot* (Aurora Press, Inc., 1984).

Hazel, Elizabeth, *Tarot Decoded: Understanding and Using Dignities and Correspondences* (Weiser Books, 2004).

Huson, Paul, *Mystical Origins of the Tarot* (Destiny Books, 2004).

———, *The Devil's Picturebook* (G. P. Putnam's Sons, 1971).

Kaplan, Stuart, *The Encyclopedia of Tarot, Vols. 1-4* (U.S. Games Systems, 1978, 1986, 1990, 1999).

Kerenyi, Carl, *Eleusis: Archetypal Image of Mother and Daughter* (Princeton, 1967).

———, *The Gods of the Greeks* (Thames and Hudson, 1951).

Kliegman, Isabel Radow, *Tarot and the Tree of Life* (Quest, 1997).

Knight, Gareth, *The Treasure House of Images* (The Aquarian Press, 1986).

———, *A Practical Guide to Qabalistic Symbolism* (Samuel Weiser, Inc., 1965).

Lao Tzu, *The Tao Te Ching*, trans. Gia-Fue Feng and Jane English (Vintage, 1989).

Lotterhand, Jason C., *The Thursday Night Tarot* (Newcastle Publishing Co., Inc., 1989).

Mathers, S. L. MacGregor, *The Tarot: A Short Treatise on Reading Cards* (Samuel Weiser, Inc., 1993).

Matthews, John, ed., *At the Table of the Grail* (Watkins Publishing, 2002).

Maxwell, Joseph, *The Tarot* (Samuel Weiser, Inc., 1977).

Moakley, Gertrude, *The Tarot Cards Painted by Bonifacio Bembo* (New York Public Library, 1966).

Moore, Daphna, *The Rabbi's Tarot* (Hughes Henshaw Publications, 2007).

O'Neill, Robert V., *Tarot Symbolism* (Fairways Press, 1986).

Opsopaus, John, *Guide to the Pythagorean Tarot* (Llewellyn Publications, 2001).

Papus, *The Tarot of the Bohemians* (Arcanum Books, 1962).

Patai, Raphael, *The Hebrew Goddess* (Avon, 1967).

Payne-Towler, Christine, *The Underground Stream: Esoteric Tarot Revealed* (Noreah Press, 1999).

Place, Robert M., *The Tarot: History, Symbolism, and Divination* (Tarcher/Penguin, 2005).

Pollack, Rachel, *The Kabbalah Tree: A Journey of Balance & Growth* (Llewellyn Publications, 2004).

———, *Seeker: The Tarot Unveiled* (Llewellyn Publications, 2005).

———, *The Forest of Souls: A Walk Through the Tarot* (Llewellyn Publications, 2003).

———, *Complete Illustrated Guide to the Tarot* (Element, 1999).

———, *The New Tarot* (Aquarian, 1989).

———, *Seventy-Eight Degrees of Wisdom* (Thorsons, 1980, 1983, 1997).

———, *Shining Tribe Tarot* (Llewellyn Publications, 2001).

———, *Shining Woman Tarot* (Thorsons, 1994).

———, *Tarot Readings and Meditations* (Aquarian, 1986). (Formerly titled *The Open Labyrinth*)

Pollack, Rachel, and Caitlin Matthews, *Tarot Tales* (Random Century, 1989).

Regardie, Israel, *The Golden Dawn: The Original Account of the Teachings, Rites & Ceremonies of the Hermetic Order* (Llewellyn Publications, 2002).

Sadhu, Mouni, *The Tarot: A Contemporary Course of the Quintessence of Hermetic Occultism* (Aeon Books, 1962).

Scholem, Gershom, *Major Trends in Jewish Mysticism* (Schocken, 1941).

———, *On the Kabbalah and Its Symbolism* (Schocken, 1965).

Schwartz, Howard, *Tree of Souls: The Mythology of Judaism* (Oxford University Press, 2004).

Thomson, Sandra A., *Pictures from the Heart* (St. Martin's Griffin, 2003).

Waite, Arthur Edward, *The Pictorial Key to the Tarot* (William Rider and Son, 1911).

Wang, Robert, *The Qabalistic Tarot: A Textbook of Mystical Philosophy* (Samuel Weiser, Inc., 1983).

———, *An Introduction to the Golden Dawn* (Aquarian Press, 1978).

Williams, Brian, *A Renaissance Tarot: A Guide to the Renaissance Tarot* (U. S. Games Systems, Inc., 1994).

Williams, Charles, *The Greater Trumps* (Victor Gollancz, 1932).

Wilson, Peter Lamborn, Christopher Bamford, and Kevin Townley, *Green Hermeticism: Alchemy and Ecology* (Lindisfarne Books, 2007).

Wirth, Oswald, *The Tarot of the Magicians* (Samuel Weiser, Inc., 1990).

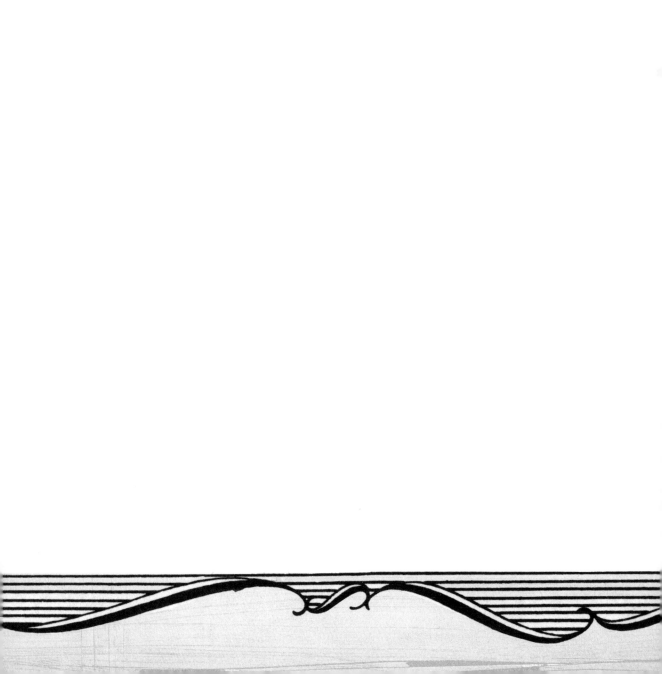

Index